The Patient Impatience

from boyhood to guerilla:
a personal narrative of Nicaragua's
struggle for liberation

TOMAS BORGE

CURBSTONE PRESS

FIRST ENGLISH EDITION, 1992
Copyright © 1989 by Tomás Borge Martínez
La Paciente Impaciente was first published
    by Editorial Vanguardia, 1989
Translation Copyright © 1991
    by Russell Bartley, Darwin Flakoll, and Sylvia Yoneda
ALL RIGHTS RESERVED

Cover photograph © 1989 by Sylvia Yoneda
Cover design by Stone Graphics
Printed in the U.S. by BookCrafters

Curbstone Press is a 501(c)(3) nonprofit literary arts
organization whose operations are supported in part
by private donations and by grants from the ADCO
Foundation, the Connecticut Commission on the Arts, the
Andrew W. Mellon Foundation, the National Endowment
for the Arts, and the Plumsock Fund.

ISBN: 0-915306-97-2
Library of Congress number: 91-55410

distributed in the U.S. by
INBOOK
Box   120470
East Haven, CT 06512

published by
CURBSTONE PRESS
321 Jackson Street
Willimantic, CT 06226

Now we exhort you, brethren,
warn them that are unruly,
comfort the weak, be patient
toward all men.
                    St. Paul
            (I Thessalonians 5:14)

THE PATIENT IMPATIENCE

Chapter One

1

Shortly before midnight one summer evening in Matagalpa, anesthetized by the twilight while my mother thought I was studying ratio and proportion problems and verbal declensions, Winnetou died. Old Shatterhand, with whom the Indian had explored all geographies and emotions, provided they were difficult, refused to believe he was dead.

If Old Shatterhand, who in his day had contemplated thousands of bloodied scalps, refused to accept the Apache's death, why did my bosom friend Adrián Blandón and I accept it? We believed without question the news of our hero's death, because in Matagalpa fiction was the only possible alternative to death from boredom.

Winnetou has died and lies buried beneath grass trodden by wild horses. His sorrel stallion searches for the master who no longer gazes at him from those fiery black eyes accustomed to detail and horizons. The Indian — half night and half day — whose silhouette emerges unexpectedly as he moves forward, neither eating nor drinking until circumstances around the campfire permit, will no longer offer his counsel, long in wisdom, ever short in words.

We never saw an acceptable picture of Winnetou, but the only way we could envision him was with perfect oblique and transverse abdominal musculature, a self-controlled nervous system that desensitized the extremities of his feet in the world's longest marches, marble molars that tore flesh from the charred ribs of buffalo and a thoracic cavity containing a heart the size of a herd of bulls. Was all this now decaying and being consumed by worms? This could not be.

Loyalty, rectitude, defense of the humble, were not buried with Winnetou.

2

Different specters swept Europe following the First World War: cold and pessimism. The wounds in the rotting bodies on the battlefields were not as deep as those left in the souls of desolate Europeans.

A German, Karl Hohental, entertained surviving youth with adventure novels. There are references from that period attesting to the popularity of these novels among the young people of Europe, above all in Germany.

Karl Hohental used the pseudonym Karl May. He traveled through Kurdistan, Arabia, Asia Minor, South America and the North American Far West. They say he was a highwayman; I don't believe it. They say he never left Germany; I don't believe it.

No one should attempt the impossible task of writing better westerns than the novels written by Karl May. His characters seem to be within arm's reach in the next room. They reproduce the virtues we ourselves would like to possess, imitate what we are in our dreams; they shake our hands and depart with the implicit promise of returning.

The main characters in Karl May's novels are Winnetou and Old Shatterhand, two intimate friends.

3

I used to play in the corners among bales of tobacco with my favorite cousin, Pastor Cordero. We would hide and play mischievous pranks on Elba and María Dolores, and we didn't always agree on everything. He wanted to play church, and I wanted to play war. Pastor became a priest; later he hung his cassock on Monsignor Octavio Calderón y Padilla's coat rack and took off for the city of Rivas at the other end of the country, fleeing scandal. He was accompanied by a girl with whom he lived to the end of his days. She reversed the color of padlocks and honeysuckle.

Lala, our aunt — in other words, our accomplice — would decide what games we could play, always on the condition that we should build her a white house with nice hallways and that when we had the money we would buy her all of Gardel's records.

Lala would rock me to sleep in her arms. I seldom saw her kiss her boyfriends. Of course, I never fell into Virgilio's trap of giving me five cents to go buy candy. That did not prevent her from getting pregnant, which caused me much suffering. I swore vengeance, but eventually resigned myself to the situation. Lala managed to find another boyfriend, marry him and give birth to another half dozen cousins.

4

On the banks of the Matagalpa River, in view of the heights that looked down on us, I read *Azul*. It was written by Rubén Darío, known even to generals. I read it when they were building the bridge that connects the city with the hospital across the river at the foot of El Calvario.

I read it with amazement there by the river, seated on a rock near where a nymph who amused herself sucking on lumps of sugar would come to bathe while awaiting a hairy satyr to make her his lover. I was self-conscious about my squalid adolescence devoid of facial fuzz and manly voice. When I greeted the nymph, it was with a voice inhabited by immature roosters; she'd look at me catlike and laugh like a little girl being tickled. Once I followed her into the dense wood and she vanished around a turn in the trail.

One afternoon as I continued to read *Azul*, together with my friend Ramón Gutiérrez, a poet turned up and told us that for some time he had been singing the word of the future. I have spread my wings before the hurricane, he said. I was born in the light of the dawn: I seek the chosen race that must await, a hymn on its lips and a lyre in its hand, the grand sunrise. Questioned, he went on: I have shattered the fawning harp with its weak strings against the Bohemian goblets and the jars foaming with wine that intoxicates without giving strength; I've thrown off the mantle that made me appear an actor or a woman, and have clad myself in a wild and splendid fashion: my rags are of royal purple.

Encouraged on, he continued: Art does not reside in cold marble wrappings nor in pretentious paintings. It wears not fine breeches nor speaks in bourgeois tongue, nor dots all the i's. Ramón, dotting all his i's, inquired about the poet's wild gestures. To which he replied: They are like two lions, sir. Between an Apollo and a goose, I prefer the Apollo, although it be of baked clay and the other of ivory.

After listening to his complaints, we came to the conclusion that, rather than become poets ourselves, it would be preferable to be mathematicians or to study jurisprudence or investigate the thymus syndrome — inasmuch as it has not been determined whether or not the thymus is an endocrine gland — although for reasons of hypochondria or ideology, neither did we wish to become bourgeois gentlemen or kings.

That same day we went by the hospital to shake hands with the tuberculosis patients and to reproach the nurses because they were unable, like us, to drink from the same glass as Juancito, the skeletal cougher who was our friend, the man who tested our fidelity to Winnetou.

Returning to the river, this time with Douglas Stuart, another adolescent friend, we encountered in *Azul* the Bengal tigress with her lustrous, striped coat, stretched out at the entrance to the grotto. There she roars and ripples her coat with pleasure. It is the mating season. The tigress inhales deeply; her breast swells; she opens her wide jaws, demands submission, sniffs the air. When she sees the male, her green eyes sparkle. He's very beautiful. He displays his white teeth and swollen muscles. The king arrives, flatters her. The tigress responds and they caress with savage ardor. Then comes the monstrous moment of bliss. The landowner approaches, shotgun in hand, as we witness the pollen, the vigor, the torrents of life. The two cats caress while the intrepid coffee planter moves closer and takes aim with one eye. Douglas leaps up like a cub and closes the book. He doesn't want to hear the outcome.

Realism is better. Let's read *El Fardo*, said Douglas. The naturalist school, brother, in Zola's style. It's like a page from Gorki, reiterates Stuart, who's also read Gogol. Rubén was given an affectionate send off by the dock workers of Valparaíso, I add, and he was received enthusiastically by the dock workers, poets, carpenters and fortune tellers of Montevideo. The Uruguayans are like that with us Nicaraguans, although that has nothing to do with *La Canción de Oro*.

We were in the middle of this when along comes a disheveled individual, a beggar, judging by his appearance, a pilgrim perhaps, or maybe a poet, who, removing a piece of black bread from his pocket, released his hymn to the winds: Let us sing to gold, king of the world, born of the fertile womb of Mother Earth. Let us sing to gold, that great river, fount of life, which makes young and beautiful all who bathe in its currents. Let us sing to gold, because from it is wrought the crowns of popes, because it spills over their mantles like fire and inundates the capes of archbishops.

Let us sing to gold, because we can be lost, yet it will erect bulwarks to conceal our abject madness, because it's going to fill the coffers of banks. Let us sing to gold, because its song is enchanted music, because it adorns the armor of the Homeric heroes. Let us sing to gold, yellow like death. Let us sing to gold, purified by fire, God the calf, marrow of rocks, resounding like a chorus of tympanies, fetus of the stars. Let us sing to gold, made sun, whose crepe shirt black with stars, is, after the final kiss, like a multitude of pounds sterling.

Ye wretched, ye drunkards, ye mirthless poor, ye prostitutes, vagabonds, pickpockets and bandits, ye poets, let us join the powerful, the demigods of the earth. Let us sing to gold!

5

Since the afternoon had already turned to evening, we went with the ragged poet to walk the streets of the city. We hadn't gone a hundred paces when we came to Morazán Park, home to bootblacks and crazies by day, by night to accumulated kisses, propositions and moist lips in the breeze. Near Morazán's statue we were joined by Ramón Gutiérrez, and the poet vanished among the foliage of the orange trees.

To our left, the cathedral resembled a sacrificial fruit, respectable like a mature widow, solid like a bureaucrat approaching retirement.

Facing the river, its towers grew in the afternoon light, while its great clock taught us to tell time and to ponder the inevitable date we would one day make with death. In those days it only indicated the time for encountering Amelia's smile, the minutes for playing hide-and-seek, the hour of 7:15 when the Buck Jones movie began, or the fragrance of incense and the *pater noster que est in celis*.

In the tower on the right is the belfry, which recalls the punctuality with which people honored the dead, the sneezes of Sunday mass, our peals of laughter beneath the full moon of Holy Week, and the lucidity with which, I'd swear, baptisms were announced.

We walked toward the neighborhood by the road to Jinotega and, leaving life's rhythms undisturbed, climbed a stairway of crickets to La Cruz or Chuga Bello Hills, from where one can view the little town below, lying like an unerring knife wound. Two main streets, animated with an impressive number of businesses and cotton dresses of every color, run parallel toward the river. To our left is Guanuca and, hidden from view, the ice factory in a place of densely foliated trees appropriate for Sunday strolls. Farther on toward El Apante is the Palo Alto neighborhood, where small adobe houses defiantly cling to the rocky banks and to the local geography. A few centimeters this side on a contour map scaled at 1:50,000, is the Laborío neighborhood, where Carlos Fonseca played with wooden toys on earthen floors.

From that hilltop one could see the sawmill and the Margot Theater, founded by Antonio Corriols, husband of the beautiful Señora Delia Morgan and father of the first automobile, the first electrical plant, the second bicycle and the first obscene flirtation to arrive in this city, as well as of the Corriols boys who played guitar and kicked a soccer ball with the same dexterity they applied to tits and motorcycles.

María Corriols and I started school together, along with the two Pérez girls, Angélica and Perfecta. One morning she discovered that I had written the word "God," without knowing what it meant, which led Angélica, whose face was as sweet as Perfecta's was severe, to prophesy that I would become a medium, a bishop, or at the very least, an appraiser of furs.

On our way back to the park, passing by the Life Isn't Worth A Damn tavern, we paused to peer through the squalid window of The 130, Angela Godoy's whorehouse. Timidly, we approached a house to the left of I'm not sure exactly what, where Clementina, the smiling, solitary prostitute lived, who in any event was too costly for our possibilities. At some distance we also passed by the yellow door behind which the good lady, Old Lion Face, offered her services. Heavily made up and ugly as a sacristan's vomit, she charged next to nothing but no one could afford a mask to stave off the horror.

We ran into Jolea, the porter. We passed by Chinche the barber, who was incapable of cutting anyone's hair without insistently whistling *Cavalleria Rusticana* and who left our heads like a helmet, like an invocation, like the face of a bluff. There goes Chavarría, said Douglas. He was the truant officer who relentlessly hunted us down whenever we played hookey.

We would get together in groups of three or more and shout at him: *"Chavarría, chavarranca, la potrilla y la potranca!"* We made him dance the minuet. He'd take off after a group on the left flank only to hear the shout off to his right, another ahead of him, and then *"Chavarría, chavarranca!"* to his rear. Just minutes before they were going to take him away in a straightjacket he decided to become the doorman at the Margot Theater.

We passed by the establishment of Pedro Culito ["Tightbuns"], whose backside was the shortest distance between two points. He was owner of the billiard parlor where Carlos Fonseca would come to sell the little newspaper, *Rumores*, and to play pool. That day we visited all the bars and liquor stores: besides the Life Isn't Worth A Damn tavern, there was Jacinta's, Pancho Camisa's near the cemetery, where they drank farewell toasts; Cheba's, a generous, fat woman who served *jocotes* and sliced mangos and bounced you out with a bump of her left hip if you got obstreperous; and Chumbulún's, where I first got drunk with Julio Cuarezma when I was fourteen.

That afternoon I made a pass at an impossible woman, I puked up everything including the milk my wet-nurse had fed me shortly after I was born, and the police arrested us while I, for some logical reason, was insulting the moon and Julio was trying to explain that, naturally, the sun was to blame. Since I behaved badly, the following morning they made me sweep Morazán Park. Two physicians were required to look after my mother, who fainted from shame.

Whenever the cloud would take on water, that is to say, whenever I could squeeze a few pesos out of my mother, I'd invite my friends to eat at the Shanghai Restaurant, owned by Chinaman Lai, a master of chop suey; or at the Cantonese Restaurant of Chinaman Po, who specialized in fish steaks and who sometimes, according to *Rumores*, served rat meat instead of Castilian pigeon. There was also Palomo's, in the shade of a beautiful *guanacaste* tree.

At the Servandita, we would drink corn, *chicha*, cocoa, shaved ice with plum syrup, barley with a straw, almond milk, Shaler Kola, fresh orange juice, contagious smiles, ice water, and, if you ordered it, coffee with gossip.

Let's go to El Molino, Ramón suggested. Couples, almost always hand in hand, liked to walk there. Why not Los Mangos? I suggested, which belonged to Consuelo Baldizón's parents. The Yoguare gorge and La Cagalera pool were too far, as was El Apante Falls. There was also La Hielera, at the other end of town, where you could eat popsicles and the Evangelicals came to be baptized by being immersed in water so cold that it surely must have left them cleansed and purged of any desire to sin against the Sixth Commandment ever again; or at least until the following summer.

It did not occur to us that day to walk along the main river with its swimming holes: El Chivo, La Carnicería, La Culebra, El Mico, Don Bruno, La Presa. Small groups of people would come there on Sundays to relax, fish or sin, as they were moved by circumstances and the gender of their motives.

6

We were on vacation. Ramón Gutiérrez and I befriended all the fruitcakes: Pantaleona, who had lost her marbles because of an unhappy love affair, painted her smooth cheeks with annatto and lifted her skirts to show the world the unreasonableness of her abandonment.

Pudgy Tomasa ate mice and seduced drunken adolescents in the flowerbeds of the park. It is said that her three blond children, handsome all, were the grandsons of a blue-eyed, freckle-faced landowner whose numerous offspring included alcoholics, good, valiant boys, anti-Somocistas, and brawlers.

Maitro Nicho was a hyperactive, intimate friend, who, convinced of his treasures, carried around a burlap bag filled with precious stones, though he had no attachment to earthly wealth. One day he asked us to watch how he could attach a hose to the clouds to provide water for a 150 story building. Ramón Gutiérrez and I saved all the diamonds and gold ingots that Maitro Nicho generously placed in our hands. To earn his daily bread he'd lug on his broad shoulders the hundred pound sacks of salt or beans the neighborhood stores ordered from my mother.

Toño Aguirre, the meteorologist, was a compendium of mental ills. He spent his time predicting perfect summers and winters, flowerings and coffee harvests greater than all the yields.

Another one was named Jesús, but everybody called him Sanamambiche. He was a huge fellow, still young. As a child, he was a shoeshine boy for the Yankees, who called him "son of a bitch." He hated Somoza's National Guards because, he said, no poet could help but hate them. One day there was a pitched battle between Sanamambiche and a squad of Guards. Sanamambiche hurled rocks with his hands and feet, though you may not believe it, and the Guards used their rifle butts. He never regained consciousness. His death was mourned by the bootblacks, fruitcakes and market ladies.

There was also a shapely woman who fixed her bloodshot gaze on people and demanded a handout for the love of God. During the brightest hours of the day she would try to divine the secret of sunspots. Everybody called her Sunflower.

Bárbara was an old lady, or seemed to be. She collected stray dogs who followed her faithfully for the bits of stale bread and scraps she distributed to them from a wooden box tied to her waist. In that box she'd deposit the leftovers people gave her and with which she nourished herself and the faithful band of flea-bitten derelicts that guarded her when she slept. There was an evil blind man with two canes named Anselmo. He would sit on the sidewalk by the market and when he heard a child's footsteps would stick one of his canes between the kid's legs. When the victim fell on his face, Anselmo would howl with laughter, scaring the wits out of passersby. It was said that his blindness was a fraud.

Abel, on the other hand, was a good blind man. He would carry sacks in exchange for food and used clothing. In his shoulders he had the strength of an ox, on his lips the smile of a new moon, whose counterpart he could divine the same as the obstacles between one part of the city and another. He knew the distances, which gave him prestige. He greeted people as though he could actually see them, while all the while carrying, as if on the wings of a mockingbird, a sewing machine, a sack of sugar, or a ton of darkness.

7

We went to bed early. In the morning my mother got me up — against my express wish — to go with her to listen to the bishop's sermon and, in passing, to serve as the young prelate's altar boy.

Near the church my mother greeted a lady with a kindly face accompanied by a young kid who wore, hanging from his nose and squalid ears, a pair of thick spectacles, and who was holding a white candle with gold motifs.

He was going to the cathedral to celebrate his first communion as part of a group of children recruited from the neighborhoods to study — in a sort of seminary — the catechism, with references to hellfire, the certainty of purgatory for venial sinners, and the undecipherable contradiction of the Holy Trinity.

My mother asked the boy's name and the lady replied that it was Carlos. I'd barely nodded to him and he replied with an austere gesture and a clear, blue gaze. They walked on ahead of us and I asked my mother who she was. Agustina Fonseca, she replied.

Chapter Two

1

Nicaragua is the land of corn. Corn that grows in unfertile soil, corn that rises up to defy the sun. Forty-day corn, sheet corn, Blood of Christ corn, highland corn. There are also native varieties called Chontales, purple husk, soft husk and mountain corn.

From this grain are made tortillas, soups, refreshments, pastries, desserts, bread, tamales, a soft drink, heavy and light dishes, and corn liquor. There are dishes such as María stew, *ajiaco* stew, slumgullion, *repocheta*, mock tongue, meat fritters, *quequerote*, marzipan, *churros*, meat and salsa tamales, and corn cakes.

Matagalpa lies at the center of this land of corn, which is also the land of coffee. Red coffee, black coffee.

No one knows when it was founded, although the original settlers are known to have been Sumo and Chorotega Indians. The aboriginal population did not constitute a single urban nucleus, rather a group of families scattered throughout Solingalpa, Molagüina and Matagalpa. From 1740 on this latter settlement dominated its neighbors and was called San Pedro de Matagalpa.

Matagalpa means "in the houses of the nets," according to the philologist Alfonso Valle; "town of the ten," says the historian Luis Cuadra Cea; "green place, place of blue clay, land of slingmen," according to the philologist, historian and martyr, Alejandro Dávila Bolaños. I'm inclined to believe that the correct place name is Land of Slingmen, inasmuch as it was the birthplace of the greatest slingman of all, Carlos Fonseca.

Among the profusion of rocks just outside the city, there are two that confounded our imagination: El Toro hill, where they say there is a horned animal carved in the rock, and La Bailadora monolith, which is visible from a great distance. La Bailadora seems suspended in space. She's the wife of the devil and, as punishment for her preferences, suffers the torment of eternal orgasm.

2

Matagalpa, the department where Rubén Darío was born — in a small locale by the name of Metapa — has as its capital Matagalpa, the city of Carlos Fonseca.

Like a luminous fish, the city lies at the bottom of a basin surrounded by hills: El Toro and La Pava, El Apante and El Calvario.

The department is situated in a mountainous region filled with unusual valleys and orographic phenomena. The mountain systems are branches of the Dariense chain, handkerchief points of the Chontales system and part of the Estrada plateau. The Dariense chain includes the Datanlí range, which reaches its highest elevation at the top of El Chimborazo, on whose slopes Ruperto Mendiola went mad while hearing people say the Holy rosary and, between Our Fathers and Ave Marías, an occasional profanity. They say he recovered his reason at the clinic of his relative, the healer and professor of occult sciences of Matagalpa, Don Juan Mendiola, where it was explained to him that what he had heard was a parrot that had escaped during a pastoral mission of Father Carmen Casco and subsequently taught short prayers and other gems to an army of his talkative feathered friends.

Father Casco wore his cassock with the ease of a Mexican cowboy in the motion pictures of Tito Guízar. He like to drink cheap rum, he had nieces in every municipality, and no one dared to challenge him. I remember him as a young and easygoing man with a certain decisiveness about him. When he was ordained as a priest, he gave an analectic sermon:

My brothers, if indeed you are worthy of being called my brothers: Here in Matagalpa it will rain fire as it did in Sodom and Gomorrah. To begin with, you have corrupted the language. You call pennies "muffins." Nobody uses the sacred noun mother; instead you say "my old stone," speaking in this absurd excuse for Castilian that you wretches call "dry spinach." When you refer to your father, you call him "the old rock." When a cloudburst threatens, rather than take cover beneath the blessed palm tree, you say "here comes the great pisser in the sky." If you see me on my little burro on my way to confess a dying man, instead of lending me a cape so that I won't catch cold, you Jews say: "there goes the profligate of Ciudad Darío." And if it's our Most Illustrious Pastor, the Bishop, who passes before your heretical eyes, not one of you calls him Excellency; instead you say: "there goes the lay sisters' stud bull." And you think you're going to be saved? Save yourselves with this!

And in conclusion, before the wide eyes of the believers, he gave them the fig, which consists of inserting the thumb between the index and middle fingers.

The Guabule range is also an outstanding feature of the Matagalpa area. Its high points, Pancasán and Kiragua, are more historical than orographic. That's where the guerrilla skirmishes of 1967 took place. And there is the Apante range near the city, whose principal feature is El Apante, not because it's the highest point but because it was right in front of our eyes and was where we'd go on Sundays to defy jaguars and drink ice-cold water from the small streams that ran down to join the river.

Winding through the entire department is the Matagalpa River, called by Christopher Columbus the "River of Disaster" because several of his sailors had drowned at its mouth in September 1501. The river covers a distance of 555 kilometers. They say it is the only one in the world that runs uphill. It does this in the winter, leaving Sébaco Valley to enter the uplands of La Picota in the municipality of Terrabona.

There's an old theory that the river once flowed into Lake Managua and that the telluric phenomenon known as the Totumbla Uplift — comprising strata of andesite and basalts that are transformed into deposits of kaolin and other clays — obliged it to change course toward the Caribbean. The river originates in Molino Norte, not far from the city, at 1100 meters above sea level; it passes between El Apante and El Calvario and makes more twists and turns than a man lost in the forest. It runs down toward Managua and then turns back to the northeast, growing quickly in volume, more and more resembling a serpent adept at the dance of sinuosity.

That river forms a part of my life, almost as much as the stream that courses through my veins and arteries. In its chill waters I felt the warmth of my first attraction to female skin; there I learned for the first time about solar flares; in its waters we caught fish, crabs and the flu. On its banks I learned that the moon is not a dusty desert, but a circumstantial accessory, an expendable adjective, as are most adjectives. That's right. The moon isn't a satellite of the earth; it's an attitude.

I learned that happiness is possible watching La Cegua bathe at dawn in La Culebra pool, and that the river, swollen to overflowing one October 4th by the seasonal squalls of St. Francis, is a spectacle that could neither be photographed nor described from the safe vantage of the house where my cousin, Pastor Cordero, lived. That day in 1940, the yellowish current, which had risen more than ten meters, carried away tranquil cows and smiling pigs with broken necks. A cadaver entangled in roots passed by with complete indifference, smashing against a tree brought down by the rushing waters; it looked for a while like it would remain in an eddy but after making several tedious circles that passed through our Adams' apples, it floated away without so much as a good-bye wave to the two trembling boys.

Pastor and I had no time to react because right behind it came a second body, venerable like an Egyptian mummy, that decided to bob on by in the middle of the current. A chest of drawers resembling Noah's ark regurgitated a doll and some green rags. Both ahead of and behind it recently deceased tree limbs took their leave.

Someone showed up in the rain and said that the *chuisles* — a Chorotega word for "stream" — had inundated the city, that the French fabrics of Don Francisco Carazo's dry goods outlets were floating desperately about, that the German crystal ware in Don Willy Hüpper's store had been shattered to bits in those showcases that at Christmas time resemble little islands of color, and that a local cook had drowned who was famous for the way she tastefully adorned rice with rose-shaped tomato slices and who made candy from sugar, eggs and red tears they called "grapes."

Pastor, who was dark-complexioned and for that reason had been nicknamed "Blackie," rolled his eyes skyward as the body of a man floated by, its dark-skinned backside gyrating wildly before disappearing from view. My mother, Doña Anita Martínez, and Pastor's mother, María, who were sisters and very close, forgot about us as they recited the rosary of the fifteen mysteries, while we remained glued to the window facing the river and its horror.

3

The Spaniards never conquered the Atlantic coast; that is, they never got beyond the so-called "edge of the frontier." One part of Matagalpa department lay beyond that edge. It was a large expanse inhabited by bellicose tribes the Spaniards called "enemies of His Majesty." A fortified line was constructed by the frustrated conquistadores between the East and the West, between the Pacific and the Atlantic, cutting Nicaragua in two.

The Spanish conquest of Matagalpa began in 1612 and was barely completed by 1787, and even then not by force of arms but by the persuasive preaching of Franciscan missionaries. The indigenous peoples were organized into localities so they could be forced to pay tribute and provide services.

The Matagalpa Indians fought with lances, bows and arrows, and used shields made of tapir hide. They practiced a wargame that consisted of tossing an ear of corn into the air and shooting arrows and hurling javelins at it until not a single kernel remained.

They marched off to war with their faces and bodies painted red and black.

In 1692, the Indians of Sébaco, a municipality of Matagalpa, rose up against the Spaniards. These hardened warriors entered the fray with their tapir shields and preferred colors. They had already rebelled fourteen times. Following independence, they rose up in 1824, 1827, 1844, 1845 and 1848, each time with their tapir shields and their bodies painted red and black. During the uprising of 1844, which took place in midwinter when the flooded river stretched like a chastity belt about the city, the Indians with the tapir shields extended a human cordon of bowmen around their enemy, tightening the line until all resistance was drowned in blood.

When the filibuster invasion of 1856 took place, Matagalpa, with its red and black Indians and their tapir shields, seized the mountain tops — the fury of tigers in their eyes, on their feet the light and shadowy wings of deer. The Yankees were terrified of them.

In every hollow, red and black Indians with tapir shields were organized under the command of a captain, under whom was a lieutenant, then a sergeant and finally a corporal. These were lifetime appointments, earned by the individual's bravery in combat.

Matagalpa then was an Indian village surrounded by compact territories comprising the indigenous community. Within this area farming and herding were organized collectively.

Between 1871 and 1877, the government established and codified a system of land tenure known as the Conservatory. Agricultural laws were enacted to eliminate the indigenous communities and communal lands attached to local municipalities. The Agricultural Laws and Police Law obliged the Indians to work without remuneration on road construction and as farm laborers, while communal farmers were evicted from their best lands under a barrage of statutes and bullets. Indians were forbidden to eat meat, make corn liquor or entertain themselves without first obtaining permission and paying a tax.

In 1880, to install telegraph lines they were forced to carry spools of wire on their backs all the way from Managua. There were accidents, deaths, injuries and such ill temper that on March 30, 1881, at 11:00 in the morning, a thousand Indians entered the city in columns four deep in the tactic known as "throwing the loop:" This consisted of forming circles that tighten to crush everything in their path like a boa constrictor, like a flash flood, like a wild and solemn bull. The Indians were painted red and black and carried arrows and tapir shields; they also carried chile pastes to apply to the genitals and anal orifices of the mestizos. After several hours of battle they withdrew, taking their dead with them. But they returned again on August 8th at 8:00 in the morning. There were 3,000 of them under the command of Lorenzo Pérez, Toribio Mendoza and Higinio Campos. They threw the loop. This time they had firearms, as well as bows and arrows, machetes and chile paste. They surrounded the city and advanced with flaming torches in the middle of the night,

27

opening passageways between the houses as was also done during the insurrection in 1979. In this way they reached the center of the city.

At 10:00 in the morning on August 10th, 200 government troops armed with harquebuses and a small cannon entered the city. The fighting was over that day. More than 500 Indians perished.

4

At the beginning of this century, one of the wealthiest immigrants in Matagalpa, the German Juan Bosche, in complicity with local authorities, obliged the entire community of Yúcul — about 10,000 Indians — to work without pay for three years in order to cancel a debt of 1,000 pesos, the equivalent of 80 dollars at that time.

In 1895, a bunch of immigrants raised a gallows in the center of town and executed two Indians. This happened because a crazy, drunken Englishman had been found dead on the road to El Apante, relieved of the gold he'd been carrying. Later, a coin appeared in the possession of an Indian at a grocery store, and that was sufficient to avenge the immigrant's death. The street where they erected the gallows has been called ever since Street of the Hanged.

The Caribbean coast, on the other hand, was conquered with good manners by English greed, which conceived the idea of advancing toward the Pacific coast with the aid of the warlike Miskitos. The English, too, were unable to go beyond the strategic line formed by the localities of Nueva Segovia, Boaco, Juigalpa, Acoyapa and the San Juan River. The city of Matagalpa formed part of that line.

In 1879, the Jesuits, intelligent as always, established the first college of higher education. It was actually a center for novices who preferred the fresh air of Matagalpa to the stifling heat of León. They also founded an annex for Indians and mestizos where they taught reading and writing, Catholic doctrine and a course for nursing the sick in their homes.

President Tomás Martínez chartered the city of Matagalpa on February 14, 1862.

The first bishop arrived in 1914. His name was Isidoro Carrillo y Salazar. He was renowned as a saint. He flagellated himself and wore a haircloth about his waist which, after his death, was exhibited in a glass case near the main altar. He was succeeded by Alejandro González y Robleto, a Somocista; Isidro Augusto Oviedo y Reyes, a poet; Octavio José Calderón y Padilla, an anti-Somocista; Julián Barni and Carlos Sancti, Franciscans.

The National Institute of the North was founded in 1937, its name changed to the Eliseo Picado National Institute in December 1964. Carlos Fonseca studied there.

Chapter Three

1

Adrián Blandón was Winnetou. He could hold a lighted match beneath his finger without altering the expression on his face or diverting his eyes from a girl — Conchita Bello, for example, the most beautiful of them all — in order to carry out a fraternal commitment. He did not lie.

One night he rescued me with his fists from a group of Somoza supporters. Estela and Yolanda Tellería, classmates of ours, watched my assailants fall to the ground as he socked them on the jaw. He accompanied me home. I was hurt, bleeding and furious. My mother met us at the door, looked at me in silence and ran her mint-scented hand through my hair.

For eight days after the Indian died we refrained from speaking to each other because we were terrified of tears. We started talking again during semester exams, when I asked my friend for the answer to some question about direct objects.

About that time I befriended Jaime Vargas, a tall, slender fellow with dark skin, radiant eyes and leadership qualities that were being wasted in his profession as a civil engineer in some U.S. city. That relationship had a certain influence on the organizing of a student directorate. We created something resembling a leadership structure and designed a rubber stamp consisting of an owl surrounded by the letters INN, which stood for the National Institute of the North. Apart from the owl nothing much happened, except for a scandal when we discovered that one of the professors was gay and the student directorate informed the principal. The teacher was suspended.

Until then the professor's affairs, concealed by fear and the stacks of books and ashen sheets that adorned the aerie of that solitary hawk, had successfully passed all the hard tests of concealment. I don't recall the exact circumstances now, but he made some sort of tentative approach, that was in some fashion rejected, who knows just what happened? The teacher, of retirement age, lived off his miserable savings, his features marked by hunger and desolation, until the need for an expert in the Spanish language overcame local prejudices.

A doctor, a priest, a barber, a musician and a beggar were also victims of scorn and social mockery. The doctor and the priest to a lesser extent, because the former was skilled at diagnosing illness, while the latter could be considered truthful, albeit not entirely, for to doubt a little bit is a venial sin while too much doubt is a mortal sin. People made vulgar jokes about the musician with musical instruments such as the clarinet, and I won't even mention how they treated the poor beggar. With the barber, on the other hand, one ran the risk of having his hair caressed in such a way as to arouse the suspicion of the neighbors, for which reason the pot-bellied barber with his supplicating gaze had only a scanty and squeamish clientele.

There was another homosexual, much beloved by the neighborhood women because of the sympathy he displayed for others' afflictions and because he was opposed to Somoza. He built altars. His Saint Joseph and Nazarene altars resembled exteriorist poems and delighted the children. He was the nephew of Eudomilia, a devout 70-year-old spinster who would accompany my mother on the Via Crucis during Holy Week. I wasn't always able to escape my mother's discipline or the tender glances of that nephew; which meant I had to endure the taunts and jibes of my friends. One day, standing before the statue of St. Francis of Assisi, following the third Station of the Cross, I rebelled and, placing my eternal salvation at grave risk, never went back. Ever again.

Doña Anita resorted to arguments, appeals to reason, supplications and lesser blackmail; she offered up Gregorian masses to saints and the saintly as well as a tempting part of the banknotes that she hoarded in soapboxes under her bed; she promised St. Anthony and St. Joseph that, at an opportune moment, I would take a vow of chastity; she offered to pay the cost of uniforms of four flashy Roman soldiers for the Holy Week procession. She begged me to continue as Bishop Oviedo y Reyes' acolyte and to take communion on first Fridays — a promise that she placed on the altar of St. Benito. All she asked in return was that I become a priest. Her enthusiasm grew when I recited the Lord's Prayer in Latin.

I almost gave in. There was already talk about a passport and visa for me to enter a Mexican seminary and they bought me a wristwatch. There was a certain atmosphere of ceremonial farewell in the house. One afternoon — one of the saddest for my mother — I was wading in the river when the waist and countenance of Rosibel appeared quivering in the mirror of the gentle current. I turned my head abruptly and her eyes and diaphanous nipples beneath her wet blouse smiled at me. At that precise moment, my mother's dream came to an end.

We collected books for a library and created student events to celebrate anniversaries. The most bombastic of those homages was the one dedicated to Bolívar. Inspired by José Martí, I pointed my index finger at the school's principal, a physician with the rank of colonel in the National Guard, and insolently told him that at the slightest ruffling of feathers the Liberator would arise from his tomb and cut off his head with a flaming sword.

In the midst of the ensuing embarrassment, the young English teacher, Matilda Morales, boosted my vanity by saying how proud she was that I was her pupil.

Professor Modesto Vargas, lawyer and, together with Román Argüello and Daniel Olivas, co-founder of the National Institute of the North, taught arithmetic and algebra. I had a particular fondness for algebraic equations. Algorithms owe their name to the Arab, Abu Ja'far Mohammed ben Musa al-Khowarezmi, Professor Vargas told us, although others claim they originate with Albiruni (al-Biruni), born in Birun of Khowarezm. Algebra, in turn, derives from the word al-jebr, which means "restoration", he continued, while I watched Consuelo. In the third century, Diophantus of Alexandria created first and second-degree equations following the form: $AX^m + BX^n = 0$.

It was Leonardo of Pisa, a native of Egypt who introduced algebra into Italy, where it came to be considered the sublime form of arithmetic, he droned on, while Consuelo gazed back at me.

With the creation of analytic geometry, Descartes gave a vigorous impetus to algebra, leading to Newton's and Leibnitz's discovery of integral calculus. And, the teacher concluded, while everyone else noticed that Consuelo and I were gazing at one another, there are two theories of capital importance: transitive substitution groups and groups of equations. She and I stopped looking at each other, her cheeks flushed, mine pale.

Anatomy was taught by Dr. Rodolfo Pérez, the black man, based on the work of Testus, from whom we learned in mid-adolescence the secret location of the Malpighian tuft — Consuelo's eyes and mine locked — that the mediastinal plura covers the pulmonary peduncle, and that it is most important to study the circulatory, nervous and lymphatic systems. And that the behavior of the anal passage — Consuelo blushes and avoids my eyes — depends on the volition of the subject, independently of whether that subject possesses a feminine or masculine urethra, through which the lymphatic fluids of the pelvic organs also pass.

When they told me in Spanish class that it is correct to ask "the hour," I inquired, and received no answer, why we couldn't ask "the hours," since an hour is always one yet they go by so quickly — as Edmundo Montenegro says — that they don't seem so long. It's true, Consuelo noted, that hours should be plural, for as soon as I ask, "what's the hour," at least two seconds have elapsed, depending on the agility of my speech, which means that by the time that you reply, it's no longer a single moment that has passed, but two or perhaps three. There is no single hour, only plural hours. "If you don't think so, ask Einstein," said Raúl Amador, who became a civil engineer. "Grammar is easier," said Miriam Ramírez, a friend of Consuelo's who became a lawyer. I understand the difference between a direct object and a dependent clause, as well as why I shall never again confuse two words: rebel and revel. Adrián Blandón rebels against everything, while Rigoberto Navarro revels in being a good student; "in being a jerk," said Orlando Vargas; "in being a Somoza supporter," said Yolandita Tellería.

2

In the early hours of a moonless night, in Mrs. Richardson's stuffy hallway, I found myself at last, timid and overcome by excitement, with Consuelo, whose kisses pleased me not only because they were our first but because they tasted of cheese and *jicote* honey.

After that, we saw each other on weekends at her parents' country house by the river at the edge of town, and each embrace was cause for shame and joy. Her body pressed against the very center of my pain; of my desperate urgency.

Once we went to Managua in a bus filled with students, and when we returned that night her right knee pressed against my left knee for several hours without the slightest wish to stop, without tiring, without speaking a word. Despite my inexperience, I was certain that in the darkness her pure face was imprinted with that seriousness expressing confusion and resentment which typically appears when it's no longer possible to distinguish my skin from yours.

Ramón Gutiérrez and I visited the Salida a Jinotega neighborhood. There we met some carefree girls with honest, slender waists: the Corrales sisters.

I liked Alicia Ampié. It was something mysterious about her eyes, a difference to her hips. She permitted me ample liberty of expression with my caresses but denied me her kisses until one night, as we sat in the drizzle on a compartmented bench against the north wall of the cathedral, she confessed that she had spots on her lungs. I kissed her, drank her saliva; we embraced until contagion, sadness, gratitude and consummation were a certainty.

Sometimes I escaped from the Institute. Together with Guillermo McEwan, Edmundo Montenegro, Julio Cuarezma and Adrián Blandón, we discovered unmapped rivers and roads. We learned to swim in La Presa, a natural swimming hole in the Matagalpa River which also attracted couples on Sundays, when the occasional adolescent would get drunk for the first time.

During those years of discovery, freckle-faced Teresita was always in the background until she convinced me that she was intelligent, that she read Balzac, and that, had she known her, she'd be a devotee of Beauvoir, or at one time of Margarita Gautier. She and her mother, Doña Teresa, were literary enthusiasts. I'd go to their house to listen to them and would die of jealousy because Teresita looked more at Adrián and her mother than at me. When I asked her to be my girlfriend, she said: "Maybe yes, maybe no." That, according to Julio Cuarezma, meant yes; according to Edmundo Montenegro, it meant no; and according to Teresita, it meant "maybe yes, maybe no."

Doña Teresa spoke to me of my friend Flaubert, although there wasn't the slightest indication that she was Madame Bovary. She was a sad widow who lived with dignity. She wasn't familiar with Pound but did know the Modernist poets; for some reason, she frequently talked about José Asunción Silva. Her enthusiasm for Gogol and Dostoesvsky led me to read the Russian classics. Once, she spoke to us of London and Hemingway.

One day I kissed Teresita on her blushing freckles. "Maybe yes, maybe no." The leaves turned red and fell in winter on Pythagorus's theorem, on our snares, on Jorge Isaacs. It was no. She married handsome Chicho, Consuelo's brother.

Marina, on the other hand, agreed to go swimming with me — in defiance of the lawyer who paid for her whims and her rent — handling my impatience and clumsiness with the dexterity of a barmaid who sells marked cards. During moonlit nights she would sing — I don't know why I relate her voice to the lucidity of her legs — *Vereda Tropical* and *Bésame Mucho*, while I told her in the voice of a baritone suffering from the flu: "I think of you, you inhabit my mind, you alone, imbedded there, endlessly at all hours, although perhaps my indifferent face fails to reflect the flame upon my forehead which silently devours me."

During that vacation I went everywhere with Marina. We visited friends, orange groves, bends in the river, the cave of crickets and absences. One day her mother, who sold rum and told fortunes, begged us to stop seeing each other. I swore I would die first, but the little shrew said that that was reasonable, that she couldn't survive without the lawyer's support, that she..., that I..."don't cry sweetheart, I really love you." She left and never returned. My mother found out about my love affairs, as did everyone else, and she reiterated her devotion to St. Francis of Assisi, that useless guardian against adolescent excesses. It was then, as part of my purification treatment, that I read — at first grudgingly, then with delight — the *Little Flowers* of St. Francis. That didn't prevent me, however, from reading Gogol's *Dead Souls*, the works of Alberto Masferrer, with their references to Sandino; Stendahl, Emily Brontë, Corín Tellado, or the adventures of Bill Barnes, Doc Savage and Nick Carter.

Chapter Four

1

In those days I was hopelessly in love with Emma Rouault, who would become Madame Bovary.

I felt such compassion for her that I wound up loving her, amazed by her ability to immortalize herself. How easy it was for that woman to transform herself into a fountain, or a tongue with which to lap up her summers! Wearing the rose of her tempest, she excited me during my adolescent years, even as I saw her languishing on a quilt of foam, expired, unhinged, with a trickle of blood that I wanted to drink, her neck motionless, with her gold threads and slender waist, made to the measure of her emotional upsets and the frights she gave her lovers.

One day my cousin, Pastor Cordero, saw me sit down beside her, heard her agonized scream as my hands restrained her dislocated hips, and concluded with the confusion of a blind clarinetist that I was head-over-heels in love with Rosibel.

The realism of Gustav Flaubert resides in him and not in the creatures of his works, whose sentiments count for nothing. What matters is not what they think, rather the degree to which they are instruments of protest against the inanity of the epoch. Flaubert used to say that more than telling a story, he was seduced by the idea of creating an atmosphere. While he was writing *Madame Bovary*, he thought constantly of the greenish color of one corner of a small-town hotel — the color of mould, to be precise. That atmosphere of congealed time is a crown of thorns upon the head of Emma Bovary.

If Guillermina, my mother's advisor in matters of ejaculatories and other complicated forms of prayer — the one who would send lemons and flowers to Monsignor Oviedo — had known Emma's story, she would have been as scandalized by it as was Monsieur Ernest Pinard, public prosecutor of the Second Empire, who was said to have secretly written poems extolling fornication.

The story of Madame Bovary is a tale of human rebellion. It's also the story of Doña Dora, who died thirty years later without having lost the anxiety in her gaze; it's the story of Señora Lucía, who loved poets, painters and guerrilla fighters, whom she provided, after the requisite ceremonies and horoscopes, with indirect enlightenment and responses to tender crossword puzzles.

No tale of love or adventure, no work of theater or philosophy or of juridical hermeneutics, has captivated me as much as the story of this lady born in France and in my heart.

Some day I'll have a daughter whom I shall name Emma. Among all the others, she will be the one who I believe is going to live her life most fully, the one whose gestures will be a premonition of pure beauty, the one who will find it impossible to take her own life or to be an adulteress, because her existence will be assured by freedom.

2

Monsieur Roualt, Emma's father, pulled back the curtain — had he not done so it would have signified his rejection of her suitor — and the widowed doctor, Charles Bovary, once more encountered a new woman.

We came to the wedding from 10,000 leagues around. The men wore embroidered shirts and the women had their hair greased with rose pomade; I wore blue trousers and a white shirt. Monsieur Bovary and I were happy. We noted the bride's rosy cheeks, her midnight hair and above all her eyes: black after sunset, blue before dawn.

Afterwards, as he set off to visit patients ill from fever and loss of blood, Charles would blow her a kiss from astride his horse and I, understanding, felt no jealousy. With open eyes and closed lips, she lamented that their honeymoon had not taken her to countries with sonorous names. Someplace, perhaps in Matagalpa, there must be a country where happiness blossoms like a magnolia.

Charles did not have an irresistible impulse to go to the theater in Paris or to the Jungles of Musún, nor did he know how to handle a saber. "Isn't it the man's duty to initiate the woman in the energies of passion?", my daughter Emma will ask once she finds herself knee-deep in words of honey and rhyme.

When the Marquis invited us to his house, we sipped champagne for the first time and the frosty bubbles made our lips and hearts tingle. When the time came for the ball to begin, she observed how a servant climbed up on a chair and broke two window panes as the lamps burned more dimly. Madame Bovary turned her head to one side while her right hand allowed the Viscount to lead her as they danced across the hall. Dizzied, she rested her head against his chest and I was jealous. Gradually, the faces of the guests, the shattering of the window panes, the dizziness, the horses and the Viscount's sideburns all faded from memory.

Emma awaited the unexpected. When they departed the small town of Tostes, I discreetly accompanied them. She was pregnant and when we arrived at Yonville l'Abbaye, she was already suffering from nostalgia. But more than nostalgia, from melancholy; more than melancholy, from expectation; more than expectation, from *Wuthering Heights*, and somehow Emma was Katherine and I was Heathcliff. There was Homais the pharmacist, counsellor, atheist, friend and neighbor, the petit bourgeois in whose presence I felt inclined toward agnosticism.

I experienced an immediate antipathy toward Léon Dupuis. "Isn't that so?" she exclaimed, fixing her great black eyes upon him. It was nighttime. The next day she saw him in the plaza — in broad daylight — with her blue eyes. Bertha was born one Sunday at 6:00 in the morning. "Have you something to do?" she asked him as she was leaving to visit her daughter at the wetnurse's house. "Come with me," she begged him. The young man's topcoat had a black velvet collar, and he took it with him to Paris. She was depressed. Her flesh burned.

3

That was when Rudolph Boulanger of La Huchette appeared on the scene. Emma saw him walking in the meadow beneath the poplars, and he thought: 'Yes...but how shall I get free of her afterwards?' I hated Boulanger. Election time came around. A hundred feet away on the fairgrounds there was what appeared to be a black Chontales bull with a halter and an iron ring in its nose. It stood as motionless as a stoplight. They chatted. The Counsellor arrived and they took their seats to listen: "Ladies and Gentlemen: Permit me to do justice to our Monarch, to this king who rules with a firm and prudent hand." They are on a platform. People glance at them out of the corners of their eyes. "I think we should move farther back," Rudolph said. "People below might see me, and with my reputation being what it is..."

"You're slandering yourself, Rudolph!" exclaimed Emma. That's the only time I thought her foolish. "Don't you know that there are tormented souls," said Rudolph, "and that because they're tormented they give themselves to all manner of caprice?" Emma looked at him as though contemplating a traveller who has visited extraordinary countries, and replied: "We don't even have that sort of distraction. Is it possible one day to find happiness?" Emma asked. "Yes, one day you'll find it," Rudolph said. He passed his hand across his face, then let it rest on Emma's. She withdrew her hand, while mine sweated.

Rudolph drew close to Emma and she inhaled the scent of the pomade that gave luster to his hair. "Why have we two met?" And this time she did not withdraw her hand. I wanted to shout at her not to be taken in by the guile of butterflies or the deceptive color of cauliflowers.

Off in the distance could be seen the rooftops and bell tower of Yonville, and in the nearby fields, horses. "Oh, Rudolph!" she exclaimed uncontrollably and, hiding her face after a prolonged shudder, abandoned herself to him, which upset me.

When she read his farewell letter, she fainted. She came down with a cerebral fever and Charles applied mustard plasters and cold compresses.

4

The crowd gathered in front of the theater. Suddenly the footlights came on and there stood Lagardy. The curtain fell. "Do you know who I ran into upstairs?" "Was it Léon?" Emma asked. My antipathy for that absurd law clerk reappeared. León entered the box. He told her he had written his will. "But why?" she asked. "Yeah, why?" I asked. "Because I have loved you so." That idiotic phrase was for Madame like a gust of wind that sweeps away the clouds. "Tomorrow at 11:00 in the cathedral," whispered León. "No," she said to herself, and at my suggestion wrote a letter rejecting him.

"Go find me a coach." The youngster ran out pursuing his impatient cry through the street of the four winds. The contraption began to move. It went down the Rue Grand-Pont. "Keep going, keep going," a voice said. Through the Lafayette intersection. "Keep going, keep going." It paused before the Jardin des Plantes. "Keep going, keep going." It passed by St. Sever, by the Hospital grounds where old people took the sun. "Keep going, keep going." On it went aimlessly.

That afternoon, out in the countryside, a hand slipped beneath the curtains of the coach and released several scraps of paper. The fragments of the letter I had suggested, torn to bits, fell like white butterflies onto a mound of red clover. I tried to peer through the slit in the curtain but could see nothing, which made matters worse. I imagined she had opened her legs, that she was without her brassiere, and other delicious and masochistic misfortunes.

Where had she learned such depravity? She undressed, pulling out the tie from her corset like a twisting serpent; hidden in her bosom were two roses that she thrust in our face. She was shameless. What pleasure! What fear! In adultery Emma found all the vulgarities of matrimony; but how would she rid herself of León and of me? Besides, she was already accustomed to the sinfulness of our kisses, to the lust etched in our wondering eyes, to the fever of our hands.

5

Felicity handed her a grayish paper. Emma read at a glance that her furniture was up for sale. She set out hastily for the beautiful mansion, reached the little park gate and entered the patio bordered by a double row of dense linden trees. She climbed the stairway to a corridor along which were arranged rooms in Indian file like a monastery. Rudolph's room was at the very end.

Rudolph made an effort to overcome his tenderness. She, ever enchanting, did not see the tear quivering on his lashes like a raindrop about to fall into a blue chalice. "As you know," said Emma, "my husband placed his fortune in the hands of the notary, who has disappeared, robbing us of everything. I'm desperate. I need 3,000 francs." I could see that she was lost.

"Ah!" thought Rudolph. "That's why she's come." And as calmly as a poker player he replied, "Well, I don't have them."

"You can't be so poor," said Emma. "When one is that poor, he doesn't have carbines with silver stocks, nor does he purchase clocks with mother-of-pearl inlay, nor gold cigarette cases, nor fancy trinkets, nor greyhounds. Even those trifles could be turned into money," she exclaimed, glancing scornfully at a pair of cufflinks resting on the mantelpiece. "I, on the other hand, would have given you everything; I would have begged in the streets in return for just one of your glances."

"I don't have them," Rudolph repeated calmly.

6

Emma wrote the date, the day, and the hour and sealed the letter. She stretched out on the bed. She heard the crackling of the fire, her husband's and my breathing as I waited expectantly, standing beside the bed. 'I'm going to sleep, and sleep forever,' she thought. She took a sip of water and again tasted the horrible inky flavor; she was overcome by such nausea that she scarcely had time to reach for her handkerchief.

The chill of death ran through her body. Charles touched her gently on the stomach and she emitted a shrill scream. Shocked, comprehending everything, he backed away. We fell to our knees and gazed at her with infinite tenderness. She felt that no one had ever looked at her that way before.

Felicity ran to Homais' house and the village kept vigil all that night. The horrible inky taste continued. "What if we apply more mustard plasters?" "Be brave, be brave; there's nothing more we can do." Her chest began to heave. Felicity knelt before the crucifix. Emma sat up like a galvanized corpse, astonished, suspended.

Bertha asked for her mother. She called out for her several times but since she never appeared, she stopped thinking about her. Children are that way. They have the powerful weapon of amnesia.

To please her, as though Emma were still alive, Charles bought himself patent leather boots and white ties. At the dinner table, he sat beside her; he placed her armchair next to the fireplace and sat facing her, undoubtedly to gaze into her eyes or look at her knees. I pitied him.

Homais the pharmacist, provider of the arsenic, proprietor of growing success, still yearned for a decoration. For Emma's tomb he proposed a kind of rotunda or massive organized ruins. All his proposals included a weeping willow symbolizing sadness.

Charles grew desperate, less now for Emma than because despite all his efforts she was fading from our memory.

While going through the little drawer of the rosewood chest where Emma kept her things, he found Léon's letters. He discovered a box and kicked it open. Rudolph's portrait reproached us. Charles' devastation was total. He no longer went out; he stopped receiving visitors. His beard grew wild; his clothes turned to rags.

Bertha came looking for him at supper time. His head rested against the pavilion wall, his eyes closed, mouth open, and in his hands was a long lock of black hair. The girl nudged him gently and Monsieur Bovary toppled to the ground. I realized that he was dead.

7

Homais received his decoration. Gustav Flaubert was never elected to the French Academy. His last words were: "*Madame Bovary c'est moi.*"

Chapter Five

1

My mother was afraid that my brain, like Don Quijote's, would become desiccated from too much reading. With an air of singular dignity, she remained ever alert to my footloose ways and roving eyes. She was severe rather than affectionate, but I loved her all the same, not only because she was my mother, but because she was beautiful — as my own memories, other people's remarks and photographs attest — and because she was as spotless as the whitest table linen. I was proud of her full lips, her washed hair, her wrinkles, her authority. I don't remember her being young as much as beautiful. I do not remember her as beautiful, rather austere; I don't remember her as severe, rather smoking as she reflected upon the Holy Trinity and her investments of the previous day in cooking oil and *Maragogipe* coffee.

It displeased me that she should be the proprietress of a store that sold grain, blue trousers, saddles and guitars, as well as of a small cigar factory. I didn't like her being so skilled at stripping away her mask to reveal the self-sacrificing air that I had always known, nor the fact that she kept her money in wooden boxes. Yet I trembled whenever the persistent smoke of a farewell, of a definitive good-bye, clouded her face.

It was a primitive but flourishing business. Fruit, clothing and grain, arriving slowly in belching trucks from Managua or other regions of the Pacific, were subjected to her expert scrutiny. Middle-aged market ladies came to dicker for rice, cacao, mangos and other incidentals accompanied by pretty young nieces, in whose homage I would lie beneath the red quilt on my iron cot with its safety railing an extra half hour until Aunt Lala came in to remind me that I had to go to the San Luis Grammar School. Sometimes the ladies would be accompanied by godsons, nephews and pretentious, good-looking sons who drew sighs from Aunt Lala and the girls who worked in the tobacco factory.

By popular acclaim, Juan Pablo Ordeñana was Rudolph Valentino. His success lay in his hairdo, his swagger, and the conviction with which he held women's arms. One day we read in the paper that he had won the lottery, and he never came back. From then on, the favorite tango of his devotees was *Volver*.

Visitors would come to stay at my house, injecting new life into the place. One Holy Week Doña Estela Munguía brought her daughter Angelita, barely more than a little girl, but who drove me wild. She made me want to cry, stroke her hair, to scratch her knees, to tickle her sciatic nerve, to close her eyes as if she had died and then revive her with mouth-to-mouth resuscitation, to tease her until she begged for mercy — above all when she crouched down, displaying dimpled buttocks, to gather rose-colored *jocotes* which had fallen complicitously to the ground. Angelita savored each *jocote* as if it were a tongue and I had to sit there in the grass with agonized lips hiding my shame. The following summer, Angelita returned in the middle of her honeymoon with a radiant, hateful, amiable young man who chauffeured her around.

All sorts of merchandise and insults circulated in the Matagalpa marketplace. Quarrels between market ladies refined and dispersed the most obscene phrases ever heard in the Spanish language, frightening children, dogs and the chickens awaiting final sacrifice in a state of catalepsy. Some of the vendors, like Big Esmeralda, were famous throughout the country. I remember her fondly because she always treated my mother with deep affection. It fills me with pride and astonishment that Doña Anita was so respected and that she was never involved in that sad clamor.

2

Despite the commercial uproar of my insignificant universe, there was an economic crisis in Nicaragua. The public debt had risen steadily since 1926 and the so-called national treasury was completely bankrupt. This obliged the government to contract new loans with

North American banks, while my mother kept on buying and selling, ever elegant in her white apron, moving self-confidently amidst that mass of small details.

My father, meanwhile, sold pink pills, prodigious bicarbonates, Bayer tonic, and perfumes. Once, while they searched for me all over the marketplace and throughout the city, I emptied the containers in a showcase where nobody looked, on top of a pile of shit and mixed in all the powders and creams against aging and skin rash.

The capitalist crisis of the '30s hit the production of coffee, rubber, lumber, and sugar, upsetting the balance of payments. The earthquake of 1931 that leveled Managua complicated things to the point that it was impossible to pay the foreign debt. There was no other way to confront the crisis than to impose exchange controls in 1931 and devalue the *córdoba* in 1934, the year that General Augusto Sandino was assassinated. Successive devaluations in '37 and '38 exerted pressures for a readjustment of the foreign debt, Anastasio Somoza García having now become the master of servants and bosses alike.

The devaluation of the dollar, as well as the *córdoba*, increased the value of gold and provoked enthusiasm among Canadian and North American mining concerns. Between 1939 and 1947, gold was our main export and the most frequent adornment in the mouths and on the fingers and necks of the market ladies.

Blacks with gold fillings came to my mother's store to buy and sell rings and chains which she hid away in cabinets sealed against our curiosity.

My mother continued to deposit her bills in coffers made more secure than a bank vault by Yale padlocks, whose keys she guarded with prodigious zeal. This despite the existence of the National Bank and the fact that our country realized operations with the Export-Import Bank that indebted us up to our ears from 1939 on. Faced with the failure of exchange controls and devaluation, a bank reform was attempted in 1940. In 1942, we owed nearly 2.5 million dollars.

I have a vague memory of the confiscation of some land my mother owned by an enterprise belonging to the Somozas. Afterwards, it was sold to the Ministry of Education and they built a school on it which has since been named Republic of Cuba School.

It was about that time that the Guard took away Prince, a dog that had brightened my childhood. They poisoned him because there was an epidemic of rabies. As far as I could see, my mother grieved as much over her lost land as I did over Prince.

A breath of economic relief increased the sale of tobacco and cigars in my mother's store, and I can still smell the shredded veins and impeccably sliced leaves, cut by a constellation of adolescent girls with crossed legs and premonitions, who gladdened the last years of my childhood and the first of adolescence.

3

During adolescence we'd go out in mixed groups without ever knowing what was going to happen; that is, nothing did happen except for Leonore's loss of her virginity at the hands, so-to-speak, of Consuelo Baldizón's brother, Rodolfo, and Auxiliadora's loss of hers through the resources, likewise a figure of speech, of Jaime Vargas's brother, whose name was also Rodolfo. Both were experts in voice modulation, placement of the right hand and eye avoidance.

Some of us collected stamps, shooting stars and Wu Li drawings cut from old oriental magazines; others collected seashells, gonorrhea and round stones. The two Rodolfos collected girlfriends, which was precisely what the rest of us wanted to do. Not until now have I given vent to the envy I felt towards them back then.

Chapter Six

1

We were in the midst of the Second World War. The heroes were the North Americans, the English and the French, according to *La Noticia*, the daily paper we read which scarcely mentioned the Soviets.

Nevertheless, in 1945 the German army is pursued relentlessly in the northeast by the Red Army and retreats kilometer after kilometer back toward the center of its arrogance. Von Rundsted's counteroffensive on the Western front briefly dissipated the Allies firm conviction that the end of the war was drawing near. In Italy, the equilibrium was broken and the troops rebelled, following along behind the triumphant armies. Eisenhower, Patton and McArthur pound their drums.

In the Far East, the Japanese have lost the initiative. In the Philippines and in Burma, the Yankees and the English take over, fulfilling Clausewitz's prediction, while the western news agencies focus their spotlights on Chiang Kai Shek, ignoring Mao Tse Tung and defeats of the Chinese Red Army. I remember the huge headlines when Franklin Delano Roosevelt died. I was moved by the disappearance of that famous and attractive cripple. Roosevelt said: "He's a son-of-a-bitch, but he's ours," referring to Somoza, yet the Nicaraguans were not to blame for the fact that the sons-of-bitches were the property of Yankee presidents.

The day the North Americans dropped atomic bombs on Hiroshima and Nagasaki, my mother said it was a horrendous crime.

Somoza, who for a while had portraits of Hitler and Mussolini hanging in his office, declared war on the Axis and avidly confiscated the property and possessions of citizens of German origin. In Matagalpa, the best-known victim was Don William Hüpper.

The Second World War, which made the word "freedom" and "democracy" so fashionable, not only had a favorable effect on the balance of payments and the foreign debt, but it also had a direct bearing on the political upsurge that swept Central America in 1944.

2

It is difficult to situate Ubico. Napoleón Bonaparte — not the Corsican but the Guatemalan — alias Jorge Ubico, made a hobby of motorcycles and shooting prisoners in the back and was crazier than a half dozen opium-smoking frogs. They say he dressed his soldiers in the uniforms of the 18th-century French Army and that on his birthday he would hang a huge, luminous star with the number 5 at its center on the most visible part of his palace, because his name and surname had five letters each.

At night, the bureaucrats kissed his hand in Indian file. Should someone be bedridden with typhoid and unable to deposit the obligatory kiss, he ran the risk — if he survived — of having his head cut off in addition to missing the spectacle of two Lacandón Indians exhibited in a cage.

Napoleón was swept from the face of Guatemala on June 1, 1944; he didn't die on Saint Helena, rather in an obscure corner of New Orleans. Following General Federico Ponce's brief stay in power, Juan José Arévalo was elected constitutional president of Guatemala.

Arévalo, a genuine intellectual, attempted some reforms and in 1950 turned the presidency over to Jacobo Arbenz, leaving as his legacy every possibility of a conflict with McCarthyism. With the complicity, of course, of Somoza, the conflict came to a head in 1954 with the overthrow of Colonel Arbenz, who plucked the petals of Margarita Gautier's daisy: yes, no, yes, no, he wouldn't give the people weapons.

Maximiliano Hernández Martínez, a Salvadoran witch-doctor, vegetarian and Theosophist, would shed torrents of tears if one of his subjects accidentally stepped on an ant, yet delighted in killing peasants, who were for him without exception a swarm of communists. He believed that humans are reincarnated and that it was not, therefore, a sin to kill them by the thousands.

They say he was a good President
because he distributed cheap houses
to those Salvadorans who remained...[1]

Of little avail were his blue waters for averting all danger, his magical colors for curing measles, and his pendulum for detecting poisons and guiding foreign policy. Hernández Martínez was dethroned in 1944 from atop his mound of skulls and deceits. His fall aroused no compassion.

He is followed by a parade of military figures: Gen. Andrés Ignacio Menéndez, tenshun!; Col. Osmán Aguirre Salinas, tenshun!; Gen. Salvador Castañeda Castro, tenshun!; Lt. Col. Manuel de J. Córdova, tenshun!; Col. Oscar Osorio, tenshun! And today, José Napoleón Duarte. Stand fast! At ease!

In Honduras, the calf-faced old man, Tiburcio Carías Andino, manages to survive until 1949.

Nothing of importance happens in Costa Rica in 1944. The central highlands continue to sell coffee and the reformer, Rafael Calderón Guardia, is succeeded by Teodoro Picado, smiling friend of Somoza and the Costa Rican communists. The election of Otilio Ulate, annulled by Congress, provokes a revolt headed by José Figueres.

The Caribbean Legion has been organized. Its authors, accomplices, and accessories were Juan José Arévalo, Carlos Prío Socarrás, Juan Rodríguez, Juan Bosch and Rosendo Argüello, all of whom aided Figueres.

The Caribbean Legion prepared an impressive number of useless, failed plans against Somoza and Trujillo. The Legion's protagonists were spectacularly successful at squabbling among themselves.

In that turbulent year of '44 the fog lifted from our consciousness and the existence of the Somoza dictatorship became obvious to us. Demonstrations were organized, above all in Managua, from where we could hear the shrill echoes and see the flashes of light from *El Universitario*, in whose pages appeared Sandino together with brief, violent editorials that took our breath away.

---

[1] Roque Dalton, "El General Martínez," in *Poesía trunca*, (Havana: Casa de las Américas, 1977), p. 63.

It was then that I fully realized I was destined to participate in that struggle and that participation was a life sentence, barely distinguishable from a death sentence.

César Carter Cantarero, Arsenio Alvarez Corrales, Andana Ubeda, Pedro Juaquín Chamorro, Enrique Espinoza Sotomayor and Aquiles Centeno were mentioned as gallant leaders of a verbal uprising that was being repressed with teargas and truncheons. In Matagalpa, the Orúe Reyes brothers led a noisy demonstration, whose immediate result was the arrest of Don Edmundo Amador, Professor Modesto Vargas and Juanillo Mairena. Sweaty, armed men patrolled the streets, keeping a leery eye on the few pedestrians moving about the difficult streets of our small town. At that point, we forgot almost completely our lunar fetish and incorporated into our routine questions of greater rotundity.

3

So it was that we became aware, barely, of the existence of Augusto Sandino. My father, Tomás Alberto, had told us about him and shown us some photographs in which he could be seen with an arm about the General of Free Men. He even told me there was a close family tie, which I have never tried to verify.

He had met Don Gregorio, Sandino's father, at the home of my uncle, Sofonías Salvatierra. Don Gregorio talked incessantly about the assassination of his two sons. He spoke with pride about his son, Augusto, and reread dozens of times newspaper and magazine articles people sent him from abroad recalling the feats of his son.

My father said that Sandino was affectionate and treated him with particular deference. Indeed, they had known each other from an early age. I suffered a certain disillusionment when I found out that the photographs in which he appeared at Sandino's side had been taken during the peace talks and not during the war, and that my father had not been a combatant in the Army For the Defense of National Sovereignty.

When I asked him about this, Don Tomás told me that he was already in his 40s at that time and was a city dweller who would not have been of much use to the Sandinista cause in the mountains, but that he had been an officer in Zeledón's army and that Don Manuel, his father — my valiant grandfather — was a veteran of the National War. I verified this with historical documents.

Sandino's soldiers would come down from the mountains on occasion and buy large quantities of cigars at my mother's factory. My mother knew who they were but never told me until I was a student leader at the university. My father quietly boasted to me that he would send the General information about the National Guard obtained from an officer with whom he was friendly. My mother, who was tight-lipped even in the confessional, never confirmed this to me.

Chapter Seven

1

My father would relate how Sandino once told him about an encounter he'd had with Somoza. When they made a toast to peace, the National Guard Chief's hand trembled as he raised his glass of champagne. Sandino asked him, "Why are you trembling, General?" Somoza smiled in reply and, according to Sandino, "His goddamn hand kept on trembling."

Sandino, my father said, was double-jointed. He could place one foot, or even both of them, behind his neck.

The night he was assassinated, they machine-gunned the house of Don Sofonías Salvatierra — my father's brother and Minister of Agriculture under President Sacasa — and killed Sócrates Sandino, Salvatierra's son-in-law, and a young boy.

Col. Santos López was wounded in one leg and escaped by climbing up a chimney and jumping onto the power lines, which broke his fall. He skirted Lake Managua and made his way along back trails to Honduras, saving himself thanks to his courage and his agility of a mountain lion.

My father had been in the machine-gunned house several hours earlier but left before the attack. It was a good thing I'd already been born. Now we'd be saying: "What a great man Don Tomás was!" He would never have been an obsessive collector of books, never gone hungry following the earthquake, nor ever have become a diabetic. He'd be a martyr, the son of a hero of the National War, a Sandinista through and through, handsome with his Napoleonic nose and eagle gaze, one of Zeledón's soldiers.

My father died calling for me at the top of his lungs while I was with the guerrillas at Pancasán. He loved me; we loved each other; we were partners: my old man, my dear old man. I saw him when he walked slowly but still flirted with the lottery vendors, and when he would discuss the genealogical tree of dignity. He was as generous as King David and a jolly prestidigitator.

My beloved old man, perhaps we'll meet along some path I envision as recently washed by the rain, covered with yellow leaves and uncomprehending stars overhead. I'm grateful that you never punished me, and at this moment I give to you, like a blurry photograph, all this accumulated love. I buried you, old man, but I keep on remembering you.

2

These tales settled into our consciousness. Influenced as we were, too, by the works of Victor Hugo, José Martí, Juan Montalvo and Manuel González Prada, or by the discontent against Somoza — which appeared quite suddenly — they were like a flowering, like the discovery of a radiance that took away one's thirst and caused a disturbance in the breast. The same thing occurred when we spoke with the Bishop of Matagalpa, Monsignor Octavio José Calderón y Padilla, who was anti-Somoza all the way to the main altar. Yes, that's when we became aware, in a political sense, of the existence of Sandino.

The General's assassination on February 21, 1934, brought to a bloody close an intense historical period, marked, according to the Yankee military command, by 515 battles. Sandino took the initial, prophetic steps in what would be a victorious struggle.

With his martyrdom an arrogant passivity takes hold, in which the apparatus organized by the North Americans — the National Guard — is at once the spinal column, army, police, prison system, grotesque parade and political party. The National Guard displaces, or rather situates in an intermediate, dependent position, the traditional political parties and other instruments of the local oligarchy.

3

Direct U.S. interventions against Nicaragua commenced in 1854 when the North American government, in its confrontation with Great Britain, ordered the bombardment of San Juan del Norte in the southeastern corner of our country. The Marines leveled the town and induced London to sign a treaty which recognized the right of the United States to construct an inter-oceanic canal through Nicaragua.

In 1855, William Walker, a North American freebooter — a cold, gray reciter of psalms and death sentences — took the city of Granada, then the seat of government, and proclaimed himself president of Nicaragua. He reinstated slavery, decreed English the official language and prohibited both noise and silence. Six months later — despite diplomatic recognition by the United States — the Nicaraguans, supported by other Central American armies, expelled the invader with stones, torches, machetes and recaptured harquebuses.

Throughout the following period the dominant classes, organized in the two traditional political parties, Liberal and Conservative, went at each other tooth and nail in battles and futile skirmishes, each encounter another drop of pus.

In 1893, the Liberal Revolution triumphed under the leadership of Gen. José Santos Zelaya, who undertook to create something resembling a nation and to liquidate the existing medieval juridical structure. In 1909, the United States withdrew its recognition of Zelaya's government and in 1912 sent back in the Marines, who bombarded Masaya and frustrated what appeared to be a bourgeois democratic revolution, which never again raised its head.

Nicaragua was obliged to sign a treaty giving the United States exclusive rights to construct an inter-oceanic canal.

The Marine occupation lasted thirteen years. They withdrew in 1925, having installed a Liberal-Conservative government. "Nicaraguan sovereignty was but a memory in the history of the American republics," in the words of Rubén Darío. What legacy did they leave us? Chewing gum, the expression "okay," some kids with more-or-less pale blue eyes, and an irreversible national rage.

That popular rage found refuge in a Liberal segment of the populace that led the struggle against the Liberal-Conservative government. The latter monopolized favors from the United States. The Marines returned in 1927 with abundant munitions, hotdogs and airplanes. But there was the General with his staff. Sandino specialized in political prophesies and ambushes. He was the General of victories and apothegms. Sandino and his guerrillas — specters of the jungle, in Neruda's words — were a tree spiralling upward, now a sleeping tortoise, now a gliding river.

We find Sandino's revolutionary ideology in his program, in the popular demands he raised for the oppressed masses and for the nation as a whole, and in the social foundation on which he based his struggle — the solid foundation of workers and peasants, the only one, as he would say, capable of carrying the struggle to its ultimate consequences: "Our war is the war of liberators, fought to exterminate the war of the oppressors." He thus affirmed that the Sandinista war was a struggle to end all forms of oppression and exploitation.[1]

Carleton Beals, who visited the general headquarters of the Army for the Defense of National Sovereignty, wrote that Sandino was "utterly without vices," possessed "an unequivocal sense of justice" and had "a keen eye for the welfare of the humblest soldier."[2]

Lejeune Cummins transcribes Beals' conversation with Gen. Feland of the Yankee Marines:

Feland: What do you think of Sandino?
Beals: He isn't a bandit. Call him a fool, a fanatic, an idealist or a patriot, as you like; but I assure you that he is not a bandit.
Feland: Of course not. In the Army we use the word "bandit" in the technical sense, meaning the member of a band.
Beals: Then Souza is also a bandit?
Feland: You really put us between a rock and a hard place.[3]

---

[1] Humberto Ortega, *50 años de lucha sandinista* (Managua: MINT, Colección Las Segovias, n.d.), p. 27.
[2] Beals, Carleton, *Banana Gold* (Editorial Nueva Nicaragua, 1983), p. 83.
[3] Lejeune Cummins, *Don Quijote en burro* (Managua: Editorial Nueva Nicaragua, 1983), p. 129.

Without being an official colony, Nicaragua was transformed into what all colonies inevitably become: a combination cemetery and whorehouse.

4

For several decades following Sandino's assassination, both the poorer and better-off peasants, beaten, taciturn, alcoholic and hungry, ceased being protagonists.

Ideological obscurantism, notes Carlos Fonseca, is one of the reasons why Sandino's death produced a long period of atrophy in the popular struggle. For him, the development of a revolutionary movement capable of achieving victory had to confront that Stone Age backwardness:

> The ideological obscurantism inherited from the colonial period has continued to weigh decisively in keeping the people from engaging with full consciousness in the battles for social change.[1]

In contrast to the majority of Latin American countries where Marxism began to be disseminated at the turn of the century, in Nicaragua it was practically unknown.

Even prior to the cruiser Aurora's cannonade, the Club of Socialist Propaganda existed in Cuba under the direction of Carlos Baliño, a companion of José Martí. And in Argentina the newspaper *El Obrero* was already being published.

At the end of the nineteenth century in Argentina, Juan B. Justo made the first translation of *Das Kapital*. I'm certain that sixty years later there were not more than half a dozen copies of *Das Kapital* in Nicaragua.

In the struggle against anarchism during the first decades of the century, Marxist ideas were disseminated by a handful of precursors. The paucity of theory and the peculiarity of our socio-economic

[1] Carlos Fonseca, "Nicaragua hora cero," in: *Obras* (Managua: Editorial Nueva Nicaragua, 1982), vol. I, p. 81.

formations led the Latin American socialist movement to assume erroneous positions with respect to the national problem and the perception of alliances in our societies.

This gap between Marxist interpretation and Latin American reality became evident between the years of the Third International, which dictated the same political tactics to all parties, be they in India, Germany, Ecuador, or on the planet Jupiter. This failure to appreciate the concrete reality of our countries is apparent, for example, in the fact that the Communist Party of Mexico was founded in 1919 by the European, Michael Borodin, and Manabendra Nath Roy, a native of India who was named First Secretary. Years later that same party, alien to the Mexican body-politic by virtue of its origins, adopted a mistaken position with regard to Sandino.

5

In Nicaragua, only distant echoes of the Continent's social struggles reached our ears. Marxism was unknown, even in its dogmatic form. The organizational abilities of Luis Emilio Recabarren in Chile, the preaching of José Carlos Mariátegui in Perú, the action of Julio Antonio Mella in Cuba, the battles of Luis Carlos Prestes in Brazil, were all remote from Nicaragua. The University Reform initiated in Córdoba, Argentina, in 1918, was felt only later and there was no Nicaraguan representation whatsoever at the conference of Latin American communist parties held in Buenos Aires in 1929.

Ten years after Sandino's assassination, on July 3, 1944, while the world was still in the throes of the Second World War and the dictatorship of Anastasio Somoza García continued to consolidate itself, there emerged in our country a group calling itself the Socialist Party of Nicaragua and influenced by the strange theses of Earl Browder, who was at that time Secretary General of the U.S. Communist Party.

In their *Manifesto to Workers*, these labor leaders — probably honest but intoxicated by backwardness, mechanistic solutions and historical circumstance and lost in the labyrinth of Browderism —

asserted that it is necessary *to seek forms that will associate the interests of the exploited classes with those of the exploiting class*...and that they were *disposed to support the policy of social benefits initiated by the government of President Somoza*....

Of course, they weren't the only ones to fall into such aberrations. Vanguardia Popular in Costa Rica — headed in the beginning by the intellectual and man of goodwill Manuel Mora Valverde, whom we respect — asserted in those fateful days that *class contradictions had disappeared.*

These deviations in the development of worker and communist movements in Latin America, while they may cause us to frown, are nonetheless explicable and can only be understood in the context of the Second World War. German Nazi fascism is a fiery hurricane sweeping Europe and reducing to rubble thousands of cities, large and small. Millions of human beings are immolated by racist insanity. European concentration camps are a stigma on humanity, which refuses to accept such barbarity. Human hair is transformed into fabric so that the ladies of the hierarchy might wear uncommon dresses. Several tons of Jewish women's hair are stored at Auschwitz. Behind those piles of hair, one sees the imploring faces, naked, trembling bodies, eyes that are incapable of grasping the unfathomable dimensions of the incomprehensible.

As is known, the Second World War produces an alliance of survival and victory between the Soviet Union, the United States, England and France — the Allies — that was interpreted by North American communists as the beginning of an eternal peace in which the hostile contradictions between socialism and capitalism would disappear.

Browder held that capitalism was repenting of its original sins, which were self-correcting. The United States was marked by destiny to lead the Latin American countries generously toward their economic independence.

Browder proposed to dissolve the American Communist Party and invited other fraternal parties to follow suit, and then to organize a new movement devoted exclusively to propaganda.

It was even said that Browder was the foremost political thinker of the Americas. The views of that *formidable brain* contributed to the ideological deformities that became the order of the day in Perú, Venezuela, Brazil, Costa Rica, Nicaragua and other Latin American countries. To be sure, it wasn't bad faith, only a sadly mistaken conception, as history, in its infinite obstinacy, would clearly teach.

6

The Nicaraguan Socialist Party supported Somoza, offering him the muscular arms of its workers to defend him from the angry street demonstrations in which students, workers, artisans and housewives, led by the Conservative Party, demanded the dictator's resignation.

This deviation from revolutionary theory in Nicaragua, and particularly on the part of the PSN, was interpreted by Carlos as follows:

> It was a matter of a leadership that suffered from an extremely low level of ideological preparation...At a public meeting in 1964, it was revealed that the principal leader of the PSN had never read the *Communist Manifesto* of Marx and Engels.[1]

In our country, Marxist ideas began to circulate in a limited way during the 1960s:

> We are in Nicaragua, a country in which not until the 1960s and '70s do scientific revolutionary principles begin to spread.[2]

In the '60s, there were no Nicaraguan university professors with a Marxist formation. The first Marxist cell, of which Carlos formed part, was created in 1956 outside the university.

Amidst this vacuum, the most outstanding Nicaraguan intellectuals wallowed in intellectual backwardness and, at certain

---

[1] Carlos Fonseca, "Notas sobre la montaña y otros problemas," in: *Obras*, Vol. I, p. 126.
[2] Ibid., p. 125.

moments of effervescence in the popular movement, some even came to identify with fascist positions.

There were diverse reasons for this cultural weakness. On the one hand, the repeated North American interventions early in the century curtailed that segment of the liberal bourgeoisie that was disposed and open to modern world thought; on the other, Nicaragua's archaic socio-economic system also exerted a negative influence. Another cause that should be emphasized was the exodus of intellectuals who held progressive ideas. The dictatorship excommunicated revolutionary ideas and exiled their bearers.

According to Carlos, this orphanage had a positive aspect, for with the introduction of new ideas and the development of revolutionary practice, "there was no fertile ground in Nicaragua for sterile polemics...In the end, this political backwardness instilled a certain positive virtue in the militant Sandinista: a lively, practical inclination for action."[1]

Nicaragua's apparent imperviousness was rent asunder by the Cuban Revolution. The struggle in the Sierra Maestra influenced Nicaraguan political life. From that point on, the Nicaraguan rebellion nurtured itself on Lenin, Che, Ho Chi Minh and other revolutionaries.

[1] Ibid., p. 128.

Chapter Eight

1

Carlos Fonseca had commenced his studies in a large house whose corridors, at the time, seemed immense. A recent visit, however, revealed them to be quite insignificant. It was called the Matagalpa Boys' High School. The National Institute of the North operated out of the same building and both were directed by an elderly man with a kind face and an insignificant goatee that resembled a brigade of burnt out matches. He smoked imported cigarettes.

The old man was a medical doctor and in his free time he would offer advice and prescribe thiamine and bicarbonates. I pointed my index finger at this National Guard colonel and threatened him with the sword of Bolívar. His name was Benjamín, and he was the brother of Don Leonardo Argüello, who, thanks to Somoza's wizardry, was the winning candidate in the presidential elections of 1947.

One day, the School and Institute were visited by Anastasio Somoza García and several of us boys refused to shake his hand. I remember Jaime Vargas' face; Adrián Blandón staring at the ceiling, faithful to his pact with Winnetou; the clear, impenetrable face of Carlos Fonseca, and the abashment of the principal.

One of the teachers, Señorita Lucidia Mantilla, was fired for being anti-Somoza. Carlos Fonseca and some other boys went to visit her. She received them with smiles and tears in her brick house, whose uncluttered tables were covered with rose-colored table cloths. Among the primary school students who visited her was Manuel Baldizón, who years later would fall in the massacre of El Chaparral.

Señorita Lucidia was given a tribute, which included a dinner at the Hotel Bermúdez. At the time, it was one of the most important political acts outside the capital and it became the target of reprisals and commentaries. Ricardo Orúe's speech — he was a pharmacist and Independent Liberal with a certain nobility in his gaze — seemed eloquent to us. I memorized his phrase: *the broom of democracy will implacably sweep away the dictatorship*. In his address, Orúe made brief reference to my first political speech and described me as intelligent, which elicited congratulations that left me blushing and grinning and filled my father, who happened to be in town, with pride.

Some days later I became conscious of my destiny. I knew it because of the accumulated obstruction in my breast and the extraordinary satisfaction I derived from being an active witness to those small demonstrations. I realized that my life would be dedicated to combat, although at that moment I didn't know the color of the uniform nor the stubbornness of my roots.

Orúe's phrase about democracy circulated in leaflets that kids picked up on the streets and took home with them. Father Manuel Salazar, who at that time was director of St. Louis College and would later become Bishop of León, took one from me. After reading it, he stuffed it into that mysterious pocket at the back of his cassock with a look on his face that told me something had just transpired of more importance than I fully realized.

One day, Ramón Gutiérrez talked me into climbing up to the cathedral bell tower with him and tolling a funeral knell because Somoza was visiting Matagalpa. We reached the belfry where a Guard of peasant extraction was carrying out orders to peal the bells joyfully. Ramón scolded him for his ignorance, arguing that during presidential visits the bells must be tolled "like this, you idiot." We rang the bells as if for a funeral until Father Navarrete, a horrified Somocista, arrived on the scene.

The priest grabbed us by our sideburns and Ramón accused him of opposing the joyousness of the dictator's visit. Only his sacred vestments kept the Guard from hauling him off to prison.

2

It must have been about 1946 when Ramón Gutiérrez wrote a book entitled *The Artists of Sin*, that was an exact reproduction of the style of Vargas Vila. With a prologue by Douglas Stuart, son of a North American and a Chinese woman and intimate friend of ours

— agile of foot and mind and whose eyes would change color with his moods — the text related a masturbation contest starring a constellation of archangels who were visiting Earth. Archangel Michael won (as members of one band or the other shouted, "Bravo!") by filling with semen a golden goblet so huge it resembled a dinosaur's yawn, a few drops spilling over the edge. The book was dedicated to "my best friend..."

His best friend was studying that year in the Salesian College of Granada, where echoes of the scandal arrived without major consequences. He had a reputation of being well-behaved and a good student, above all because of the prize he won — causing Don Tomás great pride — for the best composition in homage to His Holiness, which I filled with beautiful phrases and declarations of fealty.

In Matagalpa, the case took on apocalyptic dimensions, and both Ramón and Douglas were ceremoniously excommunicated. I was on the excommunication list, but the Clerical Council removed my name — they either pardoned me or judged me an insignificant sinner — which saved my mother from certain death.

Inasmuch as Monsignor Calderón y Padilla bought and burned all three editions that were printed, the author and editor received modest dividends. Above all the editor, of course.

Banished from daylight, Ramón paid semi-clandestine visits to certain homes where he was looked upon as a curious object. Girls had a certain sympathy for the skinny, bespectacled Gutiérrez, who one day promised me that the next morning he would wake up crippled; and sure enough, he appeared with a cane and dragged his right foot around for the next year.

Monchita, daughter of a landowner grown wealthy from inflated coffee prices, held the keys to a coffer filled with bills of every denomination and bought splendid gifts for the friends of her sweetheart, Ramón, each Christmas and birthday while their idyll lasted. Monchita was pretty. She completely dominated the aging coffee grower and landlord, whom the neighbors called "the opulent donkey." I always liked the old man because he was as genuine as an x-ray of a fox. His children graduated as medical doctors, civil engineers and lawyers' wives and all left for that land of so many millions of square kilometers that people are swallowed up and disappear forever.

Carlos Fonseca, on the verge of adolescence, and ensconced in that small town — compact inferno and obvious paradise — remained a spectator of those initial skirmishes.

Some years later, Carlos, Douglas Stuart, Ramón Gutiérrez and I would chuckle over our deviltries and share them in all their detail with Guillermo Rothschuh Tablada, director of the Ramírez Goyena Institute, whose library Carlos organized and directed.

3

Victim of each winter's mud, Carlos walked all the streets of Matagalpa, a city as long as the legs of the mailman, the candy seller or the expert in wrong addresses. On moonless nights, we suffered a city subject to fusillades of fireflies and besieged by columns of crickets, frogs, rabbits and deer. Unemployed bricklayers and students, spitting and laughing, hung out at Pedro Culito's billiard parlor.

There, for example, we celebrated the latest Nicaraguan triumphs in the baseball championship, Stanley Cayaso's inopportune catch that permitted a hit and run, Chino Meléndez' narrow victory over Cuba, and the sins against the Holy Spirit of the manager who was always to blame for losses and never credited with wins.

Our conversations, sometimes in lowered voices, redeemed the *cariocas*, which is what the Matagalpans called the whores who came from Managua for the Patron's Day celebrations in September and offered their favors in "El Ciento Treinta," a mysterious refuge for city toughs where adolescents were denied entrance.

Carlos confined himself to playing pool. He knew how to make the ball hook, knew the secrets of the cushions and the set-up and the path to the chosen pocket where he sometimes placed the number 15 ball.

He sold *Rumores*, a squalid local weekly, from house to house. When he arrived at the pool hall, he'd hand his packet of unsold papers to a friend who would read the four pages aloud while the others, except Carlos, drank Xolotlán beer. They laughed, because after all was said and done it is possible to laugh at a German joke, or a parochial witticism, or even the news account in *Rumores*. The reader would declaim in a hoarse voice:

> Chela Ugarte and Julio Bustamante were colossal dancing the Apache. María Auxiliadora Ugarte stole the applause for the marvelously magic way in which she regaled us with the privileged enchantment of her golden voice.

"Vapid!" the reader exclaimed.

> *Rumores* truly celebrates the girding of Queen María Delia Corriols' temples with the emblem she displayed with maximum elegance, with perfect graciousness, after receiving it from the hands of the sublimely beautiful, incomparable Amelia Navarro.

The reader continued:

> Rumors have circulated that millionaire Don Joaquín Lanzas has decided to invest the millions he will receive from the sale of his crop in the purchase of several houses in Matagalpa. It is said that he is negotiating the purchase of the house occupied by the Social Club, the home of Doña Elisita Eger and the valuable building of the Hüpper family, across from the Bank. If this be true, Don Joaquín will shortly be the owner of more houses than any other capitalist in this city.

"Do you want me to keep reading?" Everyone cheered and whistled. "Listen to this:"

> I, Crescencio Hernández Muñoz, known to all and resident of Los Limones Valley, of my spontaneous, free will, do declare: I have belonged to the Conservative Party and, as of today, belong to the Somoza Liberal Party, which has given us peace for more than twenty years, as well as beautiful highways in all directions. Long live Somoza! Crescencio Hernández Muñoz.

"And this:"

> Last Tuesday at 11 p.m., young Santiago Rivas Haslam was operated on for appendicitis.

"And listen to this:"

> Inasmuch as evil-tongued individuals are spreading the false information that young Mrs. Eva Pineda struck her mother, that simply isn't true. What happened was that Eva was quarreling with her sister, Marina, and their mother got in the way trying to separate them. We publish this clarification...

"And I'll bet that cost Evita a fistful of money," the reader remarked.

> ...for its moral and so that people not think that Evita committed an act which conflicts with her excellent upbringing.

"And listen, brothers, to this:"

> Undoubtedly, a criminal act has recently been committed in Matagalpa. Yes, sir, a man has been killed! The police should investigate IMMEDIATELY to find out who is the victim and who the assassin in order to punish him with the full force of the Law. We are in a position to put the police on the right trail, since chance has placed in our hands the indispensable object with which the crime was committed. In the first place, we can affirm that a pistol was used, inasmuch as we have in our office the empty cartridge which the assassin was unable to retrieve when he fled and which we discovered in a trashcan. We suggest to the police as the quickest way of discovering the existence of the crime and the identity of the victim, that they proceed immediately to count the city's inhabitants, and of the two persons who prove to be missing, one will be the victim, and the other the person who fled the scene of the crime.

They ask Lorenza, who serves soft drinks and beer, to take over the reading. She does so, declaiming in youthful bell-like tones, which is the best way according to the experts:

One of the most splendid weddings of the year is that of the young couple Tito Navarro and Perla Amador: 8 a.m. Sonorous bells peal, announcing to the couple that the immutable pontifical hour has arrived. The streets and bridges are thronged with people. "How beautiful she is!" they exclaim. She is accompanied by her maids of honor, dressed in blue. Silvia...Lesbia...Lucy and Janet...gladden the chorus of skylarks that sing the morning hymn of love...She, the beautiful bride, inviting, magnificent, so delicate, so feminine, with her high heels, with her grace, her elegance and charm, with her incomparable beauty, and smooth, diaphanous skin, walks and smiles. As she climbs the temple steps, illuminated by her presence, she is greeted by 2000 fresh, fragrant lilies....

"Don't go on, please!" The first reader, who had been completely displaced, reclaimed the newspaper and read:

The festive prayer meeting for San Pascual will be held this evening at 8 p.m. There will be a ball at the home of María Rivera who each year collects food and clothing for the prisoners. It will be most enjoyable.

4

Carlos never spent much time playing pool. He had to earn his keep. Estelita, his younger sister, had already been born. Arithmetic is easy, but it is easier if you spend some time studying and he had to take advantage of the afternoon light, because candlelight is not recommended for the nearsighted. And before going to bed there was an hour devoted to reviewing the day's events with his mother: a sharing of tenderness and the sharing of communication.

The next morning was devoted to homework: the memorizing of Canadian rivers, European capitals, ancient history and natural science. Carlos was the best student. He knew the multiplication table better than anyone. He never learned to divide. Nobody could beat him in spelling or in the number of tributaries of the Amazon and Coco rivers.

At times he was seized by guilt for spending too much time having fun, because he only had a few hours after school. Vacations were another matter. And on Saturdays and Sundays, when the kids would go swimming at La Presa, he had to deliver the late mail. Once in a while on Saturdays he'd go see Tom Mix and Jorge Negrete, if he was able to manage the severe discipline of scarce change.

At age 12, Carlos had already heard of Sandino. Carlos was proud of being related to a Sandinista combatant, whose name was also Carlos Fonseca. Sandino extols him as follows: "I am speaking to you, traitors, swindlers, gangsters, wage slaves, choir boys. On your knees, all of you! I'm going to invoke the blessed names of my comrades-in-arms who have died defending the freedom of Nicaragua: Rufo Marín and Carlos Fonseca."

When Carlos no longer distributed the weekly *Rumores* nor delivered telegrams nor sold candy, he received a small allowance from his father, a high-ranking employee who administered Somoza family holdings.

On Sundays he went to 7 a.m. mass. His mother was a pious woman but she was never a *Daughter of Mary*, which is reserved for those who have preserved the desert and the fig, for old maids and those who soon will be, and who confess every time they quarrel with a neighbor, just as before each fright they're about to receive. She believed in Santa Teresita and every year, together with her children, she would spend the nine days of the Purísima at a neighbor's house where they passed around roasted cornmeal, bananas, and caramels wrapped in pink paper.

Besides that, on the first Friday of each month she had to reiterate her repentance for major sins and take communion while kneeling, her eyes on the floor, avoiding the professional gaze from behind the golden spectacles of that short young man approaching obesity, Monsignor Isidro Augusto Oviedo y Reyes. The cleric enjoyed preaching in thunderous tones from the pulpit, which was located before an inscription to the devil: *the gates of Hell shall not prevail against her,* and above the figure of Satan, who covered his ears so as not to hear the Word of God.

Monsignor was an expert on hellfire, which is the true fire and not the miserable flames we know that merely scorch the skin. Earthly fire is a paper tiger; hellfire is a real tiger with the appetite of a rabid dog that licks, passionately, cruelly and eternally, the skin of sinners who suffer without being consumed for life everlasting, amen.

The *Daughters of Mary* had to cover themselves from neck to ankles in loose-fitting dresses that allowed not for the slightest suggestiveness. Dancing was a sin. There are no known cases in which it has not provoked temptation, as is well-established in the annals of the confessional. Dancing, albeit unintentionally, produced heat, humidity, and if care weren't taken, an odorous pool resembling saliva, tears and crushed grapes.

I recall dancing with Rosibel; we didn't talk, just danced, and right there, my eyes disengaged, I felt the expansion of sin.

Guillermina, the girl who worked at the tobacco factory, would walk with me every Sunday in gardens and lemon orchards, and, while watching me out of the corner of her eye, picked bunches of flowers and filled baskets with lemons for the attractive priest. He recommended that girls, particularly wealthy ones, should not marry. Undoubtedly, it was not a sin, but the Holy Virgin looked benevolently upon the sacrifice of family life, amen.

Chapter Nine

1

Carlos gained his first notions of revolutionary consciousness at the end of his secondary school years, around 1954. At about that time, a Student Committee was formed at the Institute in response to the Guatemalan experience, with links to the feeble workers' movement in Matagalpa.

Ramón Gutiérrez, son of Don Erasmo — artisan of leather, a lean man, expert in dirty looks and ladies shoes — had run away from home, fleeing I know not what family drama, to El Salvador. There he became embroiled in Marxism.

On his return, in 1953, he befriended Carlos Fonseca and initiated him in the study of revolutionary theory. Ramón, who was an expert plunderer of libraries, carried off some Marxist texts in French, and the two of them were forced to study that language, which they came to read almost perfectly.

When Carlos became a leading activist, things got more serious. During Holy Week, the *jocotes* were ripening at Lala's house, next to the Matagalpa River. You had only to go down a winding path to wash clothing, pots and pans and your own skin. Beneath the trees, distracted by the thighs of girls bathing nearby, a group of adolescents gathered to read Marx.

Carlos would snap his fingers, interpret, reread, and grow impatient. For years, until his death, he lived in a patient impatience. Something had to be done, but we didn't know exactly what. Reading Marx wasn't enough. All right, there would be *Segovia*.

Even his father, Don Fausto Amador, did not recognize him as his son. Except for the regular pittance of an allowance. Perhaps, from afar, some obscure memory, a more or less explicit nod from Fausto, his half-brother, son of the legitimate wife.

It was important, moreover, to be conscious of the inequalities, of the backwardness, of the religious fanaticism, of the slow pulse of commerce, of the rise of the new rich, the offspring of coffee, who painted their houses seven different colors and reverently illuminated the dining room, where you would always find beans, butter cream and a depiction of The Last Supper.

But that and historical materialism were not enough to satisfy Carlos.

Carlos' secondary studies ended with an evening ceremony of hushed youths and parents who smiled a little more than usual. That day, March 2, 1955, he, a circumspect graduate, was awarded the "Gold Star" by Dr. Heliodoro Montes. Looking on, also with near-sighted eyes, was Carlos Arroyo Buitrago, who was addicted to the norms of dignity and the use of rhetoric. I was present when Carlos gave a speech in the name of his classmates, not a word of which I remember.

His senior thesis was entitled *Capital and Labor*.

In it he argued that *the three factors which intervene in production are nature, labor and capital, and that labor is the premeditated conscious effort made to satisfy needs.*

At that point, Carlos Fonseca was not yet 19 years old, and one must remember that those theses were written in a bare two hours. The student, seated at his desk, was given a theme to develop without consulting any books; it was a total improvisation. His was the ninth graduating class of the Matagalpa Institute. In *Segovia*, Ramón Gutiérrez had the following to say about the prize pupil:

> Carlos Fonseca Amador, editor of *Segovia*, spent his childhood confronting the realities of life at the side of his working mother, amid scarcity, high prices, poor pay, candlelight and the privations that are the lot of a lone woman. Carlos sold toffee on the street with his short pants and large cat-like, myopic eyes. He was a newsboy and bill collector; he tasted necessity and trod with bare feet on the prejudices that cobble the avenues of the rancid bourgeoisie. Carlos Fonseca Amador has triumphed. His talent has not

been wasted. I am proud to be his friend. I have a predilection for humble people with good minds, whose hearts are heavy, large and spotless.

His secondary studies were a formative schooling. Amidst poverty and dictatorship and the revolutionary upsurge in Guatemala that provoked anti-imperialist student movements, two periodicals appeared in Matagalpa edited by a group of youngsters: *Espartaco* (Spartacus) and *Vanguardia Juvenil* (Youth Vanguard). Their political and cultural consummation, *Segovia*, organ of the students of the National Institute of the North, appeared for the first time on August 1, 1954. Carlos Fonseca was its director and its editor was Francisco Buitrago, co-founder of the FSLN, who was born in Terrabona, near Matagalpa, and fell during the guerrilla campaign of 1963 around the Coco river and Bocay.

Segovia became notorious. Disrespectful of commonplaces and scandalous on local customs, it dared mention the law of the powerful and brought to its astonished readers the aggressive metaphors of the Vanguard group. Eleven issues of *Segovia* were published, the first seven edited by Carlos; the eighth by Cipriano Orúe; nine through eleven — the last — by Francisco Buitrago.

Drawings of local personages alternated with photographs of graduates and their teachers on the cover of the magazine. The pages of *Segovia* insinuated, suggested and stimulated the organization of cultural groups, which in turn organized anniversary celebrations and visits by national and foreign speakers. Articles dealt with poetry, natural science, there was even one dealing with gonorrhea and another on the development of capitalism in Europe.

The magazine had a little bit of everything. Modernist rhetoric and a declamatory style predominated. Mixed in with advertisements for local businesses were short stories, historical references, poems and essays on poets such as Rubén Darío, César Vallejo, Manolo Cuadra, José Coronel Urtecho, Fernando Silva, Ernesto Mejía Sánchez, Azarías Pallais and María Teresa Sánchez.

Carlos not only directed *Segovia,* but also published articles and even a poem of Vanguardist inspiration entitled "16 Verses From the Grist Hauler":

Animal of wood
rare vulture
without wings, quadruped
without vulture song
back flattened
earth
soiled, earthbound.
Thrice daily
the dish bath,
transitory cemetery
of broken dishes.
Occasional eater
of cats.
You're unlike your carpenter father.
The rich feed you scraps,
lacking even scraps the poor make you fast.
End.[1]

[1] *Segovia*, nos. 6-7 (January-February 1955): p.6.

Chapter Ten

1

I had been in law school four years when Carlos Fonseca arrived at the University. University life in León is a tale of nymphs recounted in a barroom among whores, pimps, booze and cards. We pawned our law books to a lovely lady, Ermelinda Somoza, who charged fabulous interest.

We lived in rented houses shared by a half dozen students and spent a substantial part of our time horsing around. One night, while Donald Osorno, a medical student, was sleeping off a binge that had lasted through four bottles of Santa Cecilia and two hundred forty-five hiccoughs, several of us pretended to play a lively game of poker with the light turned off, calculating the precise moment when the victim would open his eyes in the darkness.

It worked. When Donald opened his eyes in total darkness and heard the betting going on — with cards being discarded, antes raised, hands called — he rubbed his eyes until, convinced he'd gone blind, he emitted a terrified scream. We replied with guffaws and wisecracks that still ring in the good doctor's ears whenever he runs into his old classmates.

One morning, as I was returning from the bathroom, they caught me by surprise, pushed me out the door and locked it. The problem was that I was stark naked and Olga, the sister of my future wife, Yelba Mayorga, was at that moment passing by.

Another time, we offered a serenade to a hare-lipped lady. We of course sang in the manner of hare-lips and I can't blame the good lady for emptying a chamberpot of urine on our heads, whose odor indicated that our assailant was in a good state of physical and mental health.

One evening, at the hour when couples bring chairs out on the sidewalk to sit and converse intimately, I saw my chubby friend, Cristóbal Alvarado, approaching. A noble, good-natured joker, he's now a successful physician in New York. I noticed that he was walking strangely. I was about to introduce him to my girlfriend, when his demeanor, something about his shoulders and his eyes, aroused my suspicions. Sure enough, Cristóbal, with effeminate voice, teary eyes and exaggerated gestures, denounced my betrayal and reproached the horrified Angélica María for flirting with an engaged man. "Engaged to whom?" she asked. "To me, darling, who else?" the son-of-a-bitch minced.

Angélica María turned red, then pale, then methylene blue; she called me a degenerate. I had to use all my powers of persuasion to convince Cristóbal to explain that he was joking.

I started my university career in Granada, on the shores of the Great Lake, the most beautiful city in Nicaragua, filled with huge old colonial houses and inimitable evenings. There is something about Granada that entraps one: a quality of light, a timely glance, narrow streets that renounced boredom, who knows what?

Somoza closed the University of Granada to concentrate academic endeavors in León. Affected in their sense of tradition and local interests, the Granadans erupted in protests. It was all in vain. A sizeable bunch of rebels had to go to León Santiago de los Caballeros to swell the population of that sprawling, dusty, sweet city of youthful combats and premature sweethearts.

In the three university schools — medicine, law, and pharmacy — learning was by rote without labs, seminars or individually scheduled exams.

Medical students practiced dissection on stray dogs and abandoned cadavers, memorized Testut's *Anatomy* and thick tomes of physiology, histology and chemistry without benefit of laboratories, although they made intensive use of the hospitals and of the rich spectrum of tropical pathologies of local patients. We law students learned the Codes article by article. It was astonishing to listen to the rector, Don Juan de Dios Vanegas, reciting the voluminous Civil Code from memory. Pharmacy students made martyrs of themselves deciphering the hieroglyphs of every conceivable chemical formula.

We anti-Somocistas were in a bind. We had to study harder than the rest so they wouldn't flunk us. Sometimes they would flunk us anyway and throw us in jail to boot. During one of Somoza's visits they arrested and expelled the clever, rebellious Aquiles Centeno from the country. Each time there was a presidential visit, I'd wind up in *la Chiquita*, a tiny cell in the prison known as Number 21.

2

There were a number of noteworthy student movements during those years. The university authorities hung an ostentatious medallion of Somoza in the auditorium which, when it was discovered, was spat upon by hundreds of students, one by one, who then declared an indefinite strike until such time as the bronze plaque was removed.

Ernesto Cruz, together with José María Zelaya, led the university protest. Ernesto was an exceptional student. We mobilized throughout the country and most of the secondary schools joined the strike, including the Institute in Matagalpa where Carlos Fonseca was studying. Somoza García and his sons arrived, furious, to take down the medallion, leaving in their wake obscene, rancorous comments.

By the time Carlos arrived at the university, the Somoza machine had organized a group of students who were paid salaries as professorial aides and given instructions to confront the trouble makers. They didn't have to exert themselves very much, since alcohol, the law books and the anatomy texts were sufficient to imbue a majority of students with indifference.

Despite this hostile environment, we decided to commemorate the eighth anniversary of the death of Uriel Sotomayor, a university student assassinated by the National Guard. When we called the meeting, the University was shut down. The university authorities, aided by a check signed by the secretary general, Pedro Reyes Meléndez, organized an outing to the Poneloya beach resort near León. The only ones to attend that political event were Carlos Fonseca, Humberto Sotomayor — Uriel's brother — and myself.

A gang of Somoza supporters armed with chains, clubs and revolvers tried to block our way. We kept advancing without anyone daring to touch us and when we passed by, one of them, Emilio

Mercado, a native of San Marcos, watched us with tears in his eyes, with respect.

Carlos was saddened by that desert. He nearly poked me in the eye while proposing that we publish *El Universitario* in order to counter that obscene ebb tide of indifference.

Two young Guatemalans, Heriberto Carrillo Luna and Adrián Vega Ruano, both persecuted by the dictatorship in their own country, were studying in León. Heriberto was short, painfully poor, pale and studious. Adrián looked as though he'd stepped out of *The Burial of Count Orgaz*. The two of them were like Carlos' shadow. Because of their nationality — actually, I think, because of their modesty — the two Guatemalans limited themselves to serving as advisors, sometimes critical ones, although they were always carefully courteous. They helped us from the shadows. Amidst great limitations, we published three issues of the student newspaper.

Noel Guerrero, a native of León who spent most of his life in Mexico as a disciple of Lombardo Toledano and a militant communist, organized a study circle in which Carlos Fonseca, Silvio Mayorga and I took part.

We had long discussions about the domestic situation and the need to organize a revolutionary party. Guerrero expressed his reservations about Sandino. Carlos didn't let himself be influenced by that fountain of words and argued stubbornly that Sandino was an anti-imperialist and a revolutionary. He lacked elements of judgment, but not intuition.

3

It was in Edwin Castro's print shop, where *El Universitario* was published, that Carlos Fonseca and Rigoberto López Pérez met for the only time. Rigoberto recited some poems and went off in a corner to exchange a few hushed words with Edwin.

They said nothing to us.

In those bitter years, it was the dream of the exiles and anti-Somoza leaders to kill Somoza. They wanted revenge for murdered relatives; they wanted to give a radical response to the fatal rule of that handsome, charismatic, insatiable dictator.

A group of politicians organized themselves — if you could call it organization — around this unstated idea and, without taking the project very seriously, gave some monetary support to Edwin Castro, who volunteered to act as the principal operational leader of the execution.

Some days later, in the House of the Worker in León, amidst dance music and calculated laughter, the elder Somoza stood paralyzed with horror as a young man aimed a revolver at him with impeccable form. There, a few meters from Rigoberto, was the man who, after offering him a champagne toast, had ordered the assassination of Sandino.

There, a few meters from the people's vengeance, stood the chief of the assassins, torturers and smugglers, intimate friend of the Yankees.

There was the strongbox which, protected by a pack of gunmen, contained the national wealth.

There he was, surrounded by wide eyes that beseeched him to return their gaze; there amid fashionable dresses that clung to the skin of women who suffered the heat with the same stoicism as the men, perspiring up to the knots of their neckties.

There was the chief of the loaded dice gang, owner of El Porvenir Spinning and Weaving Co., the Nicaraguan Merchant Marine, Nicaraguan Air Lines, the Montelimar Sugar Mill, the Momotombo Match Company, La Cementera cement company, the National Insurance Company, and Gadala María Textiles.

There was the owner of the daily newspaper, *Novedades*, and the La Salud pasteurizing plant, to which would be added Metals and Structures, Inc., Central American Savings Bank, Nicaraguan Hotels & Co., Hotel Irazú in Costa Rica, the Corona Vegetable Oil Co., the Nicaraguan Tobacco Co., Nestles, Fabritex, Hercasa, Pennwalt Electrochemicals...and over 500 corporations.

There was the corpulent titleholder of 30 percent of the country's agricultural lands, the possessor of a thousand medals and 20 mistresses, that arrogant sack of fat; there was the Yankees' "son-of-a-bitch" shitting in his linen drawers as he faced that single, small, enormous revolver. When the bodyguards reacted, Rigoberto López Pérez fell wounded and, lying on the floor, continued to fire at that horrible, beautiful target until he had spent his last cartridge.

Who was this man? According to Carlos Fonseca, he was "the hero and poet...who in 1956 gave his life to bring to justice the U.S. Embassy's hired assassin of Augusto Sandino."[1]

Hardly had the echo of the shots died out amid the screams of the wounded, the body of Rigoberto López Pérez having been dragged from the ballroom leaving behind a long trail of blood, when a wave of repression was unleashed throughout the country. Tens of thousands of Nicaraguans went to jail. But that extraordinary act marked the end of an era of frigid silence that had commenced on February 21, 1934.

4

Edwin had given me a general outline of the plan, and I said nothing about it to Carlos, who was spending his summer vacation with his mother in Matagalpa. All of us political and student leaders were immediately seized.

Carlos was arrested in Matagalpa. He didn't know about the plan beforehand, but he was a personal friend of several of the participants. For many days we were subjected to harsh treatment, solitary confinement and beatings. Nevertheless, as Carlos put it, "We'd had no baptism by fire and went through that experience of repression as a test."

I was held in isolation and it wasn't until the night of September 22 — after acquainting myself with the deepest secrets of fear and thirst — that they brought me bound and now fearless before Capt. Nicolás Valle Salinas. There were the mother, brother and sister of Rigoberto, and Armando Zelaya. Together, bound hand and foot, they transferred us to El Hormiguero prison, in Managua, and locked us up in the same cell.

[1] Fonseca, Carlos: "Notas sobre la carta — testamento de Rigoberto López Pérez," in *Obras*, vol. 1, p. 393.

At night, and sometimes during the day, the jangling of keys announced yet another interrogation. They hauled out Rigoberto's brother a number of times and he would return at dawn, trembling and delirious. From behind the bars we could see them shove numerous citizens down the corridor, treating some of them with extreme violence. One well-known torturer — Gonzalo Lacayo — was the cruelest of them all. We saw how with professional hatred he beat a man respected for his Montalvo-like writings, which were published in the newspaper, *Flecha*. Don Ulises Terán, who was already quite elderly, maintained his dignity. Lacayo ripped off his glasses and smashed them joyfully to pieces. Years later, Carlos Fonseca would marry María Haydée, Don Ulises' daughter. Sergeant Gonzalo Lacayo would be executed by a Sandinista commando unit led be Oscar Turcios and made up of Edmundo Pérez, a gentle little Chinese baseball player, Daniel Ortega, Hugo Medina and Gustavo Adolfo Vargas.

One morning I saw Carlos. He had to pause for a moment near my cell while they opened his and he said to me, his blue eyes flashing: "The only thing I told them is that you and I are communists." I indicated I'd understood.

Afterwards, they transferred us to the Air Force prison where we occupied an overcrowded cell in which men of all ages came and went. Those who had no record of political activity were astonished; some were afraid, others outraged. There were prayers and obscene jokes and a lot of speculating.

I kept Edwin's confidences secret. One day, a story appeared in *Novedades*, the government newspaper, to the effect that they'd decided to release me. But instead of freeing me, they brought me before Anastasio Somoza Debayle.

Seated astride a chair, chain-smoking cigarettes down to the filter, wearing dark glasses that failed to conceal the sinister pouches under his eyes, that tall, arrogant man was convinced that his presence alone would break me. I remember the cold eyes, the self-assured attitude of Anastasio Somoza, future dictator, condemned to be executed.

He asked me: "What did Edwin Castro tell you?" I remained silent. Edwin appeared flanked by escorts, wrapped in a towel; his bruises and wounds were evident. He showed me his crushed fingers. I said: "It's true; Edwin said something to me about it." Somoza turned his head sharply and said in a low voice, almost sadly: "And you even say so, you little twerp." They didn't torture me.

A great many of those who were thought to be implicated in the execution of Somoza were tortured. They were placed in one of twin cells with lions and a panther in the adjoining cell.

I was so ashamed of having confessed my knowledge of the facts that during my trial — before a military tribunal that condemned us to several years in prison — I committed the additional weakness of telling my comrades in misfortune about atrocious tortures that I never received and that, in a vicious circle, heightened my shame.

The execution of Somoza had no immediate consequences. Luis, his eldest son, was named President of the Republic, and Anastasio, the younger son, Director in Chief of the National Guard. The hydra had been decapitated, but two younger heads, very confident of their power, had sprouted in its place.

5

Amidst cannon volleys, speeches, scandalous masses and crocodile tears, Somoza García was buried with the honors accorded a Prince of the Church.

Rigoberto López Pérez' sacrifice inaugurated a political renaissance.

That man, wrote Carlos Fonseca, became the great precursor. "Surrounded by darkness, what lightning flashes guide Rigoberto's footsteps?" [1] The son of Sandino, as Nicaraguans called him, revived once again the name of our immortal hero. And, Carlos adds,

> ...only two years after 1956, surviving veterans of Sandino's army picked up their guerrilla rifles under the leadership of the elderly Ramón Raudales, white-bearded patriarch who falls in his beloved Segovian mountains. And

[1] Ibid., p.395.

five years after the deed of September 21 — that is, in 1961 — the revolutionary force is organized that will call itself the Sandinista Front of National Liberation and will earn in armed combat the leadership of the popular struggle. [1]

This deed, extraordinary in human history, is carried out by one man. Armed only with a cheap revolver and his own courage, he was determined to inaugurate — as Rigoberto López Pérez himself said and as Carlos Fonseca afterward emphasized — the "beginning of the end" of the dictatorship.

Rigoberto was not a man of abstract projects. Even from the moral standpoint, he was a man of concrete acts, a rebel whom Prometheus and Camus would have admired. Carlos Fonseca describes him as "an indomitable militant of the ethic of the exploited."[2] For this reason, the Founder affirms: "With revolutionary and proletarian pride, we say that Rigoberto is an unmistakable representative of the exploited." [3]

[1] Ibid., p.397.
[2] Ibid., p.405.
[3] Idem.

Chapter Eleven

1

Starting in 1956, hopes begin to flutter and their butterflies to reconnoiter the terrain. In 1958, prior to the triumph of the Cuban Revolution, the guerrilla struggle begins anew in Nicaragua.

The marquee of the González Theater in León announced the coming premier of *Attila Before Rome* as the daily drizzle to achieve university autonomy became a downpour. We were confronting Attila and his barbarians to achieve a conquest that, in other parts of the continent, had been won decades earlier.

Outstanding among those who participated in these demonstrations were Silvio Mayorga; Mariano Fiallos Gil, who would become rector; Mariano Fiallos Oyanguren, who shines with his own light; Ernesto Cruz, who was opaque despite his brilliance; Carlos Tünnerman, Leonel Argüello, Alvaro Porta and the brothers Roberto and Jaime Incer Barquero. Roberto Incer would become president of the Central Bank and a full-fledged Somocista; Jaime, an expert in geography, flora, fauna and other herbage of nature, such as astronomy.

In March 1958, the dictatorship finally gives in and promulgates the decree of University Autonomy. It was the same program, with a few minor revisions, that Fernando Silva, Carlos Molina del Campo, Jaime Rodríguez, Ramón Espinal, Julián Guerrero, Noel Lindo, Salvador Gaitán and I proposed. In December, speaking on behalf of the student body, Carlos Fonseca inaugurated the first school year under the autonomy code, saying: "This act, which we are celebrating in Nicaragua, in 1958, is being celebrated after 40 years delay." [1] He was referring to the University of Córdoba autonomy reform of 1918, in Argentina.

[1] Testimony of Carlos Tünnerman Bernheim.

By then, the principle protagonists of the September 21, 1956 action — Edwin Castro, Cornelio Silva, Ausberto Narváez and Juan Calderón — had been tried and sentenced to many years in prison. They, and many others, were victims of torture in the very garden of the presidential mansion itself.

That garden was surrounded by a high wall and was very well-maintained, with brilliant grass and a blue-tiled swimming pool, where the chirping of birds was only interrupted by the roars of large cats. There were two African lions, a gift of the Guatemalan dictator Castillo Armas — the one who, with the help of the Yankees, overthrew the constitutional government of Jacobo Arbenz — and a black panther.

This is how Pedro Joaquín Chamorro describes that paradise of cruelty after he was forced, against his will, to "form part of the Somoza family's new family":

> The lion paced and so did the man. Man and beast in adjoining cells of a single cage, divided only by thin bars, intelligence and instinct united in brotherhood in an indescribable picture, enclosed by the same lock... The lions and other animals ate abundant fresh meat; the prisoners, rice and beans. The prisoners were taken out twice daily to the nearby toilet and had a water spigot at their disposal in the garden. The lions relieved their physiological necessities in the cages and were bathed daily...[1]

Each morning and afternoon, Luis, Anastasio and the rest of the Somoza family — those "modern Borgias" — strolled before the caged animals and men. The torture sessions commenced in the evenings and consisted of inhuman beatings; the no less ferocious "well" — a pool filled with water into which prisoners bound hand and foot, were lowered and left until on the verge of drowning, at which point they would be raised up and then submerged again before they had regained their normal breathing rhythm; electric cattle prods; and confinement in tiny cubicles beneath stairways.

[1] Pedro Juaquín Chamorro, *Estirpe sangrienta: Los Somoza* (México: Diógenes, 1980), p. 87.

It was in those difficult days when Edwin Castro designed a continuous curve of honey that gave escape to our anguish. Carlos appreciated the prophetic poetry of that brother, with whom I shared interminable hours of nightmares and confidences in prison.

Edwin wrote poems that Ruth, his Honduran wife, smuggled out of jail hidden in her clothing. The one entitled "Tomorrow, My Son, Everything Will Be Different" became famous. The son, named after his father, is an active member of the FSLN.

On January 10, 1959, Edwin Castro dedicated a poem to me entitled "Fraternity":

> Your hand planted itself in mine,
> and they flowered together
> and matured together
> in fraternal fruit of affection.
> It was a single harvest,
> long and continuous,
> like a rail
> of unsuspected length
> laid across
> the fields of our joint anguish.
> Your hand planted itself in mine
> and still they flower together!

2

I was tried on the charge of complicity in the action carried out by Rigoberto López Pérez, that is, for having concealed the crimes of murder, attempted murder and rebellion. The National Guard found out that Edwin Castro, some days before the attempt on Somoza García, had told me that "something big was in the works." In actual fact, he had told me the tyrant would be eliminated.

I placed my defense before the military tribunal in the hands of Dr. Ernesto Cruz, a most lucid of the lucid students of the law. Cruz was my friend, godfather to my first daughter, feared by the Moors and loved by the Christians. A ray of hope for the good guys. He possessed a disconcerting eloquence. From his lips flowed flowers and dagger thrusts.

Ernesto Cruz refused to defend me. He later received a scholarship to Harvard and became rector of the Central American Institute of Business Administration (INCAE). He awarded a Doctor Honoris Causa to Somoza Debayle. I'm not sure exactly what became of him. Brother of the former revolutionary leader Arturo Cruz, they say he's now a prosperous attorney.

I then named as my defense counsel Dr. Enrique Espinoza Sotomayor, a valiant lawyer and eloquent connoisseur of his profession, now deceased, together with my friend and brilliant classmate, Carlos Tünnerman. In his plea, the latter argued that "the law obliges one to denounce but not to inform, and between denunciation and informing there lies an abyss separating the moral from the immoral...."[1] I was sentenced to nine years in prison.

Carlos Fonseca was held for fifty days at the Air Force prison and when he was released, before departing for Costa Rica, he inquired after the prisoners who had been tried and took the first steps — fulfilling promises he'd made to us while behind bars — to organize a movement that would work for our release. For us prisoners, this was a reason not to despair. The agitation in support of our release was the most unanimous, most voluminous, and most important movement in the student struggle up to that time. Students of all grade levels participated in the strikes. During these activities, in an interview between Luis Somoza Debayle and a university delegation headed by the rector, Mariano Fiallos Gil, the family president of the moment was aggressive toward Carlos Fonseca. It was on that occasion that Somoza coined the celebrated phrase: "I was educated to be President." A few days later, the famous humorist G-R-N, sent him a message asking at what university he had studied, because he too would like to be President.

Carlos mentions the student movements of 1958:

[1] Testimony of Carlos Tünnerman Bernheim.

99

For the first time in years, the name of Augusto César Sandino is heard once again, after a quarter century of shadows, paralysis and popular atrophy in Nicaragua.[1]

3

During our imprisonment in 1958, there occurs the first guerrilla movement of the period, led by Gen. Ramón Raudales, who had been one of the chiefs of the Army For the Defense of National Sovereignty.

During prison visits our families told us of Raudales, moving their lips in slow motion. Raudales' campaign is not mentioned in the newspapers, except, naturally, the day he falls in combat, which was October 4, 1958.

The visits took place in a narrow corridor under the close scrutiny of a guard whose complicity, purchased with trinkets, made matters easier. That is, the prolonging of kisses as much as decency allowed and the passing of written messages from friends who felt obliged to feed our hopes of amnesty and of popular mobilization.

Newspaper clippings mentioning the possibility of our release cost one package of Sphynx cigarettes, while the introduction of a transistor radio into our cell cost Anita Gil, Edwin Castro's beautiful sister-in-law, 50 *córdobas*.

The ingenuity and patience of Cornelio Silva, from Chontales, transformed a bottle of Santa Cecilia and some soaked cornmeal into a dazzling afternoon of drunkenness, tears and mariachi yells.

Cornelio got drunker than we did, drunker than any other prisoner in the long history of Somoza repression and a few moments before slipping into unconsciousness he shouted *vivas* for Sandino and for Rigoberto López Pérez, with the same enthusiasm he had shown in street demonstrations and in his dreams.

The prison warden, Major Agustín Boldán, lapsed into an incoherent, stammering rage, and there's no way to describe his

---

[1] Carlos Fonseca, *Entrevista a Ernesto González Bermejo,* in: *Obras,* Vol. I, p. 217.

expression when Cornelio spat at him: "Rigoberto's coming back and he's going to stick it to you, you old goat."

There was a patio on one side where we had watched a pair of deer grow and reproduce and with whom we became intimate friends during the time we were allowed outside to take the sun. Major Boldán lined us up in Indian file and the idiot called out: "*Derecha, deré!*" which meant we should turn to face him. Cornelio, staggering, was supported by Edwin and Ausberto. Major Boldán kicked at the deer, who escaped gracefully, innocently. Juan Calderón dared to say something in their defense, I'm not sure what, in the name of the Deer Lovers' Protective Society.

Boldán shouted for someone to bring him his pistol and at last he began to breathe normally again. He locked us up — not without condemning us first to death — in a pitch-dark cell where we remained for months. Family visits, needless to say, were suspended.

We felt we had been sentenced a second time: the rice became opaque; the beans like rabbit shit. When we were finally returned to our previous cell, the light coming in through the bars of the wide window penetrated like bullets and the rice once again turned white, in contrast to the beans.

Cornelio Silva was the leading jokester of Chontales and perhaps of his entire generation. He owned a cattle ranch near La Libertad, the small town where he was born. He would plan his trips to Managua to amuse himself with a wide range of practical jokes.

One afternoon he walked into a hardware store and asked the price of their shirts and ties. When the salesgirl told him they only sold hammers, saws and nails, Cornelio asked her to Christmas-wrap two pairs of blue jeans and thirty handkerchiefs. The girl insisted irately that this was a hardware store, not a boutique. So Cornelio asked her to also include blouses and brassieres for his wife, who had large, shapely breasts. "If you could only see them, Miss...", "Please, Sir, you're making fun of me." Just then the owner showed up and Silva announced loudly that for the past ten minutes he'd been trying unsuccessfully to purchase two padlocks and 30 pounds of five-inch nails. That poor girl!

For an entire year he visited a barbershop, all the while pretending to be mute. One day he whispered in the barber's ear, "How much is a shave?" and the poor man nearly died of fright.

Cornelio was a composer and, as I recall, arranged romantic tunes I've not heard since.

4

Carlos Fonseca left for Costa Rica, pleading reasons of health, to attend the Sixth World Festival of Youth and Students which was to be held in Moscow during the summer of 1957. Manolo Cuadra, who developed a close friendship with our founder, made the necessary arrangements for the trip. Carlos called Manolo a "people's poet," and he really was.

Manolo Cuadra was born in 1907 in Malacatoya, a village on the edge of Lake Nicaragua. He was a boxer, telegrapher, soldier, globetrotter, radio operator, healer, hotel clerk, banana cutter, poet.

> I'm sad like a policeman
> one of those who blossom on street corners...
> But I forgot my nightstick
> and carry my soul in my hand.[1]

He fought as a soldier in the Guard against the Army For the Defense of National Sovereignty where, though it seems paradoxical, he initiated his admiration for Sandino. An opponent of Somoza, he suffered prison, persecution, exile and confinement on Little Corn Island, where he wrote what he considered to be the best of his books.[*]

He participated in all sorts of struggles and, in contrast to his companions in the Vanguard movement, which he joined in 1924, he was a man of the Left.

---

[1] Manolo Cuadra, "Perfil," *Antología* (Managua: Editorial Nicaragüense, 1963).
[*] *Itinerario de Little Corn Island*

He spent the last years of his life in Costa Rica, only returning to Nicaragua to die in 1957.

He was, and remains, Nicaragua's poet of the people *par excellence*.

Carlos had been sent to the Festival by the Socialist Party. He recounted, grinning, that our country's delegation was the most disciplined, always punctual, never dispersed, and always arrived together at the meetings. Nobody was missing when our delegation arrived to plant the tree of friendship. Carlos, of course, was its sole member.

He recounts his celebrated trip in agile, precise prose:

> My trip to the Sixth Festival gave me the opportunity to know not only the Soviet Union, but to know the whole world as well. More precisely, I had the opportunity to know the best part of the world: its youth. I didn't fly to Egypt to contemplate the famous pyramids, but in Moscow I was able to shake hands with the youths who seized rifles in 1955 to repel the aggression of the English colonialists. Nor was I in Greece looking at the ruins of ancient civilization, but I did give a fraternal embrace to the Cypriot youths who were fighting to free Cyprus from the English yoke.... The Festival brought together in Moscow the world's best: its youth. For I believe that the most valuable thing in Panama is not its canal, but its youth. And the most valuable part of Cuba is not its sugar industry, but its youth.[1]

It was on that occasion that he met the extraordinary Salvadoran poet and revolutionary, Roque Dalton, with whom he established an enduring friendship.

"Whatever his quality, his level, his excellence, his creative capacity or his success, the poet, for the bourgeoisie, can only be: a servant, a clown or an enemy," Roque wrote shortly before his death, having opted for the last of these roles.

[1] Carlos Fonseca, *Un Nicaragüense en Moscú* (Managua: Secretaría Nacional del FSLN, 1980), p. 50.

That is, enemy poet. "One who claims his wage, not in praise or dollars, but rather in persecutions, prisons, bullets. And not only is he going to lack regalia and tuxedoes and fancy clothes, but he's going to possess fewer things with each passing day until all he has left is a pair of patched, albeit clean, shirts as his only poetry."[1]

From his youth, Roque was a writer, combatant, prisoner of fortunate metaphors and implacable executioners. He was about to be shot by a firing squad in 1960, but was spared by a hair's breadth of four days when the dictator who'd condemned him was toppled.

He was a poetic globe-trotter in Guatemala, Mexico, Czechoslovakia, Cuba and other countries of Europe, Asia and Latin America. He joined the People's Revolutionary Army (ERP) and returned to his country, where he was assassinated in 1975 by internal political rivals. Roque studied and rigorously investigated the history of his country. In the process he adopted almost every literary genre. Julio Cortázar:

> To talk to Roque was like living more intensely, like living for two. None of his friends will forget the stories... Dalton the pirate... The memories of his prisons, of prowling death, of his flight at dawn, of his exiles, his returns, the saga of the combatant, the long march of the militant.[2]

When Carlos was imprisoned in Costa Rica, Roque made extensive fraternal references in solidarity with the prisoner:

> From the beginning we were good friends, inasmuch as we both enjoyed political discussions of unlimited tone and duration; we shared a dislike for solemnity and grimness and we believed in a Central America united at the grassroots level.[3]

---

[1] Roque Dalton, "Como declaración de Principios," in: *Poemas clandestinos* (N.p.: Resistencia Nacional-FARN, 1977), p. 5.

[2] Julio Cortázar, "Una muerte monstruosa," in: *Recopilación de textos sobre Roque Dalton* (La Habana: Casa de las Américas, 1986), p. 556.

[3] Roque Dalton, "Solidaridad con Carlos Fonseca Amador," *Nicaráuac*, No. 13 (Managua: Ministerio de Cultura, 1986), p. 113.

Carlos returned to Nicaragua on December 16, 1957, and in January 1958 began writing *A Nicaraguan In Moscow*. In pursuit of simplicity and accessibility he read it several times to his mother, with whom he had a close relationship. He spoke of the standard of living of Soviet workers, the extraordinary housing projects, the people's love of art, the spectacular chandeliers of the Bolshoi Theater. These things bring to mind his beautiful phrase:

Little Vladimir seemed an adult when he spoke of peace. And adults seemed to be children when they spoke to me of peace. In reality, we all resemble each other when we speak of peace.[1]

Carlos talked for hours on end with his mother and when she didn't understand some of the concepts in the book about his trip to Moscow, he'd change the words. Carlos said that if Doña Agustina understood his language, everyone would understand it.

In March 1959, together with Silvio Mayorga, he organizes the Nicaraguan Democratic Youth, an act which he states "should be seen as the first effort of different strata of youth — students and other groups — to gain political independence and play their historical role." The Nicaraguan Democratic Youth was violently repressed and Carlos was arrested by Somoza's Office of Security on the 17th of that same month. In April, he was expelled to Guatemala, and in May he left for Honduras to join the Rigoberto López Pérez Column that was then preparing to invade Nicaragua.

5

The mobilizations and demands of the student movement finally produced results. A number of people involved in the events of September were placed under house arrest. Emilio Borge and Dr. Enrique Lacayo Farfán escaped to Costa Rica. The latter was

---

[1] Fonseca, *Un Nicaragüense en Moscú*, p. 8.

renowned because of the publicity he'd received for his long hours of interrogation under a lamp more blinding than the sun.

Luis Cardenal — Somoza's cousin by marriage and first cousin of Pedro Joaquín Chamorro, known for his elegance — organized my escape from Matagalpa, where I had been purposefully sent.

Dressed as a street walker, drunk to appease my machismo and the object of flirtatious innuendoes by the guard assigned to watch me, I escaped to Honduras, where I arrived with a colossal hangover. I was captured on the border by a Honduran Army patrol. Edwin Castro, Cornelio Silva and Ausberto Narváez remained behind in prison, sadder than the dead.

Otto Castro — a brother of Edwin's and intimate friend of the Honduran president, Ramón Villeda Morales — got me out of jail and a few days later I arrived in El Salvador with a false passport. From there, I left for Costa Rica with Pedro Joaquín Chamorro.

Chapter Twelve

1

At that time an armed movement came into being in Costa Rica with the support of the National Liberation Party and its head, José Figueres. I joined the military training program at La Lindora ranch, which belonged to representative Marcial Aguiluz, near San José.

I almost went with them. In fifteen minutes of referring to the laws of social development and the class struggle, Silvio Mayorga convinced me it was a mistake. One had to have patience, he said as he wrinkled his nose, pressed his lips together and rubbed his hands enthusiastically, almost furiously, in a gesture characteristically his. One had to wait for the opportunity, which would soon arrive, to risk or give up one's life for a truly revolutionary project.

The movement was led by Pedro Joaquín Chamorro, Luis Cardenal and Reynaldo Antonio Téfel. The group went in by plane, landing in the Olama-Mollejones area. It was detected by Somoza's Air Force and bombarded daily. The Somoza Battalion — some 900 men — surrounded them and secured the surrender of the majority. Eleven rebels managed to escape — among them the leaders — but a few days later as they prepared to rest, exhausted and hungry, they were captured. The commander of the Guard unit, Lt. Gastón Quintana, did not kill them, as was customary, and as a consequence earned the nickname of Lt. Pardón among the enlisted men.

2

One day Guillermo Duarte turned up. He was a former National Guard lieutenant with a calm gaze. He invited us to lunch at an inaccessible restaurant where, for the first time, we ate shark fins. During the apple pie he suggested, with such good manners it seemed like an order, that we join his guerrilla column. Duarte was to be the chief of the second column of the armed movement led by another former Guard officer, Rafael Somarriva.

We received a telephone call from Carlos Fonseca, in which he demanded that we come to Honduras, even if we had to swim. We were making enthusiastic arrangements when, on June 24, 1959, the El Chaparral episode occurred in Honduran territory.

The guerrilla column led by Somarriva had been surprised and cut to pieces in an infamous ravine. Against all tactical prudence, they had camped there for several weeks. The sentries were few in number, carelessly distributed and without practical training. The Honduran soldiers had approached the encampment the previous night. In the full light of mid-day they took up comfortable positions and, when the signal was given, began firing at point blank range with Garand rifles and M-1 carbines at the inexperienced column.

José Manuel Aróstegui didn't even have the privilege of astonishment, since he was the first to fall. The Cuban, Marcelo Fernández, followed him moments later. And thus, victims of the torrential fire fell: Antonio Barbosa, Aníbal Sánchez, Manuel Canelo, Enrique Morales and Adán Suárez.

Manuel Baldizón, Somarriva's second in command, who had the reputation of being affectionate and distrustful — his eyes alight like lanterns with sparks that inspired confidence — collapsed while firing an M-3 submachine gun. He had acquired it when two Cuban planes arrived with a cargo of arms sent by Che Guevara, a shipment made possible thanks to the complicity of President Ramón Villeda Morales, who admired Che.

Major Andrés Espinoza, re-baptized "Chaparral" from the day of the massacre for having been the chief of the assassins, had interviewed the Yankee ambassador in Tegucigalpa and then recounted the story to Somoza in a radio conversation which was intercepted by ham operator Fanón Herrera.

In the virtual execution by firing squad, Carlos Fonseca was seriously wounded. A bullet from an M-1 carbine pierced his lung. It is said that before transferring the wounded to Tegucigalpa, the Honduran soldiers were going to bury Carlos Fonseca, inasmuch as chance and conviction allowed him to play dead. When, having set down his stretcher and lit up cigarettes, they started digging a shallow hole two meters long, one of the soldiers had the foresight to uncover the dead man's face while going through his pockets. The poor soldier leapt backwards when he saw the life and intense defiance staring back at him from those blue eyes.

Once out of danger in the San Felipe Hospital in Tegucigalpa, his mother came to visit him, bringing homemade bread from Brigitte, in Matagalpa, along with *pinolillo* and greetings from the neighbors in the Laborío district. Doña Augustina and Carlos had a very special relationship; they respected each other and he treated her with delicacy, expressing his affection without inhibition. She became practiced at dissimulating tears and reproaches in her son's presence.

3

Silvio Mayorga and I were in Costa Rica and proved quite incapable of hiding our sorrow when the rumor circulated in San José that Carlos had died. Silvio, taut as a violin string, proposed that we organize a group at whatever cost, even with shotguns, hunting rifles and machetes. In Nicaragua, students reacted with demonstrations. On July 23, a massacre took place in León. Víctor Tirado wrote about it as follows:

> In June 1959, the kind of date the calendar typically commemorates, a guerrilla column about to enter Nicaragua and confront the National Guard, was decimated on El Chaparral mountain, in Honduras...
>
> It was a massacre in which workers, peasants and university students gave their lives. When the news arrived in Nicaragua, the university student movement denounced such crimes and the president of the University Center called an assembly to divulge the facts. There was uncertainty as to whether Carlos Fonseca and Aníbal Sánchez Arauz were alive....

In response to these events, the students organized a wake and a mass that could not be celebrated because the National Guard forbade it....

Meanwhile, university classes were to begin on July 23, 1959. In accordance with tradition, there was to be a parade of "The Bald Ones," so called because the marchers were first year students who, in accord with established ritual, had their heads shaved. Nevertheless, the memory of El Chaparral was still fresh in the minds of the students and the parade took on a tone of denunciation and political protest....

Once under way, there is an altercation between the National Guard and the students. At 6 p.m. on July 23, 1959, the National Guard, under the command of Lt. Tacho Ortiz, opens fire.... Erik Ramírez, Mauricio Martínez Santamaría, José Rubí and Sergio Octavio Saldaña González are killed....

A year later, in 1960, secondary students take to the streets to protest the massacre of 1959. During these demonstrations, Julio Oscar Romero, an invalid student from the Ramírez Goyena Institute in Managua, is killed.[1]

Due to public pressure in Honduras, Carlos was sent to Cuba. He entered the Calixto García Hospital in Havana, where he was visited by Pedro Monet and his wife Rosita, who with that visit initiated an historic relationship of lifelong solidarity.

Pedro Monet's house became our refuge. He was a lifelong communist and poor as a churchmouse. He lacked bread as well as vanity. It was in his house that we satiated both our hunger and our craving for life. He lived in Old Havana in a dinky apartment at the end of a stairway that seemed an evil omen.

Pedro was captured by Batista's people, who could not shake the dignity of that broad-shouldered man of the clear-eyed gaze. They say his torturers tried to make him cry, but only when Fidel Castro announced the advent of socialism in Cuba did he break into tears.

---

[1] Víctor Tirado López, "El FSLN: un producto y una necesidad históricos" in: *Nicaragua: una nueva democracia en el tercer mundo* (N.p.: Vanguardia, 1986), p. 25.

Carlos told Pedro and Rosita: "When the revolution triumphs, you two will be our first invited guests." Monet's now deceased but he was in Managua for the celebration of the 20th Anniversary of the foundation of the FSLN. Rosita has also made several visits to Nicaragua.

Carlos also met Flavio Bravo, who at the time of his death was president of the National Assembly of Popular Power in Cuba.

4

In Costa Rica we had serious economic complications, because we had established families while still very young. Silvio's daughter, Silvita, and my own, Birmania, tireless consumers of milk and diapers, were born in San José. Anna María and Bolivia, unfortunately for me, were gluttons and susceptible to cold.

Carlos was not yet our chief, but he didn't hesitate to make demands on us and was a careful planner. We walked from one end of the city to the other organizing and cajoling, using all the resources of language at our disposal.

We met in a rather elegant hotel with Indalecio Pastora, a young landowner from northern Nicaragua, freckle-faced, pleasant and anxious for the limelight. We made an effort to understand one another, but the man was an anti-communist from breakfast until he awakened the next morning. One day he proposed that we take photographs of ourselves at some nearby ranch and publicize our presence in Nicaragua at the head of two guerrilla columns. He looked at me with astonishment when I told him he wasn't being serious.

Adolfo García Barberena, a Nicaraguan shoemaker and lucid, persuasive communist, spent long hours talking with Indalecio but when the latter exceeded the limits of political common sense, he beat a hasty retreat.

Adolfo García joined the Southern Front during the war of liberation and died fighting in the vicinity of Guinea.

Indalecio Pastora vanished into that gray country called oblivion.

5

There were other guerrilla movements after El Chaparral. General Ramón Raudales' was the first. Julio Alonso Leclaire led the 15th of September Column which, in October 1959, attacked the villages of Susucayán, Santa Clara and Quilalí. Among his combatants were Julio Molina, Julio Velásquez, Renán Montero, Heriberto Rodríguez, Bayardo Altamirano and Pedro Pablo Ríos. In January 1960, they were joined by a veteran Sandinista, Heriberto Reyes, who led another group.

Some of these men joined the Sandino Revolutionary Front led by the brothers Alejandro and Harold Martínez. A newspaperman, Manuel Díaz y Sotelo, also led a small group that was annihilated.

These movements, as well as that of Chale Haslam, a Matagalpa rancher, expressed the natural inclination of Nicaraguans to confront the military dictatorship with armed opposition.

6

We had organized the Nicaraguan Revolutionary Youth when, in November 1959, Carlos turned up after having spent a couple of months in Cuba. Carrying his meager suitcase, he installed himself in our house and participated in our projects with a group of Nicaraguan cobblers who were scattered around the outskirts of San José.

These émigré workers, nearly all of them from Nicaragua's Pacific Coast, were drawn together in their reading of the small newspaper put out by the Popular Vanguard Party. Some of them spoke with pride of the main communist leader of those years, Don Manuel Mora Valverde, a personage with a long political career. To publish something like that was a remarkable feat in a country where the entire communications establishment had persuaded even the coffee trees of the central highlands that communists were sons-of-bitches indisputably sired by Satan.

The cobblers, knives in hand, sat around in intimate circles cutting up cured hides, talking politics, and saying nasty things about the Costa Ricans. Nicaragua was always a theme in these conversations and even more so after we organized the Nicaraguan Revolutionary Youth which managed to attract to its ranks the weatherworn Nicaraguan banana workers, many of whom had grown old in that territory of exploitation and nostalgia.

Carlos, Silvio, José Reyes Monterrey, all of us, took turns flying to the banana zone in a plane that might better have been in an aeronautical museum, where we were received with overly confident but encouraging enthusiasm.

We spent long hours persuading them of what they were already persuaded: of how perfect our return would be; what a son-of-a-bitch Somoza was; that the peasants would be owners of the land; that this wasn't living; that life began across the border, whenever we'd have the guts to risk it; that sovereignty is not open to discussion; that Sandino said....

If we arrived on a weekend, they'd take us to a nearby whorehouse, which Carlos never entered and where Silvio Mayorga became a reformer of wayward women. Our compatriots would leave part of their wages there and another portion in the hands of local physicians, who always had a supply of antibiotics on hand for the treatment of gonorrhea and syphilis.

The Nicaraguan workers contributed to our maintenance, but we frequently went hungry. The supportive leaders of the Popular Vanguard Party found housing for us in the homes of their collaborators. I came away from one of them disconcerted when the head of the family — as well as of a party cell — forbade me to talk politics during meals or in the presence of his family because he was a communist but would not permit his children to be.

We spent most of our resources on the publication of *Revolutionary Youth*, which had a wide weekly circulation and was edited by José Reyes Monterrey.

7

I was with Silvio Mayorga and José Reyes Monterrey listening to Radio Reloj from Havana, when they announced the death of

Camilo. Camilo had died. Camilo Cienfuegos. He died the 28th of October. We heard Fidel confirm the news on November 12, 1959.

How he reminded me of El Cid, Winnetou, Hans of Iceland, Perseus, Achilles, Rufo Marín, Túpac Amaru, Benjamín Zeledón, Mella! I couldn't compare him with Germán Pomares, because the latter was not yet dead, but I could say that he resembled Ulysses, or better yet, a Cuban *Mambí*.

There are heroes who have the face of a hero. Camilo was a hero with the lucidity of a jaguar, with an explosive, honeyed smile. Not only was Camilo Cienfuegos a hero, he even looked like one.

We heard the details of that painful event on the radio — in Paso Ancho, a crowded San José neighborhood — in the house of a fellow Nicaraguan living in Costa Rica.

"To have some idea of how we feel," said Fidel, "you have to live among us..."

I tried to imagine the Cubans' afflicted hearts. At that moment there still existed a vague hope of finding the famous guerrilla fighter, or at least his body.

A few days earlier, a voice simulating Camilo's announced on the radio that he had been saved by a ship that was en route to Havana. Cuba shot off fireworks, danced, laughed, fired weapons in bursts of thanks to the heavens, wept. It was delirium. The information was a trap, an atrocious felony, a perfect wad of spit in the face.

Fidel asked: Where did Camilo come from? And he answered: Camilo came from the people. The laws of history that explain where leaders spring from during social convulsions pose the question, and those same laws of history respond: Camilo came from the people.

Camilo was uncomplicated, a janitor, cordial, a window washer, intelligent, a bar waiter, audacious, a restaurant worker, valiant, a tailor, the son of my old friend Ramón. He wanted to be a sculptor but was unable; or rather, he sculpted his own light. He was also a soldier — the best, according to Che — a captain, son of a unionist, a major, blood brother and intellectual twin of Osmani. Che's friend, a worker, Che's brother, a man of faith, Che's son, a revolutionary. "How am I doing, Camilo?" He was all that and also chief of the General Staff of the Rebel Army, Raúl's righthand man, eyes laughing, the son of sweet Doña Emilia, treader of long roads. "You're doing fine, Fidel."

Blue Eyes is out there, encountering now the enemy, now a white ginger lily, twin sister of the *sacuanjoche*.*

Camilo is a born rascal. He plays practical jokes on Che, Raúl, Ramiro Valdés, William Gálvez, José Quevedo, on everybody. For Fidel he has only a knowing smile, nothing more.

Camilo was a friend of Rafael Sierra, the runt of Cuban youth, and of Jack Dempsey in the United States, where he lived for a while and came to know the belly of Manhattan, that great, neon-lighted sewer. "I'd rather live as a *cloucharde* [beggar] in Paris than as a rich man in New York," said Henry Miller, and Camilo Cienfuegos might have said the same thinking of Havana rather than Paris.

In Alegría de Pío, Juan Almeida said: "Here, no one surrenders," and Camilo took that phrase as his own motto.

Now, Camilo remains Camilo in his continuous and immortal renewal. Camilo is a reflection of the people, said Che, of us. Fidel's voice captures the essence of the man: "Today, our memory of the invasion, of all his deeds and feats, fills us with amazement... this man is a man of the people; he came from the people." He won glory, true enough, but nobody handed it to him in a package with Christmas wrapping. He earned it with the strength of his wings, with his alligator smile, with his calloused hands.

Fidel spoke for several hours. He interrogated pilots; he interrogated experts; he interrogated himself. With millimetric precision, he explained to the Cuban people the details of the drama. I thought — like Martí — too much life, oh Lord, in too short a time; like Martí — too much death, dear Cubans, oh mother mine, for so much time. The resurrection will come later: that small, prolonged disturbance that will receive flowers in an immense tomb of salt.

* Nicaragua's national flower.

8

The successes and failures of the period 1958-60 demonstrated that without a revolutionary leadership it was impossible to overthrow the dictatorship.

The political agitation in 1960 — demonstrations, acts of sabotage, armed actions on the borders — was the framework within which a new popular organization was gestating. Back then, in an interview for the April 4, 1960 issue of the newspaper *Impacto*, I said:

> We have a profound faith in the combative spirit and valor of our people. The problem is not to look for leaders but to get on with the struggle. All peoples, when they struggle, produce leaders. Leaders are not prefabricated nor are they born of agreements reached in small assemblies. Popular leaders arise in the heat of battle, frequently spattered with gunpowder and the smell of blood. Consequently, our present position is: organize for the struggle.

In January 1960, a group of youngsters, among them José Benito Escobar, Germán Pomares, Fernando Gordillo, Jorge Navarro, Manolo Morales, Julio Buitrago — all since deceased — Daniel Ortega, who at that time was 14 years-old, Joaquín Solís Piura, Róger Vásquez, Orlando Quiñónez and others, organized the Nicaraguan Patriotic Youth (JPN).

Nicaraguan Patriotic Youth was a predecessor organization of the FSLN.

Sandino's anti-imperialism, their own identification with the Cuban Revolution, and a democratic program formed part of the political ideas of the JPN.

Under the slogan: "For the salvation of the fatherland, for the union of youth," they proposed the social and political transformation of the country, the reestablishment of democracy, national sovereignty, human dignity, political freedom, economic and social justice, and respect for the heroes and martyrs who died for the liberation of Nicaragua.

In its few months of activity, Patriotic Youth established itself as a pioneer in the integration of workers, peasants and students.

Patriotic Youth denounced crimes. They mobilized in repudiation of the assassination of Edwin Castro, Ausberto Narváez, Cornelio Silva, Julio Romero and Ajax Delgado. They also denounced the imprisonment and deportation of Carlos Fonseca.

There was a coming together of revolutionary youth and the workers' movement when Patriotic Youth gave its solidarity to striking construction workers.

According to José Benito Escobar, the weakness of JPN lay in its lack of previous organizing experience and in not having a clear revolutionary consciousness.

The dictatorship dismembered JPN with the carrot-and-stick technique, jail for some, scholarships for others. In November 1960, following an attempt by traditional politicians — including some with progressive ideas — to seize the fortresses of Diriamba and Jinotepe, the dictatorship declared a state of siege and cracked down on popular organizations. The JPN was not prepared for the repression and therefore disappeared.

Chapter Thirteen

1

Carlos arrived in Venezuela on March 2, 1960, together with Silvio Mayorga and José Reyes Monterrey. They were representing the University Center and Revolutionary Youth. In Caracas, they made contact with Guillermo Urbina Vásquez, principal leader of the Nicaraguan Unitary Front, and his comrades Salvador Peña, a worker, and Alejandro Bermúdez, a poet and shrewd man of proven generosity.

In June 1960, Carlos returned to Nicaragua once more, clandestinely and defiantly, to establish contact with the Nicaraguan Patriotic Youth. He went skinny-dipping on a moonlit night in Lake Cocibolca with his friend and guide of nocturnal routes, Julio Jerez.

His subversive experience clashed with the leadership of the Socialist Party, which opposed the audacity of his return. In a vain attempt to cloak the imprudent youth's presence in legality, they published an item in the party newspaper announcing the "youthful and valiant student fighter's" arrival. The National Guard captured him in the most infantile of hideouts: a home for the elderly. He was expelled from national territory for the second time in an Air Force plane straight to Guatemala. He was confined in the jungle of Petén, where a young officer by the name of Luis Turcios Lima was stationed. The future chief of the Rebel Armed Forces (FAR) gave him a book on military tactics. Both of them — Turcios and Fonseca — always recalled this meeting that took place on the edge of coincidence and the jungle.

On June 10, 1960, there appeared in the Cuban weekly, *Combate*, a communique from the University Center of the National Autonomous University of Nicaragua and the Nicaraguan Unitary Front protesting the expulsion of Cuban diplomats, the use of

Nicaraguan territory to attack Cuba, and the rupture of relations with Cuba by the Nicaraguan government.*

2

In December 1959, I arrived in Cuba. I was received by Noel Guerrero and the illuminated streets of Havana in full revolutionary effervescence. I was moved by the slogans that overturned idols and reduced tons of rubbish to ashes. Everything on that island seemed sacred to me. I cannot describe what I felt when I took part in popular demonstrations where the speakers suggested that the firing squad might be the appropriate solution for slavery, exploitation, injustice and lies. They were, in fact, shooting the torturers and assassins of the defeated regime.

I came to know the gossamer mind of Blas Roca and the discerning and amiable silhouette of Carlos Rafael Rodríguez. Both leaders of the Popular Socialist Party gave us humble and warmhearted refuge and good counsel.

I was housed somewhere in El Vedado. One December afternoon, I was invited by a compañera from the Socialist Youth to drink *guarapo*, go to the movies and have dinner. It was late by the time I accompanied her to her house and, as I was leaving, she said to me: "Ciao, Tomás, I love you." And she closed the door.

"Well," I said to myself, "don't I have the touch! And I didn't even suggest anything." The following day, a dark, good looking fellow, also from the Socialist Youth, invited me to the movies and dinner. As we were parting, he squeezed my hand firmly and said: "Ciao, Tomás, I love you."

I stepped back in surprise and he looked at me, nonplussed. It wasn't until several days later, after everyone I met said they loved me when taking their leave, that I understood this affectionate custom of the Cuban people. Something similar happens in Nicaragua, where they say — where we say — regardless of one's sex: "Thank you, love," "See you tomorrow, love," "How're you doin', love?"

---

* See text of communique at the end of this chapter.

One day, Flavio Bravo and Noel Guerrero turned up. They gave me instructions. I was to meet a ship in Honduras carrying the fabulous quantity of 600 rifles, and I don't remember how many machine guns, bazooka-type rocket launchers and 60 mm. mortars. A portion of these weapons would be for the Sandino Front — led by the brothers Alejandro and Harold Martínez, who subsequently went over to the counterrevolution. I was supposed to wait for them at a spot near Puerto Cortés.

The ship arrived. The weapons arrived. And the Honduran soldiers arrived. Who blew the whistle? Supposedly some of our Honduran accomplices. It was said that the light signals gave us away, that the unloading point was practically in downtown Puerto Cortés, one thing and another, that "such are the risks of the trade, old buddy." I think we'll never know the truth. The weapons remained in the hands of the Army.

Rodolfo Romero and Wilfredo López, Nicaraguans who disembarked along with the weapons, were captured. Waiting in San Pedro, and surviving on the $100 dollars that Noel Guerrero had given me, I returned to Tegucigalpa hungry and consumed by anxiety. Quintín Pino Machado, who had been Cuba's ambassador in Nicaragua, appeared out of nowhere and helped me return to Havana.

In August 1960, I participated, together with Wilfredo López, who had been freed, Uriel Molina — not my friend, the Franciscan priest — and Julio Briceño, who became the principal leader of one of the factions of the Socialist Party, in the First Latin American Youth Congress. There I met young people who were to make names for themselves in the coming years.

The congress concluded with an address by Fidel Castro in El Cerro stadium. That night, Fidel lost his voice. Raúl went on to read the law of nationalization of North American enterprises. With the demise of each company, the crowd roared: "Good riddance!" At my side, a son of the great Nicaraguan poet, Salomón de la Selva, wept. Fidel recovered his voice and read the final articles. The stadium reverberated as if each one of his words were a home run with the bases loaded.

3

I visited Che Guevara at the National Bank, together with Noel Guerrero and Rodolfo Romero. I told the legendary *comandante* that I brought him greetings from Nicaragua's youth. He replied: "Let's forget the greetings and get to the point."

I insisted: "Major, I beg you to accept this greeting. It's an honorable greeting, not a demagogic one."

Possessed of unlimited admiration for, and lacking any inhibition or doubt in the presence of that man who absorbed light like parched earth absorbs water, I launched into the lengthy speech I had memorized. Che's eyes softened as he listened to me. He asked me a few questions and, when we parted, he embraced me and said: "I accept the greeting."

He gave us $20,000 dollars that Noel Guerrero utilized for the Río Coco and Bocay guerrilla expedition.

We began assembling Nicaraguans who arrived from different places: from Venezuela, Costa Rica, and other countries. Among them were some who formed part of the Sandino Front: Faustino Ruiz, Modesto Duarte, Pedro Pablo Ríos, Ramón Raudales, Jr., Bayardo Altamirano.

In the rush towards Havana, there were Nicaraguans of all tendencies and conditions. Adventurers, adolescents, astonished old men, reactionaries with false passports and authentic ideologic suspicions, professional Somoza opponents, Socialist leaders who came to declare that a popular victory through armed struggle was impossible, youngsters who wanted above all else to be reproductions of Fidel Castro, professional revolutionaries who wanted to comprehend how the Cuban revolution had swept all the pieces off the board, so joyously discrediting mummies, formulas, and how-to manuals.

It gave us goose bumps whenever we'd listen to the fascinating pedagogic discourse of Fidel Castro.

Fidel is not a revolutionary merely because of his ideological lucidity, but because he was the author of a veritable metamorphosis. To reduce cliches to dust is not a game. To achieve coherence in the application of a scientific concept of society while at the same time avoiding rigidity and dogma, is a very serious matter.

Carlos was one of the first to arrive in Cuba and if the system of State Security had been a bit more developed, it would have detected how that thirsty, thin man followed every appearance of the Cuban leader so as not to miss a single word.

The most impressive thing about Fidel Castro is his intransigent devotion to the truth, his never-ending search for an answer to hieroglyphics, his personal courage and the singular delicacy with which he treats his comrades in the struggle. He is a chess player, an assiduous examiner of differing perspectives, inexhaustible. Carlos resembles him in his purity, while he resembles Carlos in the way he conveys the certainty that he's telling the truth. If it's true that we have achieved what we desired, that we've interpreted reality and tried to transform it in accordance with our own perceptions, then it's only just to say that, after Carlos Fonseca, no man has influenced us more than Fidel Castro.

Carlos Fonseca said that it's good to criticize to one's face and to praise behind one's back. But it's also good, though it be only once, to recognize publicly the merits of our brothers.

4

We took a mortar course. A Czech instructor and two Cubans taught us how to turn a mortar inside out and still hit the target. It required physical strength, coordination and a knowledge of mathematics. Eduardo Heras León, an admirable teacher who is now a writer and a good man, a veteran of Girón and other difficult ordeals, recalls:

> It was in 1961, I don't remember the exact month, because that year of incredible tensions is lost in the twists and turns of memory. The Battle of Girón swallows up all the rest.
>
> I was a militiaman and we had completed a course for 82 mm. and 120 mm. mortar instructors given by Czech

advisors at the Baracoa base where the Major Manuel Fajardo Artillery School was located. The director of the school at that time was Capt. Octavio Toranzo (who was to die some months later in an automobile accident).

One day, Capt. Toranzo met with me and my brother, Nelson Heras León, and proposed that we give a brief, intensive course of mortar instruction to a group of Nicaraguan comrades. It was an urgent and very secret mission. It fell to me to teach the theory of artillery fire; my brother handled the practical aspects of the course.

I retain a crystal-clear image of that first class: a group of silent, very serious young men fix their eyes on me. Suddenly, there's a distance between us that I try to surmount: I say two or three phrases, clear my throat, and smile. "In order to master this weapon in such a short time, you'll need to work very hard," I tell them. That breaks the tension and we go to work. At first, they were a bit intimidated by the quantity of mathematical formulas — trigonometry in particular — that they had to use in their calculations.

I remember that one of them — the leader of the group — said to me: "Don't worry, professor. You give the classes and we'll do the rest."

We devoted mornings to the theory of mortar fire and afternoons to target practice. We forged ahead at a surprising rate and, particularly in the practical aspects, the results exceeded all our expectations. In a very short time, the group surpassed the time norms established for the mortar teams of the Cuban armed forces.

They'd turn out, silently as always, in their olive green uniforms, which were too large for their short stature, wearing those inferior Soviet boots that meant martyrdom for one's feet. I can never forget my first impression: that mixture of vulnerability and dignity which was translated into an air of serene discipline. Standing behind the mortar, they waited tensely and on the command: "Prepare for battle!" they'd hurl themselves like children on their deadly toy, competing among themselves and with the stopwatch brandished as a fraternal threat by my brother Nelson. Every second gained in that special race against time was cause for celebration.

Weeks later, when they conducted simulated combat and finally graduated as artillerymen, the celebration was double.

That's the way we did it.

The graduates were Carlos Fonseca, Silvio Mayorga, Iván Andrés Argüello, Modesto Duarte, Bayardo Altamirano, Rodolfo Romero and myself.

5

Carlos Fonseca founded New Nicaragua in July 1961. The overthrow of the dictatorship required an instrument that linked the armed struggle with the popular struggle. For the Nicaraguan revolutionaries, it was imperative to organize the masses in support of the guerrilla struggle. Such was the thesis that Carlos Fonseca proposed, thus confronting both the sadly legalistic approach of the traditional Left and the heroic adventurism of the armed movements of 1958.

To overcome this stagnation, Carlos entered Nicaragua clandestinely for the first time in June 1960. His arrest and subsequent deportation by the Office of Security delayed the realization of his plans.

When Carlos Fonseca returned to Nicaragua in July 1961, his intention was to reiterate the proposals he'd made the previous year. It was necessary to have a political force with no connection to groups of the Right and which transcended the limitations of the traditional Left. To accomplish that, it was proposed to create an organization with its own political line that used armed struggle as its primary strategic instrument and was able to incorporate other forces as well.

With the collaboration of Julio Jerez, Germán Gaitán, Guillermo Mejilla and José Benito Escobar, Carlos Fonseca founded in July

1961 the New Nicaragua Movement (MNN), a key predecessor of the FSLN.*

Carlos generously proposed that I become Secretary General of the MNN. The idea had no support. They objected, rightly enough, that I was outside the country.

The MNN adopted the anti-imperialist thought and class positions of Sandino; it declared itself the continuation of the Nicaraguan people's struggle against their oppressors — from the time of Spanish colonialism to the imperialist intervention. Its methods of struggle were inspired by Diriangen, Andrés Castro, Zeledón, Sandino and Rigoberto. It defined as an historical necessity the formation of a movement that would organize the masses and support armed struggle.

It adopted the programmatic proposals of Sandino and raised them as its banner: national independence, struggle against exploitation by the oligarchy, national unity and unity of the Latin American peoples.

Germán Gaitán, who as a companion of Carlos Fonseca experienced the ups and downs of the incipient struggle, recalls the following with respect to the emergence to the New Nicaragua Movement:

> The Nicaraguan Unitary Front (FUN), made up of Nicaraguan exiles, met in Maracaibo, Venezuela, on February 21, 1960, at the meeting of revolutionary organizations from Latin America and the United States. Carlos, who attended as a delegate from the University Center of the National University, observed that the FUN was promoting a struggle directed toward a profound change but that, because of the heterogeneous composition of its participants, it still had not resolved the problem of gathering the revolutionary elements into an independent body influenced solely by the ideology of the workers.
>
> On his return to Honduras, intent on forming the first guerrilla group, he called Julio Jerez and me to Tegucigalpa and proposed that we create the New Nicaragua Movement.

* See statutes at the end of this chapter.

Under this name, we attracted as a first step the Popular Insurrectional Movement (MIP), which had already organized student cells in Estelí and León that immediately came under the control of the MNN.

Inocente and José Benito Escobar, Rigoberto Cruz ("Pablo Ubeda"), Augusto Tercero and Guillermo Mejilla, among others who had been members of the Nationalist Revolutionary Youth (JRN), joined the new movement.[1]

The MNN carried out propaganda activities. It published for the first time *The Ideas of Sandino* on an underground press, something no political organization had been able to do. It supported the first comrades who returned to the country clandestinely. Its emphasis on unity led the MNN to create the United Sandinista Movements of the Revolution, an organism that was the immediate predecessor of the Sandinista National Liberation Front (FSLN).

The MNN held it first politico-military school in Casa Colorada in April 1962. It was discovered by the enemy and Germán Gaitán, Julio Corrales, Luis Fisher, Constantino Baltodano, Denis Barquero and René Pérez Sandoval went to prison in San Juan del Norte.

In this same period, Carlos Fonseca clandestinely sent Blanquita Segovia to Cuba. Silvio Mayorga and Germán Gaitán were in charge of this operation and were aided, in turn, by Julio Vidaurre and Dr. Emilio Flores Obregón. Blanquita, General Sandino's only daughter, was accompanied by her husband, Enrique Castillo, and her sons, Augusto Enrique, Rodolfo Antonio, Julio César, and Walter Ramiro. To elude Somoza's security force, she traveled a thousand byways using the name Petrona Pérez. She arrived in Cuba on August 15th.

The most visible antecedents of the FSLN then, are the Nicaraguan Revolutionary Youth, the Sandino Front, the New Nicaragua Movement, the Democratic Youth, and Patriotic Youth, as well as the armed movements of Ramón Raudales, Chale Haslam, Manuel Díaz y Sotelo, Julio Alonzo and the veteran Sandinista, Heriberto Reyes.

[1] Testimony given the author by Germán Gaitán in 1988.

Its founders were of different backgrounds. Some of us were students, such as Carlos himself, Silvio Mayorga, Jorge Navarro, Francisco Buitrago and Modesto Duarte. Others were workers, like José Benito Escobar, Rigoberto Cruz and Germán Pomares, while still others were peasants, as for example, Faustino Ruiz and the veteran of the Army for the Defense of National Sovereignty, Colonel Santos López.

DOCUMENT 1
Nicaraguan University Students Reject
Expulsion of Diplomats*

The expulsion of the Cuban diplomats by the tyrannical Somoza regime in Nicaragua is a clear warning that Yankee imperialism is accelerating its plans of aggression against Cuba and its Revolution.

The Somozas are the footmen of the North American monopolies in the Central American area and it is well known that their actions are ordered directly by the Department of State in Washington. Armed aggressions in the Caribbean area frequently follow on the heels of diplomatic provocations by the Somoza tyranny.

In December 1948, immediately after breaking relations with the government of Costa Rica, the Somozas invaded this sister republic with the forces of their National Guard. In 1954, the Somozas broke off relations with the democratic government of Col. Jacobo Arbenz of Guatemala and, at the behest of John Foster Dulles and the United Fruit Co., delivered arms to the traitor, Carlos Castillo Armas, and made available Las Mercedes airport in Managua for the bombers of the North American Air Force to strafe the population of this other Central American sister republic.

North American imperialism's offensive against Cuba is growing in intensity. It is no accident that at the precise moment in which the Yankee Department of State sends a new aggressive note to the revolutionary government, Gen. Stranagan of the U.S. Air Force arrives in Nicaragua to coordinate the plans for aggression against Cuba and, on the other hand, bloodthirsty Tachito Somoza reaches an agreement with Díaz Lanz in Miami. To cast a veil over their criminal plans and to heap wood on the fire of their provocations against Cuba, the Somozas expel the Cuban diplomats from Nicaragua under the absurd pretext of intervention in the internal affairs of the country.

---

* Communique of the University Center and the Nicaraguan Unitary Front published in the weekly, *Combate* [Havana, June 10, 1960].

The president of the University Center of the National Autonomous University of Nicaragua, Joaquín Solís Piura, echoing the solidarity of Nicaragua patriots with the Cuban Revolution and with our people's repudiation of the Somoza tyranny and Yankee imperialism, valiantly denounced the preparations for aggression against Cuba currently being made on Nicaraguan soil by the Somoza regime.

The Somozas, owners of 200 agricultural properties, and the large landowners, who together run national politics, fear that the Nicaraguan peasants, following the example of the Cuban *guajiros*, will seize the great expanses of land now in the hand of a few "gentlemen," and in union with the city workers, the middle class and democratic forces, will topple the Somoza regime and establish a revolutionary government born from within the people as a whole. It is because of this that Somoza and the reactionaries in Nicaragua are so anxious to serve imperialism by helping to prepare the aggression against Cuba and its Revolution, thereby defending their own ancestral system of exploitation of the land and of the farm workers.

The Somoza family confronts the increasing discontent of the people of our country, because we Nicaraguans have realized that the path of the Cuban Revolution is our own path.

We are certain that the Nicaraguan people will stand guard in solidarity with the Cuban Revolution and will do everything possible to frustrate on our own soil the criminal plans of imperialism and the Somozas against Cuba.

We particularly condemn any attempt to make Cuba appear to be a base of aggression against Nicaragua. We know that imperialism and its agents are trying to organize this sort of provocation in order to facilitate its aggression against the Cuban Revolution.

We denounce this new maneuver of imperialism and of the enemies of Cuba.

Cuba is a safe asylum for the politically persecuted, but it is not a base of aggression against any country, nor does it export revolutions.

We Nicaraguan patriots will defend the Cuban Revolution, weapons in hand, and we will fight unceasingly for the overthrow of the Somoza tyranny, the enemy of peace, democracy and progress.

[signature] For the University Center of the National Autonomous University of Nicaragua: Tomás Borge M. (Delegate in Cuba); Carlos Fonseca Amador (Delegate in Costa Rica).
For the Nicaraguan Unitary Front in Cuba: Silvio Mayorga D., Wilfredo López B., Rodolfo Romero, Noel Guerrero.

DOCUMENT 2
Statutes of the "New Nicaragua Movement"

1.-The "New Nicaragua Movement" has the historic mission to organize the Nicaraguan people to occupy the vanguard position in the patriotic struggle to achieve a profound revolutionary transformation of the country.

2.-The emblem of the "New Nicaragua Movement" is the same as that raised by the "Army for the Defense of Nicaraguan Sovereignty" led by Augusto César Sandino. Said emblem is constituted by a banner whose upper part is red, signifying "Free Homeland," and whose lower part is black, signifying "Death." That is, it symbolizes Sandino's phrase: "I want a Free Homeland or Death."

3.-The "New Nicaragua Movement" proclaims that the people determined to stand and fight, are the only source capable of supplying the immense energies necessary to overthrow their criminal oppressors. Such action achieves its fullest potential when the people have their own organization, whose doors are closed to the political party hacks representing the voracious economic and military oligarchy.

4.-The "New Nicaragua Movement" declares itself the faithful continuer of the great struggles for freedom that our people have waged throughout their national history. Our methods of struggle take their inspiration from the examples of sublime courage bequeathed us by the immortal heroes: Diriangen, Andrés Castro, Benjamín Zeledón, Augusto César Sandino and Rigoberto López.

5.-The "New Nicaragua Movement" struggles to carry out a true Revolution. To liberate the country from the oppression of foreign imperialism that it has suffered for more than four centuries. To realize a Revolutionary Agrarian Reform that liquidates feudalism. All of this to impetuously promote the material and spiritual progress of the nation and to put an end once and for all to the tremendous poverty suffered by the people and an end to the criminal extravagance of the oligarchy.

6.-The "New Nicaragua Movement" expresses its solidarity with the fraternal peoples of Latin America and the world who are struggling for the definitive triumph of justice.

7.-A militant of the "New Nicaragua Movement" is only that person who is acquainted with and accepts its Program and Statutes, who contributes actively to their application, who forms part of a member organization, who carries out the decisions of the Movement and who meets the established dues.

8.-A militant of the "New Nicaragua Movement" has the following duties: a) to protect and defend the unity of the revolutionary movement; b) to be an active combatant; c) to strengthen links to the people; d) to raise his level of revolutionary consciousness and to study revolutionary ideology; e) to observe strict discipline; f) to practice honest criticism and frank self-criticism; g) to be sincere and honest; h) to be discreet and to conceal under any circumstances the secrets of the revolutionary movement; i) to combat contempt for the people; j) to join the popular organization most appropriate to his situation; k) to pay dues of at least one percent of his monthly salary or income.

9.-A militant of the "New Nicaragua Movement" has the following rights: a) to voice his opinion in the meetings and publications of the Movement with respect to the problems, orientation and decisions of the Movement; b) to criticize honestly, in the meetings of the Movement, any of its militants; c) to demand personal participation when sanctions are contemplated against him or when his conduct is being discussed; d) to appeal to a superior organism should he be sanctioned by a subordinate organism.

10.-Militants of the Movement may be sanctioned for violating the programmatic principles, for violating its Statutes, for violating or failing to carry out the agreements of the organisms of the Movement or for conduct prejudicial to the prestige of the Movement or to the interests of the people. Depending on the gravity of the fault or crime committed, sanctions shall be censure, separation from responsibilities, suspension or expulsion from the Movement.

11.-The "New Nicaragua Movement" operates on the principle of democratic discipline. All committees and militants of the Movement, upon adopting a resolution by majority vote, must carry out that resolution, including those who voted against it. Subordinate committees are obliged to respect and carry out the resolutions of superior committees.

12.-The supreme authority of the "New Nicaragua Movement" is the "Supreme Committee," which governs the internal life of the Movement and sets its fundamental orientations and activities. A National Directorate will assist the Supreme Committee in its functions and will transmit to it the opinions of the organisms of the Movement. The Supreme Committee will seek assistance in carrying out its work from whatever special commissions it deems necessary.

13.-The Departmental, Municipal, Neighborhood and Regional committees will direct the organisms included in the territory indicated by their respective names.

The life of the Movement resides in the grassroots organizations. These organizations are called Committees. Committees are constituted in work centers, institutions or residential zones where there are no fewer than three militants of the Movement.

Nicaraguan revolutionaries residing outside the country may organize themselves with the same duties and rights as the militants who reside within the country.

Chapter Fourteen

1

Between 1960 and 1963, the Sandinista National Liberation Front (FSLN) was forged around an anti-Somoza, anti-imperialist, revolutionary strategy.

From 1958 on, various attempts were made to develop armed struggle as a political response. In all cases, the struggle was organized abroad. In nearly all cases, that is, for one has to accept the guerrilla group organized by a Matagalpan plantation owner, Chale Haslam.

For that very reason, the armed movements of the period had an invasionist character that underestimated forms of organized support within the country. The leaders of these groups, some of whom are remembered with respect, were dominated by subjective criteria and were particularly interested in seeking personal prestige.

The FSLN had come into being by 1962. Of course, it did not appear by decree, nor was it founded with a ceremony. It arose from a process that started even earlier than 1960, that began to define itself in 1961, the official date of its foundation, and which was consolidated in 1962.

> In reality, it was a process of gestation, growth and consolidation that operated over a period of years.
>
> Until 1963, this movement was not called the Sandinista National Liberation Front, but simply the Front of National Liberation. At that time, its social composition was heterogeneous, its leader was a professional, a lawyer from León. I don't remember whether he was a lawyer or a pharmacist...* He was an older man. But in practice, the generating nucleus of the movement was made up of Carlos Fonseca, Santos López, Tomás Borge, Silvio Mayorga and Jorge Navarro.[1]

---

* The reference is to Noel Guerrero. [author's note]

[1] Jaime Wheelock Román, *Nicaragua: el papel de la vanguardia* (Buenos Aires: Contrapunto, 1986), p. 50.

Our vanguard — the FSLN — wrapped in humble swaddling clothes, torn by early sufferings and surrounded by darkness, required a visionary, a guide, a mystic, a generous person, a leader of stature heightened by self-effacement and the masterful way he combined energetic criticism with the comradeship that permeated every cell of his singular frame. Carlos Fonseca was the principal founder of our dreams, the leader, once and for all time, of the Sandinista National Liberation Front.

Our organization was born as a political front to unify forces — if possible, all groups opposed to the dictatorship.

Such a bloc never came into being, but the original structures gave birth to a political vanguard that responded to the aspirations of broad sectors. The Sandinista Front was the result of a multiplication of contradictory factors, a social necessity.

Even though that generation of young revolutionaries was scarcely acquainted with political theory, they managed — "out of shame rather than awareness," as Carlos Fonseca once put it — with great ideological effort to identify the correlation of forces at that moment; they photographed the detested face of their immediate enemy and distributed the rules of the game throughout the countryside and in the cities.

> The importance of the countryside, then, was emphasized as much because it contained our exploited peasant population as because it afforded topographical advantages for armed struggle. The cities were considered the best zones for political work, so that while the military effort was concentrated in the countryside, political work prevailed in the cities.
>
> From the viewpoint of political strategy, the leadership conceived of the creation of a united front of all the people and progressive political forces around an armed vanguard, which would have the task of preparing the conditions of struggle against the military apparatus of the tyranny and in that way powerfully ripen the general political conditions, leading to the military unity of all forces,

which in turn would lead to an *insurrection of the entire people*.[1]

To accomplish this objective, which resembled a distant mountain range, as unreachable as a fish that must be captured with blistered hands, it would be necessary to carry out a war with no expectations of short-range resolutions. At that time, it was called "prolonged warfare." That was the integral idea, but its principal form was armed struggle and within that concept, guerrilla warfare.

In practice, the infant guerrilla struggle was contaminated at birth by the malady of invasion and had no base of support inside the country, except in our imagination and desire, nor even a minimal infrastructure in the zone to be invaded, as had been conceived in the initial projects.

There was, on the other hand, an excessive emotional identification — translated into a mechanical reproduction of the drawing — with the armed experience of Cuba. With a keen olfactory sense we abandoned, both in conception and in practice, the mistaken synthesis attempted by Régis Debray, and this kept our project from dying.

The FSLN not only survived but became a magnet, because its principal founder elaborated unerring strategic responses, refused to be discouraged by repeated failures or to become self-satisfied by successes and the flowering of our efforts. Nor did he entertain any illusions about being handed a pirate's map that would lead him to the buried treasure.

2

The political leadership in 1963 was concentrated in Noel Guerrero Santiago. When he joined the Nicaraguan revolutionary movement, he entered the Socialist Party — whose leaders claimed to

---

[1] Wheelock, *El FSLN, su carácter de vanguardia y el trabajo entre las masas* (Managua: Archivo del Instituto de Historia de Nicaragua, 1974), p. 5. [unpublished]

be Marxist-Leninists — where he became involved in serious arguments that soon distanced him from their ranks.

The first militants of the FSLN always thought Guerrero's positions were correct at that moment. He gave us political instruction in León, when he was still a member of the Socialist Party. His students were Carlos Fonseca, Silvio Mayorga and myself, who had formed a cell for study and political activity.

Guerrero was erudite and knew Marxist theory. At that time, he was very patient and fraternal and discussed things with us.

"Sandino," Carlos once said, "is a sort of road. It would be frivolous to reduce him to the category of an anniversary ritual. I think," he added, "that it's important to study his thought."

Noel Guerrero replied: "A road? That's poetry! Don't forget how suspect the exaltation of his image by bourgeois ideologues is. Sandino fought against foreign occupation, not against imperialism. He was never a Zapata, which is to say he never posed the problem of land ownership."

Carlos expressed his doubts about such arguments. He proposed to investigate Sandino's thought in depth. I remember his delight and the severity of his gestures when he read *Sandino or the Calvary of the Segovias*, a book edited by Somoza with the pretension of discrediting Sandino and his struggle. Somoza committed the error of reproducing the guerrilla leader's correspondence. This is the first bibliographical source we had before we became acquainted with Sofonías Salvatierra's *Sandino or the Tragedy of a People*. Afterwards, we read *With Sandino in Nicaragua*, by a Basque author whose name is nearly as long as the book itself: Belausteguigoitia. We also devoured the work of Calderón Ramírez and, above all, the books of Gregorio Selser.

Carlos jotted down notes rigorously and constantly, pulling out phrases from the varied and rich letters of Sandino. These notes became *Sandinista Ideology*, the manual of initial concepts that still circulates among militants of the FSLN.

Guerrero left the FSLN, permanently, after being accused of mismanaging the financial resources of the organization, a charge that was never proven. We've tried to locate him — inasmuch as he was not considered a traitor, rather a victim of personal weaknesses — but it hasn't been possible. We don't think he's died, but that he is lost in the increasingly dense jungles of Mexico City.

Silvio, Carlos, Noel and I participated in the meeting in Tegucigalpa. Noel proposed the formation of what he wanted to call the National Liberation Front. Carlos thought it should be called the Sandinista National Liberation Front. I proposed — and I think this is the first time I mention it — that it be called the Peoples' Liberating Front. I wanted that name so that, like Bolívar's, its military arm could be called the Liberating Army.

Silvio backed Noel's suggestion and Carlos' proposal and my own were defeated. While I abandoned the idea that it should be called the Peoples' Liberating Front, Carlos insisted and we could not dissuade him — or Noel could not dissuade him — from calling the organization the Sandinista National Liberation Front. His arguments were rejected. Carlos argued that it was not possible to form a broad front but only an organization embracing Nicaraguan revolutionaries, and that the word *Sandinista* would give a revolutionary stamp to the organization without being sectarian. Sandino had been converted into an archetype, a national figure who had even been exalted in 1944 by the parties opposed to the Somoza regime. Years later, referring to the obvious weight of Sandino, Víctor Tirado would summarize the primary source of the FSLN as follows:

> In the first place, the true father of the Sandinista Front, Gen. Augusto C. Sandino. In second place, the son of Sandino: Rigoberto López Pérez. Carlos Fonseca, principal inspirer, leader and maximum conductor of the Sandinista Front. Col. Santos López, who fought alongside Sandino against the North American intervention and who later joined the new generation of Sandinistas. Silvio Mayorga, Jorge Navarro, José Benito Escobar, Francisco Buitrago, Rigoberto Cruz, Faustino Ruiz, Germán Pomares and Tomás Borge, the only survivor of that historic enterprise.[1]

[1] Víctor Tirado López, "El FSLN: un producto y una necesidad Históricos," in: *Nicaragua: una nueva democracia en el tercer mundo* (N.P.: Vanguardia, 1986), p. 37.

In 1944, university leaders Arsenio Alvarez Corrales, Rafael Córdova Rivas, César Carter Cantarero, Hans Raven, and Pedro Joaquín Chamorro used the figure of Sandino. *El universitario*, the student newspaper, tried not to give an anti-imperialist character to Sandino, but rather to show him as a simple victim of Somoza.

Noel Guerrero prevented Carlos Fonseca from participating in the armed group but could not keep him from directing the small internal structure. Within a short time, he had created the conditions to do wall graffiti, distribute leaflets, carry out bank robberies, occupy radio stations, and edit *Trinchera*, our historical publication.

Its first issue appeared on August 1, 1962, with the name *Trinchera de la Revolución,* under the slogan: "Against the dictatorship and imperialism." Starting with its 14th issue, which appeared in December 1962, it was identified as an organ of the Front, and its motto was: "Under the banner of Sandino, against the tyranny, a Free Homeland or Death." Jorge Navarro played an important role in the foundation and direction of *Trinchera.*

Using Jorge as intermediary, Carlos sent all the funds obtained in the first bank assault to the guerrilla units. Despite the limitations imposed by secrecy, we managed to extend our underground contacts to El Viejo, Chinandega and León.

3

The first guerrilla action was organized along the banks of the Patuca River, in Honduras. The operational center — where we stored provisions and received correspondence — was Catacamas, and in particular the house of Remigio González, the local healer. At times, we spent entire weeks in this small locality.

One night, Heriberto Rodríguez and I decided to see a Pedro Infante film and we walked to the local movie house. From the moment we sat down, a girl with languid eyes wearing a full yellow skirt smiled at me. I struggled against my timidity, trying to get up the courage to sit beside her, and just when I felt brave enough I began to worry about being criticized. "You're mixed up in this other thing, Ramiro," I told myself — Ramiro was my pseudonym — "and you're not looking for amorous adventures."

The fear of an accusing forefinger was stronger than who knows how many centuries of unsatisfied desire, and I did not move from my seat, although during the show I did turn my head several times to find the eyes of that Catacamas girl drilling into me through the darkness.

The next day, Heriberto said to me: "You saved your neck."

"From what?"

"That wasn't a girl."

"Who?"

"The one who was making eyes at you last night. It was a fag. Can you imagine what would have happened if you'd started fondling his leg?"

If I had started romancing in the Catacamas cinema, the ridicule would have lasted until the day before my demise.

4

Sixty men armed with M-1 carbines, Garand assault rifles, M-3 and San Cristóbal submachine guns, and hunting rifles — the latter much sought after because of their telescopic sights and the light weight of their .22 caliber cartridges — gathered near the Patuca River. Along its mountainous margins there's an abundance of turkey, deer, tapirs, mosquitoes and jaguars. In the summer time it teems with ticks and all year round with bands of curious, shrieking monkeys that eat wild bananas and insolently mock the rubber tappers.

Between tributary streams, two or three neat houses of primitive construction look out over the dark waters. Although a corn patch announces a certain inclination toward permanence, their inhabitants — Miskitos and Sumus — impose the threat of sudden departure. There is something of this in the very structure of their humble dwellings, in the oblique shape of the dugouts in which they paddle up the rivers, in their gestures, in I'm not sure what.

The Patuca is long, though not as long as the Coco or a bad marriage. It overflows its banks, borders on perversity, talks to itself in the night, and, when one navigates over its surface, intoxicates him with something like corn liquor or desolation. There's an abundance of fish and alligators in its waters. Its islands are marked with the trails of turtles that deposit beneath small mounds of sand more eggs than necessary to defy the world.

The Patuca, tributary of my dreams, is Honduran in its source and is really a combination of rivers: the Guayape, which is born on La Flor Mountain; the Juticalpa, which is born near a small town; the Grande, which is the smallest of all; and the Galán, which, during the summer, approaches uncertainly from the department of Tegucigalpa.

The first to go up the Guayape to Piedra Chata on the Patuca itself were Carlos Fonseca and Col. Santos López. The young explorer of possible guerrilla encampments and political programs listened with amazement to the interminable stories of the veteran Sandinista, while their dugout nosed its way downstream, infallibly sniffing out the dangers of rocks and whitewater. The rapids are the only danger on the river. The boatmen respect them. They shout at them, but do not insult them. Upstream the passage is slow but safer, while downstream one goes like lightning, although at any moment there may be a thunderous roar and the accompanying fright.

5

Col. Santos López, together with other adolescents, joined the Army for the Defense of National Sovereignty as a waterboy.

The Sandinistas did not camp by the edge of rivers or streams, but rather on the geographical heights or a military crest, and water had to be brought to them along difficult trails. The task was difficult because the water had to be carried in cans on one's shoulders, uphill, besides which it was mandatory to erase one's tracks and straighten out any bent branches. For that reason, the waterboys worked in pairs. One would carry the water, while the other erased their tracks.

The waterboys were organized into an agile, astute group. They were trained in the craft of cutting off Yankee heads, of surprising the Marines at the proper moment, and of fabricating bombs out of sardine tins stolen from the invaders. At that time, they were known as the Angels' Choir.

At the age of 17, Santos López was a colonel and had received seven bullet wounds, which were cured with water, mud and soap, materials that had antiseptic and antibiotic properties that modern science still has not studied in depth.

When a Sandinista combatant was wounded, they would seek refuge for him with some peasant family. A wounded man never rejoined his column without first having impregnated a girl. Col. Santos López was wounded seven times in the legs, arms and chest, and fourteen times in the heart. He was the father of fourteen children.

During their visit to Piedra Chata, he and Carlos discovered a small group, which, under the leadership of Harold Martínez, was planning to enter Nicaragua. Harold was the brother of Alejandro, who a year earlier had been the chief of the Sandino Front column, which had many excellent members. Some of the survivors joined the FSLN.

Harold Martínez was accompanied by Edén Pastora, a Mexican, and a number of Sumus. We spoke with them and suggested we join forces. Harold proposed that we resolve the problem of unification by naming the strongest among us as chief: the one who could hike the longest without tiring while carrying the heaviest backpack. Carlos loved our reply: "That solves the problem; let's appoint a mule as our chief."

I was pleased by a gesture Pastora made when, during one of our many river crossings, he gave us his deluxe first-aid kit. Neither he, nor Harold, nor the Mexican joined our group. The Sumus, on the other hand, collaborated immediately.

When the Revolution triumphed, the archives revealed the name and activities of Harold Martínez as an active agent and confidant of Somoza's security forces.

Months later, the first combatants arrived at Patuca, among them Víctor Tirado; the medical doctors Manuel Andara Ubeda and Napoleón Quant; Bayardo Altamirano, whose father, Ramón, was a persistent collaborator of the FSLN; Heriberto Rodríguez, Francisco Rojas, Rolando Rosales, Pedro Pablo Ríos ("The Indian"), Iván Vaca, Vicente Casco, Leopoldo Rodríguez, Andrés García ("Wiwilí"), who later, as an officer in the Ministry of the Interior, was killed by the counterrevolution; Francisco Jarquín, Cristóbal Guido, Alberto Rugama, Sebastián Montoya, Antonio Escorcia, Ramón Raudales, Jr.; Chele ("Whitey") Eduardo Kalix, current whereabouts unknown; Boanerges Santamaría, Francisco Buitrago, Jorge Navarro, Mauricio Córdova, Pedrito ("The Honduran") and Iván Sánchez.

Noel Guerrero was, for practical purposes, the chief and we had disagreements with him, as I've already said, that prevented Carlos from participating in the guerrilla column. Carlos was obliged to enter Nicaragua clandestinely and could not, as he had wished, remain with the armed group during those long, hallucinatory months of winter and brutal, tick-infested summer.

> In Honduras, the man who for all practical purposes was the chief, was Noel Guerrero Santiago. He had not been appointed to that position by any consensus, but the fact that he personally controlled the funds made it possible for him to decide the most important questions. This was true in terms of overall responsibility, inasmuch as strictly military leadership was in the hands of comrade Santos López.[1]

During 1962, we spent all our time coming and going from the main river to its tributaries, which we followed almost to their headwaters hunting peccaries, tapirs, turkeys and monkeys. If we discovered honey, we'd fill our canteens after filling our stomachs. We gutted the animals we'd killed and, if we had a long way to go, roasted them to preserve the meat. The return was always arduous, as we almost always had to carry an excessive load on which depended the survival of our encampment.

The river we got to know best was El Guineo, a shallow, pleasant stream with a white, sandy bottom. We set up camp on one

---

[1] Carlos Fonseca, "Interrogatorio auto el juez, 19 July de 1964," in: *Obras*, Vol. I, p. 187.

side or another of this tributary of the Patuca, not far from "Hell's Gate," its darkest, most dreaded stretch of rapids.

I'd taken a number of courses in Cuba and taught tactics and weapons, but the real master was Col. Santos López, who gave his guerrilla course as though he were having a conversation. He was fifty years-old and a chainsmoker who rolled new cigarettes from butts whenever he ran out, and when there were no longer any butts, he smoked palm fibers.

He'd grow tired during the marches and as we climbed hills he would stop when he ran out of breath. Then, so we wouldn't make an issue of his weakness, he'd give us details of Sandinista ambushes. He would tell stories about the Old Man, whom the Yankees called a bandit and the guerrillas called the Supreme Chief. "One time, when the Old Man got tired, we had to carry him," the Colonel told us. "Another time, he was wounded by a stray bullet from an airplane and we of the Angels' Choir carried him like a feather along the most difficult paths of Nicaragua."

Between the Patuca and the Coco lies the hunchback range of Entre Ríos. On the banks of the Coco — better known as the Wankí on the Atlantic Coast — in the vicinity of Wiwilí, we had acquaintances, contacts and sympathizers: Don Ramón Altamirano, an artisan from Estelí who cobbled strong boots that protected one from the water and rough roads; Andrés García, whom we called "Wiwilí" for obvious reasons; and Sebastián Montoya ("Alfonso"), all had family and friends in the region.

Everything recommended that we move in that direction. We talked of doing political work, exploring, setting up caches. Common sense and the combatants themselves so proposed. But Noel Guerrero decided that the fate of our guerrilla band should be otherwise.

During our first months in the region we adopted the cover, successfully, of rubber tappers.

Remigio González ("The Doctor"), a healer from the Honduran village of Catacamas, was our guide and counselor. He was well-versed in herbs, bewitchments and philters [magical potions], an old rubber tapper known in the area for his consultations and visits to patients, even by the children he'd treated for indigestion and diarrhea over the past fifteen years.

He led us to Guayambre, a place that nature had decided was ideal for concealment. Remigio González had a motive for helping us: his father was Gen. Simón González, a fierce anti-Yankee Honduran who'd fought alongside Sandino.

Together with Faustino Ruiz ("El Cuje") and Pedro Pablo Ríos ("The Indian"), we set up our encampment, which we baptized "MP" in honor of Manuel Pastrana, who had fallen in the guerrilla campaign of the Sandino Front. He was a combatant with natural leadership qualities who'd won the affection and admiration of "El Cuje" and "The Indian."

For the first time, I learned about the appetite of a guerrilla. We ate cooked rice, beans by the bushel, and monkey meat. Sometimes we'd run out of rice and beans, but there were always monkeys, which we hunted with .22 caliber carbines. It was a shame to kill a monkey, especially when they were wounded and they'd look at you with the air of a victim, beseeching compassion. As they died, their eyes would flash with something resembling reproach, a vague accusation. They screeched like spoiled, hungry children.

When they were taken to the river to be dressed out, thousands of worms spilled from their stomachs and intestines and swam in the water like living spaghetti. To the guerrillas, monkey meat was delicious. The greasy soup adds dynamite to marchers' legs, stimulates fatigued lovers and illuminates one's understanding.

Guerrilla fighters newly arrived at these encampments would lose their appetite for several days. The veterans — after a week everyone's a veteran — would wait, discreetly and attentively, for the newcomers to scorn the food and then ask offhandedly for their portions, promptly wolfing them down.

The guerrilla's appetite is the size of the universe. A guerrilla is forever hungry and is capable of eating the genitals of a chameleon, as Silvio Mayorga did on the banks of the Wankí; or the head of a monkey, which is the exact reproduction of that street urchin, Quincho Barrilete, as I did on the banks of the Patuca; or the leather straps from our backpacks, oiled, as we all did on the banks of the

Umbra; or banana peels and stalks, boiled, as Faustino Ruiz's group did on the banks of the Guayape.

When they give you a serving of rice on a leaf, you eat the grains one by one and, when you're done, lick up the very aroma they have left.

Among the first to arrive were Narciso Zepeda ("Chicho") and Germán Pomares ("El Danto").

Faustino Ruiz, at the head of a small group, moved to an advanced position from which to approach the territory where the Patuca and the Coco come into close proximity. This was in preparation for the explorations of the Coco that we had planned, where with a group of Miskitos we would take the first steps to develop the social basis of a Sandinista support network.

Some of us held that it was indispensable to create such a social basis and to establish supply points and lines.

Faustino Ruiz fell ill. From what I know now, all the symptoms indicated paratyphoid. "Cuje" and his people had used up all the provisions and we didn't even have salt to sprinkle on a *jocote* or an aspirin for a headache.

"Cuje" distinguished himself by his nobility, generosity and courage. He wept easily, wasn't a bullshitter, carried a heavy backpack and was as skilled at cooking as he was equitable — with millimetric perfection — in the distribution of the rations. It was said he was the only man in history who, when it came to love, could make a girl talk who'd been mute from birth. This occurred, according to legend, in El Vedado, Havana, Cuba, to be more precise, during the Year of Agrarian Reform.

The son of peasants, he was poor at spelling, which didn't prevent him from becoming a voracious reader of historical materialism and the works of José Martí. He was dependent on phenobarbital and *difenil lidantoína,* since he had a slight cerebral lesion.

They said that if he didn't receive medical attention and proper nutrition, he could die. We filled the dugout with sacks containing the essentials. Since the trip would take several days, we loaded barrels of gasoline for the outboard motor. Dr. González prescribed chloranphenicol for the patient.

The river was in flood and seemed to be of ill humor. According to Santitos, the little Sumu, the river was less dangerous in winter than in summer, when the water was low.

Cipriano, captain of the dugout, and the other boatman, were both Miskitos. Cipriano had mythological strength; he'd pick up trees when storms had toppled them across the road. He was blond, freckled, and his skin was the color of ripe bananas. His muscles would swell whenever he'd swerve the dugout with his paddle to avoid smashing into a rock. He'd shout at the furious river to give himself courage.

We were still on the Guayape River when a man signaled us frantically from shore. Since he looked familiar, we pulled in by him. It was Julio Corrales, from Somoto, a very young man, a good hiker, impulsive, who knew with his eyes closed all the trails used by smugglers and guerrillas between Honduras and Nicaragua. On several occasions he'd guided Carlos Fonseca along those same trails. I don't remember what he was doing there. He had brought some help to friends along the river and was heading for the "MP" encampment.... Anyway, he came with us.

As we approached the Yellow Waters rapids, close to the house where Cacimiro ("El Potroso") lived, a curtain of foam struck the dugout, which went over a waterfall. In seconds we foundered and went under. The sacks of sugar and rice kept me from resurfacing immediately. I was the last to come up. I heard Cipriano shout: "Hang onto the dugout!"

I grabbed one of the boatmen by the legs and nearly dragged him into the current. I clung to the dugout as it floated belly up. I watched a carton of Delta cigarettes float impetuously downstream. A few meters away, Julio Corrales, wearing an incredulous smile, clung to a half-empty gasoline barrel that was spinning around like a top. We shouted at him to let go of the barrel. I shouted at him to let go. The last thing he heard was my insults. He struck against something, lost his grasp and sank. We saw no more of him.

We managed to drag the dugout onto shore; it wasn't difficult. We were all in undershorts and barefoot, and that's the way we arrived at "El Potroso's" house. I spent the whole night staring at the river, thinking of the drowned boy, fighting the temptation to ask time to turn back its clock so that what had happened might be undone.

We found Julio days later. The Miskitos buried him at Piedra Chata.

I returned to Catacamas in borrowed clothes and rags, barefoot.

6

With two loaded mules, I set out looking for "El Cuje" and when I arrived at a house where they sold canned sardines and rubber boots, I heard someone shout happily: "Here comes Ramiro!"

Fair-haired Eduardo, one of "El Cuje's" group, was looking for provisions. I asked him to return to his chief and notify him of our presence. We rested, since we had made a horse-killing journey, and set out at dawn.

We couldn't have been far from the encampment, because at about 3 p.m. we ran into "El Cuje" who came staggering toward us half dead from hunger.

The next day, we returned to the little store, where we rented a horse for "El Cuje."

Chapter Fifteen

1

In July 1963, we were in mid-winter. We insisted on exploring the area around Wiwilí. We had tried it months before, but with little sense of urgency, hiking upstream along the Guineo River.

Pedro Pablo Ríos headed that incursion beneath torrential downpours. They returned in a few days, blaming the cruelty of the winter and the flooding of the streams which, at that time of year, were really out of control.

Since the exploration produced no results, we made a spur of the moment decision to hike beyond the impossible Hell's Gate and construct rafts there. Singlehandedly, with the aid of the devil and his own arms of mahogany, Cipriano guided the dugout through the Gate.

By this time, nearly all of us had *leishmaniasis*, mountain leprosy. *Leishmaniasis* or *espundia*, the rubber tapper's ulcer, was caused by a parasite called *leishmania*, which is something like a bureaucrat who sets up office in the bodies of rodents, foxes, armadillos, dogs and men.

It's almost never found in urban areas, rarely in cultivated rural areas, but quite frequently in mountainous zones where gnats abound, robbing tranquility from hands, necks, faces and other exposed body parts. The microbe develops in the infinitesimal intestine of the gnat. When the tiny beast bites, it transmits mountain leprosy without further ado.

I don't recall having met any Miskitos, Sumus or rubber tappers with *leishmaniasis*. Gnats and the *leishmania* parasites seem to have a particular predilection for guerrillas who come from the cities. Lesions appear in the skin or the mucous membranes; the ulcer grows and resembles a festering puddle, a little sewer.

When the lesions appear to have healed, they can reappear years later inside the nose and in the throat, in which case, you can be sure they're fatal.

Some of the guerrillas had the disease in strange places: on one of their buttocks, or on the face. It attacked me on the right elbow.

Francisco Buitrago, who had studied several years in medical school, informed us that there is no preventative vaccine against either *leishmaniasis* or the need to be a guerrilla. So there we were.

Jorge Navarro and Francisco Buitrago arrived with supplies purchased with the loot from a bank hold up. Among the treasures that dazzled us, besides canned fruits and "Maggie" soups, was the sure-fire drug for combatting *leishmaniasis,* repodral. Jorge Navarro and Francisco Buitrago exuded mysticism in their looks and smiles, their knapsacks growing lighter every day as they gave everything away.

Francisco was anxious to serve anybody, any time and any place.

Jorge Navarro, cheerful, optimistic, even in the face of adversity, a teller of jokes and anecdotes, ventriloquist, singer of Mexican *rancheras*, replaced his smile with a harmonica and his harmonica with political discourse.

They were sent to the mountains for the purpose of bringing back to Managua reinforcements for the guerrilla groups' strategic rearguard. Guerrero convinced them — he was facile with words — to remain with us in the mountains.

2

With the guerrillas on a raft and the chiefs in a motorized dugout, we set out into the unknown.

At the place where the Cuyamel River empties, or a little beyond, when the land between the Patuca and the Coco narrows like a dancer's waist, we disembarked and began our approach to the Coco.

Our pace was rapid, despite the fact that we were loaded down with flour, rice, sugar and ammunition, in addition to our rifles, blankets and plastic tarps. During brief rest periods, we'd use our backpacks as pillows and doze for ten minutes until someone would say, "Let's go!"

We finally reached the banks of the Coco a little above Raití. We made camp there. It seemed like a dream that on the other side of the river lay the promised land. The Coco River is sacred. Yellow and stubborn, an aphrodisiac. It traps spirits. It marks men with eternal melancholy; it shrinks women's waists, rounds out their hips and lights a glow in their eyes. Whoever drinks of its water falls ill with parasites and nostalgia.

We crossed the river on rafts. When I set foot on the other side, I felt joy and an intense desire to urinate. I resisted, ashamed, long enough to scoop up a handful of dirt and caress it as if it were a woman's breast.

We made our way toward the small village of Raití. The Miskito population received us with surprise and without realizing exactly what was going on. We captured the storekeepers.

The most important of these, Chabelo Olivas, from Matagalpa, was the only one among the inhabitants of Raití who understood precisely who we were. From the terror in his eyes could be read his conviction that he was condemned to die. He must have found it very puzzling when we gave him his freedom after first distributing his canned goods, boots, pants and earrings among the population.

We used his food to put on the biggest feast the Coco River had ever seen. All the inhabitants of Raití lined up for the sweetest rice pudding, the greasiest rice and beans and the thickest oatmeal made with milk they'd ever tasted. We butchered a cow and gorged ourselves with oranges. The children ate as much candy that night as their parents would have doled out to them in a whole year.

The next morning in the Moravian Church, Noel Guerrero gave the residents an erudite talk about agrarian reform. I asked some of them who was the president of Nicaragua, and they didn't know. I also asked them who owned the surrounding land, and they told me the peccaries and tapirs did. Most of them did not speak Spanish or spoke it very badly. None of them understood it well. All of them practiced the Moravian religion.

The adult males collected rubber in the mountains and sold it to the storekeepers in exchange for different items, which were frequently trinkets. The women and old people cultivated corn and beans or fished.

Their houses were clean huts built on stilts. We noted the inhabitants' proximity and devotion to water by the cleanliness of their skin and by their few, lowly possessions.

In dugouts seized from the merchants, we set off for Walakistán, a settlement without streets consisting of four houses, where the inhabitants enjoyed another banquet of food confiscated from the commissary and another speech by Guerrero on the topic of urban reform.

3

We stealthily crossed to the other side of the river and hid several dozen sacks of edibles that later proved to be invaluable.

We decided to split into two groups: one, under the command of the Colonel, would attack Bocay; the other, led by a general staff with Silvio Mayorga as its initial chief, would remain as a reserve force to resupply Bocay using the dugouts seized in the last village.

Noel Guerrero waited several days. When Cipriano returned with empty hands and an empty dugout explaining that the Colonel's group had split up, Guerrero decided to return to Tegucigalpa to organize a new column and to seek additional arms and money.

As our small column approached Bocay, it became evident that the enemy had detected our presence. Air Force planes were searching the area and the local garrison had received reinforcements.

The Colonel decided the time was not right to attack. Jorge Navarro, Francisco Buitrago, Iván Sánchez, Pablo Ubeda, Mauricio Córdova, and Modesto Duarte were determined to attempt an attack but Narciso Zepeda, Germán Pomares and Aureliano Carrasco, ("Chicón"), together with Col. López crossed over into Honduran territory and advanced through the jungle toward Wiwilí.

Noel Guerrero took Cipriano, our only guide, with him, as well as Dr. Andara, the column's physician.

We decided to attack San Carlos and we also split into two groups: one, comprising, among others, Silvio Mayorga, Bayardo

Altamirano, Faustino Ruiz, Boanerges Santamaría, Ramón Raudales, Pedro Pablo Ríos and myself; the other remained in reserve in the Yeluke encampment under the command of Dr. Orlando Quant.

On the march toward San Carlos, we got lost in the mountains.

By coincidence, I remember it was the month of August. We were lost in that dark, humid mouth that seemed to be — and was — the headwaters of a river. Relentless starvation had set in when the sky decreed a brief pause in the rain while we rested on a sand bar. Bayardo Altamirano took out four cans of condensed milk, one of Quaker oats and three packs of Delta cigarettes.

Bayardo recovered his old malicious glee and announced: "Today is Ramiro's birthday!" It was the 13th of August.

That stash from the Thousand and One Nights was mixed with spring water, warmed, and devoured slurp by slurp without speaking, savoring each drop as if it were our first and last, next to the bonfire that was drying our wet clothes. Afterwards, we chatted about the immortality of crabs, about women, about the bean soup at Cucaracha's in León, or the pork loin in Cara de Macho's bar in Jinotepe, while smoking the most delicious cigarette in modern history.

The next day we decided to follow the river. At first it only covered our feet, then it reached to our knees. With elephant-sized hunger, in the rain, shaking with cold, alone, with the sensation of being nowhere, we built rafts because the water was now up to our waists. It was the Umbra River, a tributary of the Wankí.

When you're marching in a group, the animals disappear. They watch from the thickets, sniff at us, and know intuitively that we are hungry hunters. We staggered along. Had someone happened to see us, they might have taken us for apparitions; or possibly our appearance was so pitiful that we wouldn't even have been up to the classification of ghosts.

No one passed that way. There were no trails, no broken branches: just insolent virginity. The downpour had begun in June — save for brief moments, occasionally a few hours, only to recapture its full cruelty — putting to shame the forty days and forty nights of the biblical tale.

Soaked through to the esophagus, lips kissed by humidity, with circles under our eyes that seemed traced in charcoal, we had grown so thin that had someone taken a frontal photograph of us, he'd have thought we were posing in profile.

New *leishmaniasis* lesions reminiscent of adolescence, feet tortured by stones and blisters, scratches and bruises on our half-naked ribs. Our hands, torn by thorns, seemed wrapped in white gloves burned by an implacable acid.

We looked like victims of a shipwreck, vagabonds, madmen escaped from their straitjackets. I try to imagine a smile, some word that surely would seem a complaint, a sinister whistling, the survival instinct converted into an imperative.

The tenuous rain of that morning was interlaced with a thick white fog, like a handkerchief waving good-bye while the river widened and a cry of agony, of victory, announced the end of the day's march.

The lead raft with Silvio Mayorga and Bayardo Altamirano had gone over a waterfall to what looked like another river flowing in another dimension. We scarcely had time to desperately reach the bank and see how the shipwreck victims had saved themselves by grabbing hold of roots that reached like grappling irons into the water. Everything was saved, except the four M-3 submachine guns, our pampered darlings.

Bayardo shouted something to us and his thin howls held a note of optimism: they'd found a well-traveled path, a sure sign of proximity to humans.

And so it was. We had scarcely walked for twenty minutes when we saw a large adobe house surrounded by pastures and a corral with calves nursing at huge udders. Two of our companions forged ahead and ran smack into a wall of barking that renewed our will to live.

The owners had cooked pork-filled tamales. We bought the whole batch, which came to two and a half for each of us. We savored the mass of cornmeal, diluting each mouthful until it was transformed into a thick saliva that slid in slow-motion through the esophagus down to the stomach, where it landed like angel feathers.

After that we killed a pig. We hung him from the edge of the gallows; Pedro Pablo Ríos approached him with a knife and the animal watched him innocently, confidently. He, with the indifference of an executioner, thrust his blade into its throat and the red torrent filled a bucket, splattering hands, arms and tattered boots.

The viscera, the haunches and even the head went into the cookpot that was already bubbling over the fire. A pack of dogs waited, tongues lolling, for the chance to gorge themselves on the remains.

Some of the comrades drank the blood, because it combats anemia and multiplies spermatozoa. Most of us waited for the bacon roasting over the coals, which we ate wrapped in toasted cornmeal tortillas. Incomparable!

4

We remained for several days in that house inhabited by mixed-bloods.

We didn't permit anyone to leave and, two days later, a man arrived to find out why the pork tamales had never reached the village of San Carlos. He was called "El Managua," another mixed-blood in a small dugout.

We befriended him. He placed his machete, his knife and his dugout at our disposal. He asked us for a weapon, but we had neither an extra gun nor sufficient confidence in him. He resigned himself to sharing sentry duty and our meat, which isn't often eaten in that lost paradise.

Beneath an orange tree, while my stomach rejected the juice and pulp, which I kept eating anyway, he related his amorous adventures. A sailor with more than one love in every port, he told us of girls he'd abducted, always when they were fifteen, and of slender ladies with graceful legs and wedding rings, who were vulnerable to loneliness and anxious for consolation.

Fleeing from a deceived husband, who, to make things worse, was a colonel with a vicious temper, "El Managua" had arrived at the Wankí River where he foundered between the legs of a Miskito girl who'd bewitched him. There was no way out.

At one time, he'd been a prisoner in León's La 21 jail because of some flings. His girlfriend, Aurora, who sold meat in the railway station market, got him out; she was a friend of Sergeant Gutiérrez, an influential man in Colonel Delgadillo's office.

"I should have married her but that's life, my friend."

He was in Managua, where he tried to become a barber but wound up as a singer in the Tellería Brothers Trio, although he wasn't a member of the family.

That was where he met the colonel's lady: in the Versailles; she was with a woman friend and he noticed that both her eyes and her legs were open. She sent him a note with the waiter asking him to telephone her.

"Want me to give you the number? But what's the use, right? All the rest, my friend, is revenge. Right now I'm here. Nobody's after me. The Miskito girl is going to have my son, my first. I'm going to name him Wankí, because that's a name for the movies."

He accompanied us for the next few days. He didn't know the terrain very well but he won us with the boastful way he moved about in that crossword puzzle of trails. He guided us, unarmed, presumptuous, distrustful in the final moments, to our confrontation with the Guard in San Esquipulas.

We decided to occupy San Esquipulas before attacking San Carlos. We believed it to be a lightly guarded locality where we could find cigarettes and recover some rifles and ammunition. We left in a flotilla of small dugouts.

We had chosen Bayardo Altamirano chief. He headed the group in a dugout slightly larger than the rest. I was behind him with Pedro Pablo Ríos ("El Indio"), "El Managua," Cristóbal Guido and Antonio Escorcia, in a dugout that was just hip wide. The boatman, nervous as we approached a settlement, made a brusque movement and the dugout capsized.

I lost the Reising submachine gun I was carrying on my knees, while shouting, as Cipriano had done in another bitter moment: "Hang onto the dugout!" Tonio Escorcia was the only one who didn't know how to swim; nevertheless he managed to save himself, but without his backpack and his weapon, which were lost forever, along with his revolutionary enthusiasm.

That happened at the edge of a settlement. It was there that we met the Italian.

The moon was shining despite the drizzle, it was possible to see faces and to remember them. The man was wearing a faded undershirt that didn't conceal his superb musculature or his superior stature.

The next day, we saw his green eyes, gray beard, a scar on his right shoulder that resembled a signature, the happy surprise on his clear brow, the resolute gestures of one who is carrying out a sacred mission. He scarcely asked us any questions.

That Apollo in rags joined our guerrilla group and a short time later was marching at our head on that mountain, scorning the night with an *ocote* torch between his teeth to light his way and ours; with a machete in one hand, opening a path for us, while he gestured with the other, or, taking the torch from his teeth, would pronounce authoritative words in the darkness.

The Italian had arrived at that outpost of the world's geography fleeing from some drama, a dagger abandoned in the breast of a traitor, some amorous disillusionment.

The Italian was there — because the Guard killed him a few days later — becoming the first internationalist martyr of this new stage in the Nicaraguan revolution. A century earlier, the *condottiere* Garibaldi had passed through Nicaragua.

5

We were close to taking San Esquipulas. We arrived after nightfall. We were in front with Silvio Mayorga, Pedro Pablo Ríos, "El Indio," Cristóbal Guido and "El Managua"; the others remained a short distance behind.

We crossed a bridge, which was a fallen tree trunk, and ducked down a few meters away from some Guards who were interrupting the darkness with the glow of their cigarettes. In our hiding place we held a whispered discussion, consisting mostly of gestures, with Silvio Mayorga. Someone held that the Guards silhouetted against the moon were exactly that: Guards. Others felt that they were Miskitos who were smoking. "For that very reason, Silvio, they aren't Indians. Why the cigarettes? Where did they get them, brother?"

So, in the midst of whether they were or weren't Guards, to our astonishment we see Silvio's shadowy figure rise up and move forward to confront the Guard on sentry duty, who was wearing a rubber raincape. The sentry reacted, firing his M-1 carbine and wounding Silvio in the right leg. One of us threw a grenade into the hut. The outcome: one officer dead and various soldiers wounded, as we learned later. The second grenade we threw didn't explode. Silvio dragged himself away.

Pedro Pablo fired a burst from his Thompson, which immediately jammed. Another of our group fired some M-1 rounds and his carbine also jammed. Heriberto Rodríguez from another position, fired a shot from his Garand and after the first round, he couldn't move the bolt.

Others tried to fire their weapons and none of them worked: they were jammed because of the constant humidity. We withdrew. Pedro Pablo carried Silvio and the sound of rifles and Garands firing moved off in the opposite direction.

We walked until we were bored and kept on walking long after that. We could still hear the sound of gunfire. The National Guard was firing insults and rifle bursts at shadows. "El Managua" died in this action, pierced by an evil 30.06 bullet.

At dawn, we came across a cow. Someone proposed we kill it and carry off a leg to ease our hunger. That wasn't acceptable but there was no opposition to stripping an orange tree of its fruit. We ate half an orange each, including the pulp, the rind and even the seeds. Afterwards, the nostalgia for a cigarette.

With our hunger still intact, we heard a suspicious noise that turned into an airplane. We froze, as motionless as shrubs without a breeze. We could see the pilot's face behind his curious goggles. He didn't see us; he didn't want to see us, because we were clearly visible. He was probably afraid.

The plane moved away from our anxiety. A short time later a salvo of gunfire startled a pair of tapirs who were hiding in the thickets. At that moment, Faustino Ruiz, "El Cuje," and Boanerges Santamaría gave up their lives.

Ramón Raudales, Jr., who took part in that confrontation, showed up begging for affection twenty days later in the Yeluka encampment to which we had returned. His eyes were unintelligible; he looked like a ghost.

Chapter Sixteen

1

We voted in assembly to return. Almost everybody decided to go to Honduras, considering that conditions were not right to continue the guerrilla struggle. The great majority reaffirmed their faith in armed struggle, but this could not continue without arms, without communications, without a social base, with half-naked men starving and crucified by blisters and *leishmaniasis*. Silvio Mayorga's reasoning was the most lucid and optimistic.

We were starving during our return, really starving, inasmuch as we only killed one tapir. Sometimes we ate snails' miniscule flesh. Between the Coco and Patuca rivers was the fourteenth station of hunger.

Hunger is a combination of subjective sensations, according to physiology, that is expressed in an *inevitable anxiety* for food. This anxiety was not only inevitable and compulsive, but as violent as arrogance, as persistent as love sickness, as totalitarian as a tropical dictatorship.

The stomach contracts like an accordion. Saliva flows into the mouth, stimulated by nostalgia, like a tributary of the Wankí. One keeps swallowing and swallowing, which leads to extreme excitation.

The centers of hunger and satiation, which regulate us by means of conditioned reflexes, are located in the thalamus at the base of the brain. I said *hambre* and *saciedad*, not *hombre* and *sociedad*, which are likewise not unfamiliar with hunger.* One doesn't eat; glucose, the amino acids and fatty substances flee, like untamed animals, from the blood. Before this stampede, the lights of the appetite turn on at the base of the cerebrum.

It is said that the sufficient or excessive presence of these elements inhibits that center and stimulates the center of satiety,

---

* A play on the Spanish words for "hunger," "satiation," "man" and "society."

producing a disagreeable state of total satisfaction, which most resembles sadness.

Because of the rains, because of our nudity, we skeletons who had been loaned a fragile skin with which to cover ourselves, suffered from the cold as if it were an additional ailment. And cold, like a vicious circle, heightens one's hunger. The colder it gets, the greater the need for calories; the fewer the calories, the greater the requirement for tenderness.

We were hungry, which is that absence of nourishment — with its physical and psychological consequences — that led us to a state of total weakness. We could not raise our arms to clear a path with out machetes because of our starvation. We had reached the point of depleting the protein reserves in our muscles, hearts and brains.

This prolonged state of hunger has the strange name of *caquexia*, a word I was trying to find for a long time to finish a surrealistic poem.

We suffered from the uncontrollable need for solid food, which couldn't be human flesh because, although there have been extreme cases of nourishment anxiety where humans have eaten each other, we still loved one another. Besides, our miserable sacks of bones would not have aroused the least interest.

Each morning in sado-masochistic dialogues we'd tell each other about our nightmares. We dreamt of scrambled eggs with incandescent slices of tomato, Valencian-style rice, malted milk, rice and beans, spaghetti with oil and grated cheese.

"You forgot to dream about a cold Coca Cola."

"And you forgot the pork with yucca."

"Did anyone dream about Brigitte Bardot?"

"I dreamt I was in a real bed."

"And I dreamt about a lake full of milk with mountains of sugar and salt."

The human groups most vulnerable to hunger are children and women; the latter care for and nourish their children, and work besides. I think that in some other time it was the poets, and in yet another the guerrillas, those poets of action.

We had split into two groups. I belonged to Heriberto Rodríguez's. On the banks of the Patuca, we ran into a strange

Yankee in a sort of encampment with a large, civilized dugout. Heriberto did not want to take him captive, so we continued our march. We didn't follow the river but cut across its serpentine curves, shortening the distance.

By coincidence we were at the river bank when we heard a motor. I grabbed Cristóbal Guido's M-1 carbine and aimed it at the craft, which without a doubt resembled Noah's ark. Its passengers were the grinning comrades of our second group who, before capturing the boat, had been marching at a snail's pace because Rolando Rosales had a wounded knee.

We climbed into the boat, we ate in the boat, smoked in the boat, and were carried by this boat to the Cuyamel river. We headed up the river until the rocks and rapids prevented further progress.

Everything I ate passed through me as though I were a pipe connecting my mouth to the ground, which left me with a total disregard for hygiene. We arrived at the house of some peasants and began negotiating with them. They were cattle rustlers. I decided to barter a revolver for food and salt. During the negotiations, I felt the stab of urgency. There, in front of an old man and several children, I deposited what resembled the leavings of a sick cow. From there, we set off for Catacamas, divided into pairs.

Pedro Pablo Ríos and I made our way together to a point near the village, where we found refuge with some long-time collaborators. Their house had a wide corridor in which a girl frequently sat. She was the living image of Margarita Gautier and was Cipriano's girlfriend.

Don Remigio González found someone to take us to Tegucigalpa. On the way, the Honduran Guard stopped us in Juticalpa; I was pretending to be sick, wrapped in a sheet like a winding cloth, with the air of a dying man reinforced by a towel around my neck that made me look wretched. They asked Pedro Pablo Ríos for his identification.

"I left it at home."

"The hell you did!" they told him. "Get down!" And they took him prisoner.

"And this one?"

"He's sick."

I was like an actor with adrenaline coursing through my sunken cheeks.

"Okay, let him go."

And so I arrived in Tegucigalpa. That's where the episode ended. I ran into Noel Guerrero, who scowled at me. "What are you doing here?"

"Don't give me a hard time," I answered, and then told him the whole story.

By that time, Silvio, Altamirano, Pedro Pablo, all of them had been taken prisoner and only Fatso Rosales, Víctor Tirado, Raudales and I remained free.

Modesto Duarte's group did not attack Bocay, but decided to seek an escape route by way of Matagalpa. Iván Sánchez was captured. Modesto got lost and they captured him as well. Navarrito, Chico Buitrago and Mauricio Córdova were handed over to the Guards by some coffee planters. All of them were assassinated. Rigoberto Cruz ("Pablo Ubeda") decided not to trust anybody. Instead, he and two companions kept on hiking until they reached a safe place near Matagalpa. Colonel Santos López made his way to Honduran territory, where he would not fall into the hands of the Guard. Pomares and Narciso Zepeda went with him. They contacted no one and reached Wiwilí where they arranged their passage to Tegucigalpa.

In any event, we could not have achieved much more, because where we were there was nothing but jungle and expectant Miskitos, puzzled by the group that spoke of incomprehensible things. There was a certain degree of sympathy on the part of local people that was reflected in a timely fruit drink, a friendly gesture or an astonished smile.

The remoteness of the place and other factors prevented the guerrillas from achieving wider success in the countryside.

The Coco and Bocay rivers had influenced the consciousness of the struggle's protagonists. Some of them were frightened: the hunger, cold and fatigue were too much for them and they were overwhelmed by a gray mood, nightmarish, otherworldly. I remember how Antonio Escorcia cried like a child locked in a closet. More than once, I heard exclamations like: "This is horrible! Death would be a relief!"

After this experience, those who defended the thesis of armed struggle were Carlos Fonseca and Silvio Mayorga. I, months later and once again legal, had my doubts. Only for a short time, but I had them.

On one occasion, in a political meeting at the home of Dr. Mario Ortiz — an honest and eloquent psychiatrist, principal leader of the Republican Mobilization — we discussed utilizing all forms of struggle without giving priority to any one.

We wanted to avoid adventurism and other herbs with which vacillation is usually spiced. I allowed myself to be influenced by these criteria, which I rejected a short time later when I joined the guerrilla struggle at Pancasán. Carlos, who always defended me, said that my words were just that, mere words, and when the chips were down I could be counted on. I was always ashamed of having wavered and I say this here to get it off my chest. It would have been a one-way trip.

Carlos maintained that the Coco and Bocay river experiences led us into reformist formulations. He pointed out that, in fact, armed struggle had been interrupted for some time. He suggested that a major element in this reformist deviation was the decline of the struggle against the Somozas. I think that, in addition to our own turmoil, the boom in the national economy was also a factor in creating this inertia.

The guerrilla movement of the Coco and Bocay rivers was, in fact, a revolutionary experiment. That defeat interrupted the task of preparing for armed struggle, although we still retained our faith in it.[*]

Víctor Tirado evaluates the guerrilla experience as follows:

> After nearly two years of preparing an armed detachment
> in the mountains of El Patuca in Honduras, the Front tried

---

[*] See Carlos Fonseca, "Nicaragua hora cero," *Obras*, Vol. I, p. 87. See fragment at the end of this chapter.

its first military action, which has come to be known in history as the Bocay Campaign.

As we all know, Bocay was a military defeat. But it was also a great school. After Bocay, at the end of 1963, the Sandinista movement consolidated itself within the Front. From then on, the Front was definitely called the Sandinista Front.

But Bocay, as we said, was a great school. It was a very instructive experience.

We discovered, for example, that we had to put an end to the old practice of preparing armed movements from outside rather than from within the country.

...We also learned the elementary lesson that in order to maintain a guerrilla base, links with the masses — in this case with the peasants — must be strong.

Another conclusion that may be drawn from the Bocay experience is that armed struggle is the principal means of overthrowing the dictatorship, but not the only one. Because if we dedicated ourselves exclusively to preparing armed actions and neglected other forms of struggle, we would run the risk of isolating ourselves and of not forging alliances; we would run the risk of converting ourselves into a sect.

To put it another way, we had to learn to combine armed struggle with other forms of struggle.

It is at this time that the Sandinista Front began to master an art that previous armed movements were unable to learn and which constituted one of their weaknesses: the art of learning to work clandestinely, the art of knowing how to work under any circumstances under whatever conditions and in the face of the harshest reprisals.

Finally, we learned that the fight to destroy the Somoza regime would be hard, long, painful, difficult, as in fact it turned out to be.[1]

[1] Víctor López Tirado, "El FSLN: un producto y una necesidad históricos," pp. 41-42.

At the outset of the decade of the 60s, coffee and cotton producers, businessmen and industrialists increased their exports — and their bad taste — as a result of the ascendancy of the Central American Common Market. Similarly, the corruption and arrogance of the gang of government bureaucrats grew as they benefited from increased foreign credit.

The expansion of exports facilitated an increase in imports: jeeps, electrical appliances, marvelous creams to unwrinkle the ladies. I can attest that some cotton farmers from León drank their Scotch whiskey with slices of mango and salted *jocotes*. The importation of capital goods stimulated the infant industrial development, which made possible an increase in the volume of credits. The Somoza government enjoyed an expanded income and this stimulated the growth of fictitious businesses and outright thievery. Investments and a larger gross national product were in evidence.

The decrease in anti-Somoza sentiment was linked to the commercial expansion within the Central American Common Market. There was even a small but sufficient shift in tariff policies that stimulated demand. This in turn stimulated the growth of the industrial sector, which drew ahead of the rest of the economy.

Coinciding with the honeymoon of the Central American markets, the unequal terms of trade were less unequal than usual, or at least abandoned a part of their sadism. The relationship between export and import prices was merciful. Would that it were always so!

Along with a ravenous appetite for luxury goods and conspicuous consumption, the favorable trade balances decreased. There was not a hint, of course, of subsidizing services such as transportation and housing, which were subject to the implacable laws of supply and demand. Even less favored were education and health programs, which discriminated cruelly against the residents of poor neighborhoods and the peasants.

The North American government, the Agency for International Development (AID) and the cold-blooded financing of the Interamerican Development Bank, acted to reduce declining imports, initiating the game of mirrors where apparent economic growth is a total mirage.

Economic hypocrisy was an obvious element in the overall picture of the time, more because of its relative magnitude than its real importance. The national economy, afflicted with Parkinson's disease, shaped the politics of the first years of the decade.

Besides, the capitalist crisis and the splendor of the Cuban Revolution put the empire on maximum alert; its leaders kept watch on the Latin American horizon with furrowed brows. From under the table they pulled out the marked deck of the Alliance For Progress, a clever conspiracy in which the stick was brandished by the local dictatorships and the sweet carrot by Kennedy's distinguished government.

In Nicaragua, nevertheless, they tried out populism, smiles, anonymous alcoholism, the distribution of marginal plots of land and visits to the pawnshop. Above all, they announced an amnesty that permitted the return of some of us militants who had remained abroad following the beneficial starvation of the Coco River and Bocay.

President René Schick promoted the image of democracy and civil government that commenced in 1963. Despite one or two swallows of government independence that never produced a summer, much less a winter, Schick's government was a gesture in the strictest sense, merely an administrative apparatus. Substantive decisions were reserved for the Somoza brothers, Luis and Anastasio, who captured the leadership respectively of the Liberal Party and the National Guard.

Already in 1964, the economy grew a scant few inches. Domestic financing inflames state investment. Despite the decrease in the prices of sugar, coffee, cacao, bananas and even cotton, production increased to such an extent that it succeeded in neutralizing the bad news.

Exports increased by almost fifteen percent during 1965, while industrial production grew by only seven percent — the lowest rate since 1961. The agricultural sector, in turn, grew by twelve percent, the same rate as manufacturing production.

Until 1964, this expansion could be attributed to cotton production, which grew from slightly less than $15 million dollars in 1960 to nearly $57 million dollars, an increase of 42 percent.

When the price of cotton declined the cotton growers, with feline agility, took over the rich lands of the Pacific. Pitilessly, without violating the law and with a tranquil conscience, they dispossessed small and medium-sized landowners so that they could make up for the drop in prices by the quantity of production. In 1964, they planted more than 134,000 hectares, whose thirsty lands absorbed 70 percent of all bank credits. At the same time, this stimulated the growth of imports, given the increased demand for nonessential goods.

Unfavorable climatic conditions affected production, and therefore exports, in 1966.

The manufacturing sector was a weak point in the economic picture; its relative backwardness is the most important structural flaw in the Nicaraguan economy.

In 1967, cotton prices rose but the overall economic deterioration was irreversible, as was the resulting reaction.

The opposition to the Somozas, led by the Conservative Party, inflated Fernando Agüero with vanity and brought him renown. People chanted: *"Con Fernando ando, y con Agüero muero"* ("I walk with Fernando, and I'll die for Agüero") during his political excursions through our small, dusty locales. They listened to Agüero's speeches, despite the fact he didn't say shit and in spite of the miserable loud speakers and the whinnying of horses.

Once again in hiding, Carlos, together with Silvio Mayorga, Oscar Turcios, José Benito Escobar, Daniel Ortega, Doris Tijerino and others, prepared what would be the decisive experience of Pancasán.

DOCUMENT 3
Nicaragua, Zero Hour
(fragment)

The movement which culminated in the Coco and Bocay River operations was an action prepared by a more or less homogeneous revolutionary group. This first attempt was a trial run by the revolutionary sector.

This first defeat set in motion a review of reformist tendencies. It is certain that armed struggle was not renounced and the conviction that this form of struggle was what would be decisive in the outcome of the Nicaraguan Revolution persisted. But the reality was that practical work to continue the preparation for armed struggle had already been interrupted for some time. It is also certain that following the defeat of 1963 our movement was seriously splintered, but we were unable to find an adequate response to the internal crisis that had arisen.

One factor which undoubtedly got us off course was that our armed struggle coincided with a decline in the anti-Somoza movement in Nicaragua. In 1963, the political upsurge begun with the struggle and victory of the Cuban people was interrupted. The basis for the decline rested in the Somoza inner circle having astutely carried out the maneuver of celebrating an electoral farce in February of 1963, putting in place their puppet, René Schick. In any case, although there was a decline in the general situation, the FSLN leadership did not properly understand that this was nothing more than a limited phenomenon, that the revolutionary movement was already moving toward maturation.

It is correct that during that period our effort turned to the rebuilding of the revolutionary organization and the accumulation of new forces to renew the armed struggle, but naturally this goal required an uninterrupted continuation of a series of revolutionary tasks: the amassing of material resources, the training of combatants, the carrying out of certain armed strikes belonging to the strategic defensive phase, etcetera.

Chapter Seventeen

1

We remained for several weeks in the comfortable house Noel Guerrero had rented on the outskirts of Tegucigalpa.

The house was occupied by a small family: a wide-eyed girl, Guerrero's mistress; her younger sister who, with glances too profound to be an adolescent's, chased after the guerrillas who came through on some mission; the mother, who kept her eye on the young girl and cooked what seemed to us bottomless pits to be the most delicious meals of the entire Central American Common Market.

The mother asked me why I only ate half of what she served me, and I couldn't answer her. The truth is, I hid part of the food under my bed to eat later, fearing I know not what. Hunger, perhaps, or that it all might suddenly disappear, or that we would be swallowed up by the jungle.

Rodolfo Romero, who hadn't been able to participate in the guerrilla struggle, was in Tegucigalpa. Romero was in Guatemala during the Arbenz government and he was a close acquaintance of Ernesto Guevara. Che learned to handle the first assault rifle he had ever held, a Garand, under Romero's tutelage before the military uprising led by Carlos Castillo Armas. The counterrevolution left the national liberation of Guatemala suspended indefinitely.

Rodolfo Romero played an important role in the initial efforts to organize a revolutionary movement in Nicaragua. He was brave, stubborn, and ill-tempered. Due to circumstances that today would not have the significance they had then, he distanced himself from the revolutionary leadership.

Less than two months after arriving in Tegucigalpa, in the month of November, I volunteered to return to Nicaragua. I went in clandestinely carrying $10,000 dollars that Noel Guerrero had given me and with some ideas acquired during the traumatic experience of our recent past. Shortly, Víctor Tirado would also make his way in.

José Benito Escobar was waiting for me in Somoto and, after staying in various safehouses, I settled down in Teodorita Rubí's place where Carlos Fonseca was living.

2

The hours pass, slow, hot, with a pistol against my skin, in an undershirt, with books, cigarettes and my own thoughts. Carlos was still a bachelor. In this house, near the Luciérnaga movie theater, I had a timid, fleeting courtship with Tina, Jorge Navarro's sister, which evolved from surreptitious glances to holding hands under the table.

We frequently visited the Pescadores neighborhood on the shores of Lake Managua, which was not then contaminated, where José Benito Escobar lived. We got from one place to another on foot or by bus. Carlos was organizing, with Víctor Tirado's help, labor union projects. Inocente Escobar worked in the outlying neighborhoods of Managua.

Carlos was studying the experiences of the revolutionary movements of Nicaragua and of other peoples. He pondered the existence of a political force inside Nicaragua, but he refused to pass judgment until he had touched the local reality with his own hands.

He would say, beside a constantly renewed pot of coffee, that the ideology of the working class is historically destined to lead a victorious revolution, despite the limitations imposed by economic development. At the same time, he cautioned us not to underestimate the role of the abused, hungry, dispossessed peasants whose traditions included armed uprisings.

The role of the working class, he would maintain, depends on the degree of industrial development, the political level of the masses and the capability of the revolutionaries. The organized revolutionary movement is the energy unleashed by the conscious participation of the working class.

Trinchera reveals the undefined political line of the new vanguard so that the Sandinistas might count on these instruments to convey the *knowledge of the strategic and tactical principles of the struggle and how to defend them.*

From those first sparks, Carlos perfected his later flexibility, persuading, demanding the unity of all the forces.

It was at that time that we and the Escobar brothers, José Benito and Inocente, drew up under Carlos' direction two documents that we have never been able to recover. The first was titled *Ten Years of Struggle* and the other dealt with the political situation of that period; in them the experience of 1963 was analyzed. Sometime later, in a cadre meeting, Daniel Ortega read a document about the experiences of the entire period, which likewise has never been recovered.

Armed struggle was not renounced, but the practical work of continuing its preparation was interrupted for some time. The factor which contributed to this lapse was that our defeat in 1963 coincided with a decline in the anti-Somoza movement.

The FSLN leadership did not understand at that time that this was a transitory phenomenon in the maturation process. Between 1964 and 1965, the FSLN gave priority to legal work among the masses in the outlying neighborhoods of Managua and León and in the rural areas. It did not neglect, in these latter areas, the use of conspiratorial methods. Silvio Mayorga entered the country, protected by the more lenient attitude toward the return of exiles authorized by the René Schick government.

After several months, those of us who had entered the country illegally, although we remained clandestine, traveled about in urban and rural buses and held meetings in public parks. One day, accompanied by a .45 and a friend, I visited a bar that was renowned for its piquant possibilities. After a bottle of Santa Cecilia, the two of us started weeping — to the astonishment of the clients and the bartender — for some reason that is still valid but which I no longer recall.

By chance, I encountered my wife, Yelba. The following month she was pregnant. I found work as a drug salesman, outmaneuvering an entire squad of aspirants, thanks to my guerrilla audacity, my quick responses and my ability to conceal the *leishmaniasis* sores on my elbow which were still ugly but no longer painful.

I hadn't visited a dozen doctors and was being counseled by my Guatemalan supervisor in a public thoroughfare when I was arrested by a patrol of Security police.

After seven days of interrogation, I was released without having been mistreated. I wasn't fired by the Genie Peñalba firm and I kept on persuading doctors to prescribe *gabromicina*, a broad-spectrum antibiotic, and *epergrasiovit*, a vitamin B complex from the European Farmitalia firm. Once a week I visited pharmacies and distributed samples of *medicol*, an analgesic and antibiotic with a protective enteric coating to prevent acidity, that was no different from aspirin except for its high price, a fact I concealed with a successful spiel worthy of a better cause.

3

The lady had a goiter. This produces suffocation and palpitations in the final stages; swallowing is difficult and painful. I saw all of this, and I also saw how it produces weakness, dizziness and asphyxiation, how it produces what they call death by goiter. I hate goiter because it killed my mother, because it has no known etiology, because it produces softening of the windpipe and suffocating hemorrhage, spasms of the glottis and, finally, cardiac arrest.

I saw all of this and also that the lady wanted to tell me something. I knew that she wanted to tell me she loved me, that I was her only son, the light of her approaching shadows. The reason for all her years of suffering from the 13th of August of 1930, when I came out from between her warm legs and landed like a cat in Aunt Lala's hands — Aunt Lala, who was disillusioned by my scandalous four pounds and the fact that, according to Dr. Argüello, I even had an inflamed spleen, and that I had to be wet-nursed, since the lady had no milk.

Her hands tried to bless me so that the oblique, stingy light of prison cells would not harm me, so that the bullets of enemy rifles would be chewed and swallowed inasmuch as I had chosen such a destiny. Her hands at the end were able to make the sign of the cross, and I felt from then on that I was invulnerable, that the gesture was a charm, a talisman, that I would be loved (since hatred was madness), lost, defeated by those hands.

She opened her eyes and I heard her say in a clear voice: "My God, I entrust my spirit to your hands."

It was a cry and at that moment I realized that the woman who had given birth to me and whose only son I was, who had suffered more from my imprisonments and beatings than I had, who had gotten more joy than I out of my life; that woman who sold grain and tobacco, who had made love with Don Tomás so that I might be a possibility, and who distributed meals, advice, Marxist seminars, prayers to the Virgin of Miracles, was leaving forever.

It was true: that woman who one day wept because someone had stolen three golden rings from her, and who another day wept because His Holiness had died, and who yet another day wept because my daughter, Bolivia, had been born, and still another laughed because Luis Somoza said he had been educated to be the president, and another day laughed because a fortune teller had said that one day I would give audiences and glass beads; the woman I loved as if she were my daughter, was dying.

I shouted at her, begging her not to die; it wasn't until six hours after she drew her last breath that Bishop Octavio Calderón persuaded me to allow the nuns to dress her. I have never dreamed of her as being dead; I am still not reconciled to the fact. She wanders about at night and I allow her to do so, because I know she is there with her hands extended like a sleepwalker, a blind woman exploring the traces left by my erring ways.

Chapter Eighteen

1

The Republican Mobilization Party threw its support to the Sandinista Front, the Socialist Party and certain of its own elements, such as Mario Flores Ortiz, Manuel Pérez Bermúdez, the Pérez Arévalo brothers and Eligio Alvarez.

A single directorate was formed, in which José Benito Escobar, Silvio Mayorga and I participated for the Sandinista Front, Mario Flores Ortiz for the Republican Mobilization, and Alvaro Ramírez González for the Socialist Party. We met in secret almost daily to coordinate legal work. Various offices were opened in Managua neighborhoods and in seven other cities around the country.

We published a weekly entitled *Republican Mobilization*, of which I was the editor. We visited neighborhoods in every city and formed committees to fight for popular demands. Activity was intense.

At one time, it was proposed that Republican Mobilization participate in the electoral process in alliance with the Independent Party and within the Unified National Opposition bloc. The Conservatives put up an unyielding opposition to the presence of the Republican Mobilization. They suggested that one or two members of our organization should present their candidacy as deputies.

At that time, we maintained that armed struggle required a fuller development of the subjective conditions and that to make such development possible it was indispensable to have a close relationship with the masses; that demands for justice should not become an end in themselves but rather a means and that we had to make use of all methods.

We pointed out the need to create an overt political organization without abandoning the work of creating proper conditions in the mountains. That is, political control in the zone of possible armed operations, familiarity with the terrain, the establishment of supply lines and storage points and concrete conditions for organizing the peasantry. Besides that, we would need an apparatus capable of singling out the best human elements to be integrated into the war and to create support networks for the armed struggle. All of this without abandoning the legal struggle.

We were all in general agreement on this thesis, which gave rise to our work in the neighborhoods and to the activity that Pablo Ubeda carried out in the mountains. We wanted to activate our contact with the masses, organize unions in the countryside and in the city, and locate the appropriate terrain for the military struggle. This began to conflict with the predominant theses within the Socialist Party and within the Republican Mobilization itself, who were in no way partisans of armed struggle. At the outset, there appeared to be no serious contradictions but as events developed the differences became clear. They were organizing for an electoral campaign while we were organizing for armed struggle.

Bayardo Arce analyzes the situation as follows:

We made efforts to find revolutionary content in those organizations, efforts that were planned in the experiences of 1964-66 with the Republican Mobilization Party, the Socialist Party and other sectors of the independent Left, when the FSLN, through two of its leaders, Silvio Mayorga and Tomás Borge, running all the risks of being legal, launched a mass project in an attempt to reproduce the experiences of the Patriotic Nicaraguan Youth that had been born in the decade of the 60s.

It was there that also began another experiment of the People's Defense Committees in conjunction with Republican Mobilization, which came to cover nearly all the departments in the country and had from the outset the strategic insight to jump from neighborhood organizing to the recruitment of workers, then to the organizing of the workplace into labor unions. This experiment was frustrated when the elections took place and Agüero and the bourgeois union and the left went after electoral seats, destroying the alliance. The FSLN then set out on its own to undertake Pancasán.[1]

Taking advantage of the work of Republican Mobilization, cells were structured that studied a mimeographed pamphlet on military tactics. In 1966, Carlos Fonseca concentrated his efforts on preparing for the guerrilla campaign of Pancasán.

2

On September 14, 1966, Carlos' mother, Agustina Fonseca Ubeda, died.

Germán Gaitán, his friend and companion, violated strict security and broke Carlos' heart by communicating the news to him. Our brother wept, lapsed into silence, lost his composure. He was unable to attend the funeral, which was held in the Matagalpa cemetery where a crowd gathered. It was the anniversary of the Battle of San Jacinto and there was a student march to that historic ranch site. They went on from there in vehicles to Matagalpa to attend the funeral.

Somoza's security waited in vain for Carlos to participate in the final farewell. Silvio Mayorga, in the name of the FSLN, delivered the homage of the Sandinista militants: "In my voice is the voice of the Nicaraguan youth; in my voice is the voice of the Sandinista National Liberation Front; in my voice is the voice of Carlos Fonseca."[2]

The Front tried to find its way out of the labyrinth. Víctor Tirado, who worked in Managua, from time to time would travel to Chinandega, Estelí and Matagalpa, where he worked with labor unions.

Pablito Martínez, a proletarian, distinguished himself in this ant-like labor. Inocente Escobar was put in charge of communal work,

[1] Bayardo Arce Castaño, *El papel de las fuerzas motrices antes y después del triunfo* (Managua: Secretaría Nacional de Propaganda y Educación Política del FSLN, 1980), pp. 20-21.
[2] Testimony of Germán Gaitán.

184

which is what we called activity on the urban periphery. It was during this period that the following initiated their active participation: Daniel Ortega, Selim Shible, Edmundo Pérez, Carlos Guadamuz, Enrique Lorente, Francisco Moreno, Jacinto Suárez, Lenin Cerna and Jorge Guerrero.

Pablo Ubeda, syringe at the ready, with analgesics and antibiotics for skin and urinary infections, remedies for diarrhea, repodral, magical lotions to reduce labor pains and exorcise magic spells, traveled all roads and mountain passes. He was a wildcat with the eyes of a deer; he knew everybody. Years after his death the peasants of Rancho Grande, Uluse, Bijao, Iyás, Yaosca, La Lana and other places, would say: "Pablito was here."

Pablo Ubeda had the mission of creating a support network in the mountains and, although widely dispersed, he created it. This force was to be of strategic value to the guerrilla movement. At the same time, Pedro Joaquín Rodríguez ("Mokorón") and other cadres, including the brothers Fabián and Antonio Rodríguez, raised the banner of peasant demands in Yucul and Uluse.

This effort was not a marginal one, rather it had important consequences. It was a seedbed and basis of support for what would become the guerrilla campaign of Pancasán.

With clarity and in a constructive spirit, without subterfuge, we attempted to achieve a critical vision of the errors committed by Conservatives, Liberals and Communists in the quest for a victorious united popular movement. Carlos recommended that we make an effort to attract the widest possible strata of the population.

This flexibility did not negate, but rather implied the use of conspiratorial techniques, which was the second rail of the strategic track we had conceived.

Clandestine work, therefore, proceeded apace in the mountains under the leadership of Pablo Ubeda. Others who participated in this were Agustín Fuentes Herrera, Francisco Rojas ("Rojitas"), Sebastián Moya ("Alfonso"), and Pedrito ("El Hondureño"). The latter joined the Guard and turned in peasants, who were then assassinated.

The work extended to the departments of Matagalpa, Jinotega and Zelaya. Labor unions and Sandinista cells were organized in Uluse, El Bijao, La Tronca, Agua María, Cerro Colorado, Kuskawás, Yaosca,

El Carmen, Cubalí, Waslala, El Garrobo, El Kun, El Naranjo, El Ocote, Fila Grande, Pancasán and El Tuma. Literacy schools were created in the mountains and peasants were sent to Managua, where an effort was made to give them a theoretical formation.

In El Bijao, Yucul, La Tronca and Uluse, mountainous regions of the department of Matagalpa, labor and political organisms were developed.

Bernardino Díaz Ochoa played an outstanding role in this activity. Writes Bayardo Arce:

> Here it is worth mentioning *Compañero* Bernardino Díaz Ochoa, a peasant organizer of the Nicaraguan Socialist Party. He and our peasant organizer, Rigoberto Cruz, better known as Pablo Ubeda, were the first organizers of peasant unions in Nicaragua.
>
> Bernardino Díaz Ochoa was a militant in the Socialist Party, as well as in the FSLN, and his work, along with that of Rigoberto, is what produced the first peasant union organizations and the first serious, sustained political work our organization carried out in the rural areas and became the social base that supported the guerrilla detachment of Pancasán.[1]

A small printshop was created. Its few, primitive mimeographs turned out an edition of the *History of the Chinese Communist Party*. Carlos wrote his pamphlet, *Social Classes in Nicaragua*. These were published along with primers for peasants and different documents concerning the political situation of the moment.

3

One morning in June 1964, while walking along a muddy street in Managua's San Luis neighborhood, in front of La Esquinita Grocery — or as they say in Nicaragua, "from the San Luis public

---

[1] Arce Castaño, *op. cit.*, p. 17.

phones half a block toward the lake" — Carlos Fonseca and Víctor Tirado were captured by the Somoza security forces.

Carlos shouted his name. Víctor shouted a false name: Francisco Ortega. The following day, *Novedades* and *La Prensa* featured the story. Their shouts were to avoid being assassinated.

Carlos was described as a tall, young white male, whom a fat, muscular agent — believed to be Gonzalo Lacayo, a torturer and avid gambler — placed in a hammerlock and shoved into a Jeep.

Reporters said that Fonseca had his headquarters in the San Luis neighborhood and that when he traveled around Managua or to other places in Nicaragua, he employed different disguises: with and without glasses, wearing a hat or a cap; sometimes he appeared to be a student, at others a worker and, frequently, a peasant. The neighbors affirmed that he also disguised himself as a poet; that at night he became a monkey and in the early morning hours a *cenzontle.* *

Ten days later, by order of President René Schick, the prisoners were brought before Judge Morales Ocón, who sentenced them to six months without parole.

The crowd that surrounded the Trébol courthouse, the judge, the newspapermen, the lawyers and law clerks, listened astonished to the allegations of one who, far from defending himself, without the slightest hesitation and with disconcerting valor, leveled charges against the dictatorship. Summarizing his defense before the judge, Carlos wrote the document, *From Prison, I Accuse the Dictatorship.* ** This title, in which Carlos uses the first-person "I" — so unusual in his writings — calls one's attention, as does the fact that he precedes it with the words "from prison." He did not want to leave the least doubt as to the provenance of the accusation or who was making it. Moreover, it calls to mind the devastating *J'acuse* of Émile Zola against the unjust, anti-Semitic government of France with respect to the Dreyfus affair.

It was a unique opportunity for the Sandinista Front to gain prestige and authority, and Carlos, with his gift for penetrating analysis, did not permit it to pass by.

---

* A Nicaraguan songbird.
** See full text at end of this chapter

This bold document was published in 1964 by the Antorcha Publishing House of León, whose proprietor was the ever-honest Ulises Terán.

On September 21, eight years after the execution of Anastasio Somoza García, Carlos Fonseca, while confined in the Air Force prison, released another manifesto entitled, "This is the Truth."[**]

At the moment when they were arrested, Víctor had only known Carlos for two months, yet their identification with each other was instantaneous. Víctor writes:

> When I arrived in the mountains of Honduras to join the group that would take part in the Raití-Bocay expedition, Carlos was no longer there. He had gone to Nicaragua to organize the urban Internal Front. So it was not until April 1964 that I met him in Managua. From the very beginning we were not only united by the community of our interests and ideas; we were also united by prison, where we found ourselves in June 1964, and after that were united by our exile in Mexico when we got out of prison at the beginning of 1965.[1]

Upon completing their six month sentence, Carlos was expelled to Guatemala and Víctor Tirado to Mexico. In the dawn hours of January 6, Carlos was obliged to board a small military plane without a word of explanation. He was escorted by members of the Office of Security, one of whom was the well-known Jerónimo Linarte. Only when they were landing, after a three hour flight, did he realize that he had been expelled to Guatemala. It was his third expulsion.

The security forces of Guatemala obliged him to cross over the Suchiate river on the Mexican border. Carlos found refuge in the house of the old cemetery keeper in Tapachula, where a Mexican named Ovidio Puente came to retrieve him. Puente, an engineer, collaborated with the FSLN for a number of years and his house served as a refuge in the Mexican capital for dozens of our

[**] See full text at end of chapter.
[1] Tirado López, *Carlos: un optimismo inquebrantable*, p. 48.

combatants. For reasons that are still obscure, Puente — who possessed historic documents of the FSLN that are now surely unrecoverable — distanced himself from the Nicaraguan revolutionary movement. It is said that he recently offered his services to Edén Pastora.

In Mexico City, Carlos renewed contacts with Víctor Tirado and Prof. Edelberto Torres, who at the time was preparing the fourth edition of his work, *The Dramatic Life of Rubén Darío*.

4

Carlos had read and admired Darío, but it must have been during this period that he became impassioned with the work and life of the poet. Carlos was intensely interested in art, above all in literature. Manolo Cuadra was his friend and one of his favorite poets, as were Joaquín Pasos and Ernesto Cardenal.

Carlos also read Pablo Antonio Cuadra and did not underestimate his poetic work, although he frowned on the latter's column, *Written on the Typewriter*, and other political incursions by the Granada intellectual. Both Carlos and Ricardo Morales left evidence of their critical reading of *Letters to a Young Lady About the Modern Novel*, published in 1955.

DOCUMENT 4
*From Prison, I Accuse the Dictatorship**

In the interrogation to which I was subjected by members of the Office of Security, along with other charges I was accused of the following: 1) planning an attempt on the life of the Director-in-Chief of the National Guard, Anastasio Somoza D., and 2) the holdup of the Bank of America.

With respect to the first charge, I deny any guilt on my part, and on the other hand can accuse Anastasio Somoza D., Luis Somoza D., and other members of their family who lead the oppression, as well as the politicians and military officers who serve as their accomplices; I can accuse them, I repeat, of not merely planning attempts on the lives of innocent citizens, but of systematically carrying out assassinations of patriots and honorable individuals.

Being a prisoner and given the haste with which I must write this in clandestine circumstances, I am prevented from elaborating a more or less complete list of such assassinations. Nevertheless, I am going to cite at least some examples:

The assassinations of peasants and other persons in Chinandega in 1963. The assassinations in 1963 at the Bocay River of my dear comrades, the students Jorge Navarro, Francisco Buitrago and Modesto Duarte and of the youths Mauricio Córdoba and Iván Sánchez Argüello. The assassination at the Coco River of my dear comrades Faustino Ruiz and Boanerges Santamaría.

The assassination in the city of León in 1962 of the youth Carlos Nájar. The assassination in 1961 of several revolutionary workers in Río San Juan.

The assassination in 1961 in the Honduran city of Choluteca of the veteran Sandinista, Heriberto Reyes.

* From *Obras,* Vol. I, p. 230.

The assassination in February 1961 of the patriots Julio Alonso, Enrique Montoya and Octavio Vílchez, as well as of the student Jesús López and various other patriots.

The assassination in El Dorado in February 1960 of the students Eduardo Medina, Víctor Arbizú, Tomás Palacios and of the Salvadoran Fabricio Paz, as well as several other patriots.

The assassination in 1960 of the youths Ajax Delgado and Julio Oscar Romero. The assassination of Carlos Haslam in 1959. The assassination of the expeditionaries of Olama and los Mollejones: the patriots Antonio Gutiérrez, Rivas Gómez, Napoleón Ubila Baca, and the Costa Ricans Segura and Sonny Boy, in July 1959. The assassination of the students on July 23, 1959; the assassination of Manuel Díaz y Sotelo and various other comrades.

The assassination of the prisoners Luis Armando Morales Palacios, José Rivas Montes, Ramón Orozco and Bonifacio Miranda in September 1956.

The assassination of Adolfo and Luis Báez Bone, Opstaciano Morazán, Pablo Leal, Agustín Alfaro and many other patriots in April 1954.

The assassination of the student Uriel Sotomayor in the city of León. The assassination of the peasant Aquileo Castillo, together with many other peasants and citizens in Cuesta del Coyol in 1948.

The assassination of the patriots Rito Jiménez Prado and Luis Scott.

And finally, returning to the first days of the tyranny in February 1934, the sinister assassination of Augusto César Sandino, Juan Pablo Umanzor and Francisco Estrada, plus hundreds of Sandinistas in Wiwilí and surroundings.

Inasmuch as the one who writes these lines is accused of imaginary plans, and since my accusers are guilty of this rosary of crimes, I believe it is my accusers and not I who deserve severe punishment.

I propose that the University Center and the patriotic organizations of Nicaragua bring criminal charges against A. Somoza D., Luis Somoza D. and other members of that oppressive family and against their military and political accomplices in order that they not go unpunished but be made to pay for the many crimes they have perpetrated. Let us hasten that greatly desired moment when the victims shall become the accusers and their murderers the accused.

In this way I reply to one of the charges against me.

I said that another of the charges against me is the holdup of the Bank of America. As in the case of the previous charge brought against me by the Somoza government, I deny any guilt on my part. But that is not all that I have to say. I accuse Anastasio Somoza D., Luis Somoza D. and other members of their oppressive family, and I accuse their military and political accomplices, not only of just assaulting a millionaire bank. My accusation is much more serious. I accuse the heads of the Somoza government of assaulting, over the past thirty years, the long-suffering people of Nicaragua, in order to accumulate not the ridiculous sum of 50,000 *córdobas*, but fabulous sums that add up to many billions of *córdobas*; or in terms that simple folk can understand, sums that must be written with seven or more zeroes after them.

Where do the ships of the Mamenic Line come from? From the robbery of the people.

Where have the airplanes of Lanica come from? From the Somoza family's robbery of the people.

Where have the 300 large landed estates come from? From the robbery of the people.

Where have Montelimar and La Fundadora come from? From the robbery of the people.

Where have the 10,000 houses come from? From the robbery of the people.

Where have the millions of dollars deposited in Yankee and Swiss banks come from? From the Somoza family's robbery of the people.

Where have the landed estates of Camilo González come from? From the robbery of the people by the accomplices of the Somozas.

How did the co-author of Sandino's assassination, the cardsharp Federico Davidson Blanco, acquire his ranch? From the robbery of the people by Somoza's accomplices.

Even if I were guilty of the robbery of the Bank of America, I don't believe that the Somoza government's gang of thieves has the moral authority to accuse me.

Another assault on the people that must be denounced is that perpetrated by the mining companies with respect to gold and other minerals from our soil. The past year of 1963 marked a decrease in Yankee exploitation of our minerals compared to past epochs. Even with that decrease, the exploitation amounted to a figure of nearly 100 million *córdobas*; which enables us to roughly calculate the billions of *córdobas* the Yankees have stolen from our mineral resources without interruption for the past fifty years.

As a consequence of the assault on the Bank of America, not a single peasant has lost his land, not a single worker has been thrown out of work, not a single child has been prevented from going to school, and not a single businessman or industrialist has been bankrupted.

In contrast, the assault by the Somoza family and its accomplices has had dreadful consequences for Nicaragua. I can say the same about the Yankee assault. Those assaults, in brief, have established the foundation for a despicable regime that has converted the life of the Nicaraguan people into an inferno.

I propose that the University Center and other partisan and popular organizations of Nicaragua file criminal charges against Anastasio Somoza D., Luis Somoza D. and other members of their oppressive family and against their military and political accomplices. This trial for the robbery of the Nicaraguan people must culminate in the return to the people of the wealth that has been plundered from them and in the appropriate punishment of these voracious thieves.

Inasmuch as the one who writes these lines stands accused of a holdup of minor importance, while my accusers are guilty of the theft of an entire empire that is the result of the people's labor, I believe that it is my accusers and not myself who deserve to be severely punished.

DOCUMENT 5
*This Is The Truth**

The Somoza government has issued a slanderous communique accusing various brothers in the struggle and myself of planning absurd acts of terrorism. What this libelous accusation actually reveals are the sinister plans of the Somoza government itself.

The Somoza government plans to step up the repression against the popular movement that leads the fight for the liberation of our homeland. Today, more than ever, the people of Nicaragua refuse to fold their arms in the face of oppression and are disposed to courageously claim their rights. The profound discontent of the popular masses, the exploited and oppressed of Nicaragua, is entirely just, inasmuch as the government stubbornly refuses to solve the painful problems that afflict the nation.

Everyday, the people struggle with greater faith, and already we can catch a glimpse of the not-too-distant future in which the popular struggle will have acquired vast proportions.

In this situation, the government desperately invents pretexts, as demonstrated by the communique we are condemning, which attempt to justify the repression, imprisonment and assassination of the defenders of the people.

This is not the first time that the Somoza government has resorted to such fictions. The same thing happened with the pretext of the movement of April 4, 1954, culminating in the assassination by the government of numerous patriots. On that occasion, the government disseminated the tremendous lie of linking the revolutionaries to Russian submarines navigating in the Pacific Ocean.

By accusing us of plans for blood and fire, the Somoza government hopes to turn the people against us. But this is a vain hope, because the people of Nicaragua know very well from experience who has the bloody hands and who are the patriots; the people know who are

* From Carlos Fonseca, *Obras,* Vol. I, p. 239.

responsible for the peasants of Tempisque dying of hunger; they know who is guilty of the assassination of innocents in Posoltega; they know who are guilty of allowing the Yankee companies to carry off our gold; the people know who is guilty of stealing millions of *córdobas* from the national treasury; they know who is responsible for the National University having a miniscule budget; they know who is responsible for the majority of our children's inability to attend school, for not one child in the countryside completing primary school; for concentrating the best land in the hands of a few millionaires, especially pro-Somoza millionaires; people know who is responsible for Nicaragua suffering the sad condition of being a colony of Yankee imperialism.

People know that the guilty parties are none other than the Somoza family and their political and military accomplices. The people know, on the other hand, that we Sandinista revolutionaries are combatants who desire the happiness of all the people. To that end, we have spilled our own blood and our brothers have heroically offered their lives.

I do not deny, rather I declare with justified pride, that in the past we have taken up arms to combat the Somoza regime. But when we have done so, it has not been in order to carry out terrorist acts or to attack individuals. We have taken up arms to fight honorably, in the same way that the people rose up against the oppressive government in 1926.

In its slanderous communique, the government states that we are planning to kill members of the opposition, including Marxist leaders, and to set fire to Conservative newspapers. The purpose of this fiction is to divide the ranks of the opposition. The fact is that the government shudders at the possibility of unification of the opposition with the people. The government knows that throughout Nicaraguan history, division has favored the enemies of the people, while they themselves have been harmed by unity. Precisely on the 12th day of this patriotic month of September we will commemorate the unity which, in 1856, the entire people — including Liberal and Conservative leaders — achieved to combat the Yankee slaveholder, William Walker, and his band of traitorous Nicaraguans. The popular struggle was victorious. Walker and his mercenaries were defeated. Unity bore fruit.

It is true that we criticize the errors committed in the national struggle by Conservative and Communist leaders, as well as those of other tendencies. But our criticism is fraternal, with a desire to learn from our experience, in a spirit of overcoming difficulties and solving problems. One of our goals is the unity of all anti-Somoza and popular forces, based on our points of agreement, however limited these may be.

In its slanderous communique, the Somoza government says that we Sandinista revolutionaries obey Cuban plans and that we have been trained in Cuba to fight in Nicaragua. The Somoza government always strays from the truth.

The Cuban Revolution triumphed almost six years ago. Though we are young, we began our struggle against the Somoza government long before the Cuban triumph. Carlos Fonseca, as a secondary student in Matagalpa, participated in the student strike of 1952, as did the university students Tomás Borge and Silvio Mayorga, to demand the removal from the university campus of a medallion representing Somoza.

As a consequence of Rigoberto Lopez's action in September 1956, the three above-mentioned brothers-in-struggle suffered imprisonment together.

At the time of these events, the name of Fidel Castro was unknown in Nicaragua. Fidel Castro was not yet fighting the Batista tyranny in the Sierra Maestra.

It is certain, therefore, that in combatting the Somoza regime we are moved by the love of our homeland and not by orders from abroad.

With respect to Cuban training, I also say that is false. I do not deny that we are adequately trained to combat the Somoza regime, but our training has not taken place outside Nicaraguan borders, rather inside our national territory. It is a training that has consisted of not ignoring any injustice, of demanding freedom, of venerating Sandino and other national heroes, of suffering from oppression, exploitation and torture. This training has given us the ability to combat the enemies of the Nicaraguan people. It is easy to see that thousands upon thousands of Nicaraguans have received such training.

The government should realize that it is responsible for training the combatants who are destined to overthrow it!

We Sandinista combatants insist that it is not Fidel Castro but the Somoza regime itself, with its ferocious anti-popular policies, that has trained us to fight for the defense of our freedom!

The government claims that our terrorist plans are similar to the terrorist plans discovered in Panama. The real similarity lies in the fact that the Yankee imperialists who massacre Panamanian youths in the Canal Zone are the same ones who arm the Somoza tyranny to massacre Nicaraguan youths.

This is the truth.

Chapter Nineteen

1

The key to decoding the political thought of Pablo Antonio Cuadra, according to Carlos Fonseca, lies in *El Nicaragüense*, an anthological parade of newspaper articles that reflect his class concepts, because the key to his poetic quality lies in other texts.

The majestic distortions of *El Nicaragüense* have received praise, but very little criticism. In Nicaragua there was an abundant interchange of friendly adjectives and self-praise, and the pages of *La Prensa Literaria* assumed the central task of discovering or ignoring our poetic values. If the short story had valuable expositors such as Juan Aburto and Fernando Silva, the novel and other genres did not achieve the requisite stature until Lizandro Chávez Alfaro and Sergio Ramírez.

Among those most widely published in the weekly — without mentioning the obvious names — are Mario Cajina Vega, whose poetry and vignettes I like; Rolando Steiner, playwright; the Rumanian, Stefan Baciú, suspect for some reason; Enrique Peña Hernández, philologist; and Octavio Robleto, poet. And among the women poets, Ana Ilce Gómez, Michele Najlis, Gioconda Belli, Rosario Murillo, Vidaluz Meneses and Daisy Zamora.

Naturally, the writer with the most visibility and largest headlines was Pablo Antonio, as much for being one of the important poets of Nicaragua as for having been the founder of *La Prensa Literaria*. Since this was the only outlet for art — the cultural supplement of *Novedades* was mostly made up of clippings from other reviews, rhymed verses praising Somoza and other stupidities, independent of the fact that it had occasional bursts of literary quality — there was no possibility of publishing a critique of *El Nicaragüense*, at least at that time. On the other hand, I do not exclude in this sense the laziness of the critics, since it is always easier to offer praise.

In the first line of the introductory note to his book — and I will not speak of the blackshirts nor his devotion to Generalisimo Franco, which do not adequately explain the present idea — Cuadra says: "Ever since I was obliged to abandon my rural life and work as a newspaperman..."[1] He confesses that he has been an agricultural landowner, in other words, that he identifies himself with other landowners. Not with all of them, of course, but only the largest. This social origin stamps him with its ideological mark as indelibly as a red-hot iron brands the flanks of cattle in his economic universe.

Pablo Antonio has been, from the beginning, the organic intellectual of the rich landowners of Nicaragua, who in the final analysis make up the oligarchy. This is why, before the tomb of Virgil, he reflects: "I still have not evaluated my debt to this Latin poet, landowner and farmer, for the direction my poetry has taken... I still keep this ancient book [*Georgicas*] with pencil-marked verses that must have gladdened my small-farmer's eyes..."[2] By his own words he succeeds Virgil, the farmer and poet. Pablo is the little Virgil of our little farm.

In a society like Nicaragua's — and like so many others in the subcontinent — along with the bourgeoisie, artisans and workers, there exists another social sector that embodies a mode of production older than my great grandfather. This sector grew out of the Colony and Independence and, hurdling like a wild colt over President José Santos Zelaya's Liberal reform, continued insisting on the needs of a primitive, mountainous country dotted by cowflops and coffee bushes. Comprised of rich peasants, or better yet, landholders, it entered into a forced alliance with that sector of the bourgeoisie dependent on foreign markets, to form the social base of the regime that prevailed until the triumph of the Revolution.

The eastern landowners were — but are no longer — distinguished, intelligent, and signorial, in contrast to the western landowners, who were — and still are — brutish, miserly, ignorant and quarrelsome. León and Granada are two ancient locales founded in

[1] Pablo Antonio Cuadra, *El Nicaragüense* (San José: Educa, 1975), p. 7.

[2] Pablo Antonio Cuadra, *Otro rapto de Europa. Notas de un viaje* (Managua: Ed. El Pez y la serpiente, 1976), p. 59.

the year of smoke by the conquistador, Francisco Hernández de Córdoba. The rivalry between the two cities was the result of political antagonisms. The Liberals (the Leonese) and Conservatives (the Granadans) led farmhands and peasants into primitive armed encounters.

Among other dirty linen now hung out in public is the intervention of the filibusterers commanded by William Walker, ("The Terrible"). This has only a symbolic relationship with William Walker, ("The Petty"), the third-rate diplomat who visits Central America with the same objective but without the great courage of the great slaver and filibusterer.

The people, understanding by that the laborers and humble residents, have demonstrated throughout our bloody history a quality that need not be explained. The people of León and Granada are like lions and grenades.

In any case, the eastern sector produced the organic intellectual of the large agricultural landowners, in whose work is reflected an individualistic character subordinated to the land of huge show windows and late model cannons — for which he feels both terror and affection in the strangest and most fascinating sado-masochistic relationship of our entire history.

Pablo Antonio is the archetype of this political geography. He is far from the being the boss who curses at everyone who approaches him and practices the law of the fist. He believed in the image of the Virgin that started sweating and complies with all Ten Commandments, except that of giving to the poor that which belongs to the rich or giving the rich the pleasure of solidarity and renouncing exploitation. He is the rancher whose library is organized according to the Dewey Decimal System, who uses an exquisite deodorant and who never violates the rigorous principles of agendas and half-truths.

In certain moments of *El Nicaragüense*, of *Cantos de Cifar* and of *Esos rostros que asoman en la multitud*, Cuadra approaches populism. Populists observe, with self-confessed delight, through the complex lenses of an abstract ideal; they are philosophical idealists. Their solidarity with the underdog, the poor and the damned does not go beyond the notion of Christian charity.

Applying the subjective method, populist ideologues try to convince us that social progress is possible without capitalism, although the socialist path seems to them more preposterous than its negation. They neither discuss nor understand the importance of the masses and seek to make the movement of history depend on an intellectual minority. The basic thesis of populism tries to demonstrate that the farm economy — popular production — is antagonistic to capitalism.

Such being the case, nobody should be surprised at the following affirmations of *La Prensa's* poet:

> For both the bourgeoisie and the communists, to make a poem is not a productive activity. Nor is it a profitable one. Yet they use and consume the material created by poets and artists and do not recognize their debt; rather they think that what they are speaking or contemplating and enjoying they themselves invented in their short and sterile lives, when it is the fruit of centuries or millennia of poets who worked at the hard and desolate labor of the word to allow them to pronounce — at least! — some phrases that are suspiciously human. [1]

Pablo Antonio's populism is accentuated in *Otro rapto de Europa*, an anthology of chronicles of a trip realized between July and November 1974. *La Prensa* — and therefore its poet — has turned, if possible, more anti-Somoza. Of course, it does not for a moment stop being anti-communist. PAC — as he calls himself, in the certainty that María Teresa Sánchez, Guillermo Rothschuh Tablada, Carlos Tünnerman and I know who he is talking about — has never committed himself to either peasants or proletarians. Who has he committed himself to, then? To Virgil, to the nostalgia of the lost paradise, to the utopia of a blond, multinational paternalism. He resigns himself to our exploitation by the empire, accepts that it orders us around, yet he hopes and even prays that it won't disembowel children or organize tyrannies.

[1] Cuadra, Pablo Antonio, "El nicaragüense", Ibid., p. 177.

As a good populist, Pablo Antonio is also a disciple of Manachaeus. Because of this, he affirms that Nicaraguans are "dual beings, with two halves that engage in dialogue and belligerence."[1] We are, he says, "a country of only two seasons: winter — the realm of mud — and summer — the realm of dust."[2] Because of that, he asks himself if we will always be "facing heartbreaking dilemmas. Or is the Nicaraguan the fusion of antagonisms, the unification of contrasts?"[3]

This is the dialectic of metaphysics. Cuadra is obsessive in his attempts to conceive of unity as duality, placing himself beside the Spaniard — who is "active, fertile, masculine, oceanic," endowed with "a universal vision," with the "temptation of distance" — and far from the Indian, who is, of course, "passive, feminine, earthy" and other vagai.es.[4] The Indian is the poor Nicaraguan, a contradictory, lazy troublemaker. The white *criollo*, he almost says Spaniard — or in other words, himself, his family, his class — is the wealthy, leading man of the film, the generous man, inasmuch as he has something to give away; the one who believes in a refined God, cultured, a connoisseur of good wines, the one who models clothing tailored on the Rue du Faubourg St. Honoré.

For Pablo Antonio, the Christian faith is a canoe that is foundering but does not sink because it is made of cork with the strength of steel. His neo-Thomism, in the style of Jacques Maritain, reinforces the yearning for the peasant commune, the agrarian idyll, the return to feudalism, not with feudal lords of knife and noose, but easy-going paternalists of noble lineage and heart. Or another alternative that resembles nothing real, unless it be ancient Venice, in which buying and selling has disappeared and there is no room for the giants Gog and Magog — money and power.

Because of this, one has to look for the new city, the third Berlin, because the Berlin of Magog is a neon-lighted garbage heap, and the Berlin of Gog is the gray face of uncompromising power.

[1] Ibid., p. 16.
[2] Ibid., p. 21.
[3] Ibid., p. 20.
[4] Pablo Antonio Cuadra, "Introducción a la literatura nicaragüense," *El Pez y la Serpiente*, no. 4 (Managua, 1963), p.10.

And in order that men should not jump over the wall from Magog Berlin to Gog Berlin or from Gog Berlin to Magog Berlin, it is necessary to construct the new city where — guess who? — the peasants will live. Preferably peasants with the vocation of monks so that, as in the ancient republic of San Marino, they'll flock around the monasteries and communal houses set in the gentle countryside.

Pablo Antonio weeps for the death of the Rhine and asks himself if the same thing will happen to the San Juan and Coco rivers; he hates strident sirens and the metallic roar of motors. To achieve that utopia, one does not need vanguards or revolutions or popular movements; salvation lies in the little man — who can doubt it? — in the peasants.

The well-to-do peasant and illustrious disciple of Virgil, laborer over his own words, the owner of laborers yesterday and the friend of laborers today, finds it easy to construct paradises from his hammock in the cool corridor of his country estate or in the library of his comfortable residence in Las Colinas. He must save himself, that is, his class, which presupposes the salvation of the poor peasant, his closest class relative: the agricultural laborer, bent beneath the 11 a.m. sun as he turns the earth with a pickaxe or picks cotton for a wage as insignificant as any of the parasites that swell his children's bellies.

None of this prevented a fragment of his poem, "May," from being included in a calendar of the Ministry of the Interior several years after the revolutionary victory. That fact gave rise to comments that, taking into account his sad, reactionary political positions, he should never have been included in that brief poetic selection. Here are the verses in question:

> In May the insects take nuptial flight,
> in the heat of May the tongue incubates
> new words, in May the kingdom of yellow
> ends and the kingdom of green begins,
> the worm becomes butterfly, the star
> descends to earth and becomes insect.

No anthology of Nicaraguan poetry that includes poets of this century can omit, for any rationale, Pablo Antonio Cuadra, who indeed cannot be left out of any objective sampling of the lyrical production of his generation in our language. And it is clear that his generation is perhaps the most prominent, down to the present, in the history of Spanish literature with Vallejo, Neruda and Lorca heading the list.

It has frequently happened that great revolutionary and reactionary novelists and poets have ignored and excluded one another. More frequently, the rightists ignore the stars that illuminate the firmament of the Left. Just try to publish something by Sergio Ramírez, Nicolás Guillén, Galeano, Gabo, Bañuelos in any resplendent literary review of the right, like *Vuelta*.

No reactionary, except Pinochet, can ignore a revolutionary intellectual, just as no revolutionary can ignore Jorge Luis Borges. Marx did not ignore Balzac, but rather incorporated him into his basic data for an analysis of French society. In our illustrious land, the reactionaries generally ignore, albeit with difficulty, Ernesto Cardenal. By way of contrast, revolutionaries cannot ignore Pablo Antonio Cuadra. To cite but a single example, how can one explain the Vanguard movement in Nicaragua without his presence? Cardenal, Carlos Martínez Rivas, Ernesto Mejía Sánchez and other poets of ours, would not have been possible without the examples of José Coronel Urtecho, Luis Alberto Cabrales, Joaquín Pasos and Pablo Antonio, just as these could not be explained without reference to the work of Rubén Darío.

Coronel Urtecho and Cabrales were the initiators of the "new poetry" in our country when they revealed to us the nearly boundless realism of North American poetry and the open vanguard poetry of Europe, tendencies that were creatively incorporated by the so-called Granada Group of whom Pablo Antonio is the most representative poet, following the death of Joaquín Pasos.

His *Poemas Nicaragüenses* constitute, in the words of Jorge Eduardo Arellano, "the first *new* book of the vernacular genre in Central America, which followed a work faithful to the Nicaraguan essence that, after four decades of labor, resulted in the most serene and beautiful universalization."[1] As long as there are readers of poetry in Nicaragua — which is to say, as long as there are Nicaraguans — the "Canto temporal" and "El jaguar y la luna" will continue to be read.

It is definitely other aspects of the life and work of Cuadra that are the subject of discussion and not his poetic quality. This, in turn, does not exempt him from ideological questioning, from forming political judgments and from challenging him by establishing the difference between the poet and the reactionary. That is, between Pablo Antonio "the Great" and Pablo Antonio "the Petty."

[1] Jorge Eduardo Arellano, *Panorama de la literature nicaragüense* (Managua: Editorial Nueva Nicaragua, 1982), p. 174.

Chapter Twenty

1

Sergio Ramírez evokes the Fonseca of the 1960s:

Between July and October of 1965, on identical rainy
afternoons, with blurred, black umbrellaed figures ascending
San Pedro Hill, Carlos Fonseca would walk into the offices
of CSUCA almost every day, also with umbrella in hand as
part of his clandestine disguise. During the long evening
sessions, we would talk about the rural reality of Nicaragua,
of the FSLN's efforts to organize the peasants, and also
about Sandino; and when not talking about these things, we
would discuss Rubén Darío. Carlos spent long hours in the
National Library investigating the poet's Costa Rican
sojourn at the behest of Don Edilberto Torres, who, from
his Mexican exile, continued writing his *Dramatic Life of
Rubén Darío*. The ancient director of the Library was a very
Costa Rican poet, Don Julián Marchena, who
enthusiastically provided Carlos with everything for his
daily Darían labors, bringing books and papers to his corner
of the reading room, where Carlos was also composing his
documents about armed struggle and the revolution....[1]

Luis Rocha tells how, during a trip with Carlos, the latter
commented enthusiastically on Joaquín Pasos' poem, "Indian Maiden
Fallen in the Marketplace," and Juan Aburto recalls that he met
Fonseca at the literary evenings held by the poet María Teresa
Sánchez and her husband, the Hungarian intellectual, Pablo Steiner.

---

[1] Sergio Ramírez, *Estás en Nicaragua*, (Managua: Editorial Nueva
Nicaragua, 1986), p. 23.

Professor Edilberto Torres, in the prologue to the fourth edition of his work on Rubén Darío, acknowledges his gratitude "to the student, Carlos Fonseca," for the discovery of an unknown text by our poet while searching in the libraries and periodicals repositories of Costa Rica: it is an anagram dedicated to Delfina y Caza.

In the early years of his political involvement, besides reading Marx, Carlos Fonseca devoured every book that fell into his hands. He became famous in the Matagalpa Institute for having read the voluminous collection of *The History of Modern States*. Humberto Ortega says that Carlos devoted himself to shaping his own thought and the revolutionary basis of his struggle. He recalls that the few philosophical and political works, as well as novels or books of poetry, that arrived in the precarious bookstores of the country, were anxiously read by Carlos. He was an habitual visitor to the National Library, together with Jorge Navarro, likewise a curious library mouse who gnawed newspapers and magazines in his anxiety to devour the world. Carlos read Neruda's *Canto General* without blinking; Steinbeck's *The Grapes of Wrath*, which led him to consider modern esthetics; and Lenin, who stimulated in him an ethical conceptualization of the world. I can imagine him reading Gorky's *The Mother*; William Faulkner and the mark he left on *One Hundred Years of Solitude*, or imagine him accompanying Vallejo in Paris or Edgar Allan Poe in his overwhelming solitude. In difficult junctures, he received an inexhaustible arsenal of arrows that later helped him to interpret reality.*

3

While writing these memoirs, I spoke to Carlos Fonseca's wife and she, slender and frank, talked to me about Carlos:

---

* The books and authors cited are taken from Humberto Ortega's "Carlos, el eslabón vital de nuestra historia," prologue to Carlos Fonseca, *Obras*, Vol. I, p. 13.

I met Carlos on May 29, 1964, in a safehouse in the San Luis neighborhood of Managua. As the daughter of Ulises Terán and by my own criteria, I was unhappy with the Somoza regime; I wanted to join the Front but didn't know how. I went to this house guided by a comrade, Guillermo Lanzas, and Carlos, who was already in hiding, showed up there. I had heard about him, because in León — which is my hometown — he was recognized as a singular leader. On that first occasion, we only talked about politics. About a month after our first encounter, Carlos was taken prisoner and I went with the poet, Octavio Robleto, to visit him, to lend him moral support. I continued visiting him, almost every Thursday and Sunday, first in the Air Force prison and later at Campo de Marte. It was there that Carlos told me he loved me; I responded that I loved him. One day he was gone; he had been deported. He spent several days in Guatemala and then settled in Mexico, where I followed him accompanied by my mother.

Our civil marriage took place on April 1, 1965, and the religious ceremony two days later in the San Miguel church in Tacubaya, in Mexico City. Father Jaime Tello was the priest who married us. Although Carlos was an atheist, he respected my religious beliefs. He was staying at Don Edilberto Torres' house and a number of friends — including Víctor Tirado — joined us there to celebrate our wedding. My mother and an uncle who was living in Mexico at that time were also present. Professor Torres offered champagne and hors d'oeuvres

We honeymooned in Cuernavaca, a beautiful city where we spent eight days in the Papagayo Hotel. From there we went to live at the boarding house of a lady named Doña Julia, located, if I'm not mistaken, on Guanajuato Street near Colonia Roma. We lived there for about five months, until August 1965, when Carlos traveled to Costa Rica and I followed him a few days later. He traveled clandestinely and I with all my papers in order.

We lived in different places in San José until March or April of 1966, when Carlos returned clandestinely to Nicaragua. I also reentered the country, but legally. I was pregnant with my first son, who was born on November 24,

1966, in León and who is named after his father. When Carlos received news of his birth, he exclaimed, "A little guerrillero!" At the time, I was living with my parents.

When Carlos was arrested in Costa Rica at the end of August, 1969, I again left Nicaragua. I arrived in San José on the 3rd of September; I visited him in the Central Penitentiary and, a little later, in the Alejuela jail, where he had been transferred. He was accused of bank robbery, of illegal possession of arms, of distributing subversive — or communist — propaganda, and of having no identification papers. The Costa Rican authorities really treated him very badly, as they did the other comrades who had been arrested.

On December 23, Carlos, together with other comrades-in-arms, attempted to escape. This failed and all the fugitives were recaptured and relocated to the Central Penitentiary, in San José. On the same day of the failed escape attempt, I was arrested. They accused me of complicity in the attempt and I was held prisoner for two months. Carlos was released on October 22, 1970, thanks to the action of a Sandinista commando team that hijacked a Costa Rican airplane in which officials of the United Fruit Company were traveling. He went to Mexico and from there, a few days later, to Havana.

When this occurred, I was in Nicaragua, where I had been deported by the Costa Rican authorities, who forbade me to reenter their country and, consequently, to visit Carlos in prison. In order to join him, I traveled to Chile — those were the days of the absurd detours to get to Cuba — where Salvador Allende had won. There I received the support of the Chileans and my fellow countrymen — particularly Jaime Wheelock — as well as of the Brazilians and the Cubans. But since there were still no regular flights to the island, I had to fly to Madrid and from there, finally, to Havana.

I arrived in April 1971. Carlos was on a tour out of the country, to Korea and China, if I remember correctly, and he didn't return until October of that year. We lived for some months in Marianao, and then we settled in the Bahía district from where Carlos returned to Nicaragua in August 1975.

The news of his death was communicated to me by José Benito Escobar and Doris Tijerino.

In April 1979, we moved to Panama and in August we returned to Nicaragua. I have returned only once to Cuba, which I consider my second homeland.

Carlos talked to me a great deal about communism, but he never asked me to abandon my Christian faith. For him — as well as for me — there was no contradiction between our ways of thinking, because we both agreed on the need for a revolution. In this sense, he was very concerned about his children; he not only gave them affection, but was also concerned about their academic progress. Above all, he tried to instill in them his ideological principles, to instill in them a revolutionary morality and character.

Carlos was a man without vices. He drank on certain occasions, for instance when a friend visited us or on our childrens' birthdays. He drank coffee and smoked very little. On the other hand, he was not a person who easily became depressed, nor was he always cheerful. He was not one to play jokes. His discretion was such that he never commented to me on the internal affairs of the Front; and of course I never asked him. I'm convinced he was not a jealous husband, although I never tried to give him reasons for jealousy.

Carlos was affectionate, refined, of good character. He hardly ever swore. He didn't know how to dance and he wasn't a glutton. What he enjoyed most was reading. He not only read books on politics, history and philosophy, but also literature: novels, short stories and poetry. I remember him reading Rubén Darío, whose complete works accompanied him everywhere. He even wrote poetry when he was very young; some of his poems were published in the magazine *Segovia*.

In Cuba, Carlos rose early and did exercises — running, mostly — and then went off to House 40, where the offices of the Sandinista Front were located and spent almost all day there with his comrades. Since he did not return until dinner time, he didn't watch television or interact very much with the neighbors. I knew he was a homebody, that he didn't chase after women, and never had to fight over him. We had only the normal matrimonial disagreements. It's difficult for me to choose the most memorable moment of my life with Carlos, although I cannot forget the day our daughter, Tania, was born: January 29, 1969, in León. He managed to find a way to come and see her. His face shone with love.[1]

4

In April 1966, Carlos returns clandestinely to Nicaragua and concentrates his efforts on preparing the guerrilla actions of Fila Grande and Pancasán. Accompanying him and assisting him in the selection of tactics and terrain, in the search for contacts and the drafting of documents, were Silvio Mayorga, Oscar Turcios, Pablo Ubeda, José Benito Escobar and Daniel Ortega.

Carlos, Silvio, Rigoberto, Oscar and Doris Tijerino — who used the pseudonym Conchita Alday — wrote the communique "Sandino Yes, Somoza No; Revolution Yes, Electoral Farce No," which was the political expression of the armed project:

The Front does not want to go alone into the field of revolutionary struggle. No Nicaraguan — we believed — can be deprived of the right to defend his homeland. Accordingly, we said to the people that even though we might not find support, we do not intend to fold our arms.[2]

In December, Carlos, Silvio and Oscar moved to Fila Grande, initiating the preparation of the chosen terrain, of the armed struggle that would culminate in the holocaust of Pancasán.

On January 20, 1967, to maintain guerrilla logistics, we held up the Bank of America branch in the very navel of Managua: the San Sebastián neighborhood, near the offices of *La Prensa*.

It was easy. Chelito Moreno, Fausto García, ("Enriquito"), Santos Medina, the painter, and I walked away with 90,000 *córdobas*,

---

[1] Testimony given the author by María Haydée Terán in 1989.
[2] Carlos Fonseca, "¡Sandino sí, Somoza no; Revolución sí, farsa electoral no!", in: *Obras*, Vol. I, p. 246.

a considerable sum for that time, and ten minutes later, in the taxi we had hijacked an hour before, we roared off in the wrong direction down a one-way street and delivered the loot to Jorge Guerrero ("Cuervito").

He climbed aboard the first passing bus and transferred the money, which he'd stuffed into a gunny sack, to a safehouse in one of the eastside neighborhoods.

The police investigation ground to a sudden halt because of the events of January 22, 1967.

5

On the morning of that tragic day, an impressive crowd gathered on Roosevelt Avenue, the gayest thoroughfare in the old city, like a girl made-up for the five o'clock promenade in the park.

The crowd set off prudently, fearlessly, toward the Loma de Tiscapa. Fernando Agüero had promised to overthrow Somoza that day. He hinted at mysterious links with high National Guard officials, murmured about his contacts with functionaries at the North American Embassy. According to him, weapons would arrive from who-knows-where and determined men would show up from all over the country.

Somoza was in León, presiding over a Liberal demonstration. It is said on good authority that prior to these events Agüero and General Gustavo Montiel had met through the mediation of the church hierarchy to organize a coup against the tyrant. This explains Agüero's conviction that Somoza would be toppled that day. Montiel was the régime's chief of security. What Agüero did not know was that Montiel remained loyal to the dictator, but he did know — because this had been agreed upon — that the Guards would open fire on the crowd.

That butchery of Roosevelt Avenue was a deliberate act, one point of their program; it was part of the hare-brained, sadistic, incoherent plan of that unscrupulous politician. When Pedro Joaquín Chamorro learned of the plan a few hours before it was implemented, he rejected it as dirty, cowardly and criminal.

The demonstrators were pushing toward El Hormiguero. A high official gave the order to open fire, initiating the brutal massacre. The soldiers, using gunrests, fired at the head and the chest. From some nearby buildings there came a reply. A lone sharpshooter with a .22 calibre rifle moved from one terrace to another and each of his shots signified one less National Guardsman.

This weak response terrified the soldiers, who continued to fire at shadows all night long wounding their own people. Several dozen demonstrators and all the leaders of the traditional opposition parties took refuge in the Gran Hotel. Some people fired from the hotel windows. The Guard surrounded the hotel with armored cars and infantry. The demonstration leaders were frightened; they crossed themselves, confessed to friendly priests, and made promises to Santo Domingo. Other refugees in the hotel devoted themselves to drinking whiskey waiting for the rebellion of senior Guard officials, to exorcising themselves and eating shit.

It has never been learned how many victims there were. They speak of hundreds, of thousands. What is beyond discussion is that the traditional parties collapsed that day and left nothing behind but ashes.

The politicians who took refuge in the Gran Hotel surrendered. Agüero made a pact with Somoza and, days later, elections were held in Nicaragua for president, senators and deputies. The candidates were Somoza and Agüero; Somoza Debayle, bird of evil omen.

Chapter
Twenty-One

1

About fifty kilometers due east of Matagalpa lies a segment of mountain chain known as Fila Grande, which contains an impressive number of little streams that flow beneath rain and fog into the Upá river. In its vicinity, on the military crest — not too far from the water, not too close to the sky — the ephemeral guerrilla encampments were set up.

The armed group was weak in manpower and firepower, empirical in its knowledge of the military art. All of them were youthful students of revolutionary theory, mystics, radicals, cheerful and pure; dreamers who had renounced comforts, studies, university professions, family, everything for a higher form of fulfillment.

Some of them had memorized poems by Rubén Darío and César Vallejo and would recite them in the growing darkness beside the dying embers of the campfire after cooking the beans which, on this occasion, were almost never missing.

When they ran out of poems, they sang "Solamente una vez," "Escúchame," "Extraños en la noche," "Esa maldita pared," "Bésame mucho." Or they would converse in low voices, remembering beans with rice, *indioviejo*, and pork chops.

Almost everyone reiterated their amorous exploits with their previous girlfriend, but they'd say nothing about their current girlfriend or wife. Whenever they mentioned a heated episode with the latter, they would attribute it to another woman or to an imaginary female.

Some of them kept photographs of wives and children wrapped in plastic to protect them from rain and sweat. These were kept in the safest place, which was next to their hearts.

Francisco Moreno ("El Chelito"), the favorite disciple of Jesús — which was Carlos Fonseca's pseudonym — memorized the "Ode to Roosevelt" in order to recite it on some occasion when the chief might be present.

We were sitting around the fire and "El Chelito", very solemn and self-assured, began:

> "It's with Biblical voice, or Walt Whitman's verse,
> that one must approach thee, Hunter,
> Primitive and modern, simple and complex..."

And with the same impetus, he finished his recitation and lowered his head.

Carlos asked him: "Francisco, is that the way Dario's poem ends?"

"El Chelito", disconcerted, didn't know what to say. "Dario's poem concludes:

> You'd have to be, Roosevelt, by God's own will,
> the dreadful Marksman and the mighty Hunter
> to be able to clutch us in your iron talons.
>
> And, having everything, you lack one thing, God!"

"El Chelito" had substituted the word "people" for the word "God".

Carlos took advantage of this moment to make a frontal attack on that territory inhabited by phantoms and masks known as sectarianism and the tendency "to which revolutionaries are still no strangers, particularly in triumphant revolutions, to distort texts and historical facts on behalf of supposed political principles." And he concluded: "If we let ourselves be guided by that tendency, we will pass on to the new generation a false or incomplete history."

The first to arrive at Fila Grande were Carlos and Silvio. Oscar Turcios and Antonio Rodríguez had already explored the area as far as a place called El Jilguero. Little by little, the selected combatants began to arrive, including a woman, Gladys Báez ("Adelita"). The guerrillas were armed with old guns, .22 caliber rifles, shotguns, knapsacks, uniforms, Dacron hammocks and warm, lightweight sleeping bags.

Near the Upá, they constructed caches and mysterious routes that led from Matagalpa to the edge of Fila Grande and Pancasán. They made paths approaching Matiguás and penetrated the humid, dark center of Kiragua mountain, where they also dug caches.

These were common pits into which were promiscuously piled, beans, rice, sugar, salt, boots, ammunition, batteries and medicines. Some were sixteen feet deep by twenty-two feet long and thirteen feet wide. Others were less pretentious. The idea was to have reserves for several months after the presence of combatants had been detected.

The acts of repossession — which is what we called bank hold-ups — financed the purchase of food, cloth and other materials which we used or laid away.

2

Carlos sent us off to construct caches. Silvio, with the bulk of the troops, left for Kiragua.

Together with Germán Pomares ("El Danto"), Narciso Zepeda ("Chicho", "El Flaco"), Víctor Guillen ("Eulalio") and "Chico Chiquito", as Denis Ortega was known, we set out for the ranch of the Rodríguez family, ten kilometers from Matagalpa.

We arrived at dawn. There was Antonio Rodríguez with his parents and sisters. It was a comfortable house with earthen corridors separated from the patio, where chickens and pigs foraged. There was a sturdy, discolored railing to which the horses were tethered. The corral was nearby and, tied to a post, a cow waited to be milked.

As day was breaking, making its way through the breeze, Velia, Antonio's sister, slender, blonde, disdainful, clad in black slacks and a yellow shirt, approached the cow and milked her, with her back to the guerrillas.

She was living in New York, where she worked in a clothing factory. She had arrived a couple of weeks earlier on vacation and would only stay a month with her family. Antonio called her with a respect in his voice that wasn't customary for that stubborn rancher and baseball player who boasted of his skill with cattle and of being an unequaled seducer of women.

After washing up and cleaning her glasses, Velia shook hands and offered us foaming milk with *pinol*.* I drank the milk, while drinking in her myopic eyes and blonde hair. When she handed me the glass, she blushed and made a gesture of rejection that alarmed me.

They kept me shut in during the day, reasoning that I was well-known in the area, having been born in Matagalpa. There was no problem with the others; they looked like peasants and nobody knew them. I had the vague sense of being discriminated against, but that's alright, Toño. What's one to do?

On a leather-covered wooden bed, using my knapsack as a pillow, I started reading Corín Tellado. At some point in the story, when I was on the verge of tears because the nurse discovers that the famous doctor is in love with her while disdaining a snooty millionairess, someone rapped softly on a window looking into an adjoining room. I opened it and my heart leapt; it was Velia, made up and with her hair loose, bringing me a plateful of eggs, rice, tortillas and cheese.

Despite the fact that I already knew it, I asked her name.

"Velia."

"When are you leaving for the States?"

"In two weeks."

"Why?"

"Because. Why not?"

"Because in Nicaragua there is a struggle going on and we are all obliged to take part... From now on your name will be Marina."

And I continued talking. I knew it was demagoguery but I wanted her to stay. She asked me to eat and said we could continue talking later. I ate rapidly, because I was hungry and so that half hour could be reduced to ten minutes.

She returned at midday. She offered some excuse and promised another talk with me without really committing herself.

Meanwhile, the nurse said she also loved him, but that the social distance between them was an abyss. What would the doctor's mother and sister say? They belonged to high society. Nobody knew how they might react. The doctor and nurse got married. The mother-in-

---

* A soft drink made of finely ground cornmeal, sugar and cocoa.

law threw a fit, but became deliriously happy when a chubby, healthy grandson was born.

I was heartily ashamed of myself, but I stuck my head out the half-open door and called her. Her elder sister, Lidia, looked at me with curiosity and sympathy. All I could do was ask her for another novel and she said, yes, of course. It appeared — I remember the title as if it were in front of me: *Nights of Commitment*.

The hero was named Cienfuegos and I must say, I remember his name because of Camilo, the legendary hero of Cuba. The girl must have been named Agnes or Marisa.

Cienfuegos was young, strong, with black hair and disconcerting blue eyes. For some reason I don't remember, he went to babysit two children in a good neighborhood. The apartment was luxurious. The woman who opened the door was blonde, slender, beautiful — like Marina. Give me a break!

"Oh!" she exclaimed hurriedly. "Come in, come in. The children are asleep."

Somebody knocked on the door and it opened slightly. I didn't even have time to feel excited.

"Someone is looking for you."

"Who?"

Following the voice, like a whirlwind, Edén Pastora entered the room. I'd sent him a message inviting him for a talk.

I conveyed our desire that he join the guerrilla struggle. I told him I had a warm memory of the time on the banks of the Patuca, when with a smile he had unselfishly given me a first-aid kit. He told me he'd been arrested shortly after the events of January 22nd, thanks to the denunciation of a character named Wilfredo Montalbán.

The prisoners had all turned on him. The fool had been picked up for shooting his mouth off. They roughed him up and he talked until they had to pay him to shut up.

"The jailer, Torres," Pastora continued, "tortured me, bashed my head and made me drink my own blood, and I won't go into the mountains until I've killed him. I couldn't go on living; life would have no meaning without my getting revenge."

I asked about his family, his cattle ranch near Ciudad Darío, and repeated the invitation to join our guerrilla organization. He insisted that first he had to kill the jailer Torres, and left with a vague and genial promise to return. That jailer is now in the same band as the fierce Pastora: the counterrevolution.

The two children were charming. They got up before Cienfuegos and prepared their own breakfast. They were only six and four years-old.

As for Marisa, Agnes, Nat — I don't remember this mysterious girl's name — the children adored her but she wasn't their mother. That marvelous, slender girl of such radiant presence and those wonderful eyes, what did she do from six o'clock in the afternoon until six o'clock in the morning? Nobody knew. Cienfuegos was intrigued. He returned time and again but learned nothing definite. Of course, he was falling in love.

Germán Pomares ("El Danto") appeared, smiling. He'd been in Matagalpa, where he talked to Dr. Clarence Silva and his wife, Lolita.

"They send you their greetings."

"But, why did you tell them I was here?"

"They can be trusted and they can be useful to us. I've found the location for the cache and "Chico Chiquito" liked it. Can I bring some beer?" The malice in German's eyes danced about like a hummingbird over carnations.

"Are you coming with us? The road is hellish."

"Sure, why?"

"I don't know." And he loosed a contagious laugh, part of which escaped through his nose, making him sound like a cracked bell.

He took me with him, that devil. I had no night vision like "Chico Chiquito", like "El Flaco" Zepeda, like "Eulalio" and Germán. But we arrived early and set ourselves to the task of breaking the ground with picks and shoveling out the dirt under the light of *ocote* torches provided by Toño, who'd been waiting for us for hours.

We had to finish the job that same night and Narciso Zepeda, "Chicho," "El Flaco," who were all the same person but did the work of three, helped me by wielding his pick in my area without anyone noticing. I was grateful for his help, his discretion and his solidarity. "Chicho" was valiant, an expert tracker, uncompromising when hiking with a hundred pounds on his shoulders, soft-spoken, and wielded a mean machete. Years later, he was assassinated in a dirty plot. The revolution lost a chieftain and a hero.

The following day, he, Germán Pomares and "Chico Chiquito" went back to erase our tracks and to camouflage the wide tomb in which all its builders would have easily fit.

The sacks of rice and sugar and cartons of Quaker Oats were to arrive in the morning, and there was no alternative to packing all that weight in by mule, even though that might attract attention.

The next day, the mystery of that girl continued and Cienfuegos was on the verge of howling like a wolf. Why was he working as a babysitter? To earn extra money for his studies? Why? Too much love, excessive mystery, the children...

Velia failed to appear all that day. She arrived at nightfall and sat down to eat with us. The cache was ready and we only awaited skinny Roque, who was bringing us money, letters and news of work in the cities, before we returned to the encampment where Carlos awaited us.

Velia presided over the table. I'd scarcely taken two mouthfuls when I felt her knees brushing against mine. I felt cold, hot, shivery. It had been too long without experiencing that. Afterwards, we played cards — "Rob the Casino." Velia and I lost every hand.

Cienfuegos finally discovered that Marisa went out at night to model and do screentests before cameras and bright lights. One night she returned pale, her eyes moist, with a strange expression on her face.

"Marisa, what's happened?" The young woman tried to talk, running her fingers through her blonde hair. She removed her fur coat and hung it on the coat rack.

"Marisa, please! Won't you explain?"

They'd offered Marisa a starring role but in exchange for favors she was unable... because of her principles, because it all... because....

"Why, Marisa?" Cienfuegos felt the flame of joy.

Toño came into the room and told me that his brother, Fabián, wanted to join the guerrillas.

It was a moonlit night and the blonde drew near slowly like someone who was about to commit a premeditated murder. He turned brusquely, joyfully. He made an extreme effort to postpone the violence. He kissed her gently, long, unhurriedly, hurriedly. The moon disappeared, everyone left. The moon remained. And they remained.

We left, we remained, Velia.

Velia never went back to New York.

Cienfuegos received a sizeable inheritance. Marisa no longer needed to be an actress. They parked their newly purchased car at a tourist motel. Marisa's voice sounded stifled.

"I love you...."

"And I love you, I...."

Everything became defused. For others, not for them....

They knew how much they enjoyed that vehement and sincere love.

The end.

3

The guerrilla effort required funds. On June 22, 1967, an urban commando held up the Kennedy branch of the Bank of London and Montreal, located a hundred yards from the Fourth Section of the Managua Police (the Air Force prison).

Participants in the operation were Selím Shible, Daniel Ortega, Jorge Sinforoso Bravo, and Axel Somarriva, who later betrayed the revolution.

According to witnesses, whose statements were printed in the main city newspapers, the events unfolded in the following manner:

At 2:45 p.m., a blue taxi, license #849, parked in front of the bank branch. A young man got out, entered the bank and went to one of the teller's windows to break a 100 *córdoba* bill. As he headed toward the front door, he stepped to one side, pulled out a pistol, pointed it at the cashier and manager and ordered them to open the safe. At that moment, a second youth armed with a pistol entered the bank and shouted: "This is a hold-up by the FSLN. We aren't going to hurt you. We want the money to overthrow the Somozas." He immobilized the rest of the bank employees.

A third youth came in and cleaned out the money from the teller's cage as well as from the safe. The bills were stuffed into a briefcase and a typewriter case. After locking the employees in two back rooms, they calmly left the bank, climbed into the waiting taxi, and headed for the center of town. They obtained 225,000 *córdobas*, an unprecedented sum.

A policeman with a Garand rifle, who was guarding the bank, wasn't aware of the robbery until the manager escaped from the locked room after it was all over and informed him.

A short time later, we received, in addition to thousands of *córdobas*, canned goods, rice, salt, candies, cigarettes, sugar, oatmeal, all the things that make a guerrilla's mouth water. We proceeded to fill all the caches that had been constructed. We returned to Fila Grande and found that Carlos was gone. For reasons that nobody could explain, he had delayed his return from a mission in which he tried to extend our radius of influence by several kilometers.

"Eulalio" appeared alone, evasive, defensive. He had accompanied Carlos as a guide.

"What happened?"

"We were coming from Matagalpa at night when we ran into a group of men on horseback, all of them drunk. They were deputies and stopped us. Carlos fired at them. They shouted: 'We're friends.' Carlos dove into a ravine and I hid behind a tree. I waited an hour and then started calling the commander, first in a low voice and then shouting, but nobody answered."

"Did the deputies fire on you?"

"Yes."

"Did they wound Carlos?"

"I don't know. I don't think so. He would have cried out. At night it's almost impossible...."

"Holy fuck!" Oscar Turcios exclaimed.

"My God!" Corinto muttered.

"Tell us again what happened," I interrupted.

"Eulalio" patiently repeated the details of the incident.

We concluded that he wasn't dead; that if he'd been killed we'd already know about it. That there was a risk of a new encounter or possible capture. That Carlos didn't see well at night. That there were no collaborators in the area. That, yes, there was a nice old guy nearby who knew Carlos and could orient him. That Carlos isn't stupid, telling others to scatter the coals but not to burn themselves. That if he was able to orient us, how could he fail to orient himself? He only orients us politically, dumbo, not in the mountains. Where he is isn't the mountains; it's a highway and there are a lot of houses. It's true, he's smarter than all of us. Just the same, you're not the only one who's worried.

"Eulalio," a simple peasant, was more upset than we were.

Our chief showed up a week later, in a bad mood and complaining of an infected toenail.

We went to Pancasán and met to examine the situation.

4

When Carlos gathered the small guerrilla unit of just over thirty men to inform them that it was rumored that the National Guard was organizing search sweeps in our zone, all the peasants except "Eulalio" and Nicolás Sánchez — "The Tiger of Cerro Colorado", as Silvio called him then and history calls him now — asked to be excused, accepting our promise that there would be no reprisals against anyone who withdrew.

"Eulalio" lived in Yaro, which is some twenty kilometers southeast of Waslala; that was far away, toward the Atlantic Coast. Oscar Turcios and Pablo Ubeda had traveled that far to recover some old weapons that had been cached there ever since Pablito had escaped oblivion and death following the Coco river and Bocay campaigns.

Those weapons were sent to the area around Musún and from there were transferred to Fila Grande. There were several .22 rifles, two .30-30s, two Garands, four revolvers, one M-1 carbine and the famous "tapir-killer" rifle.

"When I saw those weapons," "Eulalio" said, "I shook my head, because I thought there were lots of them and not just that handful. They were rusty and we had to boil them, grease them, shine their shoes and try firing them." They were tested out in the jungle and they worked.

Other weapons arrived: M-1 carbines and two M-3 submachine guns. Oscar Turcios was so delighted, that he came into camp firing into the air, knowing that Carlos would chew him out, which in fact he did.

"Eulalio" survived the campaigns of Pancasán and Fila Grande. Today he's the leader of a cooperative and even at this stage of the game I still admire his courage and conviction. When Carlos, our undisputed chief, got lost in the jungle, "Eulalio" had returned to camp alone, knowing full well that he might be shot. "Eulalio" and Gladys are two of the three survivors of that period.

Chapter
Twenty-Two

1

Carlos said something to Oscar that the latter resented; then neither of them wanted to back down until Silvio intervened.

During this rift, Otto Casco and Danilo Rosales, the doctor, arrived.

We continued our conversations at Doña Luisa Alonso's place. It was a big house, or so it seemed to me. When you're in the mountains, a deer trail seems like a highway. When you leave the mountains, a highway takes on the dimensions of a freeway and a simple roof seems like a temple.

The house was surrounded by gardens and when one approached it along the damp pathway it looked like a picture postcard.

Once in the house, comforted by cups of Matagalpa coffee served by Gladys Báez, Carlos read Danilo Rosales' letter to the university rector in which he resigned his post as a professor. This letter made a deep impression on students and faculty alike. Among other things, it said:

> The political situation in Nicaragua has led the sons and daughters of our people to understand that the rights and freedoms trampled by years of dynastic oppression in alliance with the oligarchies and imperialism, can only be regained by means of the purest form of revolutionary struggle: namely, armed popular insurrection. For that reason, I have decided, with profound conviction and revolutionary consciousness, to submit my resignation as Resident and Instructor of Pathology in the Faculty of Medicine of the National Autonomous University. I consider it the duty of every revolutionary intellectual to join the

Army of Nicaragua which, holding the ideals of Sandino, marches under the banner of the FSLN.

To you, Mr. Rector, to the university professors, to the professionals and students, I say that the definitive struggle for the liberation of Nicaragua has entered its decisive phase and that it is here where you have a role as patriots and as Nicaraguans.

Danilo died, but numerous students and professionals would heed his call.

2

We were still at Doña Luisa's house when, on July 25, 1967, we heard on the radio that the young poet, intellectual and Sandinista militant, Fernando Gordillo, had died.

Fernando died at the age of 26 and was buried on July 26th, the fourteenth anniversary of the assault on the Moncada barracks.

He was the victim of an absurd disease, a pathology that is a monstrous roulette wheel with a million possibilities. And perhaps by the whim of his patron saint, the wheel stopped on the number that sealed his fate.

Miastenia gravis is characterized by a progressive and stupid debilitation of muscular strength. It can appear at any time following adolescence. Fernando closed the last door of his childhood and the gods of the shadows trapped him.

He couldn't even whistle; his voice acquired a nasal tone. With that voice he had shaken and persuaded half the National University. It was no accident that he had won I don't know many international oratorical competitions, including the one sponsored by *El Universal* of Mexico, where he competed against Latin American university students.

Breathing difficulties appear in the musculature of the chest. In the final stages, the patient can no longer raise his arms. Severe cases, such as Fernando's, develop respiratory complications that lead rapidly to death.

The only treatment is complete rest: impossible advice for a combatant. Fernando died while holding onto a telephone receiver with great difficulty and talking to the woman who meant the most in his life: his comrade, sister, sweetheart and lover, Michele Najlis.

Gordillo was co-founder of the magazine *Ventana,* which was published for four years and united the literary group of the same name.

The proclamation of the Ventana Front appeared in February 1960 over the signatures of Sergio Ramírez, Alfonso Robles and Fernando Gordillo:

Since God has descended neither to the Fisherman's Village nor to Juan Pedro's hut, and since the darkness in the mines prevents him from seeing the lungs of the silicosis victims, we believe it is not of interest to us to know whether or not God has descended in Harlem.

We do not believe in exile; we know we are on a battlefield and the least we can hope is that our machete has a sharp edge.

We do not despair of the present. We do not fill our lives with emptiness. The clamor of our people wrenches our hearts and we seek to be their bell tower. We know that beans are more essential than chewing gum. We can find people who are tired of drinking whiskey in the Dakotas, New Jersey or on Broadway. Among ourselves, we can only get tired of drinking *pinol.*

Of course, we ourselves are in agreement. We don't agree with the people of our time. Our song will not be dedicated to the beauty of the young lady whose parents spend the wages of ten servants on her nor to the success of men who believe that money is the measure of success. Nor to the virtue of those who believe that prayers are deeds. We know that it is necessary to destroy. We want to destroy but we want to destroy the seed that is rotting in order to produce a new plant. We want to encourage the hand that wields the machete, but only to prune, not to annihilate. Authenticity above all. Authenticity before all else. An ulcer is more important than a diamond.

We believe that poetry is the voice of the people. As long as there is one man who is desperately hungry, longing for comforts is excessive. Social protest lies in redemption and not in abandonment. Poetry is a whetstone for sharpening and not a precipice of despair. Young people were born to live their lives, not to be suspended in meaninglessness.

Mary Rose Thomas and Burt McCastle, two U.S. adolescents who died at dawn on the freeway on their way home from a rock concert, arouse pity. But José Ruiz and Manuel López, dead in the mines, provoke a greater sorrow, the epitome of grief. There, poetry must tremble, must strike like a lightning bolt.

Our time, Nicaragua's time, is not saturated with exact mechanisms nor with mechanical superstructures that leave no room for the spirit. The site of the soul in Limay, Siuna, Alamikamba, Teustepe or Niquinohomo is as vast and profound as the sadness of a sick peasant, as the grief of a child with no toys. A plane passing overhead is less infuriating than "a man passing by with a loaf on his shoulder". A bored millionaire and his children, infatuated by so much precision on the highway, arouse less feeling than a woman giving birth in the street. And that woman's children will not protest against their miserable time. They will pass it on to their children if we abandon them. For this reason, and for everything else that is left unsaid, we, the bell tower of empty stomachs, mud for the tracks of those who come after us, not for those who return, invoke God so that he might descend in Siuna, Bonanza and Pescadores. And if he descends in Harlem, let him not pass among us leaving behind wads of used chewing gum. Is God also Made in U.S.A.?

We proclaim the poetry of the defenseless, not of desperation; the song for the dead Miskito Indian, not a prayer response for our own bones; the betrayal of the men in the factories, mines and ranches, not our personal betrayal.

We elevate beauty to its ultimate degree, and as long as birds do not desert the trees and stars don't wander from the sky, we will be here as we always have been. We are not the betrayed generation.

We are the generation that must not betray Nicaragua.[1]

Sergio is already part of history as a writer and government leader. Alfonso Robles, according to my friend and comrade, José Reyes Monterrey, became a successful lawyer and got rich. In other words, he went to hell. Fernando, had he lived, would have been in the top cultural and political ranks of the country.

Carlos sent by guerrilla mail the order that the Sandinista Front of National Liberation should be present at his funeral with the flags of the FSLN and the FER (Federation of Revolutionary Students). Chelito Moreno, in the encampment with us, whispered Fernando's poem "Adivinanza" ["Augury"], which might as well have been entitled "Somoza and Sandino":

> Two deaths:
> one, within the view of all
> in the heart of none.
> The other, within the view of none
> in the heart of all.

3

Gladys Báez was in a Managua safehouse with Selím Shible when she received orders to join the guerrillas. She was accompanied by Daniel Ortega — who was in Fila Grande and Pancasán four times, dividing his time between the urban and rural fronts — Efraín Sánchez, "Eulalio" and Chico Chiquito.

Efraín Sánchez was driving the car. Due to mechanical failure, accident or overloading, at the point where the primitive road started up the mountain in a steep upgrade, the jeep started rolling

[1] "Proclama Frente Ventana" in: *Taller* (León: Editorial Universitaria UNAN, 1977), No. 14, p. 17.

backwards. Slowly at first, then more rapidly. Step on the brake. It doesn't work. Shift into four-wheel-drive. It doesn't have four-wheel-drive. Turn it to the left. That's what I'm doing. Then turn to the right, brother. They plunged into emptiness. A tree stopped them.

Daniel was the first out. Chico Chiquito had eight long gashes on his forearm and "Eulalio" had a cut on one leg. Gladys was unhurt.

They took out their knapsacks, food and rifles. Daniel Ortega ordered them to push the vehicle over the cliff where everyone would have ended up if it hadn't been for Gladys Báez's guardian angel.

Another angel, named Martínez, to whom we gave the pseudonym "Juan Pueblo", gave them refuge for the night and helped bandage their injuries.

The following day, Daniel and Efraín returned with Chico Chiquito, who was still bleeding.

Days later, we learned that the Guard had concluded that the vehicle's occupants were thieves and that they had all perished. None of the soldiers that were sent to investigate dared climb down to the bottom of the abyss, because "not even the buzzards go down there."

"Eulalio" recovered in a hut, a needle in the mountain haystack. Gladys, when she finally set out for the guerrilla encampment, carried so many documents and letters that when she tucked them between her navel and her belt she looked pregnant. This was a perfect disguise, since it is the natural condition of peasant women. They walked at the pace of a pregnant woman with a crippled husband, accompanied by "Juan Pueblo."

They were approaching a creek when, from the opposite direction, five Guards appeared on horseback driving before them like cattle a group of six peasants who were tied together. "Eulalio" recognized them, as did Angel. They recognized "Eulalio" and Angel. Gladys stuck fingers down her throat to induce vomiting. The bound peasants remained silent.

"Who are you?" the Guards insisted.

"I'm a carpenter," Eulalio said. "I'm on my way to Washington to work for my boss, Don Miguel." Angel said he was Eulalio's assistant. Gladys made eye contact with one of the peasants, signalling gratitude for their silence. The Guards continued on down the road with their prisoners.

The introduction of a woman into the guerrilla movement is like placing a loaf of bread in the oven: she's untouchable, yet her gratifying presence is there. Nobody prevents you from looking at her or helping her with her knapsack. At first it was embarrassing, because our daily provisions consisted of beans, which generate intestinal gases that the guerrillas discharge in short bursts whenever the need strikes.

I think Comandante Silvio Mayorga — who knew Gladys ("Adelita") the best — was the one who first broke our self-imposed courtesy with a sonorous fart. After that, when we had to urinate, we merely walked a few steps away and turned our backs. Gladys smiled. She was in the middle squad and I will always be grateful to her because, in addition to her many other merits, she was a stimulus and refuge for Silvio during those transcendental days which for him would be his last.

The Comandante was born clever. He managed sarcasm as a cardsharp manages a deck of cards. He was studious, demanding and spoiled.

Among the people I know, the one who most reminds me of him is Bayardo Arce, just as the one who most reminds me of Francisco Moreno is René Núñez. Carlos Fonseca doesn't remind me of anybody and nobody reminds me of Carlos Fonseca, because he wasn't like anyone else, and yet he was like everyone.

In July 1964, Silvio wrote some notes that demonstrate his exceptional mystique. He is the most relevant, most respected figure, after Carlos Fonseca, in the history of the FSLN:

> I have had the great good fortune to participate in the struggle for the liberation of Nicaragua, and this has been the most satisfying experience of my life. I think I could have been a better revolutionary.
>
> May those who come after me understand the treasure that being a combatant for the future of our people represents.

The only thing I regret is not having contributed more to our cause.

Patriotism is not some laboratory formula. It is an unshakable determination to liberate one's Homeland.

I feel proud to be a militant in the FSLN.

Future years will see hard-fought, decisive battles. It is the duty of revolutionaries today to prepare ourselves, because so much is at stake: FOR THE FIRST TIME THERE EXISTS THE REAL POSSIBILITY OF LIBERATING NICARAGUA. What sacrifice or what effort could seem to us to be too great?[1]

4

We moved camp. Near a small branch of the Upá, we set up our umpteenth encampment.

That evening after dark, around the campfire, Carlos, Silvio and "El Chelito" Moreno complained of chills. Soon they were feverish with splitting headaches. Carlos was the first to begin vomiting. They all took to their hammocks. I didn't know much about treatment but I was more or less a paramedic, drawing on my precarious knowledge as a former pharmaceuticals salesman. I presumed from the symptoms that they might have paratyphoid and I took the risk of treating them with that dangerous assassin of intestinal flora, chloranphenicol.

In addition, we sent an urgent message to the city and a few days later Dr. Sócrates Flores arrived. The patients were recovering and Sócrates' arrival gave us a chance to catch up on what was happening at the National University and within the political parties.

Everything was more or less tranquil as political life was going through a quiescent period.

[1] Silvio Mayorga, letter, July 1964, Archives of the Nicaraguan Historical Institute.

5

One afternoon before dinner, we made a head count and discovered that one of the peasants, the youngest of them all, had disappeared.

We immediately organized a small patrol. At dawn we surrounded his humble hut, and there he was, surprised, trembling, and younger than ever. His head hung so low that it seemed about to fall among his hungry brothers and sisters who looked on curiously, without understanding the drama of the situation.

His mother, who judging by the age of her smallest children must still be young, looked as old as Methuselah's grandmother. That's what country life does to people. She begged us in an adolescent's voice: "Forgive him, I beg you. It was a crazy thing, but he's only fourteen years-old." Carlos remained silent for a moment then said: "It's alright. Let him be." The boy returned the revolver we had given him. Sometime later, he joined the guerrilla forces in Zinica and died in an encounter with rural deputies.

6

Carlos sent Germán Pomares and me to the region of El Bálsamo, near Cerro Colorado and a long way from Fila Grande. The peasants led us to a large cave that protected us from the rain, but which, according to Pomares' cat-like instincts, was a death trap.

There we established a small training school for youngsters of both sexes. There were fourteen of them. We explained, over and over again, how to set up harassment and containment ambushes, the tactics for wiping out small and large units, the enemy's military structure, and how to assemble and disassemble a Garand semi-automatic assault rifle, an M-3 submachine gun, M-1 and M-2 carbines and a Browning .45 pistol.

It was in precisely this place that Carlos, one translucent morning, told us: "Also, teach them to read."

Chapter
Twenty-Three

1

During those days the need to structure our activities became clear. Until then we had regulated ourselves by means of obvious principles of loyalty, comradeship, firmness and discipline, all of which were tacitly understood.

By now it was necessary to formalize symbols, oaths, rites and duties, to affirm the practices of criticism and self-criticism and to adopt an organic structure. Carlos recommended that we rid ourselves once and for all of both liberalism and straitjackets.

Thus it was that between holding classes and digging caches, while sitting on a tree root beside a stream, interrupted by that caution ever present in the eyes and ears of a guerrilla, we drew up the *Statutes of the FSLN*, which were later polished by an ad hoc commission, in Cuba. The Sandinista Oath, written by Carlos read as follows:

> With my heart and mind focused on the immortal patriotic example of Augusto César Sandino and Ernesto Che Guevara; before the memory of all the heroes and martyrs for the liberation of Nicaragua, Latin America and all of humanity; before history itself, I place my hand on the red and black banner that signifies: A Free Homeland or Death. With weapons in hand I swear to defend our national honor and to fight for the redemption of the repressed and exploited of Nicaragua and the world. If I fulfill this oath, the liberation of Nicaragua will be my reward. If I betray this oath, a dishonorable death and disgrace will be my punishment.*

* *Estatutos históricos del FSLN.* See complete text at the end of this chapter.

2

Carlos Reyna, sent by the organization, taught literacy classes in Chonta, Castillo Blanco and El Bálsamo. In El Bálsamo, the students — several dozens of all ages and both sexes — belonged to the Ochoa family, all from one village, who earned the right to pass en masse into the history of collaboration with the FSLN.

Carlos Reyna, whom the peasants called "professor" and we called "El Teacher," frequently accompanied Carlos Fonseca on his endless rounds.

During these marches, the top guerrilla chief carried an enormous backpack. On one occasion, Eulalio offered to help him, and another time Oscar Turcios offered to share his burden. Carlos Fonseca rejected both offers. Eulalio said: "If you don't want help, it's probably because your backpack is more bulky than heavy." Carlos asked him to pick it up and when the peasant, who was no weakling, tried to lift it, he found to his astonishment that it weighed more than 100 pounds. On this occasion, Carlos was also carrying a Garand, a .22 carbine and a .45 pistol.

3

In the Sisimique encampment, a site selected by Pablo Ubeda, we organized another training school. Carlos Fonseca took the course like any other guerrilla, although he had an aversion to barked orders.

The assault on the fortress of Matiguás was planned in that same encampment. Before the attack, having taken into account the time, distance, level of training, and number of enemy guards, we felt it was necessary to finish the construction of caches.

We completed eight in Fila Grande, four in Kiragua and one in Matapalo, twelve kilometers from Matagalpa. This last one was never discovered by the enemy.

4

We were scattered when the National Guard discovered the presence of guerrillas. Silvio Mayorga was moving toward Kiragua with a small group to deposit food and clothing. Others of us were at the Rodríguez family farm near Matagalpa.

One of the pockets in Chelito Moreno's olive green pants tore open during the march and some 30.06 cartridges slipped through this fatal hole. They were found by the Guard, who had already been alerted by some women coffee pickers a few days earlier after they had seen a group of strangers — perhaps cattle rustlers — pass by.

When the enemy entered from Matiguás, Germán Pomares, Chicho, Eulalio, Chico Chiquito and I returned to Fila Grande, where Carlos, Oscar Turcios and Daniel Ortega were waiting. We didn't know the whereabouts of Silvio and his people.

We decided that Eulalio and Fausto Heriberto García ("Enriquito") should go looking for them. They were given a map with a scale of 1/50,000 on which was marked their return route. Carlos ordered Daniel Ortega to return to Managua with Leopoldo Rivas, who was ill. Daniel left under protest, because he would have preferred to share our fortunes.

5

Days went by without our learning anything. Carlos ordered me to go with Germán Pomares to the Rodríguez farm to make contact with the father of Lolita, who was the wife of the doctor, Clarence Silva. Her father owned the El Castillo cattle ranch near Kiragua. Silva would be asked to take me to the small unit that was the object of our concern.

The same day we arrived, dead tired, Antonio Rodríguez's sister, Lidia, appeared with information picked up by a ham radio operator about a battle near the Washington ranch.

The command post, located in the house of a local exploiter by the name of Miguel Láinez, informed National Guard headquarters that a number of guerrillas had died in the encounter, and that others were wounded, among them Silvio Mayorga. There was at least one unwounded prisoner, Otto Casco.

I immediately sent a messenger to Managua to have this information broadcast over the radio in the hope of saving the lives of Otto and the wounded men. The information was given to Manuel Espinoza Enríquez and he, in turn, broadcast it without hesitation on his news program, "Extra."

We didn't sleep. Then, the next morning, the Guard issued a communique announcing that all combatants of the column were dead. Those who died that August 27th were: Silvio Mayorga, Rigoberto Cruz ("Pablo Ubeda"), Francisco Moreno ("El Chelito"), Otto Casco, Fausto García, Carlos Reyna, Ernesto Fernández ("El Masaya") and Carlos Tinoco.

Not appearing on the list were Nicolás Sánchez ("El Tigre de Cerro Colorado"), Eulalio, Chinito Edmundo Pérez and Danilo Rosales. Nevertheless, we gave them up for dead.

What had happened?

When Eulalio and Fausto García located Silvio, the guerrillas were constructing caches. Silvio called them together, but they decided to finish the job which delayed their return to Fila Grande.

Three days later, they started their march, but by a different route than the one indicated on the map. Pablo Ubeda, Genaro Díaz and Fausto García had an inconsequential encounter with the Guard. Silvio sent Eulalio to Fermín Diaz's house. The latter was a guerrilla contact and it was learned that he had been captured.

They decided to withdraw by way of a place known as Portillo Grande in the direction of Jabalar. As they were climbing La Mona hill, "El Tigre del Cerro Colorado," who had lagged behind erasing their tracks, ran into a man who said he was looking for the captain's mule. "El Tigre" didn't detain him and the man informed the Guard.

Eulalio warned Silvio of the danger. They continued the march. Ernesto Fernández — whom we also called "Lencho" — said that he felt it was an ambush. They hadn't walked more than 500 meters when they heard a long burst of gunfire.

Pablo asked Eulalio to investigate. The latter went back cautiously and saw that they had killed Lencho and that El Tigre's right foot had been destroyed by a bullet. Eulalio carried him on his back and Dr. Danilo Rosales gave him emergency treatment.

Eulalio and Paul — Chinito Edmundo Pérez, who was ill — hid in the brush, caring for El Tigre, while the column continued its march. El Tigre died in Eulalio's arms three days later, because they were unable to staunch the hemorrhaging. His body was placed between the gigantic roots of a *ceiba* and covered with leaves and bits of wood. Danilo remained in El Bálsamo. He was captured in the cave where we had given military training with Pomares. Indeed it was a death trap. Danilo was assassinated.

Three days later, they heard the news on Paul's small radio that the rest of the unit had fallen. Paul was taken to Matapalo by Eulalio, and the FSLN organization in Matagalpa brought him to Managua.

It had been an unequal encounter. Squads of soldiers, armed with automatic rifles and hand grenades, surrounded the small guerrilla unit. The hail of gunfire did not prevent the Sandinistas from defending themselves with their damaged shotguns and carbines. It was said that the Guards themselves commented admiringly on the bravery of the guerrillas. One National Guard Corporal told how Pablo Ubeda, with his entrails hanging out, kept firing until they finished him off as he was drawing his last breath.

I left, with "El Danto" and Velia, for Managua. When Chinito Edmundo Pérez appeared a few weeks later in the safehouse we had in the Monseñor Lezcano neighborhood, Oscar Turcios embraced and kissed him unrestrainedly, possessed by a savage joy. That day we got drunk on *Flor de Caña* rum.

On October 23, 1967, Gonzalo Lacayo was executed. "El Chinito" participated in the operation. On November 4th, in revenge for Lacayo's death, "El Chinito" — whose name was Edmundo Pérez Quant — Casimiro Sotelo, who had been president of the student center of the Central American University, and the students Hugo Medina and Roberto Amaya, were captured and assassinated.

DOCUMENT 6
Statutes

STATEMENT OF PURPOSE

NATIONAL LIBERATION must be won by the workers, peasants, students and progressive intellectuals. To struggle for this goal is not to fight for new class privileges but for the abolition of the entire system of exploitation and misery that oppresses our people.

The economic submission of the exploited classes to the usurpers of power signifies a whole regime of slavery that manifests itself in social misery, stunted intellectual growth and political influence-mongering.

National Liberation is the great goal which all political vanguard movements must pursue.

Thus far, we have had in our hands an important factor for achieving victory: IDEOLOGICAL UNITY. But this is a decisive factor only when an organization provides that UNITY and projects it toward a conscious end.

The National Directorate of the FSLN has elaborated these Statutes to achieve organizational unity, to strengthen our discipline and to permit the total fulfillment of our revolutionary tasks.

CHAPTER I. GENERAL DISPOSITIONS

Article 1. - The FSLN is a politico-military organization that has as its goal the seizure of power by means of a People's War and the putting into practice of its Program.

Article 2. - The FSLN is an armed detachment of the vanguard of the Nicaraguan people, constituted as a voluntary group of revolutionaries committed to a general strategic concept, to a program, and to these Statutes.

Article 3. - The motto of the FSLN: "A FREE HOMELAND OR DEATH."

Article 4. - The Banner of the FSLN is red and black in two equal, horizontal strips, with the symbol, FSLN, in white letters in the middle.

247

<u>Article 5</u>. - The Hymn of the FSLN is: "STRUGGLE AND WIN."

<u>Article 6</u>. - The Sandinista Oath is:
"With my heart and mind fixed on the immortal patriotic example of Augusto César Sandino and Ernesto Che Guevara; in the memory of all the heroes and martyrs for the liberation of Nicaragua, Latin America and all of humanity; before history, I place my hand on the red and black banner that signifies: 'A Free Homeland or Death.' With weapons in hand I swear to defend our national honor and to fight for the redemption of the repressed and exploited of Nicaragua and the world. If I fulfill this oath, the liberation of Nicaragua will be my reward. If I betray this oath, disgrace and a dishonorable death will be my punishment."

CHAPTER II. OBJECTIVES

<u>Article 7</u>. - The objectives of the FSLN are as follows:
a) To overthrow the Somoza Dynasty, which for more than 35 years has robbed and murdered the Nicaraguan people and handed the national wealth over to foreign interests.
b) The establishment of a revolutionary people's government that is anti-imperialist and anti-feudal.
c) To achieve unity in our struggle with all progressive, revolutionary and popular forces in the country.
d) To create and strengthen a consciousness of anti-imperialist and anti-oligarchic struggle that goes beyond the liquidation of the detested Somoza tyranny.
e) To construct a solid, independent economy and to better the living conditions of all the people.
f) To expropriate and nationalize the large landed estates, factories, mining enterprises and other properties usurped by the Yankee monopolies and local traitors.
g) To carry out a popular, radical and integral Agrarian Reform.
h) To build a culture that is national and democratic in nature. To eliminate once and for all the ILLITERACY that has immersed our people in the most degrading ignorance.
i) To maintain combative solidarity with all peoples who struggle for their liberation.
j) To create a new man, educated in the beautiful revolutionary traditions of our people, in patriotism, in steadfastness, in the

integrity and heroism of the many combatants who have fallen throughout our history.

CHAPTER III. MEMBERS

Article 8. - The FSLN recognizes only one type of member: the militant.

Article 9. - Militants of the FSLN are all those persons who, having complied with the requirements for membership and having been duly admitted, submit themselves to the discipline, program and line of the organization.

Article 10. - Membership requirements for militants are:
a) To have the conscious will to struggle to the death against the Somoza dictatorship or any other like it.
b) To have not participated directly or indirectly in the crimes and thefts of the regime, which is the enemy of the people.
c) To have been recommended by at least one militant of the organization.

Article 11. - Any person who fulfills all the requisites set forth in Article 10 and who communicates in writing, verbally or by any other means his desire to join the FSLN, has the right to be accepted by any person authorized to do so. The applicant may be subjected to investigation and testing should the appropriate FSLN command structure so decide.

Article 12. - The following have the authority to admit new members:
a) The National Directorate.
b) The Executive Secretariat.
c) The General Staffs of the Guerrilla Forces and the Resistance.
d) The Regional Committees.

Article 13. - The FSLN, in accordance with the principles of revolutionary internationalism, admits to its ranks citizens of any nationality.

Article 14. - It is indispensable that nationals of other countries be accepted by the National Directorate or the Executive Secretariat.

Article 15. - Once the new militant is accepted, he will take the Sandinista Oath before any person designated to administer said Oath by the Membership Authority.

CHAPTER IV. DUTIES

Article 16. - The duties of militants are:

a) To unselfishly and resolutely struggle for the Revolution.

b) To adjust his/her conduct to the Statutes, Program and lines of the organization.

c) To be integrated into a specific organism.

d) To constantly study and apply the politico-military line of the FSLN.

e) To promote unity and cooperation within the organization as well as between the organization and the people.

f) To strengthen links to the masses on a daily basis. To lead the struggle in defense of the interests of the workers, peasants, students and the people in general, firmly raising their demands and fighting to secure them.

g) To raise the level of discipline and one's own moral conduct, as well as that of his comrades', making appropriate use of revolutionary criticism and self-criticism.

h) To immediately obey orders without question or hesitation.

i) To exercise creative initiative within the framework of orders received. By this is understood the use of all means and ideas not specified in the order, but not contradicting it, to enrich the content of the mission that has been assigned.

Article 17. - In addition to the above, the following are particular duties of persons in positions of responsibility:

a) To assure that orders are strictly carried out.

b) To modestly and simply issue rational orders.

c) To be exemplary in carrying out his/her revolutionary duties, in studying, and in his/her personal conduct.

d) To consult with militants concerning the nature of their orders whenever the importance of those orders warrants and circumstances permit.

e) To show concern for and make every effort to resolve militants' needs.

f) To carry out all routine tasks, so long as they do not interfere with his/her assigned activity.

CHAPTER V. RIGHTS

Article 18. - Militants have the following rights:
   a) To express themselves freely and to be heard through their respective organisms.
   b) To elect and be elected as members of the directive bodies of the FSLN in accordance with the dispositions of the Statutes.
   c) To participate in the elaboration of the politico-military line of the FSLN through their respective organisms.
   d) To receive official reports issued by the National Directorate or the Executive Secretariat concerning such activities or matters as do not constitute military secrets.
   e) To receive political, ideological, military and cultural instruction.
   f) To be protected by the organization to the degree such protection is feasible.

Article 19. - The wives, children, parents or other family members who are economically dependent on a militant who has died or been taken prisoner will be supported in so far as possible.

Article 20. - The following incentives are established for relevant deeds:
   a) Private congratulations.
   b) Public congratulations.
   c) Promotion within the Revolutionary Army.
   d) For acts of extraordinary heroism, the decoration "SANDINISTA HERO" is established and will be awarded by the National Directorate or the Executive Secretariat.

CHAPTER VI. CRITICISM

Article 21. - Criticism and self-criticism will be practiced and developed in the grassroots and leadership organisms of the FSLN alike to opportunely identify and correct defects and errors in operating methods, as well as their causes, which likewise shall immediately be corrected. When the criticized comrade is absent, she/he shall be informed of said criticism in writing.

Article 22. - In any session, at whatever level, the necessary time shall be taken to analyze work that has been done, to identify the cause of errors, to propose concrete measures to avoid such errors in the future and to improve our style of work.

Article 23. - Criticism must be:
   a) Just: based on concrete facts and objectives.
   b) Political: oriented toward identifying political and ideological deviations, while refraining from invoking personal aspects of the individual criticized.
   c) Serious: related to transcendental errors, without falling into banalities or gossip.
   d) Opportune: allowing no time to elapse between recognition of the error and criticism of the same.
   e) Fraternal: in content as well as in form; seeking to improve the comrade while refraining from insidious personal attacks.
   f) Energetic: expounding in its full dimension the error committed.

Article 24. - Criticism should always be accepted calmly and positively, with the firm intention of rectifying mistakes.

Article 25. - The criticized party may not allege in his or her favor the defects and errors of the comrade making the criticism.

CHAPTER VII. STRUCTURE

Article 26. - The FSLN is structured as a complex of organisms and not as a sum of its members; it has a common purpose and a shared discipline; democratic centralism governs the life of our organization.

Article 27. - Organisms of the FSLN are as follows:
   a) National Directorate.
   b) Executive Secretariat.
   c) General Staff of the Guerrilla Forces.
   d) General Staff of the Resistance.
   e) Regional organisms.
   f) Cells.

Article 28. - The system contemplated in the preceding article does not preclude the formation of working commissions and other control mechanisms in order to facilitate the functioning of the organization.

Article 29. - The Cell is the organization that links the Front to the masses. Its principle functions are:

a) To take the lead in advancing the demands and struggles of the masses in its own immediate area and in advancing the popular struggle generally. To defend actively the demands and to win the hearts of the masses by trying to link these struggles to the general fight of the people against their domination by the reactionary ruling class.

b) To organize the defense and self-defense of the masses against attacks by the repressive forces of the regime.

c) To participate in labor unions, student organizations or any other combative popular organization within its jurisdiction, endeavoring to improve such an organization if it suffers from deficiencies, or organize it if it does not yet exist.

d) To recruit new members and proselytize generally. As new friends are made, the cell should attempt to heighten its political and ideological level and to improve its revolutionary formation by means of collective and individual study.

e) To carry out the task of mobilizing and organizing the Front, developing efficient methods of agitation and propaganda in accord with local requirements.

f) To strengthen ties with militants of other revolutionary and progressive organizations. To concern itself generally with the task of building unity.

g) To oversee the attainment and maintenance of the spirit of the approved lines of intransigent conduct against the enemy.

Article 30. - The Regional Organism is the instrument of Executive Leadership at the regional level. Its functions are:

a) To direct work at the regional level, to check on the functioning of commissions located in the region, to elaborate and implement operational plans, and to carry out simultaneously guidelines or orders from higher organisms.

b) To elaborate periodical reports and forward them to the National Directorate and organize the sharing of experiences with other Regional Organisms.

Article 31. - The General Staff of Urban Resistance will be appointed by the National Directorate. Its function is to lead and develop the Popular War in the country's urban centers, coordinating its activity with the general strategic line of the organization.

Article 32. - The members of the General Staff of Urban Resistance may or may not be members of the National Directorate.

Article 33. - The General Staff of the Guerrilla Forces is appointed by the National Directorate. Its function is to lead and develop the Popular War in the countryside.

Article 34. - The General Staff of the Guerrilla Forces is autonomous within its own internal organization and may create the sections it deems necessary for its proper functioning. It answers only to the Executive Secretariat when the National Directorate is in recess.

Article 35. - The members of the General Staff of the Guerrilla Forces may or may not be members of the National Directorate.

Article 36. - The Executive Secretariat is the organism that directs and implements the politico-military line set by the National Directorate.

Article 37. - The Executive Secretariat originates from within the National Directorate and is charged with convening meetings of the National Directorate. It is the direct representative of the National Directorate.

Article 38. - The National Directorate is the highest organism of the FSLN and is responsible for appointing the other organisms of command at the national level.

Article 39. - The number of members of the National Directorate will be determined by the growth and capacity of the organization.

Article 40. - The powers of the National Directorate are as follows:
a) To elaborate the politico-military line and organization of the FSLN.
b) To oversee compliance with and respect for the Statutes and programmatic platform of the organization.
c) To represent the organization internationally.

d) To elect from its body the Executive Secretariat and its respective alternates.

e) To adapt the Statutes to special situations.

Article 41. - The decisions of the National Directorate are taken by simple majority.

CHAPTER VIII. OFFENSES, ERRORS AND PENALTIES

Article 42. - The actions or voluntary omissions penalized by these Statutes are considered to be offenses or errors. The following are offenses:

a) Desertion.

b) Denunciation and betrayal of secrets, even under threats or tortures of whatever nature.

c) Insubordination.

d) Fractionalism. This is understood to be the creation of internal groups outside the authority of the organization.

e) Disobeying orders.

f) Flight from combat.

g) The abandonment of wounded comrades or effects of the organization.

h) The abandonment of one's post or sleeping while on duty.

i) The wrongful use or waste of goods belonging to the organization or of goods captured from the enemy.

j) The theft of food from guerrilla supplies.

k) The abuse of alcoholic beverages, the use of drugs, disorderliness, abnormal behavior, and sexual practices that prove detrimental to the organization.

l) Gossip and calumnies.

Article 44.[sic]* - The following penalties are established:

a) Private or public rebuke.

b) The carrying out of certain routine tasks.

c) Disarming.

d) Temporary suspension.

e) Expulsion.

f) Execution by firing squad.

* Error in sequential numbering of articles in original Statutes.

Article 45. - For purposes of implementing the provisions of Article 44, a Disciplinary Tribunal shall be created, consisting of three members and a Prosecutor.

Article 46. - The Accused may appoint a defender or conduct his or her own defense.

Article 47. - In cases where the penalty imposed is temporary suspension, expulsion or execution, the sentenced party will have recourse to appeal and review, which must be granted by the Disciplinary Tribunal.

Article 48. - The National Directorate, or, in its absence, the Executive Secretariat, will be apprised of all cases in which the penalty imposed is execution, whether in consultation, on appeal or in review.

Article 49. - The aforementioned appeals shall be communicated to the next higher organism.

Article 50. - Repetition of offenses and the rank of the offender will be considered aggravating circumstances.

Article 51. - The voluntary, spontaneous confession of the offender will be considered an extenuating circumstance.

Article 52. - Group Chiefs will be apprised of minor offenses and they themselves will impose the penalties.

"A FREE HOMELAND OR DEATH"

THE SANDINISTA FRONT OF NATIONAL LIBERATION (FSLN)

Somewhere in Nicaragua.

Chapter
Twenty-Four

1

We have abandoned the mountains without losing faith. Velia and I are in Managua. She had fled to the United States after being abandoned. Her rival was more skillful and her fiancé broke off their engagement. In the small neighborhood of Guanuca, Matagalpa, the gossip ate her alive. That's why she left, because loneliness is a lesser evil.

Now she is in her own country. She has found love once again, healing the ulcerated feet of a guerrilla who caresses her with words she never found in the dictionary, words left in those interstices where the devil organized temptations.

She feels liberated, beyond the sinful self, and has the courage to shout with joy on a mattress from the Oriental market in a hot room, invulnerable to agonies and resurrections.

The eyes of the new woman look at me, myopic and beautiful. They watch how my eyes gaze on you, how they recognize your nude body. They are a handful of blind feathers from so much looking. I don't see, I see by touching, and I touch until I see your body without looking, a font of holy water.

We are within these walls, pursued, exhausted, but our existence is as real as the mirrors. If we weren't here, there would be no risk of tears, orgasms, life, the proximity of death.

2

It was in that house, rented by Velia, where Casimiro Sotelo and other comrades were destined to be captured, that we learned about the death of Che in Bolivia.

Che is as impertinent as Christ, as Quixote, as Bolívar. So impertinent that he mounted Rocinante, demolished chess bishops and frontiers and was crucified in La Higuera, I thought while Velia wiped away my tears and her own.

It is our duty to rescue his thought without separating it from his actions, Carlos Fonseca reminded us. Che has sufficient stature for both. His preaching about the new man is a tolling bell, a conflagration. It is true: the development of consciousness leads to a new society. That is something serious, historic, daring.

The material stimulus exists, but it's a mere trifle compared to the moral stimulus. Some dwarves could walk into our consciousness and leave a basketful of electrical appliances and salary increases, and we'd say to them: "Thank you." Some giants could walk into our consciousness with empty hands, give us a handful of stardust, and we'd say: "Stay here forever."

The revolution makes no sense if we reduce ourselves to being machines, if in addition to producing and reproducing things, we fail to produce and reproduce consciousness. Our labor is not for the purpose of grinding ourselves up in the mill of alienation and selfishness. Labor must be for the purpose of creating material value for renewed human beings. The metamorphosis is possible if in your consciousness you set off on the road of no return, Oscar Turcios reflected.

That man, born in Rosario on June 14, 1928, that sharpshooter who always hit the bullseye with his moral principles, died on October 8, 1967, only a few days after we had withdrawn from Pancasán. One day he would talk about economic controls, about advanced accounting systems, he would defend the principle of economic planning, analyze economic computation and be opposed to the free play of the law of value. The following dawn he would relate anecdotes of the revolutionary war and recite poems by Whitman and León Felipe.

Shitpot "Colonel" Andrés Selich: Che is written without an accent mark. He is a smile which contradictorily unites contempt for one's enemies with love for people. I have reached the age of 39, Che, and I am inexorably approaching the stage where it is difficult to be a guerrilla. For the moment, he said, I am whole. Our memory of him is also whole, the ache in our breasts, the sharp-edged silhouette of that creator. Che didn't manufacture bank notes or prefabricated buildings, anyone can do that. Che manufactured a new consciousness.

I have always had difficulty talking about Che. Each time I have wished to tell about our encounter in Havana, each time my memory returns to that day when all Latin America turned pale at the martyrdom in La Higuera, words and images fail me.

It must be because what I wish is to invoke his life as an example.

Che is the man we all would have liked to be, if only for a few hours. It must cause infinite pleasure not to know what arrogance is, never to have been scarred by a double standard of morality.

Che, at that time, had the mirror of Cuba, in which he recognized Latin America. Later on, there would be two mirrors. Two, three, many mirrors in which the peoples of Latin America could see to the hilt of their political geography the perspectives and heights scaled.

It is said, and it must be true although I haven't confirmed it, that at the moment when he was about to leave for Bolivia, Che sat down on a tree trunk next to Fidel in the encampment where the future guerrillas of Bolivia were gathered. They sat there side by side for more than an hour without saying a word.

Finally, still without speaking, Che's hand fell on Fidel's shoulder and Fidel's on Che's shoulder and they slapped each other heavily on the back.

Their empathy was such that words were unnecessary. Nothing had been left unsaid in that silent communication which is only possible between such men.

CHE

If yet again we divide history
it must be from that October day
when some learned to tremble
seeing that the fire of the gods
burns in the hearts of men.
It is dangerous to disturb the ashes,
to close your ears to the discordant
concert of guitars.

From that day forth no one can pretend
that the dead remain silent,
that they no longer speak out,
nor any longer have need of their drab roses.
Doubtless, the hour of their deaths
is a category unto itself,
the gentle renunciation
of short-lived fires.

We learned, Che, that it is possible to be —
what's the name of that wandering knight,
the one who arrived like a triumphant king,
that gentle vagabond consumed
with resolving fantasies?
Glory is but a match struck
behind the lines, and life's as beautiful
as your mother's nipple, as a plot of corn.

We learned, Major, that no one
can console us, for those who might
do so must themselves be consoled,
and after all is said and done, what we require
is something else —

How to kill death
how to resurrect life
how in hell to visualize utopia.[1]

It's true, Fidel. Che contemplated his death as something natural.
In whatever place death might surprise us, welcome it. So long as the
cause for which one dies is redemption. Words cannot express what I
might wish to say, but other lands in the world reclaim their power.
The moral responsibility for Pancasán, and before that, for Raití and
Bocay and Wankí, is yours, Guerrillero, and for what lies ahead in the
coming years, for our victory, someday and always. So be it. And so
it was.

[1]Translation from Tomás Borge Martínez, *Have You Seen a Red Curtain in
My Weary Chamber?* Poems, stories and essays with introduction,
translation and notes by Russell Bartley, Kent Johnson, and Sylvia Yoneda.
(Willimantic, CT: Curbstone Press, 1989), pp. 119,121.

3

Carlos spoke, from sunset until sunrise, with Ernesto Cardenal.

The poet left us speechless with his simplicity, with his complexity. My liberal prejudices — like Robespierre, of course, and not Virgilio Godoy — against priests, swiftly retreated after meeting him.

The period when we inaugurated the anti-Somoza struggle was for me, looking back now, like the tolling of a distant bell. Ernesto, poet of such clarity, moves forward through so much darkness, not the darkness of memory but that of the bloody viceroyalty. I remember him with his premonitions, with his anguished honesty, with his measured words, unequivocal and defiant.

Together with Pedro Joaquín Chamorro, he was close to Reynaldo Antonio Téfel. He was not yet a priest; I was almost a child. We all participated in the anti-Somoza struggle.

Afterwards, we didn't see each other: the university, my first incarcerations, trials and sentences, conspiratorial travels, founding of the Sandinista Front, the Coco river and Bocay, the outlying neighborhoods of Managua and León, resumption of the armed struggle, Pancasán.

I read his poetry before Pancasán. His "Epigrams" are the love poems I would like to have written:

> On losing you, you and I both have lost:
> I, because you were the one I most loved
> and you, because you were the one I loved most.
> But of the two of us, you lose more than I:
> because I can love others as I loved you
> but no other will love you as I loved you.

In Colombia, where I arrived with Henry Ruiz in 1969 after being expelled by the Costa Rican police — who tortured me for three straight nights — I read the poem of his I like the best: "Prayer for Marilyn Monroe." But no, it wasn't in Colombia; it was in another state: what they call a state of mind.

A love poem that is also political, that dignifies poor Marilyn, the orphan who was raped as a child, the little store clerk, and along with her all the young girls lost in capitalism and because of capitalism. A poem that condemns the cruelty of cosmetics; of sailing on a yacht with an inside swimming pool filled with champagne and colored fish; of a kiss in Singapore in return for half a pound of opium; of a dance in Río with the delegate of death.

It is not she who is pardoned, but God: that Marquis de Sade, stern creator of eternal flames, is the one who must be pardoned. It is he who must answer for her suicide. Ernesto pardons God in the name of Marilyn Monroe.

By then, Ernesto belonged to the literary history of Latin America and was on his way to belonging to world literary history. And while I don't believe it is possible to separate the priest from the poet, or the poet from the priest, being acquainted with his poetry was fundamental if we were to approach him.

The Front already had a contact of extraordinary historical value in Monsignor José Arias Caldera. His quarters and his sacristy had been converted from time to time into a safehouse that had sheltered Carlos Fonseca, Silvio Mayorga, José Benito Escobar, Oscar Turcios and Daniel Ortega. Another priest, Manuel Salazar, who became a bishop and turned into a counterrevolutionary, had taken José Benito Escobar from León to Managua. But the political relationship filled with fertile contradictions was produced upon meeting Ernesto Cardenal.

It occurred to us to contact him at the end of 1967. We had returned from Pancasán and after that military defeat had initiated a new retreat: the silent accumulation of forces.

I wrote him a letter — that was a time of letters — saying that I wanted to talk with him and, in broad outlines, expressing our interest. In the letter, I spoke of how I had renounced my fear of hellfire and I spoke of our love, a shield against bullets and rhetoric, for the poor.

Ernesto burned that letter as a precaution against a house search but it has been reproduced by a publication of progressive Christians who, through the pages of that publication, sent us signs of life and understanding. The magazine was called *Testimonio* and was edited by Tito Castillo. Here is the letter:

Father Cardenal:

I am realizing a long-time wish of mine: to write you. I thought of writing you a long explanatory letter, but changed my mind. I would prefer to speak with you.

Because of the particular conditions in which I live, it is impossible for me to visit you, as would be the proper thing to do out of courtesy and respect. It is you who will have to come to me. To speak with you will be to receive the visit of a long-awaited friend.

We have renounced the pleasures of life. We cannot even satisfy the elementary need of seeing streets and the incomparable spectacle of human beings coming and going. In a certain sense, we are monks, with the difference that we are closer to death. But we are content.

I was educated in the Catholic religion, the practice of which I abandoned with repugnance.

I knew a Church that jubilantly rang its bells and celebrated when General Somoza visited my Matagalpa. A Church that haughtily received the candle offered by the rough hand of a peasant, but refused to redeem him from his poverty, placing itself on the side of the landowner. A God who pardoned the abundant sins of the rich and denied entrance into His temple to poor girls who were expecting an illegitimate child.

For me, this situation is responsible for my Manichaeism, which I have now overcome.

I killed the God of that Church within myself. It seems, however, that He does not want to die.

In the jungles of Colombia there has been a new Bethlehem. Camilo Torres Restrepo told us so before he died, or perhaps as he was dying. And he also told us that there are other Bethlehems and other mangers. Might not the Council be a new Bethlehem?

I have seen this new God being born within myself — I don't know why this brings to mind the memory of my mother — and I have watched Him growing. But it is not spontaneous growth. He grows because He is nourished by the preachings of Father Juan Carlos Saforoni in Uruguay, or the sermon of Father Cardenal at the funeral of Fernando Gordillo. Of course, this God's life is precarious in me. The more He grows, the more nourishment He requires. It will depend on the immediate attitude of the Church, or at least of its honest and progressive sector, if He is to grow vigorously. Otherwise, He will die of hunger. Father, I await you.

P.S. The person who delivers this letter does not know my identity.

Ernesto did not reply to the letter but came immediately to the appointment in a house located in the center of old Managua. We had a meeting and when, days later, I told Carlos Fonseca about our conversation, he called for another meeting. He wanted to meet and speak with Ernesto himself.

The poet showed up punctually. I waited for him on the sidewalk in front of the house, disguised as a National Guard officer. After a momentary shock, he went in to talk to Carlos. It was a long conversation.

These and other conversations focused on what should be the role of Christians and, specifically, the role of Catholic priests in this country. One of our concerns was that, when the Somoza dictatorship fell, a wave of excessive reprisals against representatives of the Somoza regime would be unleashed. At that moment, which was as inevitable as the sunrise, the Church should exercise a role of containment. Together, we would be able to neutralize that drama.

Naturally, the arguments and themes grew more extensive on both sides. There were understandings and contradictions. Ernesto, as happened afterward with Uriel Molina and other progressive priests, understood us but at the same time were distrustful. The ebb and flow of these conversations in the catacombs bathed both banks. They were afraid that we would use them to further our political objectives and we had reservations that their ideas would contaminate the ideological purity of Nicaraguan revolutionaries.

These shared reservations were the object of long discussions; we tried to convince them that the Church should carry out that humanitarian role and that the philosophical contradiction was irrelevant. The essential thing was survival of the country, rescuing the people, and saving their bodies and souls from the Somoza inferno. Besides, we reassured them that the religious beliefs of the people would be respected and that — for reasons of political realism and common sense — their survival was assured and that the Sandinista Revolution would not attack Christianity, but on the contrary would make efforts to form something closer than an alliance with the Nicaraguan Church.

Carlos had great confidence in the poet's honesty and sense of responsibility. Ernesto offered himself completely in his gaze. One had only to see — as anyone can see today — the eloquence of his eyes.

In some of these conversations, I proposed to Ernesto that he join the movement, not as a guerrilla, but that he go to the mountains and become a peasant priest in Matagalpa and Jinotega, in the manner of the worker priests of Europe, who labor in factories and live with the workers, because, given the conditions of economic development in Nicaragua, such an experience was possible.

Ernesto thought the idea an excellent one but there were objective obstacles that prevented him from carrying it out. He agreed that the Church should restrain the violence at the moment of political change. Carlos went much deeper than I in analyzing these problems and thus a permanent relationship was established.

Carlos was interested in the Solentiname experience. We were going to visit the archipelago but obstacles at the time prevented us from doing so. A person living there was suspected of being an agent of the enemy's security system. Today, we know Solentiname to a certain extent through the poetry of the peasants, the assault on the San Carlos fortress, its martyrs — Elvis, Donald, Felipe and Laureano — of fragrant memory, the landscapes in the primitivist paintings. But our trip to Solentiname is still postponed. When we arrive there, it will be like meeting Ernesto Cardenal anew, as though we have always known him. Solentiname to me is still paradise lost.

I will have to settle for having known Ernesto even though I do not know Solentiname, which is a part of Ernesto: a landscape he invented, a painting, a sigh, water, a bite of land, a paradigm. I settle for having known Ernesto the poet, a great poet; for having met the underground priest. But after getting to know him as a priest and brother, it is better to know him as he is: an exceptional man, incapable of burning a grain of incense to his own glory. Ernesto is not timid; he's as simple as an orange leaf, as humble as St. Francis of Assisi.

As an exemplary priest and a famous poet read in every language, including the language of the poor, he is above all a man who lends prestige to the revolution.

One must love and respect Ernesto as though he had died and been resurrected. One must love him here and now. Nicaragua has reason to feel proud of certain men. How can we fail to be proud of Darío, or Sandino, or Carlos?

I would add, at no risk whatsoever, how can we fail to be proud of Ernesto Cardenal!

4

The later convergence of revolutionary Christians and Sandinista militants was virtually a natural process.

In Nicaragua, as in many Latin American countries, Christianity is also a political fact; and political facts favor or oppose dictatorships and imperialism.

With the barriers to the participation of Christians removed, the FSLN grew in strength:

> At times, the base communities acted as sources of raw material and political propaganda. In this sense they were extremely important inasmuch as they broke down the taboo of incompatibility between Christians and Sandinistas. A vision of Christianity favorable to the popular interests was disseminated through them.[1]

In this convergence, lucidity took priority over dogma; concrete interests over interminable philosophical expositions. Ricardo

[1]Luis Carríon Cruz, in: Margaret Randall, *Cristianos en la revolución. Del testimonio a la lucha.* (Managua: Editorial Nueva Nicaragua, 1983).

Morales Avilés played an important role together with certain other priests like Uriel Molina, Fernando Cardenal and Félix Jiménez, in giving the Christian movement an increasingly political orientation.

5

I was given the use of a safehouse only for a week. I was stuck in a room all day long without going out, without speaking, without sneezing from 6 p.m. on. What heat! What boredom!

"In the morning you can express yourself freely," Ruth, the owner, told me. "Everybody's at work; even I, who work in a bank and am alone and with no commitments. And I don't want any commitments, lengthy or otherwise, just so you're clear about that. I rent the other bedroom to a couple. If I ask you not to talk or sneeze, it's because you can hear everything in this house. They're a young couple...well, not so young. He's 50 and she's 39. They are Catholics and they say the rosary aloud every night. At least they do it in their room. That's their thing. I'm a Catholic myself, but not to such an extreme," Ruth finished.

That night I remained silent. And I heard them saying the rosary.

Good God! I couldn't believe it: the two of them begged the Lord's pardon for the sin they were about to commit. As I heard their ejaculatory prayers pronounced in strange, suffocated voices, I understood what sin they were referring to. It was no more nor less than the sin of the flesh.

Their ejaculatory prayers accelerated like the hoofbeats of a horse trotting in the sun; they grew agitated and in the midst of huffing and puffing the woman cried out, "Fantastic!" He was snorting. There was no doubt about it. Those two good Christians were making love.

I had no chance to talk to Ruth. I waited the following night, but nothing happened. They didn't pray. Nobody said, "Fantastic!" No huffing or puffing. Everything was quiet. In the morning I was awakened by the invocation and, a bit later, the storm broke.

Ruth returned during the day and I told her about the singular episode. She didn't believe me. According to her, they visited altars, recited *novenas* before the heavenly corpse, blessed their bread, and even a cup of coffee merited a brief prayer. "Now that I think of it," Ruth said pensively, "when they invoke Heaven, his eyes shine and hers roll upward." I invited her to hear the 10 p.m. performance. She promised she'd come, a bit skeptically, but with a gleam of curiosity in her eyes. During the day, I read Jorge Amado's *Clove and Cinnamon*, which helped shorten the hours. Ruth appeared at 9:45 and was about to give up when that strange liturgy commenced. Nevertheless, he interrupted their prayers to say: "Don't you think it's more of a sin to beg pardon for sinning? Haven't you noticed..." Ruth perked up her ears and closed her eyes, while I opened my eyes and pressed my ear to the wall, "that we are using our prayers as a pretext to sin wholeheartedly?"

"That's true," she said. "with just this little bit I'm already wet."

"Don't say another word or I won't answer for myself."

"We ought to consult Father García."

"No, I don't trust him. I don't like the way he looks at you. He starts praying and at the first indiscretion you'll fall."

"Don't be silly; you're the only one I like. I don't offend you even in my thoughts. Besides, he's a priest, he's sacred."

"Aha!"

"We can consult Father Navarrete, he's an old man. Perhaps it isn't a sin to ask forgiveness for delightful things. Maybe it's the prize they'll grant us for our faith and devotion to Jesus."

"Promise me that tonight we're going to pray, and tomorrow we'll talk to Father Navarrete."

Ruth was dying of laughter and after the whole thing was over, she ran out clutching her stomach with both hands, while I was left alone.

Chapter
Twenty-Five

1

One afternoon I was sitting in the safehouse in the San Sebastián neighborhood, dying of heat together with Velia ("Marina"), when Daniel Ortega arrived to warn me that they had captured Lesbia Carrasquilla, a beautiful girl in every way.

Daniel left and a short time later a young man on an asthmatic motorcycle appeared and addressed the owner of the house from the doorway: "Señora," he asked, "do you know where I can find a house for rent?"

"No señor."

"Why don't you rent me a room?"

I turned my back to him, listening intently.

"I've got to find a place to live."

"No, I don't rent rooms," she replied.

After scanning the layout of the interior the man left.

"Marina," I said urgently, "we have to get out of here immediately!"

"I'll get a few clothes together."

"Hell no! We go as we are!"

An hour later a National Guard patrol led by "No Neck" Torres jumped over the wall, broke in through the windows and searched everywhere, even the larynx of the toilet.

We looked for any place to hide and found an abandoned house that had rats as big as cats and holes in the roof the size of windows. A few days later, Carlos arrived and stretched his long legs out on the floor. We gave Velia the only mattress. A week later we had five safehouses in that neighborhood.

Daniel Ortega was captured on November 18th, beginning what would be one of the longest imprisonments in the history of the FSLN.

2

One night before I left for Havana, Julio Buitrago arrived from Cuba. We exchanged pistols, ideas, expressions of affection and talked until dawn. I slept all day clinging to Velia, who wept.

I left for Cuba with Germán Pomares. I left Velia behind with the promise I would send for her.

Some weeks later I was in Havana and, on instructions from Carlos Fonseca, I was put in charge of the heterogeneous group that was training in Cuba.

We raced like marathon runners, swam like Johnny Weismuller. When we went on marches in the Escambray mountains, I was reminded of the garden of my house.

My substituting for Oscar Turcios as leader of the group created internal problems. The decision had been unjust because it was based on erroneous and superfluous information which, coming from Nicaragua, was difficult for us to evaluate.

I was not magnanimous enough to renounce my command, and Oscar felt he had been badly treated. In the end, maturity imposed itself on us and we decided we would all return to Central America.

I left in the first group with Germán Pomares and Oscar Benavides. In Prague, we stayed at the International hotel while we made arrangements to get to Switzerland and, from there, to fly to Costa Rica. This spiderweb of an itinerary was imposed on us revolutionaries by the blockade of Cuba.

In the Czech capital, we met a beautiful Spanish-speaking woman who befriended Germán. Benavides and I devoted ourselves to touring one of the most beautiful cities in the world. While our infatuation with the Street of the Alchemists lasted — I later learned that García Márquez created the figure of Melquíades, the magician in *One Hundred Years of Solitude,* there — we looked up some Latin friends. Two weeks later, we left for Switzerland.

There we found the brothers Gustavo Adolfo and Oscar René Vargas, Sandinista militants, and Constantino Pereira, who, as an FSLN collaborator, had been imprisoned in Managua for several months. Tino, intelligent and cordial, took us to the cafe where Lenin and Tristan Tzara played a legendary game of chess. Nobody knows who won, although the Dadaists say it was Tzara and the Marxists say it was Lenin. I think that Lenin won, despite the fact that he protected neither his king nor queen, but only his pawns. Tino took me out on a newly built freeway in a newly bought car, with which we broke the sound barrier. I still don't know why we weren't fined, and more to the point, why we survived.

3

Oscar Benavides spoke in a strange, solemn manner. He wouldn't say it's raining, rather that a pluvial precipitation is falling upon us. Instead of complaining that he was tired, he'd lament being caught up in a state of fatigue; and if he had a cramp, he'd confess that he had suffered an involuntary muscular contraction. If it was nighttime, he yawned happily at being ensconced in nocturnal hours, and if he caught a cold he'd ask for a tablet of acetylsalicylic acid with its analgesic and antipyretic properties to alleviate his pathology. At breakfast, he didn't drink milk but the pearly liquid of the bull's consort. A chair was the place where one would set down his gluteus maximus, and the sky was a distant point in the universe where stars, planets and satellites floated, to be admired with the optical organs.

Oscar was valiant and had a revolutionary mystique the size of an army. As we boarded the plane in Geneva, when he was on the last step and chatting happily, his Browning pistol slipped from under his suit and fell clattering down the metallic stairs sounding like the trumpet of Final Judgment. He scurried down to retrieve it, while I tried to look like I'd never seen him before in my fucking life. I gestured to him to sit far away from me. I was also armed with a pistol and a grenade between my legs forming a bulge that, somehow, the stewardesses failed to notice. They must have thought I had a hernia. The plane delayed its departure for several hours. At least that's what it seemed like to us. Back in those days, airplane hijackings were rare and pre-boarding searches nonexistent.

We arrived in Panama. From there we entered Costa Rica by ground transport, with false passports.

274

4

Sometime during this period, Carlos Fonseca, using Napoleón Chow as an intermediary, held an interview with the intellectual José Coronel Urtecho.

Coronel Urtecho was something else, or the same thing in another dimension. At the time, I didn't know him except through *Rapid Transit*. Eighteen years later we would be friends.

When he turned 80, he told us with the shrewdness of a watchman: "When I was young and fell in love with a woman, I was afraid she'd say no. Now when I fall in love, I'm afraid she'll say yes."

Carlos Fonseca, while still an adolescent, had foreseen José Coronel Urtecho.

In the mid-50s, in the magazine *Segovia* Carlos introduced a number of Nicaraguan poets, among them Coronel Urtecho. His article, which included a fragment of "A Little Ode to Uncle Coyote," a poem representative of the way the Vanguardists handled our folklore, reads as follows:

> The extraordinary figure of José Coronel Urtecho, a Nicaraguan who writes good verses, appears as little more than a name or rank to the majority of Nicaraguans who know how to read...
>
> We *nornicaraguanos* are those Nicaraguans from the north who know a great deal about coffee and cattle and not much about poetry...To introduce José Coronel Urtecho is a literary obligation of *Segovia*. This is no military man; he is a Colonel but only by name. He was born in Granada back around 1906; he attended Jesuit school (Centroamérica) and later went on to study humanities at various universities in the United States. With the vast knowledge he acquired and his own creative talent, he was able to inspire the generation from Granada that a short time thereafter would be called the Vanguardist movement, in which flowered poets like Pablo Antonio Cuadra and Joaquín Pasos.

He has been a deputy to the National Congress and represented Nicaragua at the centennial celebration of the University of Salamanca. His refuge was always the Hacienda San Francisco del Río, on the banks of Nicaragua's San Juan river. He has distinguished himself in the Western Hemisphere as the best translator of U.S. poetry, and recently, in his book *Rapid Transit*, he has described brilliantly the life and work of the people of the United States at the time he was there studying. Through this book one comes to know San Francisco, California, the waters of the Mississippi, a little history of the San Juan river, and vague recollections in which the reader himself seems to participate in the adventure of the protagonist: Coronel Urtecho.

He has cultivated all phases of poetry. Among his popular poetic works is his "Little Ode to Uncle Coyote," especially popular for its nursery rhyme flavor:

> And the critter, tooth broken
> tail smokin',
> drowned in the lagoon
> diving for the cheese in the moon.
> And there begins his glory
> where ends his worry,
> thus also did go
> Li-Tai-Po
> Chinese Poet.

His best known poetic works are: "The Parks," "Ode to Rubén," "Mombacho," and "Portrait of Thy Neighbor's Wife." In prose: short novels or *noveletas*, as he calls them, and theatrical works like *La petenera* and *Chinfonía burguesa*, which he wrote together with Joaquín Pasos. His most recent work is *Rapid Transit*. At present he resides in New York.*

---

* "José Coronel Urtecho," *Segovia*, Nos. 6-7 (January-February 1955), p.8. This translation from Tomás Borge Martínez, *Have You Seen a Red Curtain in My Weary Chamber*, pp. 135-136.

When Carlos met José Coronel Urtecho, he spat out the following phrase: "After Somoza, you are the one most responsible for the disgrace of this country...."

Why Carlos Fonseca's juvenile interest in introducing us in the pages of *Segovia* to a Nicaraguan who writes good poetry? Why Carlos' interest as a mature politician in conversing with that singular man, accusing and confronting him from the outset? In any event, the incident verifies the FSLN founder's intuition: his own frankness and his confidence in the personal integrity of Coronel Urtecho, which was vital for a person in hiding.

Coronel Urtecho was reborn when poetry came looking for him again and he had the lucidity, in this case both political and moral, to recognize the volcano and accept the invitation of the lava. One night at Ernesto Cardenal's house, in front of many friends, he read us the certificate of his rebirth:

> After 20 years of poetic silence, or rather sterility, which I unhesitatingly confess, morally crushed under the sense of guilt suffered by much of the country, excepting the oppressed and exploited, the youth, and above all the Sandinista Front, which redeemed the country, freed it of ignominy and led it to victory, I have once again felt the irresistible need to write impersonal, objective, concrete poems that help give verbal form and graphic architecture to the immense content of Nicaragua's irreversible, invincible, incomparable revolution.

If a poet is faithful to his people and faithful to poetry, he is honest, and that, in almost every case, leads to revolution. For a number of years now, the Nicaraguan bourgeoisie —*fat, ostentatious and brainless* — has accused José Coronel of being a traitor to his class, which is definitely a great compliment.

Coronel Urtecho will receive much recognition. People will speak of his prolific production in verse and prose, of his pleasure in conversation, of his capacity for happiness. They will accuse him of being one of those responsible for the Nicaraguan cultural boom.

We, however, wish to refer to his principal virtue, which originates in his principal sins: to have achieved the highest level of decency by means of a relentless exercise of self-criticism.

Only the senile and the dead are incapable of self-criticism. Of course, there are too many dead and too many senile; but José Coronel — who is alive, with no possibility of dying, and very youthful — has strongly criticized his class, the Vanguard Movement and Coronel Urtecho.

Ever since the 1930s, when he returned to Nicaragua and formed a group of young intellectuals, right down to his latest poems, Coronel Urtecho has devoted himself to transferring the center of cultural creativity from the western to the eastern part of the country.

The generation of 1927 did not escape the trauma of the inter-war and post-war years nor the crisis of western culture. The men of those years, as Matthew Arnold used to say, were caught between a world that had just died and one that had yet to be born.

It is his generation, then, that inaugurates the debate between two antagonistic economic, political, ideological and cultural systems; the generation that suffers the impact of the first socialist revolution, the Spanish Civil War, and the sacrificed voices of Miguel Hernández and Federico García Lorca.

It is the generation of the University Reform in Córdoba, Argentina; that of Vallejo and Neruda, of Carpentier and Borges, of Mariátegui. It is the generation of Sandino, the scale by which, without exception, all Nicaraguans of the time were weighed. It is a divided generation, predestined by history to choose sides.

The Nicaraguan literary vanguard took possession of our natural beauty — landscapes, trees, flowers, fruits, birds, lakes and volcanoes — as well as the products of a poor, peasant handicraft industry — hammocks, hand-carved gourds, woven mats — and they also purloined vernacular speech. The literary vanguard was the ideological and political rearguard of that period. In *Three Lectures For Private Enterprise,* Coronel Urtecho affirms:

> In the late '20s and early '30s there appeared among the so-called Vanguard group in Granada some young iconoclasts, or at least irreverent youths, who together with

me tried to free both our speech and our lives of all bourgeois hindrances and adiposities or expressions, calling things not only by their proper names but also at times calling bread wine and wine bread, as if changing through words the very form of things, but perhaps now with the intention...of one day in Nicaragua changing bread into real bread and wine into real wine, not just the imported kind but also, perhaps, bread and wine produced in our country and available to everyone.

They appeared in politics with the name of reactionaries and they were reactionaries out of snobbishness and conviction. That word, which in their mouths meant seeking roots in the past, or rebelling against their parents on behalf of their grandparents, as the poet said, restating — I believe — Jean Cocteau, or — according to Cardenal — Ernesto Psicary, but in reality it was in accord with their class origins. Their grandparents were their predecessors, the ones from farthest back, from the colonial period.

Coronel Urtecho sneezed, reacting against his class background, as one who curses his mother while remaining — until much later — by her side. Commerce and business speculation were for him the opposite of culture, the counter-culture, rather than the bourgeoisie itself, wherein lay the root of the problem. This is also the reason why he once expressed his support for the Somoza dictatorship.

All of this explains why the literary vanguard was contradictory, irresponsible, brilliant and influential. It is not possible to absolve politically this literary movement, but the revolutionary vanguard — can there be any doubt? — has absolved José Coronel Urtecho.

His ideas remain recorded in his written work, but the poet also teaches, stimulates and illuminates in his conversation. There is complete coherence in his aesthetic ideas. The great iconoclast greatly respects, that is, assimilates, accepts and reworks universal culture. From the time of his first visit to the United States, he learned the modern poetry of the English language, particularly that of Ezra Pound, T.S. Eliot and William Carlos Williams.

He does not deceive us, though on the other hand his guileless face scarcely reveals the seriousness with which he plays chess, or his propensity for leaps in multi-colored parachutes, or the passion of his skirmishes with adjectives and their placement. Behind this apparent spontaneity lurks the rigorous intellectual, attuned to others' cultural creativity, vigilant of the meaning and form of contemporary poets.

The sad self-sufficiency of post-Darían modernism, the arrogant, unintelligible language of the Central American Institute of Business Administration (INCAE) — with which the poet makes his final ideological concessions; the cliches, errors and half-truths, the platitudes and verbal burro dung of the tyranny; the cruelty, the philosophy of contempt and foreign domination, all led to a crisis in which the only possible response was revolution. That is, the possibility of a new aesthetic, capable of revealing the true coloration of everything.

The intellectuals, the poets, were in José Coronel's opinion the ones called upon to confront the inflation of language, to make a final attempt to interest the bourgeoisie in a modern response. What he failed to understand is that the bourgeoisie, in accordance with its own true nature, was comprised of charlatans, incompetent technocrats, and stupendous villains: ants in their labyrinth.

With rare exception, it was the poets and other artists who executed the first Somoza, who had five fewer lives than a cat. It was they who brandished metaphors, paintbrushes, rifles and hand grenades; it was they who identified with the classes that made possible the triumph of the revolution, they who contributed to the epilogue and the opening of new chapters in this history — which grew less and less noisy, in contradiction of Montesquieu.

It was also Coronel Urtecho — whom we should promote to the rank of General — who reminded us that Rubén Darío, baptized by him the "Bolívar of Culture," was a leader of the cultural independence of Hispanic America and, therefore, the hero of our own national culture.

Coronel knows how the relationship between politics and intellectuals developed and how these two fields have come together and separated. Ever since colonial times, politics was the only outlet for the worker of words who had something between his ears. Thanks to the intellectuals, he says, certain words had meaning and even a degree of reality.

280

In the 19th century, Rubén Darío is — to be redundant — an exemplary case, because with him the separation between the poet and everything else, between the reality of the word and the verse, between the political and economic reality of his "dense municipal epoch" reaches its peak.

Nevertheless, the modernist legacy that evolved purposely into aestheticism — the opposite of a modernism with leopard's claws, immaculate swan whose wings attest to the struggle against the barbarians and Nimrod's poisoned dart — left no tradition, and the following generation — that of 1927, Coronel Urtecho's generation — marched off in the other direction. In the difficult year of 1936, however, this intellectual, acting as a politician, did not achieve the stature of his words. *Life Lived and Shared as the Life of the People* is merely a desire. But from that time on, he denounced the accelerating militarization and commercialization of society which amount, as he says, to the "de-intellectualization" and "deculturation" of the country denounced by Ernesto Cardenal, who, from the mid-1940s on makes his actions conform to his words.

For Coronel Urtecho, giving due value to poetry and to intellectuals is, above all, to defend culture from the monetarist spirit of the Granadan oligarchy, in the moldiest sense of the term. We agree with this part of his thinking, but we insist: one must go to the root of the matter, to the class itself and confront that class if the spirit of the new revolutionary culture is to flourish. That is what Coronel Urtecho himself would say later on, referring to Leonel Rugama.

For Coronel, culture was that which was born of culture, which is constantly changing; culture was the synthesis "of all knowledge relevant to man in our time" — a thesis that would later be surpassed. At that time, he explained it as follows:

Culture is not a matter of possessing a great deal of knowledge, nor even less of possessing specialized scientific knowledge, rather of one's knowledge and experience forming an organic, living whole that is revealed in the activities and expressions of a person or a collectivity ... I believe it was Max Scheller who said or quoted the saying that the cultured man is the one who if he knows, no one knows he knows, and if he doesn't know, no one knows he doesn't know.

From the revolutionary viewpoint, culture cannot be private property nor a monopoly of intellectuals, rather it must belong to the people, concepts which, in the end, José Coronel Urtecho himself would accept.

For such a culture to exist, it must be rooted in new values: a universal culture because it is a culture of our reality and of our time.

It is not my place to play the role of the Lone Ranger, settling accounts with the ideological consciousness of the past. I believe, from a general point of view, that the Vanguard Movement, and therefore José Coronel Urtecho, contribute artistic elements that the revolution appropriates, above all through Leonel Rugama.

The new politico-literary dimension occurs in a context where the struggle for culture is not separate from the struggle for revolutionary transformation. But it is indisputable that this rupture, on the political level, utilized the metamorphosis of language created by the Vanguard Movement.

José Coronel Urtecho himself admits this; but what seems to us most worthy of recognition, we repeat, is his decision to accept the responsibility he bears for some of the sins of our history.

It is not just rhetoric to say of José Coronel Urtecho, already in his 80s, what he himself said about his wife, María: "So much life after so many years!" And this vitality is not only manifest in his criticism of the past, but reveals itself as well in his constant effort to understand the revolution — a sort of lucid agony that is life rather than death that he might share the perspective of the people.

This is reflected in his three great poems, written under the influence of the popular victory: "Panels of Hell," "The Past Will Not Return," and "Conversation With Carlos."

His fondness for cards, his continual reiteration of arguments and his use of dialectics in the field of aesthetic expression are, among others, characteristics of the poet. But José Coronel Urtecho's profile is defined by María Kautz, a woman who is one and many women simultaneously.

Aside from his political commitments, the conjunctions that Coronel Urtecho sets marching like erect little soldiers of tin and pollen through his poetry of pronouns, nouns, verbs and occasional adjectives are required by his fusion with that woman who has been the poet's very existence:

> It's sufficient that you are here, that you are
> That I can call you, that I call you María
> To know who I am and know who you are

This is not a play on words; the distance between this man and woman does not exist except that he might be, while she already is. It would be unjust to speak of José Coronel Urtecho without mentioning María Kautz, or to speak of María while avoiding mention of José.

The sluggish, middle-brow Nicaraguan bourgeoisie rejected his offer. The revolution adopted him once and for all: the bread was transformed into bread and the wine into wine. And now, José Coronel Urtecho, we can share the wine and the bread.

5

I arrived in Costa Rica from Switzerland. After several months in San José, living in the house of Santiago Martínez, Henry Ruiz ("Modesto") and I were arrested while attempting to purchase arms.

They deported us to Canada by plane, but we didn't get past Mexico. We were arrested in Benito Juárez International Airport and a blond, violent character started insulting us: "Communist sons-of-bitches, we're going to kill you here!" I had to restrain Modesto who, despite the fact we were in an office next to a holding cell, wanted to give the bastard his just desserts. They returned us to Costa Rica. A rescue attempt was planned at Juan Santamaría Airport with a squad led by Germán Pomares, who hid in the grass next to the runway, armed with a Garand rifle. The squad's mission was to provide getaway vehicles. But it proved impossible to pass us the pistol with which we were to initiate the operation.

They sent us to San Andrés Island. Once aboard the plane, I suggested that we hijack it using a razor blade. Modesto was in agreement, but in the end I was possessed of too little resolution and too much realism.

Once on the island, the local bishop helped us board a plane to Medellín, Colombia, an industrial city, cradle of Phoenicians and poets: Tomás Carrasquilla, León de Greiff, Fernando González, where Porfirio Barba Jacob strolled his horse-like figure.

I recalled that Ernesto Cardenal had studied for the priesthood in the village of La Ceja, near Medellín. We went to the Seminary. The director, a bishop, gave us money and a letter requesting the general secretary of the Foreign Ministry in Bogotá, a man named Londoño, to attend to our needs.

In the Antioquian capital, a revolutionary priest, Vicente Mejía, offered us refuge. He was a young man with the gentle features of a prophet; his whole body vibrated with energy. In the Caribe neighborhood where we were living, Mejía had organized the slum-dwellers, who form a gray belt encircling the bustling city. He was soon withdrawn and replaced by a priest who was even more reactionary than Monsignor Pablo Antonio Vega, a militant of the far right lane of the avenue to the right of the right side of the Nicaraguan right.

We were arrested and sent to Bogotá. We were held for 15 days in the district jail in the center of the city. A fat cop, the chief, who resembled a wounded elephant, locked us up in a corridor. While we were there, we read in *El Espectador* that a group of Sandinista combatants, among them Julio Buitrago, had died in battle. It was July 15, 1969.

6

Julio Buitrago politely took the book out of Doris Tijerino's hands and looked at the title: *Rayuela*. He didn't have to ask the name of the author, because the young law student was not unfamiliar with Julio Cortázar.

In that house Colonel Aureliano Buendía, who was riddled with solitude, had already been talked about. Most of the underground militants devoured Mario Vargas Llosa's *The City and the Dogs*. We also tuned our violin strings to works by Carlos Fuentes and Mario Benedetti.

Juan Carlos Onetti was read in narrower circles. Once Ricardo Morales had a collection of the Uruguayan's books. Nobody read Borges, despite the fact that he is the best.

Inasmuch as his centennial had just been celebrated, the poetry of Rubén Darío passed from mouth to mouth. Carlos, years before, had already pointed out that Rubén was not only a lyrical, but also an epic, anti-imperialistic voice. There was not a single combatant with a university background who hadn't memorized his ode "To Roosevelt." Others recited the "Triumphal March" and "The Motives of the Wolf" and commented on his sonnet in homage to Caupolicán.

Nevertheless, the best known and most widely discussed books were *Sandino, General of Free Men* and *El pequeño ejército loco* [The Crazy Little Army], both by Gregorio Selser. *La patria del criollo* [The Creole's Homeland] by the Guatemalan, Severo Martínez Peláez, would be read some years later.

We read and reread until we knew the whole book by the Czech national hero, Julius Fucik, *Report From the Foot of the Gallows*. Many years later, I met his widow and despite myself broke down and cried like a weanling, much to the astonishment of Gusta Fucikova. I had to explain to her that I also cry whenever I hear "Bésame mucho," not because it evokes any particular woman I have loved and lost, but because it reminds me of Germán Pomares. Germán used to sing that song in our guerrilla encampments. The degree to which Fucik's book influenced the Sandinista mystique is immeasurable, particularly its closing words: "Men: I have loved you. Stay alert."

Selser's works were printed in Nicaragua through the initiative of Silvio Mayorga, and they were distributed by Germán Gaitán. These underground editions were read in safehouses, almost as a moral obligation. The result of that fact cannot be measured, according to Carlos. Sandino on his white mule with his political principles tucked into his belt, rode into the consciousness of the combatants and established his general headquarters in their minds.

Doris had finished drafting a document about the Women's Patriotic Alliance and had begun talking to Julio Buitrago about the demands of Mirna Mendoza's family that the FSLN political activist, Ramón Rizo, marry her in a church wedding.

Someone voiced the opinion — Doris doesn't remember who — that it was absurd to oppose such a desire, that it was good, that marriage has a thousand faces and it didn't contradict Sandinista principles, when they heard the rapid footsteps of a man approaching the front door of the safehouse, located in the Frixione neighborhood of Managua.

The man knocked loudly and Gloria Campos, who was sewing buttons onto one of Julio's shirts, went out to the patio and saw that they were surrounded by the National Guard. She shouted the news to those inside. Doris Tijerino tells what followed:

A Guardsman immediately broke the door down with his rifle butt and started shooting. Julio gestured to me to evacuate Gloria and her daughter, whose father was the slain Sandinista, Enrique Lorente. I took the child in my arms and guided Gloria toward an escape route. When I returned I saw Julio in a combat position on the stairs because the Guard who'd broken in was firing at a height that kept Julio pinned down on his back half way up the stairs.

The Guard didn't notice my return. I took advantage of that to stretch out flat at the very moment when a Security agent crossed the threshold, pistol in hand.

From his position, Julio signaled to me that someone else had entered the house. When the man passed in front of me, Julio fired. The agent fell, wounded, and the soldiers behind him retreated. Julio took advantage of the disorder to get up and climb to the second floor. I, on the other hand, could not move because the wounded man was hanging onto me in desperation. The only thing I could do was toss my revolver up the stairs where apparently Julio was able to grab it. The other Guards managed to shove me out of the house in the midst of the crossfire, leaving me on the sidewalk expecting to be hit by some of the bullets.

Shortly, an officer Cuadra ordered them to put me in a jeep.

In spite of all the shouting and gunfire, I was aware of what was happening. A shout of "Long live Sandino!", "Long live the Sandinista Front!" made me think that Julio had been wounded. He was singing some verses of the National Anthem while firing.

An hour and an half after the battle began, they moved the jeep I was in and parked it alongside the building. A newspaperman with a tape recorder came up to ask my name, whether or not I was wounded, and who was inside the house. Thinking that Julio might still survive, I would give his pseudonym, "Alvaro," but because nobody in the house was returning the enemy fire, I presumed that Julio must be dead.

Turning to the newspaperman, I explained: "It's Julio Buitrago. He's alone and he's probably dead."

The Guard, for some reason, thought that somebody had escaped into the neighborhood from the house where Julio Buitrago had been shooting. They mistook a poor kid who had been asleep in his underwear for the supposed fugitive. He was a 17 year-old boy, José Bernardo Carrión, who worked nights as a baker and slept days. They made him run out in front of the besieged house, and they shot him down. That's the origin of the legend that Julio had come running out of the house firing a submachine gun.

Julio had been fighting from the second floor. After it was all over, they took me up to view his corpse riddled with bullets and shrapnel.[**]

That man fought alone against an army equipped with machine guns, tanks and planes. Carlos Fonseca frequently said there might be heroes as great as, but never greater than, Julio. Few such deeds have been recorded in human history. Perhaps the case of the combatants Marco Antonio Rivera, Aníbal Castrillo and Alesio Blandón, who on the same day they assassinated Julio, resisted the Guard in the Santo Domingo neighborhood. Perhaps Leonel Rugama. Perhaps Leónidas or the priest Diakos who, in 1821, fighting for the independence of

---

[**] Testimony given the author by Doris Tijerino in 1988.

Greece, defended himself from behind a pinnacle of Thermopylae against 400 Turkish soldiers. Lord Byron also made his way there from the Port of Genoa, bringing all his money to finance the liberation of Greece; and it was in Greece that he died of a deadly fever at the age of 36.

Chapter
Twenty-Six

1

They ordered our expulsion from the country, at which point we asked for and received the solidarity of the Colombian Communist Party.

They gave me refuge in the Pablo VI neighborhood of Bogotá, in the house of an engineer. There I met María Cristina, slender of waist, timid, peppered with freckles, who was about to become engaged to a surgeon with thick spectacles and correct features.

María Cristina came to lunch one day. The owners of the house sat on one side of the small table, while she and I faced each other. The little table was low and when our knees touched, we both trembled.

It was difficult to eat and look at each other; we opted for silence. I could see in the engineer's crafty eyes, in those of his wife and in María Cristina's that we all knew, without saying anything, that something had happened, and I was certain that we would make love that night. And so we did, in María Cristina's house, on the living room sofa, while her mother feigned sleep upstairs. She told me she was afraid I would think her a prostitute; I told her that everything depends on the circumstances. And I fell in love.

2

They had given me false identity papers, which allowed me to go to concerts with María Cristina — she played the piano and loved music — and to lectures on various subjects. She came to see me in the house they finally moved me into. There was no hot water there and the sheets were gray despite the fact they had been bought new in a supermarket. There was a knife-edged chill in the room, which was on a second floor in the Las Cruces neighborhood, but it was there we loved each other.

She abandoned her timidity to tell me of her life, of her brothers, of her dead father, of her mother — who had the same name as mine — of her friends, of her first kisses. I told her of my people's struggle, of my father, of Doña Anita, of my being an only child. I concealed my true name from her for months and only told her the day before we left Bogotá.

It was during those days that I read *One Hundred Years of Solitude*, which was already well enough known to be commented on by two attractive, divorced housewives, who discussed the hidden signs of Remedios the Beautiful in the waiting room of Dr. Velásquez's clinic. I tried unsuccessfully to get them to look at me, while pretending to read one of those magazines that are supposed to distract impatient patients.

Those women, of course, didn't know that Gabo [García Márquez] had written 38 chronicles for *El Universal*, in Cartagena, and some 400 installments for the satirical column, "The Giraffe," in *El Heraldo*, of Barranquilla, under the pseudonym "Séptimus."

I don't think they knew — and, of course, neither did I — that Gabo had written more than 200 movie reviews in *El Espectador*, that he had studied filmmaking in Rome, that he had lived in Paris, and that he was in Caracas when Marco Pérez Jiménez was overthrown, much less that he arrived in Havana a few days after the revolutionary triumph, that he had tried his luck while in Mexico in advertising, and that he was a screenwriter.

When I read *One Hundred Years of Solitude*, I was convinced that Macondo is not merely an astonishing locale burdened by the heat of Colombia's Atlantic Coast, but that Macondo is all of Bogotá, that Macondo is the Caribe neighborhood of Medellín, that Macondo is a unique island named Colombia although who says there is only one Colombia? There are several, as the poet Aurelio Arturo said when he spoke of "the countries of Colombia." The whole overwhelms you.

Bogotá is introverted. Medellín bulges outward, whereas the coast is extroverted: it is the curious eye of Colombia. Only there and in Nicaragua — Carlos Fonseca said — could *One Hundred Years of Solitude* have been written; only in Colombia and in Nicaragua — he insisted — is there that much imagination. I had read José Asunción Silva since childhood and while I was in Medellín I read Porfirio Barba Jacob and Luis Carlos López, the half-blind satirist:

> "Hurrah for peace! Hurrah for peace...!"
> Thus
> a hummingbird happily warbled
> warm-hearted, innocent
> from flower to flower...
> And the poor little bird
> trilled just as gayly, perched on the coil
> of the ferocious *mapanare* serpent.
> While in a papaya tree
> a squint-eyed, half-cynical parrot
> gravely scoffed:
> Cuá! Cuá!

The first person to write about the massacre of banana workers was Alvaro Cepeda Samudio in *La casa grande*. The chapter in *One Hundred Years of Solitude* that describes this episode is unforgettable. I read Jorge Zalamea, León de Greiff and Aurelio Arturo — the mysterious, the lyrical, the discreet:

> In the *mestizo* nights that mounted the grass,
> young horses, curvaceous shadows, glittering,
> made the earth shudder with their bronze hooves.

Many years later I would read Juan Manuel Roca, who invites us into a new Colombian poetry, in which we discover Luis Tejada, chronicler of idleness, bullets and proletarian strikes.

I am not sure that what Gabo says about the literature of his country is true, that "the history of Colombian literature from colonial times can be reduced to three or four individual successes." Remember, Gabo, that only a week before *One Hundred Years of Solitude* appeared in Bogota's bookstores, a literary poll was taken in your country which concluded that Colombians have a total inability to create novels.

Tomás Carrasquilla, Eustaquio Palacios, Jorge Isaacs, José Eustasio Rivera, Eduardo Zalamea, José María Vargas Vila, José Félix Fuenmayor, Héctor Rojas Herazo and Alvaro Cepedio Samudio. That's more than three, without mentioning you yourself, Gabo. And you're worth every year of the Buendías' history.

I don't believe that Spanish literature is the same since *One Hundred Years of Solitude*. José Emilio Pacheco claims that "it is a perfect novel, insofar as that adjective can be used without sounding false." I agree with him.

3

It was during those days — January 15, 1970 — that we learned of the death of Leonel Rugama. Consternation congealed Henry's features and my own as well. María Cristina tried to distract me. She took me to the Salt Cathedral of Zipaquirá, an old abandoned mine where we experienced a basilican chill that banished our sorrow for a while.

I wrote to Costa Rica asking them to send me details of Rugama's death.

It was about 3 p.m. on Thursday, and Managua was intensely hot. The poet was reading inside the house. Two National Guard patrols pulled up in jeeps and braked suddenly. They were units of the Special Brigade Against Terrorist Acts, better known as BECAT.

The armed men jumped out. Zoila Esperanza Rodríguez, mother of the Sandinista painter Santos Medina, who at the time was a prisoner, shouted: "The Guard!" and slammed the door shut. Róger Núñez and Mauricio Hernández were also inside that safehouse.

When the officer in charge saw one of his fellow agents, Luis Navarrete, felled by a bullet, he jumped the cyclone fence, dropping his pistol, which was retrieved by a passerby. The other Guards withdrew.

There was an intense exchange of gunfire that lasted two hours. Another officer, Lieutenant Bayer, shouted to the Sandinistas to surrender and they replied: "Go tell your mother to surrender!"

To wipe out the resistance of the three Sandinista combatants required more than 200 soldiers, armored vehicles and military aircraft.

On November 4th, their revolutionary cell had held up a branch of the Bank of Nicaragua, in León, in homage to Casimiro Sotelo, a student leader who had been killed two years earlier together with Hugo Medina, Roberto Amaya and Edmundo Pérez. On that same day, Pedro Arauz and Juan José Quesada, in another act of homage to Casimiro, hijacked a Lanica aircraft and took it to Cuba.

Rugama took refuge in the house of his close friend, Rogelio Ramírez, who was also a Sandinista, and from there departed for Managua.

Six days before he fell, the FSLN held up the Boer branch of the Bank of Nicaragua in an action in which Polo Rivas, Emmet Lang, Olga Alvilés, Julián Roque and Igor Ubeda Herrera participated. Ubeda was fatally wounded during another action a few months later. These revolutionary operations provoked increased repression and searches for guerrillas by the National Guard.

In the little house in the El Edén neighborhood where Rugama was staying, the Sandinistas shouted: "Long live Julio Buitrago!" and all eye witnesses agree that the boys sang the National Anthem. At first it sounded as though their voices were being transmitted by loudspeakers, overpowering the noise of the weapons, and little by little, as their arteries were opened and their riddled breasts lost strength, the hymn died away.

There ensued a consternating silence on the part of the multitude of witnesses to that event, whose only precedents were Julio Buitrago's battle against 300 Guards, and the Battle of Thermopylae. The Catholic priest, Francisco Mejía, appeared on the scene and rebuked the Guards. He was struck down by a rifle butt and hauled off to jail. Before he was freed, he wrote a note confessing that on one occasion two young girls had attended a meeting at his parish house. They were Doris Tijerino and Gladys Báez, who had just joined the Patriotic Alliance of Nicaraguan Women. As we have already recounted, Doris at that time, was already in prison.

On January 15, 1970, Róger Núñez, Mauricio Hernández and Leonel Rugama, the poet, were killed. Rugama's death sent a wave of shock and sorrow through university and intellectual circles. I believe that the sacrifice of this singular youth decisively influenced almost all Nicaraguan poets and writers to join the revolution.

Never before had the poet, the 20 year-old youth, the hero, the martyr and the revolutionary been so steadfastly united in a single individual as in the case of Leonel. From the union of a carpenter and a schoolteacher, only a poet or a redeemer could be born.

Raised in a small, combative city — Estelí — one of those places that frowns just as easily as giving you an eternal embrace, Leonel Rugama was both poet and redeemer.

He had an aura of the nearsighted and the mystic. When he was in the seminary, he modeled himself after the missionary, Francisco Javier, and perhaps that is why in the underground he was called Francisco and why, when he joined the FSLN, he did everything possible to be as moral as Che.

Leonel assaulted hyperboles and banks.

From the early '60s, with that immutable vocation of taking heaven by storm, the FSLN, stubborn, iconoclastic, erupts in our depressing history with the shots fired on the Río Coco and in Bocay. Premonition and hope, an intention and a sign rather than victories, yet a path to pursue toward freedom after long years in the shadows. Later this initial spark ignited the prairie fires of Pancasán and the North. And from the North, to the Segovias and all of Nicaragua. From hope to faith, credibility, and confidence. Children of the Río Coco and Bocay and Pancasán, the new generations, stirred by banners of heroism and redemption, would be enriched by stages of struggle that were still in their infancy.

Leonel Rugama is a true son of that milieu.[1]

The primary antecedent of the poet is freedom in the Vanguard Movement's use of words — which has nothing to do with freedom of the word — that is, Joaquín Pasos, Luis Alberto Cabrales, José Coronel Urtecho and Pablo Antonio Cuadra.

---

[1] Jaime Wheelock, "Leonel Rugama: en el gozo de la tierra prometida," in: Leonel Rugama, *Obras* (Managua, 1980), p. I.

Manolo Cuadra was something else. They say he was a little less illustrious — which has not been proven — and a bit sharper — which can be demonstrated. In political and ideological terms, in any event, he was the most advanced.

Manolo was the first revolutionary poet of the period. He foresaw the Vanguard before the FSLN was founded, inasmuch as he died in 1957. According to Pablo Antonio Cuadra he was the first to leave the group and take a leftist position. Included in this legacy is an irreverence — never abusive — toward Modernism and its totalitarian chieftain, Rubén Darío.

Ernesto Cardenal, Carlos Martínez Rivas and Ernesto Mejía Sánchez are the jaguars who explore the jungles of a new literature. Perhaps one should add Mario Cajina-Vega and, a bit later, Fernando Silva and Guillermo Rothschuh Tablada.

Leonel Rugama is very close in time to the generation of Fernando Gordillo and Sergio Ramírez, and he thrusts his head out of *Ventana* to discover astonishment through a pair of binoculars purchased in the Oriental Market. His language took an unexpected turn. Rugama writes — as suggested by José Coronel Urtecho — a mathematical poetry.

Like Roque Dalton and Ernesto Cardenal, he belonged to that poetic trend called Exteriorism, but from within. It appears that nearly all of his poetry was written in the midst of the political storms of those years. Some of his words fly like sparks, and that was not accidental inasmuch as he had taken his position on the firing line.

Leonel's poetry is sustained by epigraphs and allocutions; no precious jewels glitter there, rather scalpels of irony. He knows how to agitate without falling into pamphleteerism or eulogy. I have in my hands Leonel Rugama's notebook, in which, alongside child-like drawings of skeletons and what appears to be a dance between life and death, are mathematical formulae, theorems, unpublished poems, revised poems, references to Rilke, T.S. Eliot and Joaquín Pasos, as well as criteria expressed in numbers.

I believe Rugama was on the verge of creating a new poetic style and, at the time of his death, was just discovering the evasive eyes of the sun.

Rugama tramples over commonplaces with common, ordinary, everyday speech; he links phrases that suddenly hit you upside the head. He aligns verbs, nouns, a few adjectives, invents where the concepts should be placed and surprises us with a ventriloquist act: he speaks, and what he says comes from the lips of shoeshine boys, market women, coastal blacks — from the Caribbean coast — day laborers and prostitutes.

He talks to them: to the charcoal burner, the taxi driver, the dust-covered truck driver, to the drunken soldier and the shoe repairman. To all the women: the fat-assed vegetable lady, servants, aged prostitutes with sagging tits and young, recently initiated ones. He talks to the skeletons that drift along the streambeds, through the streets of sin, in Acahualinca and La Fossette; he even talks to spiritualists and witch doctors, from whom he buys love potions. He asks them all to tell everyone for 400 kilometers around that Sandino has not died; that he lives on in Che, in Miguel Angel Ortez, in Jorge Navarro, Selim Shible, Jacinto Vaca, and Julio Buitrago; and he asks travelers to announce in Sparta that here we die fulfilling their laws. Rugama kisses the blood-soaked earth and promises: Now, we are going to live like the saints.

And, moving on to something else, which is more or less a variation of the same thing: "Dogs piss on lightpoles..."

"Light," when I first read this verse, had for me a metaphysical connotation until, caught by surprise, I realized it also had a physical meaning; in the final instance, it cast light into my surrealistic corners as well as on the road, where an imbedded stone endeavored to hinder my passing, which was not divorced from realism, but there was something else there. When he says that the novel, *Lost in the Deep Jungles of Borneo*, is "illustrated with gorrillas," I think he's going to say that the gorrillas are illustrious, that they smile, but no, what he says is that "they kidnap the women." Was King Kong among them? The tender woman brings the monster to a fantastic orgasm that sprays the steel and concrete jungle with terror and tenderness in order to give his magnificent uncle the necessary support of a poem, written when Leonel was 19 years-old, which is the precise age at which uncles inspire poems.

One morning his uncle, "of tall race" and "fine Costa Rican boots, did not awake in his bed;" he'd left forever to become a gorrilla: not one of those murderers who abound in such jungles, but one who resembles King Kong. At least that's how I understand what Leonel suggests.

Rugama gathers his chessmen or he smashes the board; he slaps and embraces us before impressing on our consciousness that "the earth is a satellite of the moon."

I don't know what to say when the poet doodles an extrasensory, erotic, automatic suggestion:

> and only its shadow remained
> and it told me
> and it told me

He was and he wasn't an exteriorist; he wasn't a surrealist, but sometimes he was. Rugama was Rugama. Tell me if this isn't perfect:

> and with your sheer skirt
> that flows like water
> over your hips

He fought without firing a single metaphor. On one occasion he wrote: "heroes never said they were dying for their country; they just died." Ah! If it were not that martyrdom is greater than death, I would have saved the poet.

"Every man must back with his actions each word he uses. And one must be very careful about this," Leonel wrote. No one can doubt that he was faithful to this view.

Chapter
Twenty-Seven

1

We went to the doctor. To learn that María Cristina wasn't pregnant was both a disappointment and a relief. We wanted her to be and not to be; it was rather complicated.

At last the problem of papers was resolved and a date was set for our long-awaited return to the guerrilla struggle.

Shortly before leaving Colombia, Henry and I spent a few days in Cali at the house of some friends. Warming our butts in Caicedo Park, we watched the longest parade of beauties in history pass by, which, according to recent reports, still continues. It's possible that others think differently, but Henry and I are persuaded by the laws of dialectical materialism and we believe there is no other place in the world, not even the beach in Ipanema, with so many beautiful women at any time of day.

From Cali we left for Peru, where we looked for a ship that would take us to Mexico. I wrote innumerable letters to María Cristina. Letters came and letters went.

In the first, in March 1970, I told her:

> I will love you by loving those around me, in danger and in thirst. I'll love you so that one day all girls can be loved by men who have no need to renounce love.
>
> From this day forth we won't be the same. We will be better without having to betray one another. I leave you in hopes of seeing you again, but with no ties. If one day you love another, so be it. In a way, I'll be present in that new love. Let no one call you to account for your past. A goodbye in this case would be a lie. Life always places me in a posture of yesterday and, at the same time, in an attitude of tomorrow. When the plane entered the clouds, something inside me broke as if sliced by a knife.

And in another letter, also written in March:

Quito is gray, even though Ecuador, I warn you, has a luminous history, captured by Guayasamín, who's more witch than wizard.

> On earth,
> Quito
> and in heaven
> a tiny hole
> to gaze down
> on Quito.

At the Intercontinental Hotel — where we wound up because of some route mix-up on the part of the airline — even smiles are expensive. Since we don't give tips, the waiters and service people masterfully zip shut their mouths each time they wait on us. Along the carpeted corridors pass businessmen and women in maxi-skirts exuding confidence in the quality of the masks constructed for them in the impatient ladies' salon. If any of them have your beauty marks, they've covered them over with the creams they've used to contrive their next anticipation.

From Guayaquil to Lima:

These days, everyone crosses the Andes by plane. Nevertheless, I got this fleeting vision. Bolívar crossed them on horseback, advancing each inch with the force of the sun; with ant-like slowness he built a suspension bridge between the cold and daring, a bridge of wood joining hunger and the consummation of centuries, a bridge of flour and fire between crags and sky, a bridge of marble between temporal space and the final judgment. First, a lone foothill and a snow-covered peak. Then the plane's shadow resembles a small oasis in the white desert, as immeasurable as the doldrums of a lonely man. I will write you tomorrow.

Now we're in Lima:

We're staying in a house where a motherly old lady waits
on us affectionately. She has a recently-married daughter and
two sons, one of whom is studying abroad. People here are
extroverted; couples walk with their arms around each other
and kiss uninhibitedly at the movies, in parks and in
restaurants.

We visited the cathedral. Inside, in an urn, are exhibited
the dubious remains of the despot, Francisco Pizarro. We
haven't gone to the beach yet, but plan to at least once.

Lima is a city where it never rains. When it did rain
some months ago, people thought it was the end of the
world. It hadn't rained in 40 years. Only Vallejo got rained
on in Paris; but Lima is 100% humidity, like a woman
about to make love. Somebody manufactured a potion of
sand, anemic sunshine and broomstraws: it's the skin of
Lima's residents. In the Amazon region there's a town called
Loreto; if one of its women gives a stranger a drink of water
mixed with thorn apple, he immediately falls ill of
gastroenteritis and love. Something like that happened to me
in Colombia, where I was robbed of my wallet and my
heart.

On April 28th, I write her the following:

I have a girlfriend. A few days ago, in the presence of her
mother and her aunts, she confessed her love for me. Her
name is Natacha. I sleep with her: a condition she required
so that later we would get married. Sometimes, when I have
to go to a meeting, she waits up for me, but I always find
her asleep. The next day she refuses to talk to me until I use
all my persuasive powers. Yesterday I confessed that I was
engaged to another. She replied that she'd marry you as well.
She just celebrated her fifth birthday.

With a certain braggadocio:

Don't think for a moment that the struggle only involves
heroic acts. No. It entails, above all, modest, routine,

seemingly insignificant tasks. Talk to Marina and Luz M.; agree on something and do it. For example, meet twice a week and study, discuss and decide on goals. Why do people have to continue with that ridiculous existence of working, eating, listening to music and sleeping? Or must it always be that others sacrifice their lives to make up for our indifference? When you do something for your own people, you're also doing something for mine. You will also find along this path — and I tell you now so you won't be disillusioned — pettiness, egoism and misunderstanding. Despite all that, one must keep on fighting. The world is drawing ever closer to the hour of decision: either you're with the people or you're against them.

On June 5, 1970, I write her about the earthquake. A dishonest letter — that same day I was flirting with a girl from Loreto:

As you already must know, Peru has suffered a tragedy. There are 70,000 dead and an incalculable number of injured and homeless. Economic losses run into the billions of *soles*. Here in Lima the quake was strong but without major consequences. Eight people were killed and several dozen injured or bruised. It is beautiful to see the solidarity of the residents. Everyone is donating blood, offering food and other necessities and volunteering to help out in the disaster area. We are doing our best to be included in a volunteer brigade. We've donated blood and will do so again if necessary. We've also given away most of our clothing. I tell you this not to be boastful, but so you can see what everybody is doing in Lima.

In another letter I'm quite ostentatious in my observations:

In the 12th century the Quechuas developed their economy, their culture and their dominion over neighboring tribes and territories to such a degree that they created the great Tahuantinsuyo empire. The Incas specialized in horticulture. For four centuries they built roads, canals and agricultural communes; domesticated nearly 100 plants; forged gold, bronze and platinum; calculated the solstices, the equinoxes and the length of the solar year. Nazca pottery is the most fragile in the world. They accumulated such abundance that the Spaniards, during the conquest, found storehouses filled with enough provisions to feed the people for ten years. Many have spoken about the socialism of the Incas. Their weaving was of such quality that some samples in museums are more than 3000 years old. Their medicine knew the value of purgatives, bloodletting and the secrets of innumerable herbs, among them quinine. They practiced amputation and cranial trepanation 1000 years before the Christian era. Although I haven't been able to visit Machu Pichu, I can say that the architecture of the Incas is comparable only to that of the Greeks and the Romans. Its characteristic features, according to the experts, are: "simplicity, symmetry and solidity." It was in Machu Pichu that Pablo Neruda wrote his best poem.

I counsel her once again with a good deal of pedantry:

Don't be contented with a law degree and those courses whose purpose is to make money. The dominant classes have to prepare intermediate cadres in certain disciplines so that they are more productive in the dense jungle of public offices. It's alright to take such classes; they're useful for earning a promotion, but don't stop there. Read, study, get involved, break with routine.

On July 14th:

I am sending you a five-*sol* bill for Juana Elvia. Don't think I'm being prodigal; it's that here there aren't any one-*sol* bills, only coins. According to Vallejo, *Trilce* meant a three-*sol* bill, which is less than what I'm sending your sister. I'm also sending her a crisp new 100-peso bill from Chile.

I always look for simple, spontaneous vocabulary. Pretentious words are horrible. You have a rich vocabulary, capable of expressing sentiments. You're capable of composing phrases that, without losing their simplicity, touch my heart. Nonetheless, the word "fire" is as simple as the word "ice." And you're last letter was like that. Last Sunday I saw a Cuban film entitled "David." A moving documentary about Frank País, a hero of the revolutionary war in Cuba, archetype of generosity, audacity and tenderness. Frank loved flowers and children, but he didn't hesitate to kill a hired thug. An interview is included in the film with his mother, who declared: "They killed my son, but that can't be helped now. This is not the time for crying, rather to vindicate the blood of our martyrs." I had to put on my dark glasses because, as you know, I'm incorrigibly sentimental and terrified of being discovered with water and salt on my cheeks. May I one day attain a hundredth part of Frank's worth.

I've finished the work about my country. It runs 100 pages, and I think they're going to mimeograph it. I'll send you several copies. It will be called *Sandino*....

On October 21st, finally in Mexico:

I live on a seventh floor. Down below, children are building toy houses. A couple is kissing in the sunshine. In the distance, workers are putting up a new building. How I need you!

I dreamt that my mother was alive. This happens a lot and I'm always surprised in the dream at my stupidity for having thought her dead. You were at my home; she asked you something and you replied: "I'm in love with someone else and I can't lie about it to Carlos."

I'm one place today, someplace else tomorrow, and the day after, who knows? Nevertheless, wherever I may be, you'll be there too, like a rider on her horse. For me, you are bread and water. Things at home are worse every day. I don't know if the newspapers in Colombia have published anything about recent events.

I've never liked Mexico City because it's too big, with a gray anxiety in the sky, in the people, in the streets. There is hospitality in some corners of this outward jungle. The people, who have an extraordinary history, are for the present asleep. As a consolation and to avoid boredom, I have my work, you, Emiliano Zapata and the murals.

On November 12th, Henry helped me explain the absurdity of her having received a letter addressed to another woman. It was simple enough: I wrote two letters and placed them in the wrong envelopes. Henry gave her an unlikely explanation, which she accepted.

December 24th:

There was a Nicaraguan party that I couldn't attend for security reasons. Inside, I'm a mass of nostalgias. Yesterday, I received my only New Year's gift: you're letter. Since we separated, I haven't written a single new poem. Sometimes I have the urge, but I sense that it will be a sad poem and I avoid it. Last Saturday I got drunk without realizing it on a bottle of brandy, because of the songs we were all singing.

Chapter
Twenty-Eight

1

I'm as naked as the day Doña Anita expelled me into the world and into my aunt Lala's arms. It had been months since I'd taken off my clothes to sleep. In the mountains it's not possible to allow yourself that luxury. And why would you? You sleep alone, accompanied by the cold, by dreams of bonfires and bakeries and burning sand, your only thought that early in the morning, before sunrise, you'll have to get up. That weighs more than a ton: you have to get out of your warm clothes and put on your damp ones. If you don't, the next night you'll have two sets of wet clothing and feel as though a dog had run his moist nose all over your body.

I had come down from the mountains to Managua, and had decided to leave my pistol, clothes, boots, cigarettes, flashlight and all security precautions at the foot of that comfortable double bed. I was hoping to see Josefina — who would eventually become my wife — known in the underground as Valeria. She couldn't find an excuse to get out of the house. I wasn't sleepy and instead of counting sheep, thought of Valeria and the backseat of the Mazda where we had made love. Ricardo Morales was asleep in the next room. Half an hour before going to bed I had phoned Valeria. She said that her mother was there, that she couldn't leave the house, that tomorrow at 10, that she hadn't forgotten me, that I must have given her a love potion. And I was thinking of her great round eyes, her splendid breasts and her crab-like scent when, without any transition, came the apocalypse.

I darted out into the street before the monstrous quake had ended, carrying my pistol, clothing, boots and cigarettes in my disconcerted hands.

Nobody paid any attention to my nudity, nor did I notice anyone else's lack of clothing. I dressed frantically, like a man surprised in the bed of his neighbor's wife. I heard a woman screaming: "Good God! Save my children!" I hesitated for a moment and the children came running out before I'd finished my thought. I went back into the house to look for Ricardo.

Ricardo was disoriented and trying to get out the back way. Once in the street, he expressed his concern for our prisoners and other clandestine comrades. We were in Doris Tijerino's house in Colonia Centroamérica, where the quake was slightly less violent than in other districts.

Fortunately, the cigarette pack was intact and I had another in reserve. I recommend that anyone wishing to savor the most delicious cigarette in the world should light up immediately after an earthquake. (As I write this, I have given up smoking and, while I know I won't go back to it, I want to express my conviction that one of the pleasures that most closely resembles death is to smoke a cigarette after having done something, or after having done nothing at all.)

Forty-four minutes and thirty seconds later — we were still in suspense as the aftershocks continued — a black cat shot by fleeing the God of Wrath, and Ricardo announced a second quake. He'd only begun to speak when some terribly powerful being gave the Tiscapa geological fault another shove.

At dawn, while we were inspecting the damage to the house, we received our first news. We learned that Gustavo Adolfo Vargas López, a lawyer, collaborator and friend, had perished — the first victim we knew of.

2

The different sections of the city flashed through our minds as we learned more about the magnitude of the disaster.

That rumbling beneath our feet had lasted 30 seconds. What caused the earthquake? A subterranean tempest, a ferocious sinking of interior strata, movements in the pyrosphere, the mechanical action of water vapor in the deepest regions of the globe? This was what the scientist Lyel maintained about the origin of all earthquakes, as did Daubré.

According to these two experts on convulsions, water can — and does — penetrate by force of gravity and capillary action to great depths (where, according to Monsignor Isidro Augusto's sermon, Hell is located). When the earth's crust, or skin, contracts, it produces folds which in turn create hollows that fill with enormous quantities of water. When the water comes into contact with the devil's dwelling place, where everything is boiling hot, it evaporates causing a build-up of pressure.

Nowadays it is believed that most earthquakes — which can be detected with instruments as sensitive as a revolutionary's heart — are of tectonic origin. The list is lengthy and dramatic: Lisbon in 1755; the Chilean earthquake of 1939; the one in Callejón de Huaylas, Peru, whose effects Henry Ruiz and I felt in Lima on May 31, 1970; or the quake accompanied by the volcanic eruption of Mount Pelée that struck Martinique.

In any event, that day — or rather that night — the giant stirred twice, which doesn't often happen, and each time he yawned and stretched he shattered 33,000 homes in Managua like a castle of cards constructed by a Peruvian sorceress, killing almost 10,000 people and rending the earth's surface over an area of 27,000 square kilometers. At that hour, people were sleeping, studying topography and chemistry, healing sores, fixing flat tires, telling fortunes, assassinating Sandinistas, selling tomatoes, cheating their neighbors or looting public coffers, making love, smoking Sphynx cigarettes, weaving hammocks and poems, opposing Somoza, watching horror movies, bathing, ordaining that butterflies should define brilliance, struggling against the established order.

José Benito Escobar, Oscar Benavides, Julián Roque, Daniel Ortega, Jacinto Suárez, Manuel Rivas Vallecillo, Lenin Cerna, Carlos Guadamuz, and Leopoldo Rivas were all being held in the Tipitapa prison. Unlike the Air Force prison, whose walls collapsed, permitting the prisoners to escape, the walls of Tipitapa resisted the quake and the prisoners could not get out.

We Nicaraguans, ever faithful to hyperbole in our speeches, poems, and etcetera, believe that our earthquake was the greatest geological calamity in history after the Flood. Gustavo Tijerino wrote a book entitled *The Most Barbarous Earthquake in History*, which is a faithful reflection of the tenderness of Nicaraguans and the way they exaggerate everything that has to do with their homeland.

3

No one knows how many earthquakes the globe has suffered. Sodom and Gomorrah, the walls of Jericho, Pompeii, Barkal in Siberia, Krakatoa in Java, and Guam in the Pacific are some of the victims. A tremor of fragmented poetry struck the author of these memoirs when he met Valeria, and another, registering five on the Richter scale, when he met the Witch. A particularly powerful quake was the one in Mexico, in the middle of the Sierra Madre, which was similar to the one in Andalusia — birthplace of imaginary beings, one of whom impregnated my great-great grandmother.

The most memorable earthquakes in terms of force and damage caused, have occurred in March, December and January, which — until demonstrated otherwise — is simply a coincidence, according to our earthquake expert Alejandro Rodríguez. Earthquakes show originality; they like to recur in the same places. In France and Belgium they prefer the winter solstice, while along the banks of the Danube they prefer the summer solstice. In Europe, there have been more earthquakes in winter than in springtime. In Nicaragua, they've chanced to frighten and set us back in the dry season, which we call summer.

Wherever they occur, seismic shocks are indeed shocking: in the Caledonian range, the flatlands of eastern England, the Rhine valley, or in the Europe of the revolutions of 1830 and 1848, which are also seismic shocks. Or in the Russian steppes, which is both subsoil and conscience, above all since the triumph of the October Revolution.

Afghanistan is a seismic zone; if you don't believe it, ask the seismologists and the United Nations. So are the Rocky Mountains and all of Mexico; in Central America, Guatemala City and San Salvador, too, are vulnerable, while Managua — can there be any doubt? — is the region's earthquake capital, as seismologists, sociologists, the CIA — and its fans — and spectators who walk among its ruins will attest.

Managua was also shaken in 1844, 1885, 1931 and 1968. The worst quakes were those of '31 and '72. Not only because they destroyed buildings, but because they destroyed systems and ripped off masks as well.

Thanks to more subtle and advanced methods of observation, it has been proven that what lies beneath our feet is subject to different pulsations occasioned by brusque changes of temperature and atmospheric pressure, by the pounding hooves of wild horses, by the prenuptial caresses of lovers, above all when they seek their pleasure right on the ground. Honeymoons generally take place in rented beds during trips preceding the onset of routine, so those pulsations are not registered. It seems that the sophisticated instruments only detect movement produced in direct contact with the earth.

4

So what, then, is a tremor, an earthquake, a seismic event? Our people call a minor quake a tremor and a large one an earthquake. For scientists, they are all seismic events and what people experience when they feel one is nothing more than the elastic vibration of the earth's crust produced by a sudden impulse, something like a heart attack caused by a cardiac fracture of the lithosphere.

Predicting earthquakes is a challenge to mankind. Chinese seismologists, using premonitory signals, such as the abnormal behavior of animals, for example, have predicted earthquakes. Nevertheless, months later they were surprised by another enormous quake unaccompanied by premonitory signs.

In our country, Carlos Santos Berroterán predicted the earthquake of 1972 based on considerations of local geology and the presence or absence of water that had filtered into the subsoil. It is said that Don Miguel Larreynaga, a Nicaraguan scientist and one of the leaders of the country's independence, elaborated his own earthquake theory, which was empirical and faulty but not nearly as bad as that of the renowned Santos, who was said to be a charlatan.

To date, there has been no evidence that seismic events prefer certain seasons, months, days or times. Earthquakes, poets and revolutionaries — and I mean real earthquakes, poets and revolutionaries — abhor routine, stagnant waters, boredom. Good poems and events that qualitatively change history shake things up and are appreciated, and there is one seismic event — Marxism — which, unlike others, is universal and predictable.

5

The center of the city was fenced off with barbed wire to decrease its value so it could be bought and sold and rebought and resold. Business, simply business, ladies and gentlemen.

We make up part of what has been called the Third World although there are some who maintain — according to anthropologists, who are confused or have been paid to confuse — that we belong to the Fourth World, that of ethnic minorities. There are certain Nicaraguans possessed of such fantasy that they claim we belong to the Fifth World, which is probably the one conceived of by García Márquez.

The truth, nevertheless, is that we belong to a universe in which demography is not a science, rather a flaw in multiplication attributable, in Nicaragua, to amorous enthusiasm and a scarcity of contraceptives, infant mortality notwithstanding.

A high percentage of the economically active population was employed in agriculture, underemployed somewhere else, busy starving to death or engaged in combat. It lacked technical skills, produced raw materials worth nothing and purchased finished products costing a fortune. This is real dependence.

Gold, platinum, copper, lumber, shrimp for the rich, bananas, sugar, quality rice, *ipecacuana*, which is a purgative, coffee, Nicaraguan *Flor de Caña* rum, which is the best in the world, and poetry. This is what we produce, what they steal from us.

We buy screws, jeeps, some tractors, a certain quantity of Yves Saint Laurent shirts, Japanese vehicles and Italian chemical products. We import English good-byes and French tears. I've known only one person in this underdeveloped world — Arturo Sotomayor — who learned German for the sole purpose of reading Goethe. We also buy mini-skirts from Miami, which use much less cloth but are much more expensive than long skirts from Masaya.

313

We also import — I almost forgot — horror movies and pornographic films. We export fear, because others fear us like the devil himself. It must be because that's who we are, or because, whether you like it or not, these poverty-stricken countries represent a threat to the tranquility of the rich. The earthquake of 1972 was a prelude to a serious social upheaval. There have been other quakes as well, and there will be more.

6

The quake of 1931 jolted a Nicaragua with a weak money economy; exports in 1930 amounted to 8 billion dollars and in 1939 they totaled the same. During the Second World War, a reserve of 15 million dollars was accumulated, only to disappear from the vaults of the National Bank when the gold was physically pledged as collateral for a miserable loan of 500,000 dollars.

Nicaragua was occupied by the Marines. Sandino's guerrilla forces threatened the Pacific zone. Umanzor's column occupied Chichigalpa; General Altamirano's forces moved at will through Chontales; Sandinista forces reached San Francisco del Carnicero on the far edge of Lake Managua; they visited students at the university and workers at incipient union meetings.

Forty-one years later, in 1972, the dictatorship was secure; the Conservatives were tranquil, the Sandinistas silent following Pancasán.

What happened after the earthquake? Managua residents, including bureaucrats and soldiers, were dispersed all over the country. In the first hours, Somoza was left without troops in the barracks. Well-armed North American troops arrived immediately from Panama.

Government officials sauntered about as free of inhibitions as someone strolling nude down Insurgentes, the longest avenue in Mexico and in the entire world. They stole the emergency aid that arrived from abroad, sneered at the suffering of the poor; they held orgies, ran over pedestrians and Christmas trees with their Mercedes Benzes. Somoza lost his inhibitions; without being the Head of State, he placed himself at the head of the National Emergency

Committee and created a Ministry of Reconstruction so that his cohorts could steal cement, bricks, birdcages, paintings, lumber, trained dogs, prefabricated houses, anything and everything.

Anyone who didn't steal was a fool, an idiot; he was looked at askance, scorned; he wasn't invited to cocktails or parties at Denorah Sampson's, where there were two swimming pools with overhead and underwater lighting. It might be added that the government failed to organize rescue brigades; each individual did what he could to save his loved ones moaning beneath the rubble. The main preoccupation of the Somozas was to assure their political survival. In the first days there was looting, repressed with bullets, which then enabled the senior officers of the National Guard to organize the looting for their own benefit. The international relief aid sent in response to the earthquake never reached the victims. It was stolen openly by the Guard.

There was talk of reconstruction but nothing was reconstructed. There was talk of decentralization and nothing was decentralized. There was talk of evaluating the damage and they didn't even take a census of the dead. There was talk of changing the order of the seasons and it never rained.

This lunar landscape was the prelude to the revolutionary developments of the succeeding years. The bourgeoisie began increasingly to fragment and divide; the coexistence between the dictatorship and this sector of society was shattered.

> By 1973, Somoza has alienated the rest of the bourgeoisie. He enters the banking field, invades finance and clashes with the financial bourgeoisie of the country. It was no longer sufficient for him to dominate the means of production, but by moving into the financial scene he threatened the rules he himself had established for the bourgeoisie... After the earthquake, Somoza breaks those rules, creating enmity and jealousy; a political opposition begins to form. In this way, Somoza tips the balance against himself.[1]

[1] Henry Ruiz, "La montaña era como un crisol donde se forjaban los mejores cuadros," *Nicaráhuac*, No. 1 (Managua, 1980): 8.

Chapter
Twenty-Nine

1

I was in Rivas, where they had sent me after the earthquake, living in the house of a couple who worked as nurses — she loyal to the revolution and her husband; he loyal to the revolution. The wife was jealous and when she threw a tantrum she bit, scratched and screamed. I witnessed their quarrels, terrified that the scandal they created would attract the Guard, whose barracks were not on the other side of the world.

The first time they fought, I was so concerned that I packed my things to leave, when the situation began to change. Thereafter, it was always the same, just like so many one-way streets. The husband resolved their conjugal bouts by silencing her mouth with a kiss and raising her skirt.

Her screams of rage transformed into muffled, confused complaints; the complaints into moans, the moans into agitated sounds like someone scaling a steep mountain. And finally, silence, the impatience of having to wait for the next quarrel; happiness and the calm that precedes another tempest.

That particular morning — it was a Tuesday — everything was tranquil. I arose early and my hosts had breakfast. A few minutes before they left for the hospital, someone knocked on the door. I grabbed my Browning and, suddenly, the doorway filled with sunlight and there, svelte, dressed in white, stood Valeria.

My caresses in a single day made up for all the seasons of the year and I was advancing slowly along the contours of her geography when the radio — which was turned up full volume to drown out the collapse and reconstruction of our hips — changed from music to the telegraphic dots and dashes that always precede bad news.

The announcer — it must have been Radio Corporación — spouted something about Nandaime, a house near the hospital, gunshots, bodies. The information meant little to anyone else, including Valeria, but to me it was as clear as if I were living it, because I had been in that safehouse the previous day.

When she saw my face turn gray and me starting to tremble with anguish, she returned to normal, to that serene state that possesses her in the face of danger. I explained things through chattering teeth. I was irritated by her calm.

She dressed and went out to telephone my contact, Silvio Casco. He knew nothing more than what we'd heard on the radio. She asked him to come to Rivas, and Silvio, with his usual discipline and decisiveness, appeared that same night. Little by little the facts became clear.

Ricardo Morales and Oscar Turcios had left the safehouse we'd rented near the hospital in Nandaime at midnight on September 18, 1973. They headed toward "the airplane," as we called the big, noisy car René Vivas had bought for 800 *córdobas*. A National Guard patrol in search of thieves accidentally stumbled upon the two guerrillas. At the moment of their capture, they barely had time to throw away the compromising pamphlets they were carrying and Mariíta, the courier and cook who cleaned the safehouses and kept them free of rubbish and telltale signs, found the papers the next morning when she returned with the breakfast milk. She thought Ricardo, who was going to distribute them at the university, had dropped them out of carelessness.

When they were taken to jail, Ricardo identified himself as Oscar's partner, while Oscar said he was a cattle rancher. Oscar had been through similar situations. On one occasion, he successfully negotiated the release of Roberto Huembes from a barracks in León after the latter had been involved in an automobile accident. Another time he was arrested and, after slipping a few bills to his captors, was released.

The following day, the barracks commandante and several soldiers went to inspect the house where Oscar claimed to have a mistress. His surprised lover, Alicia Bervis — of the most renowned family of long-time collaborators in Subtiava — who was expecting Pedro Arauz's baby, delayed them while Jonathan González and Juan José Quezada reassembled the M-3 submachine gun and .45 automatic they'd been cleaning.

When they gave her the signal, Alicia opened the door and the Guards were wiped out as they entered. During the confused exchange of gunfire, Jonathan was wounded. They left together and headed for the highway.

In Managua, the Office of Security was informed of the facts and it was decided to transfer Major Alfredo Juárez, along with two other officers, to Nandaime.

Juan José Quezada, the karate blackbelt and airplane hijacker, aided the wounded Jonathan during their march. When they reached the Pan American highway they tried unsuccessfully to stop a passing vehicle.

They made their way to a place called Mendoza's mountain, which they judged a suitable hideout. They were discovered by a patrol and defended themselves. One of the Guards was killed. Juan José and Jonathan had no way out. Both of them died. According to the Guard report, it happened at noon.

It is not known whether they fell in the exchange of gunfire or whether Lt. Coronado Urbina, who commanded the patrol, ordered them killed when they ran out of ammunition.

Another patrol had been sent to search the house where the confrontation had occurred. There they found political propaganda and baby clothes. Oscar and Ricardo were taken to a lonely road where, in a simulated escape attempt, they were shot at 4:30 in the afternoon.

It was never established whether or not the identity of the two had been learned before the decision was taken to kill them. The operational report of the Guard, dated September 20th, says the two were not identified until their bodies were in the morgue.

2

Some weeks later, it was made known that the unidentified guerrilla was not Carlos Fonseca — for whom black coffee, a coffin and floral offerings had been prepared in León — but Juan José Quezada. Omar Cabezas assumed the difficult task of breaking the news to his family.

Sometime later, the students of the School of Psychology at the National University asked me to prepare a paper on Ricardo Morales. It was a period when certain sectors opposed to armed struggle were criticizing the "adventurism" of the FSLN and, in the name of revolutionary ideas, called on us to remain passive. I undertook the task and wrote the following:

The first thing Ricardo Morales asks himself in his cell at the Air Force prison is: "What will be my fate?" And next, without worrying overly much about his immediate future, he invokes the cause to which he has dedicated his intellectual capacity and lifeblood: "The important thing is that we are on the side of the people and are shaping their history." At another point he reaffirms his commitment to national liberation and, in accord with this postulate, states: "Revolutionary activity is the art of infusing life itself with the value of an historic mission."

Ricardo Morales devoted himself, knowingly and passionately, to revolutionary struggle. In his politicizing and operational movements, he exemplified self-commitment with all the tenacity of a gardener who cultivates men to put them to work as political cadres. He was slow to cast blame, passionate and precise in his criticism, direct and fraternal. In his eyes was a controlled tenderness that occasionally gave way to flashes of lightning.

He was everywhere and always at the opportune moment: at the university, in proletarian strikes, in any crisis, in the lonely contentment of sentry duty, in his extended hands, as well as his clenched fists. The enemies of our people don't know who they killed — and we speak in the singular because Ricardo Morales and Oscar Turcios were two individuals in a single, complementary whole. In their ignorance and arrogance, they fail to recognize the river whose course they seek to erase; in any event, their happiness will not last long.

Ricardo Morales was born on June 11, 1939, in Diriamba. He spent his childhood and adolescence there, distinguishing himself as an athlete. He graduated in Psychology from the National Autonomous University of

Mexico, where his revolutionary concern was awakened. He participated with other Nicaraguans in some of those exile political organizations where exaltation is the inevitable response to nostalgia and patriotism. In 1968, he returned to Nicaragua and immediately joined the Sandinista National Liberation Front.

Although Ricardo was a passionate person, as is every true revolutionary, this was not an impetuous act. The FSLN was and is the national response to imperialist domination and backwardness, the necessary synthesis of our people's struggle. For a revolutionary like Ricardo Morales, who combined theoretical ability, honesty and determination, joining the ranks of the Sandinistas amounted to a blood oath with history.

On December 15, 1968, the revolutionary leader was captured — when his revolutionary activities were detected by the regime's repressive police — after attempting to flee in a car that turned over. At that time, Ricardo was — and continued to be after he got out of prison — a professor at the National University. Tortured by his interrogators, he refused to say a word — not a single word — about his activities. Some individuals with whom he had superficial conspiratorial contacts and with whom he was confronted in prison, lowered their gaze in shame when his flashing cat eyes stubbornly refused to acknowledge what he'd already denied under torture.

It is known that, just as a prisoner of war captured in action gives only his name, rank and serial number, he firmly declared: "I am a revolutionary and a militant of the Sandinista National Liberation Front."

His conduct conformed to a clear awareness of what a revolutionary's behavior must be, even in the most difficult situations. Sometime later, he wrote from prison: "In the environment in which we find ourselves, it seems that it's not enough to be a revolutionary; you also have to resemble one."

Prison was, for Ricardo, a constant questioning, to which he sometimes responded with further questioning, but also on many occasions with categorical affirmations: "I ask myself if I can't transform this monotony into something momentous." Or:

"Nothing happens here. Nothing but tranquil lockups. The peace of this country is adorned with prisons and the stench of death. Would someone care to make another commentary? To add something else? What is needed is to open and smash what must be opened and smashed, and to clear the way for hope."

Sometimes he shows signs of discouragement: "What weighs on me is this isolation and monotonous inactivity..." But then, immediately and firmly: "The struggle must lead to an outcome in this situation."

The response to solitude can only be achieved in the paradise that men construct with their own hands. "I am doing nothing. Perhaps I'll do nothing, yet I keep on dreaming. My dreams continue to grow, while my vision fails to capture the world of the future." In his reflections, he does not forget one of those transitory cellmates who remained behind someplace for all time:

"Juan Pérez was like an old shoe and he died of incarceration. We were cellmates. We'd go out together to take the sun, line up together to receive our meager food rations. We also shared our rations of silence and oppression. Suddenly, he was no longer with me. They say he died of sickness, of hunger, of sadness, of solitude, of hatred, of a lack of sunshine, of anger. Why not of politics?"

He continues to dream of a flowering, upright society, of a world that has consigned chains to museums. He dreams of his beloved, who also is a combatant and who, like himself, has been subjected to torture. He tells her:

In this solitude I have your smile as compensation
and nobody knew
how my memory placed it on your face.
This morning the scents of your body
remain imprisoned in my senses.

Be happy, little one,
I'm going to bring you our daily bread:
a million kisses
to fill every last recess of your body.

Pain for Ricardo is not the torture with which they try to subjugate his body, trained to resist; it's the anguish of his companion that inspires this message:

...the beasts don't go into the jungle
and the pack in full cry
presses in on those bodies
discovering as many tortures as necessary
to achieve victory.
Neither slander nor violation suffice
to drain you of blood
nor any secret that conspires
to gnaw away
so many inevitable middays...

Doris María Tijerino, his companion, had been raped. Ricardo gathered her tears and donated them to the revolution.

Prison and solitude test the revolutionary's fortitude. His determination not only withstands the test but overcomes it and scales new heights. The bars offer little deterence to Ricardo's decision to surpass individualistic boundaries and commit himself to the revolutionary cause. He states in his prison writings: "It seems very strange. I feel as though I'd prepared myself for this many years ago." Ricardo is free even while in prison. He says so himself in one poem:

Prison
— perhaps it's worth saying —
is no prison for my bones.
It's madness,
to lock up dreams is madness.
— Rage, impotence, bile
of a class already extinct —

324

In prison I'm on the outside,
the jailors are inside...

In his poem "Pancasán," Ricardo announces his own
death and resurrection:

We died so many times we closed memory's eyelids
and we enshrouded with dreams our millions of wounds,
so death no longer exists..."

When he got out of prison, he gave new content to the
internal relations of the FSLN. He moved from the
university into conspiracy, reappeared in workers' strikes,
then in the lecture hall; he returned time and again to
conspiratorial work; and so it was until his death.

There are those who, to justify their own cowardice and
indifference — those who, in the words of Lenin, belong to
the party of the satiated — criticize over coffee the
"imprudence" of Ricardo Morales and Oscar Turcios for
walking around in a small town in the middle of the night.
It's enough to make you puke! There'd be no reason to
mention the "critiques" of such observers — who on top of
it all call themselves revolutionaries — were it not for the
fact that sowing panic can have consequences in certain
misinformed sectors. It's impossible to participate in the
revolutionary struggle without running risks. In the hard
profession of militancy there is a real possibility of having
to make the ultimate sacrifice. To defend itself against this
possibility the revolutionary movement takes security
measures to neutralize the enemy's repressive measures.

We would not do justice if we failed to reaffirm our faith
in Sandinista strategy, and there is no more appropriate way
of doing so than to confront head on the vacillation of the
reformists and the attempts of reactionaries to sow doubt and
pessimism. In Nicaragua there has been no real polemic, no
theoretical confrontation around the objective conditions
needed for a process of armed struggle. Contradictions have
appeared not so much in words as in deeds.

The pronouncements of the traditional left lack
consistency, inasmuch as it is difficult to persuade someone
that the earth is square or that Cornelio Hüeck is a

cosmonaut or that revolutionary warfare is not the fundamental and obligatory form of the Nicaraguan Revolution. If it is true that the "socialists" do not doubt — or don't admit to any doubt — that communism will someday rule the world, or that Cornelio Hüeck is a scoundrel, they do question the validity of armed struggle as the means of achieving our national liberation. It is our obligation to forcefully confront reformist vagaries and foolishness.

In a recent document issued by the university chapter of the Socialist Youth, in which they criticize the declarations of the Fifth Congress of the University Students, we find an expression of the most "radical" thought of the so-called left. It's inexplicable that some people have been unable to comprehend that in this country the dividing line between the exploited and the exploiters is the weapons of the National Guard, whose gunsights are aimed at the exploited.

From the other side of this lethal barrier, we hear the frivolous advice — the threats — that workers in the city and countryside must not try, nor even think about invading the forbidden terrain that is the domain of private property, free enterprise and imperialism. True revolutionaries try to clear away that tangle of wire and bullets which is not only a threat but actively impedes workers from realizing themselves as human beings, from enjoying the product of their labor, from being free. There are those who call this effort by revolutionaries "adventurism," desperation, pessimism.

The situation of Nicaragua is neither new nor unique. The peoples of Latin America suffer capitalism's spurs and goading. Cuba, in its worst hour, was the victim of exploitation, as were Czarist Russia and China. These three countries launched a violent assault on a new reality in which experimentation, failure, repression and apprenticeship were inevitable. No revolutionary victory has been easy. Only the difficult serves to stimulate, says José Lezama Lima.

Fidel Castro was defeated when he tried to take the Moncada fortress by force. It is not superfluous to add that after this failure, Fidel and his comrades were showered with epithets: adventurers, madmen. Other people — or perhaps the same ones — spit back in our faces the failures of the FSLN and complain about the repression. Since when has the revolutionary struggle, even when wielding ideas, not carried within itself the certainty of enemy repression?

Ricardo Morales wrote: "Repression is the ultimate technique, the best invention for overthrowing governments." That's true. Repression, together with organizational and ideological work, is a stimulus for the incorporation into the revolution of important peasant and working class sectors who have come to understand that unions, consumer cooperatives and pleading signatures on manifestos are not enough; that the most important thing is political organization.

Organization allows one to see beyond gastroenteritis and hunger and to struggle for a better life. Trade unions are a school for reaffirming the class struggle and for studying the preliminaries to the seizure of power, that is clear. If unions are used later to confront the bureaucracy that inevitably springs up after the seizure of power, that's alright; but if unions are celebrated as an end in themselves, they're nothing more than a poor magician incapable of pulling out of his hat the solutions that the working class requires for its survival.

Ricardo Morales maintained that while armed violence may be debatable in developed countries, to question it in these preserves of primitive, brutal violence is absurd. In Nicaragua, the situation and its solution are so obvious that even the reformists — amidst sighs and whimpers — admit its possibility; the pseudo-socialists, in Lenin's phrase, "have replaced class struggle with dreams of class conciliation, imagining a socialist transformation not as the overthrow of the dominant exploiting class, but as a peaceful submission of that class."

Affirmed the Bolshevik leader: "Only the bourgeois parties are interested in strengthening the apparatus of repression," that is, the machinery of the State. The revolution, on the other hand, is obliged to "concentrate all its forces of destruction" and to propose as its objective not the perfecting of the State apparatus, but "its destruction, its annihilation." Leninist thinking on the option of revolutionary violence leaves no room for doubt. In *The State and Revolution*, Lenin says: "The need to systematically educate the masses in this, precisely in this idea of revolutionary violence, constitutes the basis of the entire doctrine of Marx and Engels." And elsewhere he affirms: "The substitution of the bourgeois state by the proletarian state is impossible without a violent revolution."

When the "socialists" say that they support "the need for conscientious organization of the proletariat" and that this "presents the possibility of a serious confrontation with the capitalist regime, which, in our country implies armed struggle for the seizure of power," we feel that they aren't taking themselves seriously. They are not deceiving anyone, much less themselves, with these demagogic phrases. When they affirm that "a step as decisive as armed struggle requires a sufficiently organized social base and technical-military capability to defeat the opposing military forces...," they are content to state a truism equivalent to saying that dogs bark or that Anastasio Somoza is a servant of imperialism.

Those who "deny that it is the hungry and exploited who will make the revolution," attempt to distinguish between these and the peasants and workers. But, aren't the peasants and workers themselves among the hungry and exploited? Hasn't it been repeated to the point of tedium that the Sandinista Revolution will be the fruit of a combative unity of peasants and workers, with the participation of students and others interested in change? When has the FSLN or the university students in the Fifth Congress ever said that the contradiction between the bourgeoisie and the working class has disappeared? To affirm, moreover, that the FSLN and the university students are inspired by the ideas of Marcuse is a frivolous toying with arguments.

Ricardo Morales maintained that Marxism is a humanistic philosophy and that the revolution must reduce bloodshed and human suffering to a minimum, but not by "weakening the bourgeoisie economically and politically" through class conciliation and demands, rather through violent confrontation with those who cause the bloodshed and kill thousands of men, women and children by means of hunger and disease. Don't the reformists know that, for different reasons, the National Guard assassinates about a dozen people each day? Are they ignorant of infant mortality due to hunger and a lack of medical care?

The bloodshed caused by the revolutionary war is insignificant compared to the torrent spilled by the crimes of the Somoza regime. The revolutionary war, in the final analysis, represents a saving of blood and lives, although it has made necessary the sacrifice of Ricardo Morales, Oscar Turcios, Jonathan González, Juan José Quezada and hundreds and thousands of revolutionary militants. It would be a serious error to launch into crazy adventures, but it would be even more serious not to prepare the political, material and technical conditions for insurrectional warfare.

Insurrectional struggle requires an organized base and a technical, military capability. The essence of the matter, nevertheless, is that one must remain true to his words, must prove with deeds what he states in phrases — phrases that on the lips of "reformists" are highly suspicious. The humanism of the reformists is demagogic, a fog of words in which they conceal their vacillation.

We would like to know where they get the notion that the "peaceful" transition to socialism is drawing closer. Recent events in Latin America demonstrate the contrary. But there is always a way to justify the unjustifiable; now it turns out that for these "socialists" the principal responsibility for the coup in Chile lies not with imperialism or the Chilean oligarchy, but with the comrades of the Revolutionary Left Movement (MIR).

In Chile, it was shown once again that revolution remains impossible without the intervention of that ancient midwife of the new society, violence.

With respect to prolonged struggle, implicit in any people's war, the reformists speak gibberish. According to them, the concept of prolonged struggle is the result of desperation and pessimism. Where are we, anyway? First they say the FSLN thinks only of the short term, and that, of course, is adventurism; then they accuse our revolutionary organization of advocating "prolonged struggle," and that, of course, is desperation and pessimism.

What happens is that no matter how one discusses revolutionary warfare, the reformists will always find a way to deny its correctness, its possibility. Prolonged struggle is a sequence of stages that begin with the painstaking preparation of political, material and technical conditions and whose breadth and depth will be determined by concrete circumstances, the ability of the revolutionaries and experience.

It's touching to watch them get all wrapped up in the varied forms of struggle: "Demonstrations, strikes, sabotage, boycotts, terrorism, parliamentarianism, guerrilla warfare, regular warfare, etcetera." At least they added "etcetera." At issue are two fundamental forms of struggle: peaceful or armed. Armed struggle does not exclude, rather pre-supposes other forms of confrontation. To speak of parliamentarianism in Nicaragua is ridiculous. With respect to guerrilla warfare versus regular warfare, they fail to realize that these constitute different phases of the revolutionary struggle.

In the conditions obtaining in our countries, the struggle begins with guerrilla warfare and ends with something resembling regular warfare. That is, with urban insurrections supported by rural guerrillas organized in aggressive columns that no longer simply hit and run but attack and advance in a full-fledged strategic offensive, which implies the maximum use of tactical offense.

It would be too simplistic, however, to speak of a people's war and to point out in advance the stages of such a process in our country. A people's war can start in an unforeseen manner and acquire new characteristics in accord with the conditions of the time and our country. These characteristics can assume different dimensions, wear a thousand faces, manifest themselves in one or in many places, but they will have a single common denominator: their popular character and their revolutionary leadership.

Undoubtedly, the strategic military inferiority of the revolutionary movement will oblige it, in the initial phase, to rely on a respectful, yet audacious tactical superiority, that is, choosing the time and place for combat. This implies technical preparation and, above all, an organized and fully aware social base. Only in this way is it possible to compensate for the material advantage of the enemy. The strategic military superiority of the enemy must be countered with strategic political superiority and tactical initiative.

The revolutionaries will have to change the correlation of material forces and strengthen their political superiority without surrendering their operational and tactical initiative. Their triumph will be the result of a combination of political and military factors. Ricardo Morales was convinced that, to make victory possible, the vanguard had to be consolidated. To be worthy of the name the vanguard had to be turned into a structured, self-aware organic collective and faithful interpreter of popular needs. It must possess audacity and agility.

This vanguard is obliged to interpret reality in the same way it prepares for war and to transmit its knowledge to the masses. This implies a connection with the most politically conscious urban and rural workers and with the poverty-stricken and backward peasants in the remote areas. Somewhat like an umbilical cord.

To speak of armed conflict in the abstract, with that irritating vagueness of opportunists, and at the same time to fail to take a single step in preparation for war is what in every time and place has been called demagoguery. At every stage of its development, the revolutionary movement must prepare for armed struggle.

A combatant cannot be improvised, above all on the psychological plane. War is a prolongation of politics, as well as an art and a science. The bourgeoisie has an army that does not neglect its military training. Revolutionaries, in so far as possible, must create an army and prepare it in every way, progressing from the simple to the complex. But they must start. This effort allows for no delay, particularly in Nicaragua where all paths of legal expression have been blocked.

Ricardo Morales and his comrades died fully conscious of the rightness of these principles and the practical philosophy of the revolution. Ricardo was a conscientious humanist; he took up arms out of historical necessity. Listen to his words:

"I do not believe that violence is a form of self-liberation. Revolutionary violence is an historical necessity to destroy the domination of the bourgeois class and to oppose the overt and covert violence of the capitalist system. Violence cannot be calibrated in terms of the individual. It can be found in the historic development of class relations and class struggle. The only form of violence that opens possibilities for self-liberation is that which pursues liberation from class exploitation."

Let us complete this image: our struggle cannot be understood as a quest for revenge. Revolutionary struggle does not signify killing individuals, rather "killing" the oppressor classes and destroying their means of domination. Armed struggle is the most effective means of "killing" the bourgeois state's instruments of power, that gangster who walks around with a pistol in his belt and the Penal Code in his hand so as to drown revolutionaries in blood or repress them in prison, or, equally important, to short-circuit public opinion.

We believe it is possible to bring together in a single front those interested in social change — as well as other sectors who do not share the same ideology but do share the same political ends — and that this unity will come about through the very process of revolutionary action. To avoid political isolation one need not seek out the enemies of the people, unless they find themselves obliged to follow in our footsteps; one must seek companionship, above all, in the comforting presence of the exploited. The "socialists" who join with the bourgeoisie in the struggle for "freedom" don't place themselves at the head of the column but at its tail. They don't even form the tail, rather an appendix to the tail. Ricardo Morales refers to this "freedom:"

"What freedom are these heralds of the bourgeoisie talking about? Is it that freedom they attribute ideally to each of us and which concrete daily experience refutes with

332

starving children, miserable wages, lack of culture, illiteracy and the oppression of the bourgeois class? The freedom we are talking about is that which we must win on the barricades and that will free us from the yoke of bourgeois exploitation. Socialist freedom is what we are talking about."

In sum, the FSLN, faithful to its pronouncements and its martyrs, has structured itself as a politico-military organism; it has survived despite the blows it has received; it has consolidated its moral authority before the Nicaraguan people; it is overcoming, as it matures, the weaknesses of all youthful organizations and is examining its tactical errors. It is preparing for a struggle in which the problem of power will be elucidated in the fire of rebel rifles drowning out the siren songs of the bourgeoisie and their "socialist" allies.

We do not doubt that this is the time to build our forces, to organize, to prepare detachments for combat. Or, as our Ricardo Morales said:

"At this moment we must be aware of a fork in the road ahead: abdication and a long night of tyranny, or revolutionary firmness and determination to found our own promised land."[1]

Nicaraguan revolutionaries have chosen the path of revolutionary firmness.

3

The above document was edited and distributed clandestinely by the student movement and reflects our thinking at that time.

The death of the two members of the National Directorate in Nandaime was a blow that left us shaken for some time. The

[1] Introduction to *El pensamiento político de Ricardo Morales Avilés* (Association of Psychology Students of the UNAN.)

imperatives of the struggle obliged us to designate replacements without delay. As Henry Ruiz says:

By that time replacements already existed. We had resolved the problem of continuity of command... We accepted the fact that we could fall at any moment, though we didn't cloak ourselves in a sense of martyrdom...of dramatic, last-minute farewells, of premonitions that we'd be shot down as we went out the door...we simply took into consideration the fact that, in accordance with the rules of the game, we might be killed, and for that reason we had a second in command.[1]

[1] Henry Ruiz, "La montaña era como un crisol donde se forjaban los mejores cuadros," *Nicaráhuac*, No. 1, p. 8.

Chapter Thirty

1

In the period following 1970, known as the silent accumulation of forces, the FSLN had a sustained growth. The men and women who would lead us to victory were getting their formation in the mountains. Henry Ruiz ("Modesto") writes:

> We were principally from the middle class, of student origin, and the mountains were like a crucible. There we learned who the real cadres were. Carlos Fonseca was obsessed with improving the cadres under the most difficult circumstances... In the mountains one tempers his will. What is written in books about guerrillas is one thing, but to be one is something else... [1]

During this same period, an underground is organized in the cities that begins to provide leadership to the popular movement. We did not engage in combat unless it was unavoidable; we developed intermediate bodies such as the Revolutionary Student Front (FER); we approached the Christians; we began to organize the women, and we succeeded in disseminating Sandinista views. The enemy believed we no longer existed.

Humberto Ortega summarizes this period in the following manner:

> With more extensive political and organizational work among the masses throughout the period 1970 - 1974, and with a considerable development of the internal structures of the vanguard in the mountains, cities and countryside, the Sandinista war makes a great leap forward in its

[1] Henry Ruiz, "La montaña era como un crisol donde se forjaban los mejores cuadros," loc. sit., p. 8.

accumulation of political, organizational, material and military strength as preparations were made for the politico-military offensive successfully unleashed on December 27, 1974.[1]

2

Following the deaths of Ricardo and Oscar, I moved to Managua. It was during this period that I met Carlos Núñez, who relates how he was recruited into the FSLN by his brother René:

> One night, René showed up in León in a taxi. He was carrying several packages — walkie-talkies — and he said, "Help me out. Take these to Aunt María's and give them to Diana." I was a neophyte. I went off with the packages, opened the door to Diana's room, and there was somebody pointing a cocked pistol at me. What on earth for?! I repented of ever having entered the room, laid the packages on the bed and left.
>
> It was Oscar Turcios. I didn't know that until 1973 when I saw his bullet-riddled corpse. I had met Ricardo Morales at the University, arguing with Federico López and Nathán Sevilla. I still remember his gaze. [2]

The National Directorate decided to undertake an audacious operation to rescue a whole group of leadership figures who had spent several years — some as many as seven — in prison. After drinking a liter of coffee and smoking a pack of Sphynx cigarettes, in the early dawn beneath a tumultuous August downpour, Pedro Arauz asked me what ideas I had for freeing the Sandinista prisoners.

"Let me think about it," I said to him. Then he suggested an idea that Carlos Fonseca had outlined as one possibility. Immediately, without saying anything, I reproached myself for the poverty of my own imagination. Yes, that was the solution!

[1] Humberto Ortega, *50 años de lucha sandinista* (Managua: MINT, Colección Las Segovias, n.d.), p. 107.
[2] Testimony given the author by Carlos Núñez in 1989.

Pedro Arauz ("Federico") was a meticulous young man, an organizer, valiant, who seemed to have no notion of fatigue. He would sleep any time, any place. He was a conspirator who zealously respected our compartmentalized structure and scanty resources. He had the gift of ubiquity.

Luis Carrión describes him and narrates the circumstances of his death in October 1977:

> The OSN (Somoza's National Security Office), with the probable collaboration of an infiltrated traitor, had managed to identify various FSLN safehouses in upper Masaya and Federico tried to withdraw to Managua. His assassins were waiting to kill him; it was a terrible blow for our organization.
>
> Pedro Arauz played a fundamental role in the strengthening and consolidation of the FSLN during the entire decade of the '70s. A tireless promoter of the underground structures and methods of work that protected and guaranteed the political and military activity of the Sandinista Front, a man who hammered on the need to link the FSLN to the masses and of participating in their struggles, as demanding of himself as he was of others. Firm, stubbornly confident in the people and their eventual victory, Pedro was one of those who, without being spectacular, work every day to strengthen and advance the organization.
>
> It was a cowardly, useless crime on the part of the dictatorship, because Carlos Fonseca's organization was already indestructible, thanks to the labor and sacrifice of comrades like Pedro Arauz. [1]

We had already discarded one rash plan: a jailbreak by the prisoners in complicity with some Guards. José Benito Escobar and Daniel Ortega wrote lengthy letters in microscopic hand insisting on the real possibilities of the escape and of their confidence in the Guards they'd recruited.

[1] Luis Carríon Cruz, *Escudo invulnerable del pueblo nicaragüense* (Managua: Editorial Dirección Política MINT, 1986), p. 9.

The letters were read by the sharp eyes of Eduardo Contreras or with the aid of a magnifying glass that Federico carried in his inseparable attache case, which he'd open with a mysterious smile, without revealing its contents.

In preparation, we selected the ranch of long-time collaborator Yico Sánchez, near Jinotepe, to hide the escapees. We explored all the access routes and possible escape routes and assembled the necessary weapons for this feat.

I was given responsibility for the details and took charge of the groups of drivers and support personnel who would await the escaped prisoners in a prearranged spot near the Tipitapa prison.

The truth is it made me shudder just remembering the frustrated escape of Edwin Castro, Cornelio Silva and Ausberto Narváez, who'd been sentenced to 30 years for the execution of the elder Somoza. The Guard — in that case there was only one — betrayed them and all three were assassinated.

In any event, we had to rescue these comrades, since, as Carlos said, it was imperative for elementary reasons of solidarity and because it contributed to strengthening our internal unity. Moreover, the cadres were invaluable, necessary for continuing our work.

3

The new idea was to seize an embassy in the midst of one of those receptions that are frequently given to celebrate anniversaries or to entertain the regime's politicians.

Once the decision was made, the first steps were taken to carry it out. Federico gave me instructions concerning the training of the group that came to be known as the Juan José Quezada commando unit.

Leonel Espinoza and Charlotte Baltodano played the part of a conventional married couple. They started looking for a country property where the future combat unit could assemble for military training.

At one point, we nearly rented a place on the banks of the Tipitapa river. I even inspected it. I no longer recall the reasons why we decided against it. At last we found a place in Las Nubes, near El Crucero, a few kilometers from the capital in the Managua hills, where it's cold, foggy and dark.

The house fronted on Callejón de los Enamorados [Lover's Lane] — where our sentries could hear the sighs, muffled screams and cars exceeding the speed limit while parked — and looked out over the lake and lights of the capital. Most of the selected combatants had gathered there by early October 1974.

On a certain day the group was assembled, each combatant was assigned a number and from then on answered only to that number. They were organized into three squads without regard to hierarchy.

Nobody knew anything. The combatants questioned each other and speculated. Germán Pomares said to Joaquín Cuadra: "It's going to be an embassy, because I heard Eduardo say as much. Federico came the other day with Tomás, and he said something. I think we're going to hit the gringo embassy."

Joaquín replied: "Sonofabitch! How do we get over those walls? The gringo embassy...that's going to be hard...there's a mountain of guards..."[1]

I still feel a great tenderness when I remember how the members of that combat unit always believed the operation would be extremely dangerous, yet never for a second did it cross their minds that it might be impossible. With their training, they came to have total confidence in its success. It was intense. They practiced hundreds of times how to break into a building and immobilize its occupants, how to improvise cover, how to repel a counterattack. They even practiced how they would ride in the vehicles.

The physical exercises were so strenuous that, despite the cold, the residence floor became as sweat-saturated as an Olympic champion's jersey. Joaquín Cuadra says: "We'd do 150 to 200 deep kneebends dying of laughter."[2] They could have done, I might add, up to a thousand.

[1] Joaquín Cuadra, "Una acción Patria o Muerte," supplement, *Ventana*, No. 2 (Managua, December 27, 1980): p. 5.
[2] Ibid.

They received a course in military tactics at the company level as well as in street warfare; they practiced assembling and disassembling weapons; they had exercises in night warfare. There was a detailed course in how to confront enemy interrogation. They studied the history of Nicaragua with Eduardo Contreras who was obsessed with analyzing our national roots.

4

By November 1974, the commando unit was ready for action, yet the training did not let up for a moment.

Clothing they would wear was ready, the nylon stockings they would use as masks, the individual first aid kits, the handkerchiefs for gagging people if necessary, and innumerable small details: jackknives, some food, a couple of hundred items. Josefina Cerda ("Valeria") was placed in charge of all these details.

The three squad leaders were Joaquín Cuadra, the favorite of Carlos Fonseca; Hugo Torres, who wears his heart like a medal; and Germán Pomares, strong and as sweet as corn and raw sugar. The politico-military chief was Eduardo Contreras ("Marcos"). I directed all the training.

We took extraordinary measures to improve the quality of training. The team members learned how to recognize and assemble, with their eyes closed, the parts of rifles and pistols, even when the pieces were all mixed together.

Each of them was subjected to the grenade test, in which the instructor pulled the pin from a deactivated grenade and "accidentally" dropped it on the ground so as to observe their various reactions to the danger.

Hugo Torres' squad was professional. Hugo, straightforward, affectionate, has the gaze of an owl. People like him. Germán Pomares' squad was extroverted. Olga Avilés López, a long-time militant, was one of its members, as was Róger Deshón, an inveterate jokester. This last group occupied the maids' quarters at the rear of the house: a strategic location.

Smoking was punished with something close to the death penalty, and drinking alcohol was like being found guilty of assassinating your maternal grandmother.

There was a red lightbulb in the room and during recreation time we'd go in, turn on the music and start dancing with the *compañeras*. Leonel Espinoza ("El Chaparro") smuggled cigarettes in to us... We took advantage of the fact that this room was some distance away from that of Tomás and Eduardo, which was the headquarters. We'd leave a sentry in the dining room to warn us if Tomás or Eduardo were coming, and we'd turn on the red light and start dancing, imagining ourselves in a nightclub. They never discovered us... It was a sort of discotheque, a conspiracy within the conspiracy.[1]

On Christmas Eve the entire team shared a bottle of *Flor de Caña* rum between them and one cigarette per squad. How ingenuous we chiefs are, nearly always! The group was insuperable — morally, politically and physically.

Our intelligence team, organized by Eduardo Contreras, reported that there would be a fiesta at the home of Noel Pallais Debayle, Somoza's first cousin, and that "El Chigüín" (Anastasio Somoza Portocarrero, Somoza's eldest son) and probably Dinorah Sampson, Somoza's favorite mistress, would be present. The latter, famed for her physical beauty and extravagance, would arrive — if in fact she came, because she didn't get along with the Pallais family, which was related to Somoza's legal wife, Doña Hope — with her entourage of make-up people and her wardrobe, since she sometimes changed dresses as many as three times during a party.

The Yankee ambassador would also be there: the eye of a small hurricane of favor-seekers. The ambassador's recommendation, or that of "the embassy" — that's how he was referred to rather than by his name, as though he were a dog — was an order strictly complied with by the Somoza government.

[1] Ibid., p. 6.

We had to cancel the operation at the last moment because — of all things! — we were unable to steal the necessary vehicles. When we checked the place from outside, there were more Somoza supporters at the party than at a Liberal Party convention. Security was so tight that we suspected Somoza himself would show up.

5

Laszlo Pataky was a fat man — I mean truly fat — of Jewish origin, who lived and enjoyed life in Managua. He was the owner, manager, announcer and program director of the radio news station El Clarín and was invited to receptions, birthday parties, weddings, baptisms, farewell parties, anniversaries, award ceremonies and the presentation of honorary degrees.

He was even invited to informal bashes, which were the best kind, because there Pataky could drink whiskey until he passed out. He always read the invitations over the radio in his ingratiating, disagreeable voice.

One morning in December 1974, somebody — some say it was Joaquín, Joaquín says it was Germán Pomares, I think it was Eduardo — heard over Radio El Clarín that there would be a reception in honor of the U.S. ambassador at the home of José María Castillo Quant. I think it was more like one of those informal bashes.

Eduardo's 180 pounds moved to the rhythm of his exceptional mental agility. Decision shown in his face with the same intensity as his frequent outbursts of tenderness.

6

The project was activated after dark. We decided not to hijack automobiles but to hire taxis instead and then take them by force. Several units of the support group, led by Alvaro Baltodano and Mario Cardenal, left the headquarters residence in their own cars. I left with Leonel Espinoza, and headed for a ranch near the León highway.

I found out later from the active participants what had happened. One of the taxi drivers who was held up protested in anguish: "Now you've screwed me, brother."

"What do you mean, we've screwed you?" Germán Pomares asked him.

"I'm Catún Sandoval's brother. Nobody's gonna believe I wasn't involved in this."

"Show me your license."

It was true; he was Catún's brother, a well-known Sandinista. He began bashing himself in the face so the police would believe he'd been subdued by force.

During the ride, Eduardo ordered his team to open and close the doors to make sure they worked. Joaquín ignored the order, which nearly cost him his life. When the time came to get out with all due speed and violence, he couldn't get the door open. Olga helped him and they were the last to arrive at the house they were to assault.

The commando unit formed a semicircle shooting at anything that moved. Hilario Sánchez pushed open the door and burst into the house.

Someone fired at the group while they were still outside, wounding Róger Deshón. Germán said to Joaquín, "Cover me!"

Joaquín thought that Germán was going to enter the house, but instead saw him run across the street to a parked car. Germán had seen that the man who'd been shooting at them was reloading and he took advantage of the pause.

He returned rapidly and entered the house to confront the terrorized faces of the Chilean ambassador, the Gallo brothers and Fatso Pataky.

"We blew it," Germán said. "Nobody here's worth our while. All I see is a bunch of women."

"If the wives are here, their husbands must be here, too," Eduardo reasoned. "We have to look for them."

They searched the closets and discovered an arsenal. Chema Castillo collected military weapons, so suddenly each of the guerrillas had three weapons and extra ammunition for each one. They demanded that the North American wife of the bald Minister of Foreign

Relations call her husband. "My dear, my dear," she cried in a shrill voice. "Come out, please!"

There was a second exchange of gunfire, this time with Hugo Torres' squad which was covering the kitchen and garage. A squad car, approaching slowly as if sniffing danger, was greeted with a hail of bullets. Some of its occupants fell, the others abandoned the vehicle and fled. The team shifted from the offensive to a tactical defensive posture as anticipated, and for which they had been trained.

The enemy tried to open the patio gate. They opened a hole and fired blindly through it. Germán and Joaquín returned the fire and several Guards were wounded or withdrew.

Chema Castillo put up a fight and was killed. This fact was kept from the guests. The youngest daughter was asked to go out of the house waving a white handkerchief and the other women were told to scream. This stopped the enemy fire.

They were still worried about the captives they'd taken. Germán kept repeating: "They aren't worth shit."

There was a door that led to the adjoining patio. At the first light of day, one of the women hostages was sent to explore it and there was something about her when she returned that made Pomares suspicious.

"Cover me," he murmured to Joaquín Cuadra and he went through the door with the agility of a ballet star. Trembling on the other side, some with wet pants, others smelling of shit, were the big fish: Montiel Argüello, the Foreign Minister; Danilo Lacayo, the Esso manager; the notorious "Chato" Lang, intimate friend of Somoza; and Iván Osorio Peters. The latter's wife, we learned later, had swallowed her diamond ring and managed to deposit it later in a white chamberpot, but not without first downing a dose of castor oil. Not quite as disagreeable as the voice of Laszlo Pataky.

Above all, there was Guillermo Sevilla Sacasa, Somoza's brother-in-law — husband of the army's queen, the gluttonous Lilliam Somoza, who was the girl on the one-*córdoba* bill, wearing an Indian feather on her forehead — an artistic consumer of alcohol and good food.

Now we really felt like kings, the combatants recalled. Eduardo Contreras initiated the negotiations. He even spoke by phone with

Somoza. The most difficult aspect was the money. We were asking for five million dollars. The other side argued that the banks were closed and there wasn't that much money in Nicaragua. Pure bullshit.

Eduardo Contreras whose pseudonym for this operation was "Zero," asked his people what they thought. Germán Pomares said that a million — the amount offered — was nothing, that Guillermo Sevilla alone was worth the five million. The majority, nonetheless, were inclined to accept the million since the basic goal had been achieved: the liberation of the prisoners and the dissemination of two communiques on the radio, on television and in the press. Eduardo accepted. The intermediary was Monsignor Miguel Obando y Bravo.

7

Some comrades were arrested after the operation began, among them, René Núñez. His brother Carlos relates the episode as follows:

December 27th approached and, as might be imagined, none of the overt cadres had the slightest idea of what was going to happen. Many of the underground cadres were also unaware of the impending action.

It appears that René Núñez Téllez, a cadre of long experience, had likewise not been informed of Operation Juan José Quezada. Pursued by the Somoza security forces in the northern part of the country, with local safehouses discovered by the enemy and on the verge of being captured, he left Matagalpa for León accompanied by Juan de Diós Muñoz and Ana Julia Guida early on December 28th to make contact with Pedro Arauz.

René hadn't slept for three days. He and his companions boarded what at the time were known as inter-locale taxis because they traveled between departments. There was a military checkpoint at the entrance to León. René was asleep and when he awoke, soldiers and civilian police agents were searching him. They discovered his weapon and arrested him, but they still didn't know his identity. René made a last attempt to save himself, arguing that, as a cattle rancher from the north, he had to protect himself against guerrilla activity. The Guards almost believed him, but an informer named O'Conner recognized him and denounced him.

Behind Rene's taxi was a vehicle carrying Marco Antonio Somarriva, a student leader and Sandinista militant since 1971. He informed my mother and sisters of Rene's arrest and the whole family mobilized to do whatever they could.

At 11:30 in the morning on December 28th, my Aunt Amanda said to me: "Carlos, they're calling you from León." I took the telephone with a strange foreboding and one of my sisters told me: "They've arrested René."

"That can't be! He's neither in Managua nor in León."

"Marco Antonio Somarriva witnessed his arrest. We have to inform the Juan José Quezada commando unit so they can get him out."

I remembered a public telephone near the Las Palmas pharmacy and I tried to call "Zero," but the lines were blocked. My poor mother came to Managua, together with Milena, in the hopes of sending word of Rene's arrest through Monsignor Obando y Bravo, who had just been named as negotiator. They went to Las Sierritas, asked for an interview and explained the case. They left happy and filled with confidence. Eduardo Contreras, up to the time he left to receive the liberated prisoners, never received the name of René Núñez Téllez. Everything seems to indicate that the archbishop, the only person with access to the residence who knew of his arrest, decided not to mention it. Four years later, on August 22, 1978, René was liberated through the successful Operation "Death to Somocismo."[1]

8

They broadcast our communiques. I heard them from the ranch where I'd gone into hiding. I had been charged with drafting Communique No. 2. No. 1 was sent from the mountains by Henry Ruiz.* There had been lengthy discussions inside the commando unit

[1]Testimony by Carlos Núñez.
* See document at the end of this chapter.

about the withdrawal, that is, about the steps to be taken once our demands had been met: how to get to the airport where a Lanica plane would be waiting to fly the group to Cuba, once the Cuban government had accepted the prisoners and their liberators. Three routes were proposed and, at the last moment, the unit selected one of the three.

The bus arrived. Monsignor Obando entered the house and assured them that everything was alright. The driver was told where to park. Joaquín Cuadra came out with Guillermo Sevilla, who resented the cold muzzle of a Browning against his temple. After making sure there was nothing anomalous or suspicious inside the bus, he returned with Sevilla. Germán ordered the driver out so he could be searched.

The team members, each with a hostage, left the house: Eduardo Contreras, Joaquín Cuadra, Hugo Torres, Germán Pomares, Javier Carrión, Róger Deshón, Leticia Herrera, Olga Avilés, Eleonora Rocha, Omar Hallesleven, Hilario Sánchez, Juan Antonio Ríos and Félix Pedro Picado.

At that moment, a car approached filled with women who stared in amazement at what was happening. Through an error, they had been allowed into the prohibited zone. The commandos, who didn't trust anyone, were about to open fire. Monsignor Obando walked over to the vehicle, briefly explained the situation to its occupants and asked them to leave.

Joaquín sat behind the driver, Eduardo and Germán Pomares next to the door. The hostages were seated by the windows, while the commandos sat next to the aisle. Joaquín indicated to the driver where he should drive and had him blow the horn during the entire trip. The bus was identified with Sandinista flags flying from its windows and was followed by motorcycles, automobiles, cameramen, photographers, journalists, everybody.

Joaquín Cuadra will never forget a single one of the many images along that route. "I read their lips," he says, "and they were saying, 'Long live something,' maybe love, maybe happiness. They waved at us with white hands, because they had plaster on their dark skin. There was a light in those bricklayers' eyes that we took with us and that accompanied us in the battles that followed. What a reward! They live. We live. They will always be a part of our lives," the commandos would say, and Joaquín Cuadra, squad leader, commando number seven would say.

They arrive at the airport. The freed prisoners are already aboard the plane: José Benito Escobar, Daniel Ortega, Lenin Cerna, Carlos Guadamuz, Julián Roque, Oscar Benavides, Alí Rivas Vallecillo, Jacinto Suárez. The plane crosses the water like a flash. Awaiting them in Cuba is Carlos Fonseca.

9

"Marcos," Eduardo Contreras, "Major Zero", knew from birth how to persuade men and manage abstract concepts. He learned how to handle rifles in Palestinian training camps, where he stood out among such singular companions as Pedro Arauz, Enrique Schmidt, René Vivas, Patricio Argüello, who died in a Palestinian operation to rescue prisoners in the hands of the Zionists, and Juan José Quezada, who was killed in Nandaime and for whom the commando team was named. He never took a course in political negotiations but he directed those of December 27th like a master.

Marcos had the air of a mythological hero. His youthful prophet's face, recently graduated in the science of daring, was intact, serene. After Marcos' death, Daniel Ortega sent these words to his companion, Marisabel Aramburú:

Restless streets, dust, flies. A midday filled with sadness. Ditches, pensive bridges. Here a sacrificed yesterday of water and plants and feathers. Here the buried flowers: the warriors' bow and arrows entombed. Here time stands still: the chieftain reincarnated, tribal voices. Here the neighborhood, cooking fires and burned rice. The little house: water droplets in the drought, breeze in the heat. A cot that leaves your feet exposed. A plate of beans, a tortilla, ten kids ready for war. Commander Marcos! The people receive you.

Carlos Mejía Godoy relates the following:

"Hey, m' man!" said the stranger who had just climbed into the front seat of the car. And that "Hey, m' man!" let me understand that I could look at his face. He impressed me: tall, husky, different somehow, from the classical guerrilla... He looked more like an architect than a Sandinista leader.

"Hangin' in there," I managed, while a BECAT anti-terrorist patrol approached from the opposite direction. He must have seen the fear outlined in my profile because he said in a clear voice, "Don't sweat it, Charlie...."

The next day, my superior said, "I have a surprise for you, *compa*. When you get back from the barrio, I'll tell you." I couldn't wait and walked him to the door explaining that I had to go to El Viejo, in Chinandega, that afternoon to do research on local folklore and would be gone for two days. He didn't want to leave me on tenterhooks, so he clarified the mystery. "Look," he said, "you made big points last night. You were driving for Marcos." And he walked off shouldering his olive green backpack.

I don't know how many times I saw Marcos... Once at dawn, in a yellow SOVIPE engineer's hardhat, twice at my house, and one final time — the best of all. We talked for nearly two hours about our work, about the organization, about my job as a singer.

The fact is that Marcos had the ability to charge the batteries of the most depressed person... I can honestly say that if I've remained forever a militant, I owe it to that man who knew how to channel my preoccupations and give form to my dreams. Thank you, Commander Marcos! [1]

Marcos is dead, I'm in prison. It's November 1976. They take me to the morgue — as they would Javier Carrión, to identify him. I see Marcos stretched out in a cold drawer. Beside him is Roberto

[1] Testimony given the author by Carlos Mejía Godoy in 1988.

Huembes ("The Quiet One"), a natural leader who at birth drank the milk of seven young goats. Next to them is Silvio Renazco, whom I didn't know.

I draw myself to attention amidst a total silence. Then I unhurriedly caress Marcos' unlined brow, remembering the hours we shared, and the contradictions, his anecdotes about France and Germany; and mine about Cuba, Colombia and Peru; the final moment when we bade farewell to each other with a feverish embrace. I remember particularly the note he sent me in prison by way of Rafael Córdova Rivas, my defense counsel, in which he wrote, "An embrace," and on the reverse side I wrote, "Unity." He received it, they told me, with an affirmative, cordial nod.

I want to kiss his hands but am afraid the colonels, majors and other waiting shitheads will think me weak. They ask if I recognize him and I answer: "It's him."

10

The pathological symptoms of political divergences have already made their appearance. A number of incidents embittered the experience of various people. I remember the discussions: the role of class, wartime priorities, the placement of cadres, even the mortality of crabs. Theoretical arguments clashed like swords, Franz Fanon mentioned this; Che pointed it out; Lenin noted it; so did Fidel. Dialectics came, concepts went; and things got worse. The common denominator was "A Free Homeland or Death." We were all Sandinistas, we were all ready to die fighting. Maturity and common sense were there awaiting an opportunity for nourishment and victory.

Carlos Núñez recalls those moments:

The crisis and the appearance of tendencies shook the Sandinista Front. We could not believe it; our organization was splitting and we were pained. Pained? Yes, pained. Even among brothers we were distrustful and suspicious of each other, yet at bottom we retained a heartfelt respect for our comrades in struggle who shared a common origin.

While I'm thinking, Pedro Arauz ("Federico") shows up. I'm in a safehouse in the Altagracia neighborhood, only a block away from the First Section police station. I wasn't expecting him. We talk about the internal situation of the FSLN and he tells me: "Your new superior is Rolando (Tomás)." And I tell him: "I don't like that. Rolando doesn't observe security precautions. One of these days they're going to capture or kill him." Federico exploded and insisted on my meeting with Rolando. I still didn't know much about the political crisis in the FSLN.

Charlotte Baltodano showed up in my Altagracia safehouse to leave me a message and give me a date for the meeting with Rolando. I wasn't there. When they tell me about it, I disappear; I go into hiding in my safehouses that nobody knows about. But I go to the meeting. No one knows anything. I walk the streets and I'm uptight; I have my .9 mm pistol tucked in my belt; I'm uptight... Tomás says to me: "Close your eyes." I didn't close them both, only one, and I must confess that I had my finger on the trigger.

After that, we talked until 2:30 in the morning. Earlier, when I entered the house, I had seen my brother-in-arms Marco Antonio Somarriva, stretched out on a mattress. He looks at me but doesn't greet me. The meeting ends and Tomás leaves. Marco watches me, then suddenly gets up and says: "How are you?"

Gloria Campos must remember well that early morning when Marco, Rosalba, Oscar Pérez Cassar and I spent the dawn talking about the situation in the FSLN, with Gloria listening in and making no attempt to hide her personal loyalty and affection for all of us.

It was December. What solitude! The closer Christmas and New Year's got, the more alone we all felt. That's how it was. One of those days, Tomás spoke with Marco Somarriva who asked him for a further explanation of the different tendencies. Tomás gave him a general analysis and when Marco asked him about Homero (myself), Tomás said to him, "Forget it; he's a good kid, and he'll soon be with us again."[1]

11

Carlos Núñez was not mistaken. I always believed in the need for audacity, which on occasion led me to be imprudent and violate the norms of security.

There are many ways an underground cadre can fall into enemy hands: a chance encounter with an informer, a traffic accident, disregard for compartmentalization, underestimation of the enemy, routine.

One mistake that nearly cost me my life was to go to the Diriamba hospital when my daughter, Ana Josefina, was born. As I approached the old building, I noticed a strange movement. A military patrol came down the street leading to the hospital. I did not know until later that they were searching for me. I passed them with a twinge of doubt and fear, and nobody recognized me.

In Josefina's room at the hospital, I picked up a bundle of wrinkles in my arms that shrilly demanded of life something like milk, landscapes and comprehension. I was still in a daze when Nubia, Josefina's cousin and an FSLN collaborator, dashed into the room stammering that the hospital was surrounded by armed guards. Josefina wanted desperately to hold me back. I left immediately and there were four men in the corridor wearing typical outfits from the Gómez tailor shop who had between their eyebrows the unmistakable scowl of security agents. I stuck my hand into the pocket where I carried my pistol. Nobody moved.

Later, when I was a prisoner in the Security cells, one of the wardens told me in a rare moment of confidence that they had recognized me, but knowing how Sandinistas would react, they had preferred not to move. Outside, the soldiers were searching

---

[1]Testimony by Carlos Núñez.

pedestrians. I walked unimpeded to the Volkswagon where Tito Chamorro — who hadn't yet betrayed us — was waiting for me.

When I recall that episode, it still gives me goose bumps, because for my daughter, the first day of her life might have been her father's last.

I took another serious risk in Matagalpa. Knowing that Velia Rodríguez had been detected by Security, I decided to warn her of the danger or else rescue her.

I went to her house. There were two agents at the door with pistols visible in their belts. By the time I saw them, it was too late to turn back, so I walked between them with my pistol drawn, as if I did that sort of thing every day. Inside the house, Velia's sister Lidia, who was pregnant, nearly fainted.

We experienced many other dangerous moments, not because we had violated security norms but due simply to the ups and downs in the life of a revolutionary. Sometimes I was saved by the Guard uniform I was wearing, at other times by the serenity and audacity of my comrades. Like the time a patrol stopped us on the road from El Viejo to the beach town of Aposentillo. Juan José Ubeda, with a characteristic nod, indicated to Israel Lewites which two soldiers he should take out. With a wink, he offered me the officer. When we were all ready to open fire, we tried one last resort: I offered a bribe to the officer. He accepted it, but not without first informing me that Guards could not be bribed.

In all our schools we taught comrades the basic rule that it was safer to go out at night than during the day. I thought the contrary, which won me the fame of being imprudent. When I finally accepted the norm of going out only at night, I stepped into deep shit and Charon nearly carried me off in his boat.

DOCUMENT 7
Communique No. 1
(Fragment)

The Nicaraguan peasant: ...his sad eyes discolored with the characteristic yellow of malnutrition, expresses a violent hope of redemption. Awash in a sea of promises of a justice that never arrives, his patience has worn thin as the organizational forms of labor unions and cooperatives have disappeared.

Following is the economic situation of the impoverished peasant [currency = córdobas]:

Salary	5.00
Salt	1.00 per pound
Soap	1.50 per bar
Gas	1.50 per bottle
Entero-vioforma	2.00 per envelope
	(he always has gastric problems)
Mejoral	20 per pill
	(he's always in pain)
Bottle of cane liquor	8.00
Average fine of local sheriff	50.00
Average fine of National Guard	80.00

He pays his fines with pigs and chickens to regain his "freedom."

His economic balance is: misery, hunger, malnutrition, night blindness, fear, premature death from mostly curable diseases, illiteracy.

Ricardo Morales, Oscar Turcios, Juan José Quezada and Jonathan González are four Sandinista brothers assassinated by the National Guard in Nandaime in September 1973.

In September 1973, 23 indigenous leaders are hunted down by the National Guard in response to an occupation of land carried out by the people of Subtiava — lands that had been usurped by a group of landowners.

In November 1973, a strike by the workers of the Licorera Nacional protesting inhuman working conditions is repressed by the National Guard.

In December 1973, the people demand freedom and justice for a Sandinista brother, Francisco Romero, and the Salvadoran professor,

Efraín Nortalwalton. The people demonstrate and protest energetically until both are released from their unjust incarceration...

In April 1974, there are new arrests; helicopters burst upon the countryside and mountains of Matagalpa, Jinotega, Nueva Segovia and Zelaya. Counterinsurgency patrols of the Guard take prisoners, torture, rape, loot and burn peasant homes...

In February 1974, our Sandinista brother Manuel Avilés C. is assassinated in Rivas. In April 1974, our Sandinista brother Ramón González is assassinated in Rivas.

Sadism and other aberrations are given free rein and the cases of Amada Pineda, María Castil and other peasant women have come to public attention, causing indignation and contempt for the dictatorial regime...

Doctors and nurses demand better treatment and better salaries. The reply is a savage wave of repression...

Union headquarters and hospitals are searched by the National Guard; labor leaders are taken captive.

Brutality grows and, invigorated, turns to torture with electric cattle prods, the ripping out of fingernails, cigarette burns, the withholding of food, enforced nudity and the exposure of victims night and day to inclement weather and the voracity of mosquitoes and gnats. As in the Middle Ages, the National Guard ties peasants to posts and slaughters them, accusing them of cattle rustling, banditry, or belonging to the guerrilla movement. The witchhunt turns surprisingly pathological when the murder of peasants and the rape of their women is declared by local and national authorities to be a mission of peace and cleansing by the National Guard. The Great Crusade!

On May 22, 1974, Luis García Cardenal is captured, along with 26 other peasants, including women and children. It is known that among them were María Felicia de García and her seven-month-old baby, Lucio Martínez, Abelina Muñoz de Martínez and their four small children, as well as Mario and Genaro Martínez, Rodolfo Martínez and others. Where are all these people?

Alfredo Medina, a Sandinista brother, is assassinated in Somotillo by a National Guard patrol.

In Nueva Segovia, the National Guard captures and tortures Andrés López, Miguel Angel Pozo, José Montenegro and Alfonso Florián, accusing them of cattle rustling and concealing arms in their homes. Where are they?

In Nueva Guinea, the National Guard, acting on orders of Somoza propagandist Cornelio Hüeck, falsely accuses and jails Teresa Zeledón Pérez and Domingo Dávila Zeledón in an attempt to force them to abandon their land so that Hüeck can seize it. In the same area, Estanislao Romero was savagely beaten by the National Guard for demanding better prices for his crop. It should be pointed out that Nueva Guinea is a concentration camp, surrounded and controlled by the National Guard.

From April to August we can say that the repression was expressed in the traditional manner of the National Guard... Crime, violence and pillage was never more highly praised by the degenerate national authorities and the regime's paid writers.

Where are the peasants Santos and Genaro Díaz, Pedro Hernández, María Castil, Víctor Flores, Juan Castil, Juan López Agustín, Agustín Mendoza, Julio Pineda, Felipe Aguilar and his father, the González family, José Angel Martínez, the Loza family (not including the traitor, Pedro), the four children and two women who were with César Flores in a cave near Yaosca Central, Sabino and Demetrio Centeno, Victoria Díaz and the four who were assassinated at Rancho Grande, the five peasant leaders who were captured in Chinandega after occupying lands in Palo Grande and Palo Alto? Where are all these people?

The helicopter flights over the sea, the tiger cages, the famous firing squad executions at dawn, the gang rapes of family members in the presence of prisoners, and the pregnant woman who aborted in the presence of her husband while being kicked in the stomach are typical expressions of the suffering of our people, particularly among the peasants. These episodes are not imaginary. They are based on actual fact.

On September 18, 1974, the Somoza Battalion occupied the city of León to repress protests over the arrest of peasant leaders who had occupied land in Los Arcos.

The cycle of accumulation of lands by the armed bourgeoisie is being repeated and, as always, the impoverished peasant is their victim.

Patience has its limits, as do stoicism and resignation. The peasant, the worker and the progressive intellectual who suffer these repressions clamor for justice and they shall find it.

We denounce these assassinations, crimes and rapes before our people, before all Latin America and before the world, and we alert them so they might lend us their support and solidarity in the face of the brutal repression of the peasantry of Matagalpa, Jinotega, Nueva Segovia, Chinandega, Estelí, León, Carazo, Rivas, Chontales, Managua, Zelaya, Boaco and elsewhere.

We alert everyone and call on patriotic personalities to make use of their connections to denounce before the world the planned extermination that the most discredited of Latin American dictatorships seek to carry out against the most stoic and long-suffering segment of our people.

DOCUMENT 8
Communique No. 2

Nicaraguan brothers, for the past four years our organization has accumulated forces in the mountains, countryside and cities of our nation so as to provide the exploited and oppressed classes — workers and peasants — with a politico-military organization capable of directing the just and necessary war that will liquidate forever the criminal, servile and oppressive system headed by the hated despot, Anastasio Somoza Debayle.

The Sandinista National Liberation Front (FSLN), in a necessary stage of apprenticeship and accumulation of experience, undertook the guerrilla efforts of 1963 and 1967 in Río Coco and Bocay, Fila Grande and Pancasán. Those efforts came to naught because of the scanty development of the revolutionary movement that was only taking its first steps. Nevertheless, the partial failures of '63 and '67 left a positive balance of valuable experience that has been assimilated with fervor by the new generations of revolutionaries. From the very beginning, our organization tried to link itself to the exploited classes of our country. It is understandable that a young revolutionary organization like ours, with all the enthusiasm of its militants, has had to stumble along in the dark looking for ways to join with the most combative sectors of the population. Having assured this commitment of the Sandinistas to the masses, however, has finally born fruit.

The guerrilla actions of 1958 - 1961 in every corner of the country are a prelude to improved subjective conditions in labor and political organizations at the national level.

It must be pointed out that the guerrilla movement of 1963 represents the appearance of the first armed organization with a coherent ideology, a revolutionary program to construct a socialist society, and the bringing together of dispersed combatants who identify with this program.

The guerrilla effort of 1967 in Fila Grande and Pancasán represented a new quality with respect to operational methods and the correction of certain errors of the past. From a political point of view, Fila Grande and Pancasán were a different response from that of the bourgeois opposition and the traditional left, who tried to find a short-range solution to the struggle against the regime of Anastasio Somoza. The short-range attitude that found expression in the events of January 22, 1967, where our people, in their anxiety for change, generously shed their blood to satisfy — without realizing it — the petty appetites of traditional politicians. The treason and cowardice of the opposition leaders translated into the historical liquidation of the Conservative Party and confirmed the dualism and opportunism of the traditional left.

The Pancasán endeavor is the resulting military expression of the political development that had been gestating in the rural peasant unions. Pancasán was the response of peasant organizations and indigenous communities to the constant aggression of the National Guard, brutal guardian of the voracious land hunger of a handful of landowners from throughout the country.

The struggle proposed by the Sandinista National Liberation Front (FSLN) responds to an historical need. Nicaragua is a dependency of North American imperialism, the dominating center that directs and benefits from — along with the Liberal-Conservative oligarchy — the looting and exploitation of our country. The instrument of imperial domination is the Liberal-Conservative government that controls the state apparatus by means of which it has unleashed violence and terror against different sectors of the populace, especially against the peasants in the mountains.

The Sandinista National Liberation Front (FSLN) makes public its broad and generous policy toward those soldiers, non-commissioned officers and officers who refuse to obey the criminal orders of the regime or who are willing to join the ranks of the revolutionary combatants. In any case, our policy with respect to enemy soldiers is to be implacable in combat and the meting out of justice, and to be generous in victory. Our organization takes this

359

opportunity to respectfully remember the names of Adolfo Báez Bone, Napoleón Ubilla Baca, Julio Alonso, and Víctor Rivas Gómez, officers of the National Guard who died in combat or were assassinated by the Somoza regime; of Carlos Ulloa, Nicaraguan Air Force pilot who died heroically defending the Cuban people; and of Lt. David Tejada Peralta, glorious militant of the Sandinista National Liberation Front.

The Sandinista National Liberation Front (FSLN) identifies fully with and deposits its most ardent faith in the beleaguered and exploited peasants and workers who will lead the coming battles and who will express with greater clarity, if possible, their heroic revolutionary vocation.

The destiny of Nicaragua is in the hands of the workers and peasants. They are tomorrow's Fatherland. The workers of the countryside and city are the flesh and blood of the Sandinista National Liberation Front (FSLN).

The Sandinista National Liberation Front (FSLN) energetically practices revolutionary violence, but wishes to utilize such violence only to the extent that it is strictly necessary to achieve a popular victory. We are aware that revolutionary violence is a painful but necessary measure and is never an end in itself, and we are also aware that this necessary violence will, in the long run, reduce bloodshed, infant mortality, cultural frustration, and hunger and cold for broad segments of our people.

We go to war to kill and be killed, but in order that our people may have a real opportunity to live.

In the particular conditions of our country, revolutionary violence manifests itself in the particular form of a Prolonged People's War, which means, in other words, a political and military confrontation of an organized populace with its foreign and local enemies during whatever period of time is required for the careful preparation and development of the conflict. The Sandinista National Liberation Front (FSLN) intends, in an absolutely responsible way, to carry out the people's war in the mountains, countryside and cities so as to hasten the day of revolutionary victory.

The Sandinista National Liberation Front (FSLN) has been obliged to carry out these actions in response to the repressive policies of the regime. We are moved by profoundly humanitarian motives. Our operational system contrasts clearly with that of the repressive forces. We are taking a group of diplomats temporarily hostage in order to achieve the liberation of our brothers who are in prison.

If there had existed in Nicaragua the slightest possibility of rescuing our Sandinista brothers from prison by any other means, the present action would not have taken place. This operation is, moreover, our first response to the illegal way in which Anastasio Somoza Debayle has decided to continue holding, with the support of North American imperialism, the title of President of the Republic.

We demand:

1.- Liberation of the following Sandinista brothers who have been unjustly jailed: José Benito Escobar, Daniel Ortega, Carlos Guadamuz, Jacinto Suárez, Manuel Rivas, Julián Roque, Oscar Benavides and Lenin Cerna, who must be placed on a plane of the Lanica Company, together with the members of this commando unit and selected hostages (named in a separate list) within a deadline of 36 hours starting from the time indicated at the end of this message.

2.- Five million dollars gathered within the same time limit by governments indicated in a separate list. This amount must be delivered to the members of this commando unit in 50, 20, 10 and 5 dollar bills, divided in proportional parts and random numbering.

3.- An immediate governmental decree raising the minimum wage throughout the country as follows:

a) General workers: 2.50 *córdobas* per hour.

b) Industrial workers: 3.00 *córdobas* per hour.

c) Agricultural workers: 2.50 *córdobas* per hour plus food and lodging.

d) Domestic workers: 350.00 *córdobas* per month plus food, lodging weekly rest and paid vacations.

In addition to this:

a) A Christmas bonus of one month's salary to workers in the following areas throughout the country:

Hospital workers, not excluding any regional center.

Construction workers.

Textile workers.

Stevedores.

Drivers and helpers.

Siemens Company workers.
Sugar mill workers.
Banana workers of the Standard Fruit Company.

Finally:
An increase in wages of ordinary National Guard soldiers to 500 *córdobas* per month.

4.- A suspension of all repressive measures. This is not an idle request. A violation of this demand will arouse the just wrath of our commando unit.

5.- The immediate and full publication of this message, in legible type and prominently placed, in the following newspapers:

La Prensa, Novedades and *El Centroamericano.*

The reading of this same message, in a clear voice and without distortions on the following radio news programs: Extra, Radioinformaciones, Reportaje, Sucesos, Diez en Punto and La Verdad, and by the television newscasts Extra Visión and Telemundo. It must also be read in a clear voice and without distortions over the national radio network at noon on two consecutive days.

6.- Absolute freedom in the spoken and written media to report the events surrounding this action. If the specified conditions are not met or arrangements have not been made to do so within the time limit of 36 hours, the first hostage will be executed; the second hostage will be executed 12 hours later and so on, successively.

Finally, we wish to add that the conditions outlined here are orders emanating from the National Directorate of the Sandinista National Liberation Front (FSLN) and are not, therefore, subject to modification. What is indicated above will be carried out with a firm hand. Let no one doubt it. Our combatants have been imbued with an iron, conscientious discipline and are prepared to resist to the end. All orders will be carried out, save one: surrender.

11 p.m., 27 December 1974

Chapter
Thirty-One

I took charge of the military schools.

I had received training in Cuba. The officers' school was in the Coronela neighborhood, in an old house that had belonged to a millionaire by the name of Pumarejo, the former owner of a Havana television station. The students were primarily cadres of the [Cuban] Popular Socialist Party. There were 78 of us, including Sócrates Flores, Pedro Pablo Ríos and myself from Nicaragua.

Discipline was strict, the study of tactics rigorous and advanced. We studied tactics at the individual, squad, platoon, company and battalion levels. There was a special course in urban warfare, as well as arms training and other traditional disciplines. The infantry instructor, Lt. Andrés Ordaz, managed to whip that heterogeneous collection of skinny workers and fat functionaries into a crack company that excelled at close order drill and was capable of running several kilometers with rifles at the ready without tiring. The political instructor, Emiliano Hernández, reaffirmed our faith in qualitative and quantitative transformations and in the fascinating necessity of historic leaps. Emiliano predicted that I would become a *comandante* and that he would be requesting an audience with me. The revolutionary victory proved him right, although, as I pointed out to him, it was I who requested the audience with him. A year later, in Vietnam, my friend and classmate, Yaúr Barrios, is almost hit on the head by a bomb of the same make as one that, at precisely the same moment, strikes down the school's director, Lt. José Claro.

The group became a family, the family a fraternity, and the fraternity our identity.

Twenty-seven years later, in Havana, I had a reunion with many of those men, one of whom had become the chief of Cuban police and another, director of customs. The majority are public functionaries, officers in the Armed Forces and Interior Ministry, or retired.

2

In the school we held near Jinotepe, at the Yico Sánchez ranch, there was sufficient discipline to make it unforgettable. Bayardo Arce and Joaquín Cuadra were there.

Yico's son, Orlando Castellón, who died years later in the mountains, was advantageously tall and ingenious. One day as I entered the classroom, I saw him in the middle of an expectant group. They ceased smiling as soon as I came in. He was raising his arms and opening and closing his fists. On seeing me, he froze, and I asked him: "What's going on, Casimiro?"

"Ah!" he said. "You've told us that when we want something, we have to invent it. I have a thirst for orange juice and since there aren't any around here, I'm inventing them."

I stifled my laughter and made him do a thousand knee bends.

Another notable school was at San Jacinto, near Telica. In attendance were Juan de Diós Muñoz, Jorge Sinforoso Bravo, Leonardo Real Espinal and Julio Avedaño, all slain, and Leonel Espinoza, Ana Julia Guido, José Valdivia and sweet, slender Mónica Baltodano.

During the summer of 1975, the enemy detected another school near Telica, where Arlén Siu was training, and I decided that instead of withdrawing into the countryside we should move toward León. This was the opposite of what happened months later in the El Sauce school where, on orders of their leader, the Costa Rican Plutarco Hernández, the combatants withdrew into the rural areas with fatal consequences. Arlén Siu died there.

We walked through the night. At dawn, near the Hermita neighborhood at the north end of the city, we stopped in a cornfield. All the guerrillas slept and I was left to keep watch.

Eva awoke next to me in that cornfield — Eva who had deranged my insides and my common sense with her penetrating eyes. When we set off once again, the two of us smelled of earth and guava jelly. We made it to León and various refuges in Managua.

We hid in the house of William Ramírez, who was still overt and worked as an editor at *La Prensa*. William is a good man with laughing eyes, tall and strong. He accompanied me without the slightest evidence of fear on many of my clandestine excursions.

We took refuge in the house of Roberto McEwan and his strong-willed companion, Silvia Amador. There we invented tricks, caresses and quarrels in the most varied range of sound and color.

Eva was later arrested, during a failed attempt against a BECAT patrol. She took a defiant stance against the enemy.

Carlos Agüero, Silvio Casco and I were nearly captured. Carlos Núñez, who was involved in that episode, relates:

> On December 29th, I was in a safehouse in the Máximo Jerez neighborhood, the same house where Tomás took me to talk about internal tensions and my responsibilities. He appeared with Carlos Agüero. There was a problem: apparently, a safehouse in which Carlos Fonseca and a group of members were preparing to go to the mountains had been detected. The house was located behind the Ocón Hospital, now named after Carlos Roberto Huembes.
>
> The problem was simple. Tomás asked if we were willing to carry out a holding action. We said we were and left immediately to help with the evacuation of the others. How romantic we were! Marco Antonio Somarriva positioned himself at the entrance to the Vélez Paiz Hospital with a .9 mm Luger, Rosalba Carrasco at Kilometer 7 with a .45, and I one block before the entrance to the Vélez Paiz Hospital with my .9 mm Browning. We were going to hold off Somoza's Guard with three pistols. The truth is we couldn't have held off anybody or anything. Or maybe we could.[1]

---

[1] *Testimonio de Carlos Nuñez.*

3

We had gathered at Ruth Marcenaro's house in Colonia Centroamérica. About 9 p.m. I decided to take Mildred Abaunza to within walking distance of her house in one of the eastern neighborhoods of Managua and when we were already in the back seat of the jeep, Juancito, the driver, alerted me to the presence of a strange car.

I knew immediately that it was a Security vehicle and I told Juancito to turn around and go past them. He did and we hadn't gone a hundred yards when a BECAT jeep and the Security vehicle caught up with us blowing their horns.

Juancito stopped and I readied my .9 mm pistol. I said to Mildred: "Time to die."

"That's right," she said. And she squeezed my arm, trembling and supportive.

The patrol officer, who turned out to be Lt. Rodolfo Sequeira O'Connolly, approached confidently holding a Thompson submachine gun. He stopped a few meters away, looked at me coldly, contemptuously, arrogantly. Before he could shoot, my bullet ripped away that mask.

I saw his eyes go blank as he fell to the ground like the feather of a bird on a summer afternoon.

I ran zigzagging some 200 meters, pursued by the unsettling sensation of having killed a man and a hail of bullets. When I reached the Masaya Road Commercial Center, having thrown myself blindly into the Santo Domingo drainage ditch, I felt myself all over and was amazed that I didn't have a scratch. I came out near the movie houses.

I stopped a car with a couple in it but desisted because the woman was pregnant. Moreover, my pistol was jammed. A patrol car came along, oblivious to the preceding episode, and arrested a man who was trying to kidnap a couple. I shouted my name and some passers-by reported it.

I was turned over to the Somoza Security Office where they stripped me and gave me my first beating. When I identified myself, they fell silent. It was 10 p.m., February 4, 1976. It wasn't until the following day, when they were sure who I was, that the interrogation began in earnest.

My capture provoked diverse reactions:

February came and Tomás fell prisoner. We didn't know what information the enemy had gotten out of him. We tried to remain calm and find out the circumstances of his arrest. But impatience breeds tension. Oscar Pérez Cassar couldn't take it and left for Honduras, abandoning us. Later he repented of his behavior and asked to return to the ranks of the Sandinista Front. I was unjust and opposed it. Daniel or Humberto gave him the opportunity and Oscar Pérez Cassar vindicated himself, as verified by his capture and heroic death alongside the General Staff of the Rigoberto López Pérez Western Front. Jaime Wheelock asked me many times to rethink the matter and change my attitude. Today I believe that we human beings are not exempt from errors; we are not perfect. But I must say that Oscar Pérez Cassar was a leader and a revolutionary combatant. Joaquín Cuadra, Dora María Téllez, Hilario Sánchez, Oswaldo Lacayo and my other comrades are or were aware of the change in my thinking.[1]

4

On the opaque floor, measuring each impulse, my memory spinning like a top, I cannot persuade myself of the absence of light, the light that escaped hours ago; of that abyss of hidden faces close to my hood; of the bitter taste in my mouth and the threatening urgency of my bladder; of my right hand cuffed to a ring in the wall which, for some reason and for the first time, acquired consciousness of its circularity, unable to conceive any other geometrical form. I don't know why that was so important.

There is in all this an element of levitation, of a dance, of useless repentance. I know beforehand that they won't believe me, that they're convinced I'm a murderer.

[1] *Testimonio de Carlos Nuñez.*

We are persuaded of our mutual deceptions, of the chess game and the marked cards. Suddenly, the wall becomes mine, it settles by my side, becomes the landscape I cannot see but which is within reach of the only hands I have, for the others flap like buzzards; more precisely, they are the swords in this war where all the advantages are mine.

They ask my name. What difference does it make? I give it to them, even though it might mean the firing squad — childhood memories — and they're astonished. Pepe Manzano, redheaded practical joker of the neighborhood, Virginia's son, who was a friend of Doña Anita, my mother. Remember, Pepe, how we were once jailed for our opposition to Somoza. That doesn't mean a thing now, my little Colonel.

The sun is so far away! Huddled in my chest is repentance for having scorned the trees, the sand, that starry night I squeezed your hand to feign tenderness when the only thing I wanted was to open your legs and sample the font of your desire. The permanent scars of optimism are ever so close to the surface. Why didn't I embrace my friend? Why didn't I tell him I respected him? The neon lights, the position on the directorate, a noise in history...it's more important to know what place I have in your heart.

A minimal voice reminds me that some place on the other side of my hood are Carlos and Pedro Arauz and all the others, and that it's almost an aberration to feel this exuberance at the challenge.

It's preferable to receive the distracting blow that inhibits reflection. The feet refine their dance; they move over your chest, they crush your ribs; they decide over and over to attack; the boots strike your kneecaps, your testicles, and once again treacherously return to the brutal minuet.

Close your eyes; take off your hood; I'm sure it's Germán Bello, colonel, pilot, boyhood friend, brother of the beautiful Conchita, my love in the days of Winnetou, the one I planned to kidnap when I took off for the jungle with Adrián Blandón and that ballsy fellow, Salvador Vílchez, who was already 20 years-old. There are only 270 days of this to go — no matter that you don't know this now — 270 days of the same thing, the salty taste, the hard, anticipated defiance that will some day become nostalgia because it is unrepeatable, like the love for a woman who has gone away forever. I must tell them something, a lengthy, deliberate, serious lie, to gain time, hoping, optimistically, that they'll grow tired, perhaps show some sign of compassion. But, careful! That's also dangerous. Not their fists, but the need for a bit of rest, the yearned for pleasure of dreaming, even if it's only in black and white; a little water. You know the value of a parenthesis so they'll stop the sadism, of giving them old directions to an abandoned cave on the edge of doubt. Not safehouses, because they've no place in my story.

I don't want to believe in the possibility of their picking up the threads; they don't have bloodhounds to follow the trail; they're stupid, brutal; they lack astuteness, common sense. They haven't been able to decipher the simple code for some obvious telephone numbers. Duty dictates falsifying addresses, throwing them off track, diverting them, but oh for a sip of water, some sleep, some rest, knowing all the while that temptation's been rejected, that the mirrors are shattered, that we are all mad...

In the final analysis, it was easy, so easy that at times it provokes a desire to be put to the test again, all that is preferable to an accusing glance some morning, to a slight shove, to the possibility that one's skin — not the one that has to do with histology but the other skin — might one day be injured. Of course they know that I know. Carlos knows that I know, that I'm thirsty. And Pedro Arauz knows that I know that I'm thirsty. They all know that, although they'll never know where we satisfy our thirst. You've already given them a comfortable margin of safety. Your voice sounds like that of a distant, disagreeable relative, sort of like an idiot brother-in-law. You don't fool anybody with the grains of sugar you add to the bile.

My ribs resound, converted into piano keys, the pain rising above the music; my sneezing and coughing above the pain. The eternal scars are here, my daughter, my love. They have their own anniversaries and I can see them whenever my faith or my happiness waver. Space and time have to do not only with relativity, but with this irreplaceable moment, with these walls that I refuse to hate because they saw me when I could not see them, because they were witnesses.

They neutralize the urine with deodorant spray so the man can ask me questions.

The pock-marked mattress in my cell upon which I rest is as old as a sword. After two weeks, the itching starts in my swollen testicles, in the innocent hairs that were the shame of my childhood and the prologue and epilogue to so much bewilderment and so much joy. The crab lice migrated from the mattress to the hair, and from the hair to the idle fingernails that were kept busy for months.

5

Those who specialize in insects call the malady pubic pediculosis, according to my friend, Dr. Elías Guevara, who prescribed rubdowns with mercurochrome so a patient would not pass it on to his wife.

I had nothing but my anxious fingernails, which put in 15 hour days of voluntary labor once they reduced the torture to occasional sessions each day.

The experts Falot and Mourion demonstrated the falsity of the belief that crab lice produce typhoid fever, but these hemipterous creatures, almost always the bastard offspring of pleasure, produce a worse itching than bad thoughts, which are always the best ones. They can also be transmitted in other ways, I know, as does the filthy mattress on which my sack of bones was deposited.

The crab louse is white in color, tending to a yellowish-gray, and its torso is wider than its head. The females are more developed than the male, growing to 1 1/2 millimeters in length, while the males — stupid, weak midgets — only reach a millimeter in length.

The crab louse has the highest birthrate in the world. After I'd killed the last one with my implacable fingernails, they'd reappear as though nothing had happened.

6

Music played 24 hours a day deafens, distracts, kills and revives you; it drowns out the screams of the tortured and the names of the prisoners. Where could Mildred Abaunza be? After firing the shot, the murderer was condemned for this and many other crimes to 180 years in prison. And Mildred? She died. They told the condemned man much later at his court-martial, when he recalled her two large, animated eyes.

When hunger grips one, it strikes like a sergeant's fist. It's not right for them to offer you the pleasure of yesterday's rice mixed with oil and today's beans only to snatch it away as your salivary glands begin to flow with what seems like your mother's milk and drag you off down the stone corridor, beating you all the way.

It's not right that they make you stand up when you ankles are swollen like baseballs and that they beat you. No one can replace the pleasure of writing a poem to little Ana Josefina whose memory is a lake dotted with colored boats.

It's already a relief to be beaten only three times a day and only now and then late at night; to receive only occasional insults; and that Whitey no longer spits in your drinking water.

When they turn on the cold — and what cold! — and the noise — what noise! — of the air conditioning, it sinks into your skin, makes you want to hear anything but that noise, even insults to your mother, anything else. But it's not to make you hear something else, rather to say something else. Cold, noise, solitude, shit, piss, dreams.

Central America is big; it should be a child's notebook, a university city. Some day — why not? — children will be children, women will be women, men will learn what this means and human beings will be cordial stars and only practice self-effacement, which is the superior form of hygiene.

The circle tightened, becoming mysterious and maddeningly familiar. The comings and goings were a constant distraction. Days of forgetting, until six weeks — centuries — have passed. There's the deliberate silence of the human voice, the shit accumulating in plastic bags, the uncontrollable vomiting of the ferocious warden who collects those packages I have sent to all of them.

7

They bring a hose to wash down the crumbs and odors; they blast me with foam and the voice starts up again: "I respect you; okay, I admire you; you succeeded, so now help me justify somehow these months of conversation; it doesn't make sense; just decipher the telephone numbers; give me some of the addresses that no longer mean anything; why do you want a soft drink when water is better for you? Cigarettes are bad for you; your family is well; why did you make the mistake of writing a poem to your daughter instead of answering a few simple questions? We know everything; maybe you're going to live; I can't promise but it's a possibility; it depends; in any case, you want to be a hero and that's vanity; if they kill you, you're a martyr, and if they don't, you're a hero; anyway, you screwed me; nobody's grateful to you for anything; nobody's going to remember this; you think I want to trick you, but I'm sincere about this; you'll see, the world keeps turning and here you are like an idiot; you like women, don't tell me you don't; so do I; but if you don't get out of here, what good does that do you? Reduced to dust, you can't raise any dust; just the godamn telephones; I'm not asking much of you; just give me one of them, the least important one; think it over, I'll be back in a while."

Slowness is comforting, as it is to move my swollen feet with the tenderness one uses to pull the pin from a hand grenade, my hand as if I were stroking a kitten, my torso without pinpricks; to assimilate the confidential, murmured news the guard passed me, that tomorrow I'm to appear before the court-martial; the honeymoon of a cigarette smuggled to me behind the back of the existing social order, the possibility, for God's sake, of seeing a bare knee, a text by Borges, perhaps to see René, Juan José, "Chiri" Guzmán, the baby girl I left a year ago and who, if she still lives, now walks and talks, Josefina, the sun, life and its contradictions, an accidental bruise, a bloodstain at the tip of a rose petal.

I won't listen to that voice; I'm deaf; from now on I'll listen to the message, watch the twists and turns with new eyes. I'll walk slowly, savoring cooking oil, the odor of the earth and the fragrance of your sex, water. I'm going to love each child, no doubt about it; I promise to forgive my torturer, I will not fear death; I'll love life as if each minute were a new resurrection.

Chapter
Thirty-Two

1

Somoza denies at a press conference that I have been captured. Before diplomats, the Cabinet and the General Staff he affirms: "Señor Borge was never arrested."

The students continued denouncing my arrest. There were small but persistent demonstrations and even some strikes.

Monsignor Miguel Obando sent a telegram to Somoza the day after the event pleading for my personal safety. Somoza did not reply.

On April 9, 1976 — two months after my detention — as he was bidding farewell to the President of Costa Rica, Daniel Oduber, Somoza Debayle held another press conference in the Officers Club in which he ardently promised an economic bonanza. In addition to the Cabinet and diplomatic corps, the shock troops of petty thieves and paid assassins headed by Nicolasa Sevilla, Somoza's long-time procuress, were also present.

Silvio Mora, a reporter for Channel 2's *Extravisión* program, asked Somoza, who appeared to be half-inebriated: "Tomás Borge was captured on February 4th at 8 p.m. on the Masaya highway in front of McDonald's. When will he be brought to trial?"

There was a tense silence. Somoza thought for interminable seconds. He adjusted his tie, coughed. Then he said slowly: "Here it's not like Cuba where your cronies murder their prisoners... Señor Borge will be tried by a Court Martial."

Somoza didn't dare deny my imprisonment in the presence of Oduber. Many people maintained, with good reason, that Silvio Mora's courage saved my life. It was necessary to mount a campaign — out of the University — to protect Silvio.

2

After six months in prison, I was called before the Court Martial.

The provost, Capt. Gabuardi, plays his role well. He does not smile. He's courteous. From the moment I saw him, as I got out of the van that would bring me to the Court every day, I recognized him.

I'd seen him months earlier when Silvio Casco was driving me from a clandestine meeting to a safehouse. He had been drunk, with only one foot in this world. The first thing that occurred to us was to disarm him. He offered no resistance when we shoved him into the car. We felt sorry for him. We were barely able to make out the address he mumbled to us where he lived. His wife, or sister, or somebody was waiting for him on the sidewalk.

I'm tempted to tell the Court about my generosity toward that man. Should I? I decide not to. I don't want to humiliate him; it would appear boastful, so I keep my mouth shut.

"Tell us what you know about the Sandinista National Liberation Front."

"Everything I know?"

"Yes."

"Including its origins?"

"Of course."

I tell what I recall of the history of the FSLN and, the next day, I espy a newspaper in the hands of a secretary, who gives me a conspiratorial wink. Before the questioning begins, she gets up and leaves the paper within my reach. She then sits down again with a spectacular crossing of her legs that distracts the young prosecutor.

I note with astonishment that they have transcribed my every word. 'How stupid!' I think. It's our history, as I remember it. It can't be. Yet there it is. For the first time, some of the activities of the organization founded by Carlos Fonseca are revealed to the general public.

At night, when I'd already raised my hopes that they would take me to Tipitapa prison along with the other defendants, they return me to the security cell. They strip me so as not to soil the clothing I am to wear at the trial. They have taken away the mattress and I'm to sleep once again, hooded and manacled, on the cold floor. My bones ache and an insidious cough keeps me awake. I ask for an aspirin and they tell me to go to hell.

A new prison guard asks: "What's your name?"

"What's it to you?"

He opens the cuffs and hangs me from the top of the bars so the tips of my toes barely touch the floor. I don't know why but I'm happy, euphoric. I know they aren't going to kill me, at least not yet, and I can afford the luxury of defying them more openly.

An officer passes by and sees me dangling from the manacles. He asks why, orders them to take me down, curses the prison guard. The next day, my eyes covered with tape, they take me out into the sunshine. After two hours, when I'm on the verge of sunstroke, a barber shows up, shaves me and pats talcum powder on my sunburnt skin.

They again take me to the Court Martial and, for the first time, I see my comrades. When I enter the room filled with prisoners, lawyers, secretaries, newspapermen, and, toward the rear, family members and curious observers, there is a wave of sound. An intense murmur bathes the desolate coasts of my heart. Everybody stands and applauds. The president of the Court shouts something, the provost impotently clenches his fists, and the prosecutor threatens I don't know what punishment.

I made my plea. I spoke of life, solitude, justice, honor. Behind me, the silence of the other defendants; in front of me, the attentive, suspicious, hostile eyes of the uniformed judges. I confessed to being a subversive, an enemy of the established order, an accomplice in the deaths of rural magistrates and the author of a homicide: "I killed Officer Rodolfo Sequeira O'Connoly, in self-defense. I fired first. Who killed Mildred Abaunza? Mildred had no weapons to defend herself, other than her sweetness and her patriotism. I understand the letter sent by Officer Sequeira's father. The letter Mildred's mother must have sent has not arrived nor will it. We do not know who fired the Garand that killed Mildred, and we'll never know. Therefore, Mildred was not killed by an individual but by a system. One day the guilty parties will be brought to trial. Today, the dawn is still only a temptation. Tomorrow, someday, a new sun will shine, illuminating all the land the martyrs and heroes have bequeathed us with deep rivers of milk and honey."

Carlos Mejía Godoy immortalized that phrase by incorporating it into the FSLN anthem.

The judges remained silent. They shared shrugs and stern glares. They laughed at my solitude and my prophecy. Too bad for them.

3

I decide to go on a hunger strike to demand my transfer to the Tipitapa prison. A physician visits me from time to time to take my blood pressure and discovers, when he taps my knees with his little hammer, that I have no reflexes. My broken ribs still hurt.

I hear music 24 hours a day. *Radio Amor* is the favorite station. Luckily, it's instrumental music: "Strangers in the Night," "Blue Moon," Paul Mauriat, Ray Coniff and, occasionally, the music of Bach, drown out the screams of the tortured coming from the end of a nearby tunnel. I couldn't make out the words, mixed with groans and screams, issuing from the interrogation rooms. One night I heard Tito Chamorro's name and thought my imagination was playing tricks on me, because Tito was in the mountains. Another day, I heard Roberto McEwan's name. Afterwards I learned that he'd been betrayed by Tito Chamorro. I never lost the hope of hearing Mildred Abaunza's dear voice. I had no idea she'd been sacrificed. I was weaker and more squalid each time I left for the Court Martial.

My hunger strike succeeded and they were obliged to transfer me to the Tipitapa prison, where I remained in solitary confinement. Colonel Nicolás Valle Salinas visited me and promised, in his soft, gentlemanly voice, to keep fucking me over until the year 2000. I assured him I'd soon be released. I asked to be put in with my comrades in the other cell block, otherwise I'd start a new hunger strike.

The first thing I received was the poem, "Conspiracy of the Earth Against Solitude" — until now unpublished — written by Gioconda Belli in May 1976. I've loved Gioconda since I first met her, when she was known in the underground as "Justina." I love her because she's good, a good poet, just plain good.

> They constructed silence
> to surround your voice
> opened a parenthesis of walls
> to enclose your eyes
> they did not suspect the earth's mysterious way
> of reading your footprints
> through the rude cement of your cell.
> In scorched Februaries and Marches
> the vapor of your tears travels underground
> entombed words escape
> through the complicity of roots;
> we find messages written in your hand
> on the leaves of trees,
> your breath mixes with
> the oxygen we breathe
> and paints vegetable cobwebs.
> We speak your prison jargon
> like ancient, illuminated apostles.
> Solitude is an illusion of sand
> to deceive impotent jailors.
> They can do nothing, Tomás,
> against the multiple trees
> of our hope.

4

The struggle to break my isolation was difficult. The predominant fear was that they would take advantage of any misstep to assassinate me and, in passing, Marcio Jaén, who was also in solitary confinement.

To weaken the enemy's will, we announced a hunger strike in both cell blocks. For me, it was the second one. The enemy took us seriously, but not too seriously, because we consumed astronomical quantities of caramels. We grew skinny, but not enough to upset the Human Rights Commission or the International Red Cross. When we saw we weren't achieving any results, except to grow a bit skinnier every day, and to thicken the carpet of candy wrappers outside out windows, we decided, with brilliant common sense, to call off the strike.

5

Days went by, weeks, months. Marcio and I decided to try again. This time, just Marcio and me, without any candy. For me, it would be my third. Later, at an opportune moment, the others would join in the strike. I, like an idiot, continued to smoke.

From the window of my cell I could see the spotlight that stared insistently back at me. It was the eye of the Cyclops, a ray of light that prevented me from escaping to the heavens but could not drown out the stars that entertained me one by one. By day, there was the treeless patio, the watchtowers, the chain link fences, an occasional skinny, indifferent dog who'd pause now and then to squirt an underdeveloped stream. At times, I read. Eugène Grindel managed to hold my interest. Like us, he used a pseudonym. Everyone knows him as Paul Eluard. A surrealist, Eluard believed that a poem is a weapon. If the officer of the guard realized that, I thought, he wouldn't even let me have the poems of Santiago Argüello. That danger, however, did not exist: I only glanced through them looking for metaphors.

A little before my hunger strike, I read *El Cid* and even *The Life of María Egipciaca,* a saintly sinner. She fasted to atone for her sins; I in order to annoy my enemies, to test myself, and to be with my comrades.

6

I remember that Valeria's fragrance was unatonable. I had met her at the Witch's house. A witch who bewitched the heart and senses, a witch because she bewitched me, because she had magical philters in her nipples, in her naughtiness, in her orgasms, a jealous witch, enravished and enravishing.

The very first night I met her I called her Valeria, kissed her, and rid her of her prejudices from the Immaculate Convent School, bringing to the surface of her round eyes the flames of Hell and the forbidden fruit.

Since then, we've been joint owners of trapezes, of desires serious and sweet, and of the lust for life.

We always wanted to have a boy child but never managed until we adopted Germancito, the son of El Danto and Julia Herrera, who also fell in combat.

Ana Josefina was born on a day I was about to die. She was conceived by mutual consent one summer night in one of the eastern neighborhoods of Managua, just as Valeria was conceived on a rug embroidered with goblins in Pyongyang the same day we shook the cordial hand of Kim Il Sung. Nine months later, God said: "Let there be light," and Valeria was born. Five years later, I kept my promise to Madame Bovary, and when the unmistakable hare was born, we named her Emma.

That history of ours, Valeria's and mine, Josefina's and mine, was resumed in the cell where I wrote *Carlos, The Dawn Is No Longer Beyond Our Reach*. There we also discussed *Trinchera*, the loveliest, smallest, grandest little newspaper in the world, which Luis ("Chiri") Guzmán illustrated with miniatures and poems and you smuggled out of prison concealed in your sex, its flame surviving the moist evidence of our being.

Chapter
Thirty-Three

1

Josefina, a graduate in educational sciences, had specialized in Spanish literature. From her I learned that the first manifestation of literature is the epic poem — the primary form of history. When his friends go in search of the Cid, they identify him because he offers water to a leper. The hero surmounts fate and death. His sole destiny is victory and loyalty: "Oh Lord, how faithful the servant were there a good master!"

I read some of Enrique de Villena, a kind of Faust. He looked like a faun and was small as a gnome, fat as Sancho Panza, with the inclinations of Don Juan. He wanted to be a marquis and could not. They say he made a pact with the devil, which moved Juan II to ask Fray Lope de Barrientos, bishop of Segovia, to make a pyre of his books, since it was not possible to burn him at the stake. The prelate was a sympathizer of the magical arts and he didn't burn all the books. Villena wrote a *Treatise on the Art of Cutting With a Knife, or the Art of Meat Carving,* a protocol of the dining table in which he also enumerates dishes and tells how to make meat pies, cakes, meatballs and stuffings. Learning about these culinary incursions of the frustrated marquis increased my appetite. I read *Amadís de Gaula.* Cervantes' war against books of chivalry was successful with respect to Amadís, knight errant who delighted St. Ignatius of Loyola and Santa Teresa. Amadís loves Oriana; I love Valeria. Amadís triumphs over the devil and Hell; I have only to triumph over General Genie and solitude. There's a similarity, however, for General Genie has horns, even though his wife is not the cause, and solitude is hell.

Have you read anything by Santa Teresa? By Teresa Cepeda y Ahumada, native of Castile, born in Avila de los Caballeros, enthusiastic reader of books of chivalry, warmhearted and passionate? She married Jesus. It was an intense marriage with an unending honeymoon. An angel with beautiful, flaming features drew near to

Teresa's left side. It must have been a cherub who introduced a long, golden dart into her heart and entrails. The pain was great, the sweetness excessive; such the sweetness, so great the pain, that she has no desire to remove it, nor is her soul content with anything less than God. It is not a corporal pain — Teresa says — but spiritual, although — she clarifies — the body does participate and greatly.

I liked this saint, this Carmelite, this barefoot woman. The book about her life is the highest expression of religious mysticism. My sympathies were with the nun in her quarrels with the Princess of Eboli. She writes from Segovia in 1574, hoping the Lord will visit much suffering and many fleas and goblins on the Princess and her nuns.

2

Josefina brought me *The Solitary Insurrection* in prison. There was a serious struggle with the officer of the guard, who feared that the book might be a subversive manual in verse. I imagined Carlos Martínez Rivas as being similar in appearance to García Lorca, or perhaps to an habitué of gambling casinos and art museums: that is, slender, with a solemn, seductive gaze.

When, during the decade of the '40s, Carlos Martínez Rivas recited his first poems in that international commentator's voice of his, with which he also would sing "C'est Si Bon," everyone, irrespective of race, religion or lyrical preference, was consumed by the flames.

The assassin was only sixteen years-old, yet he had already constructed the only authorized airfield for butterflies. José Coronel Urtecho and Angel Martínez Baigorri didn't dare correct him, as, when asked, they did so many others.

How to change a word of these whispered lines?

Day and night I pounded at the foot of your smile.
But you didn't hear me. I called you with bees...

to no avail. With sparrows...no response.

With horses...

and your breast remained closed.

Until one day...

"Of all the poets of our time," says Coronel Urtecho, "Carlos is the one I most admire." States Ernesto Cardenal: "Not even Rubén Darío, perhaps, has enjoyed such a poetic gift, such a state of grace as he." And Mejía Sánchez concludes: "Martínez Rivas, unrivaled poet."

Octavio Paz also appreciates him. Occasionally, distance is a spyglass that permits objectivity. The Mexican says something — I don't quote him textually — to the effect that the Nicaraguan is a new version of the poet as rebel, which is the key to his radiance.

What does Carlos Martínez Rivas rebel against? *The Solitary Insurrection* expresses his rejection of a dehumanized society. Those who rebel are as dangerous as those who reveal themselves, and not simply because William Carlos Williams has said so. It's true, the purpose of writing is to reveal — rebellion takes care of itself — and revelation occurs when we regurgitate the inner self, when our inner being is recreated in the image of our outward appearance.

A poet in revolt, though his insurrection be solitary, is like an angel. Poets have the gift of transforming themselves into demons, on earth as well as in heaven. The little Luzbels of the past century are, also in this case, our point of reference: Baudelaire, Rimbaud, Verlaine. It is possible that one should add Whitman — the favorite of so many — to this family; and Pushkin — Lenin's favorite; and Lorca — everyone's favorite, who as Paul Eluard says, were "heroes or victims, nostalgic for a greater light, the incarnation of man extenuated by heaven...suppressed and rebellious, a slave who dreams of freedom, desperate, illuminated." Carlos Martínez Rivas is a descendant of this breed by way of the same state of grace and lyrical subversiveness.

There are other poets who are serene and have angelic faces, such as Shakespeare, Dante, Goethe. They are the conscience of their time. Among them I would include Ernesto Cardenal.

That is why our poet is impelled toward a rude, self-induced, private hell.

Is this man — the question's worth asking — a rebel without a cause? An officious interpreter of European solitude? A snob?

To begin with, there can be no doubt that his solitude is American and that he does not plagiarize concepts and attitudes. He reiterates that he's from this side of the Atlantic:

> I also saw the mothers
> of our America, in Paris, promenading
> along the great boulevards
> with the cadavers of their daughters
> wearing plumes and high heels. Ready.
> Embalmed for marriage.

He's American; he's Nicaraguan, which exalts and comforts me. The poet knew our purgatory — which is an historical hell — and he knew that daily life, the yapping of lapdogs, the megaphone broadcasting "the Fifth Symphony" was all predetermined by the Somoza dictatorship. That's why he says:

> Sleep now, while you have not yet to wait
> for that all-powerful signature from the hill: the safe conduct,
> the tax exemption, the pardon for your rebellious nephew,
> inclusion on the Roll, the Order of Merit...Everything!

For those who do not know, it's a "Cradlesong Without Music," a reflection of the uneasiness and dread in the clogged veins of Latin America.

The past applauded him as a Bohemian. For that world what matters is that he's a poet of such magnitude; it's enough, though few understand this, that he is called a poet. The Revolution recognizes him as a creator, understanding him and, in any case, if there is something to lament, it's the Bohemian element in its destructive sense.

He was a rebel in accord with his time and circumstances. As a rebel, like many others — though in another sense — he served his sentence.

Following the revolutionary victory, Martínez Rivas escapes from his condition of "hibernation and fear," he deciphers some of his enigmas and his subjective insurrection begins to metamorphose; his insurrection remains solitary, possessed of a poetry that doggedly follows its aesthetic intentions, with the result that he rends himself, plunges into the abyss through tunnels from which he emerges dazed and bewildered. His aesthetic intentions are superimposed on a project of terrible unknowns. He has the same harshness as Vallejo, although he now builds with images that are closer to more densely populated territory.

In his "Two Leaders Analyze Ortega's Words," obsessed by children, he affirms that Nicaragua today is not only "the imaginary image of the world," but — and I would say above all — "the darling daughter of the peoples of the People." He condemns Bermúdez's chaplain to suffer in the most elaborate chamberpot of Hell, not because Monsignor is a reactionary, but because he doesn't give a damn that children are murdered by the counterrevolution.

It's worth reading the other poem by Martínez Rivas, written when Archbishop Obando returned from his campaign to win a Cardinal's purple. Upon receiving it he was given a pompous reception. Let's look at this other "Welcome":

> Welcome.
> Only a few will be missing at the reception.
>
> Such as the Nicaraguan mothers,
> for whose sons fallen in combat
> His Holiness John Paul the Second
> did not deign to say a public prayer.
>
>   (There was a moment of silence
> in the square for a full, eternal second.
> That silence still hangs suspended, I hear it now.
> But the Pontif relented not. He remained unmoved.)
>
> Those boys, sons of those mothers, won't be there,
> nor other mothers of other sons killed later;
> fallen during your recent visit to the Vatican
> for the purpose of consolidating in Rome,
> Capital of Christianity, your relations

with Washington, Capital of Capital.
They will not be present at your Welcome.

You will miss the children
from the Alliance of Sandinista Children.
Luis Alfonso Velázquez Flores won't be there with flowers
for you. Nor will the dead or the living or those
who will die *(morituri)* greet you.
You will miss the pampered of the Gospels.

Only the Magnates will receive you.
The last Tycoons!
The High Church, The High Clergy, The Highest Baseness.
And, yes, your dozing congregation.
Those who, according to Jesus, comprised the blind flock:
"I came into this world, that they who do not see may see,
and they who see may become blind." (John 9: 39)

We write anew what we have seen and lived
for twenty glutted years, but as up-to-date
as tomorrow's newspaper.

             "Before
you have tarnished the miter, raising it
in your trembling pastoral fingers
in defense of oppression...,"
                         reconsider,
Pastor. The blind will receive you.
Your sleepy flock. The Armada of Fear.

The wakeful will not see your pomp. They,
far away, hugging the earth
with pounding hearts,
will watch for the aggressor on the border.

Forgive their absence at your Welcoming. Absolve them.

Carlos Martínez Rivas is singular, a wise man — he speaks
living and dead languages and he has, besides, a tongue as fertile as
the pollen on the beak of a hummingbird — enigmatic in practically

the full sense of the perfect crime he commits each time he recalls Joaquín Pasos or explains a poem.

After reading Martínez Rivas, one asks what is the secret of such discoveries, what is the source of all that earth, fire, air and water? I'm speaking of his clear brow, his ears sharp as a carpenter's chisel, or fingers made to mold hypotenuses, or his unobstructed nose for detecting bellies and obstinate mirrors.

It's difficult to forgive Carlos Martínez Rivas, because, no matter how hard we try, it's impossible to reach him. There is nothing to do but feel admiration, for he's extraordinary, and to love him because he is, after all, imperfect.

Chapter
Thirty-Four

1

In my cell, damn it, there are fleas and hunger.

One day of many, from that world of mine, I saw Julio Cortázar bound by like a startled deer.

Ah, Julio! In that solitude you were my companion. I never supposed that you would come to be such a friend, such a brother, such a... You were there in prison with me, and this you did know.

It was Josefina who brought into the prison and introduced me to *A Manual For Manuel, Hopscotch...* The ignorance of that herd of animals comprising the military censors, men who didn't know Cortázar existed, whose name must have sounded to them like some author of Greek myths, made their presence possible. They did not permit me many books.

The titles of publications were decisive: if they raised any doubts they ended up in the fire; if not, they might be spared and remain in prison. On one occasion someone brought me the work of an unknown North American author: *Mental Energy*, by Orison Sweet Marden. The inquisitors, of course, would not let it pass, because that "mental energy" would surely provide me with sufficient secret weapons to make my escape. They unexpectedly let George Politzer's *Elements of Philosophy* through because it had to do with philosophy, which they deemed inconsequential and inoffensive. Had someone sent me Gunter Grass's *The Tin Drum*, they would have prohibited it simply because of the word, "drum," although they might have allowed it because of the word "tin."

The stupidity of the censors permitted mc to read and reread Cortázar. That's where I got to know and appreciate him. He'd enter and leave the prison through imaginary cracks in the walls. He slipped in clandestinely and we'd talk. Julio never proposed any plan of escape. So I never did escape, in any sense. The solitude was torture, but Julio was there keeping me company. His construction and reconstruction of worlds, his *62/A Model to Build* and *All Fires the Fire* were a moral and literary stimulus for me, for at that time I was writing *Carlos, The Dawn Is No Longer Beyond Our Reach.* Julio's story about Che Guevara entitled "Meeting" made an impression on me. Influenced by that story and using it as a reference I wrote a letter/story to Carlos Nuñez about Carlos Fonseca. And, of course, there were the enigmas of *Hopscotch,* enigmas that even in my subsequent personal relationship with Julio I have not dared to try to decipher. I prefer that these enigmas remain intact.

I read *Hopscotch* in a linear fashion, which is one of the ways Julio proposes in his preliminary "Table of Advice." I also read it from end to beginning and from beginning to end. A multi-layered work; two, three, four worlds; different novels; a true piece of literature where we the readers end up being the authors. Cortázar's literature, in or out of jail, is a call to the imagination: never ever was it an escape from consciousness. Nothing is more exciting than a revolutionary project. For me, *Hopscotch* is as necessary as *Faust,* or *Dead Souls,* or *Under the Volcano,* the *Divine Comedy* and the *History of Genji.*

Cortázar manages an irony filled with tenderness yet which at the same time does not conceal its identity as irony. I imagine this ironic style comes from the River Plate, but Cortázar synthesizes it and raises it to universal dimensions. He's audacious with language, with the everyday street language of this America of ours. This language of ordinary folk, of our sibling and our neighbor, took the new Latin American literature by storm and enriched it. His audacity never loses touch with reality, nor is it lacking in content, for it seeks to create and recreate symbols and intelligible individuals: the *cronopios,* the sorceress, or his jazz musician.

When Cortázar would leave and I'd remain behind in prison, we would continue to communicate in some fashion. Perhaps by remote control; perhaps in the secret language of the *cronopios.* At the time, Cortázar was in Paris writing, in Mexico, or in Rome with the Bertrand Russell Tribunal, or in San José, Costa Rica; and I, isolated, protesting and skinny in the Tipitapa Model Prison. One day I had the intention of writing him, but it remained unrealized. I was certain he would answer me. Although I never did write him, Julio responded. He also responded to the needs of the Nicaraguan people. The proof is that at that very moment Cortázar signed a message expressing his solidarity and personal identification with our people's struggle. That was his response to the letter I neither wrote nor sent. His letter, which appeared in Sandinista papers, in magazines and solidarity newspapers in America and Europe, read as follows:

Although widely known throughout the world, one appreciates the tragic political and social situations of the people of Nicaragua more intimately and with greater clarity when he sets foot on the soil of a neighboring country, as is the case of Costa Rica, for the firsthand accounts of that situation multiply as you meet the exiles and the relatives of innumerable victims and prisoners of the Somoza regime.

That is why I do not wish to leave San José without registering my repudiation of so many endless violations of human rights and of the most elementary laws of a democratic society. The Bertrand Russell Tribunal, of which I was a jury member and with which were associated the most eminent personalities of our time, on numerous occasions expressed its energetic condemnation of the ruling regime in Nicaragua. I feel that that condemnation must be tirelessly repeated by all who believe in democracy and freedom; I believe that the government of Nicaragua must be obliged to respect the laws and rights of man. My protest is not merely personal; I know that it embraces millions of people in Latin America and throughout the world who will never accept regimes based on hate, oppression and disdain for human values.

(signed)   Julio Cortázar

In mid-October 1979, shortly after the revolutionary victory, General Omar Torrijos telephoned me from Panama offering us the opportunity to invite Cortázar to Nicaragua, since he was close enough to hear and feel our national euphoria as it spread over the Isthmus. Julio, of course, had already decided to come to Nicaragua.

Torrijos and we limited ourselves to facilitating his inevitable reentry. We immediately sent an airplane, the "19 DE JULIO", to pick him up. But it turned out that a day or so prior to the arrival of our plane Cortázar had been mugged and his passport and money stolen. Torrijos, for his part, had also placed an aircraft at his disposal in order to facilitate the trip. Thus Cortázar found himself without documents and penniless, but with two airplanes fully ready to transport him, so he took off.

This was the second time he had come to Nicaragua — once before he had been clandestinely, with his lanky and thoroughly unclandestine figure, in Solentiname together with Ernesto Cardenal, the local community and Sergio Ramírez — but it was the first time he had arrived in a liberated and revolutionary Nicaragua. On that occasion I went to the airport to receive him as befits a respectable writer and there I had the good fortune to meet in person my old friend who had visited me in prison who had seemed so inoffensive to the blind eyes of the military censors and had breached the military security apparatus put in place to keep the Sandinista prisoners incommunicado.

Cortázar and Carol settled in Nicaragua; they came and went, they'd leave and return, stay and live and come back again. Cortázar circled the day in eighty worlds and stopped in Nicaragua.

Although he had an address and post office box in Paris, Cortázar is a Latin American and has never ceased being one; that is, he's never stopped experiencing the pleasure and suffering of being Latin American: the banishments and struggles, the pains and hopes. Nicaragua was his home. Cortázar discovered Nicaragua each time he came here. He wanted to see it all. He went everywhere: among the people, to the volcanoes, the rivers, the Atlantic Coast, the cooperatives, the literacy program.

He gave readings in the patio of the Casa Fernando Gordillo of the Sandinista Cultural Workers Association, inaugurated the Ministry of Culture's Poetry Tuesdays, and drank *Flor de Caña* rum with his friends. He joined a peace vigil on the northern border, and he received the Rubén Darío Order of Cultural Independence.

Cortázar suffered a personal tragedy and I was anxious about his return, for this country's landscape might prove disagreeable to him.

But he reappeared and I saw the same Cortázar as before, rising above his pain and transcending it. The explanation he gave us was that his love itself consoled him. When one has known how to love, there is no guilt. While it might seem a contradiction, he who is capable of love suffers the loss of a loved one less than the person who has been unable to show or demonstrate sufficient love. Grief is sometimes accompanied by remorse. The loss of another human being hurts in large measure because of guilt complexes that don't exist when one — as was Cortázar's case — has been able to love his spouse; which also reflects Cortázar's capacity to give of himself. So it is that, in such situations, people like him are less vulnerable than those who give nothing of themselves. They don't feel the impact of grief as much. Love alleviates our sorrow and defends us from death. One night Carol asked to speak with me alone. She had severe pain in her bones. With hands full of mystery and tender eyes she communicated to me the secret that she had only a few months to live.

What moved me when that secret was revealed through its own drama were her words: "I wish Julio might die first so that he could be spared the pain of my death."

When Claribel Alegría communicated to me the news of Carol's death, I became aware of the magnitude of that love.

Cortázar is such a tall person, so profound, that he manages to make himself smaller and to reduce his frame in order to walk through life simulating the stature of ordinary men. Cortázar is man-sized, that is, a man who is taller than he really is. He's a man in whom coexist naturally and unmistakably simplicity, tenderness and modesty. Julio's stature rises above his literature. I noted in him a series of virtues which, insofar as possible, I have sought to cultivate in myself, if indeed I possess any at all. I would like to be like Cortázar, not as a writer but as a man. I would like to grow as a man, even were I incapable of becoming an artist. And while it certainly is true that I could never aspire to be a writer like Cortázar, I do have the right and the obligation to aspire to be a man like Julio.

2

Josefina also brought me *The Open Veins of Latin America*, which tells of the development of underdevelopment and exposes the keys to the international structure of plunder.

The Open Veins relates that when Columbus discovered America, he witnessed a formidable volcanic eruption. It was like an omen of what would become of the immense lands of America, festering beneath the feet of its ancient and modern conquerors. And what would become — I add — of the little country where Sandino's bones lie lost and scattered.

I imagined Eduardo Galeano as having a reflective, ceremonial face. I never supposed him to be a young man with a frankness that leaves one dazed and anxious to continue listening to what he has to say. Galeano, who was to become my fraternal confidant, is, above all, a man of principles.

3

Despite the hunger strike, they do not suspend visits except one or two afternoons. They even permit them more regularly. During these visits, they take Mario and me out of our cells and we can be together. He's visited by his mother, his brothers and a pale young girl as thin as a profile.

Josefina arrived punctually, wearing foam rubber sandals, alert, serene, indefinable, together with Ana Josefina, that small explosion of 200 shooting stars.

My children by my first wife, Yelba Mayorga, also visited me. Yelba would be assassinated by the National Guard in 1979 — in March it must have been — three months before the revolutionary victory.

She was trying to find Birmania, Dominique and Michelle, unaware that the first two were underground manufacturing contact bombs near Chichigalpa, nor that Michelle, the youngest, was in Managua and would take part in the famous withdrawal to Masaya that June. It was useless for Yelba to tell them she hadn't participated in any activities, that she was innocent. They raped her, beat her terribly and machine-gunned her together with some of the witnesses who were accompanying her in the taxi where she was captured, between Chinandega and León.

4

My children by Yelba had neither a roof over their heads nor a school. They went hungry. One day they stayed with an aunt, another night they'd sleep in the house of a collaborator. The FSLN lacked resources and the little we obtained barely sufficed to maintain the full-time combatants. Families dependent on the professional cadres experienced deprivations.

Yelba arrived one day and our daughter, Bolivia, spoke to her harshly, in a way I rejected because Yelba was her mother, because it was unfair and because she was confused. And she, my daughter, the walking photograph of my first gestures and whom I loved like a wounded bird, took an overdose of tranquilizers. Her heart, which always quickened the sources of my tenderness, stopped beating.

Josefina brought me letters.

Gioconda Belli wrote: "You are not nor will you ever be alone."

Pedro Aráuz ordered me to get it off my chest: "Cry as only the wretched can cry."

Henry Ruiz comforted me, saying: "My brother wolf is a tiger," and he committed himself to victory with a phrase that later became famous: "We will bury the enemy's heart in the mountains."

Rosario Murillo, who had lost one of her sons in the earthquake, wrote me a letter urging me to go on living:

> That's how it was with me. I wasn't there to save him either, or to try to save him, from the earth.
>
> You can't say good-bye with your own hand. Because you cannot hate love, much less *that* love. We need your hand, your face, your smile. Here we are. Always raising our song.

Bolivia was a prostitute from age sixteen on. That's why I loved her so. Was that the reason? She sold herself in order to live, because I didn't give her a penny for survival, because that was the price I had to pay. My contribution to the struggle was the red lights, the vomiting, the horror, her flesh stained out of necessity or out of weakness, what the hell difference does it make? She smoked marijuana, got pregnant very young and had a son whom she named after me.

Since that day when I bashed my forehead against the bars, screaming like a wounded animal, my life is incomplete, for it lacks that quota of warmth I was unable to give her during that long winter.

They didn't let me see her. That was best. I don't want to see her with her eyes closed, hands folded. Since that day at two o'clock in the afternoon, I have been hoping for her resurrection. I don't want to see her surrounded by dirt on all sides, her feet, her breasts sold to the highest bidders, those breasts on which I recline my head as I reject her memory.

Even now, as I write these knife-jabs I continue to forget you without destroying the mirror in which I see your hands that caressed and clawed me, your spotless sex from which issued Tomás, your son whom I never knew because he died in a green phosphorescence while I was blinded by the hood and far from your labor pains. My project of forgetting, my useless project: I had to tell it, defy the hurricane, relive this pain once more. If you only knew how much I needed to forget, my little girl.

Chapter
Thirty-Five

1

We sat on the cot to watch the days marching by, to read and to smoke. I imagined at night — before entering the dark tunnel that in prison is cast iron and outside is called sleep — that I am playing baseball, that I'm insulting the warden, that an unknown girl in a long, wide dress comes to visit me. She sits in the wooden chair and seduces me and I seduce her in a long ceremony whose coronation of thorns and oranges I leave for the next apparition.

In the morning there are throbs of happiness. I do exercises for two hours, sometimes three. Stealthily, I write doggerel verse sometimes deliberately, sometimes spontaneously; I write letters to Bayardo Arce and to Josefina, with which one could compile the encyclopedia of faith. Allusions to the war, in which I defend and attack with the theories of an unemployed, subjective intellectual; conceptions that delved into our strategic and tactical possibilities. I don't know if the letter has been preserved in which I announce that the bourgeoisie has been incapable of creating a political party and that the theoreticians of INCAE were forming, together with bankers and industrialists — opposed to Somoza in the roundhouse of economic contradictions — a new political party.

Somoza never represented the bourgeoisie — as I said in my letter — but only small groups of technocrats and enriched military men who, like Somoza himself, had no need to compete because they enjoyed fiscal and banking privileges, virulent business opportunities and smuggling operations conducted in plain view.

The economic contradiction between those bankers and businessmen, whom I characterized as modern, and the others who were in Somoza's corral of wild and domesticated bulls, would — I asserted — find expression in the rise of a political party of the Nicaraguan bourgeoisie, irremediably shipwrecked on shores occupied by the Sandinistas.

A little later, with the appearance of the Nicaraguan Democratic Movement (MDN), I gave myself airs — I now understand the matter was more complex — of having prophesied the rise of the party headed by the young millionaire (Casanova seventy something), Alfonso Robelo, who would become a member of the Junta of the Government of National Reconstruction, of the counterrevolutionary directorate and of the Society for the Protection of Demagogic Phrases.

2

"A" was a karate blow with closed fist aimed at the ceiling; "E" was two blows; "I" was three, "O" four and "U" five; in the same way and the same direction, clear and amnesia-proof, these are, as common sense would indicate, the vowels.

"B"—as in *bien, bollo, burro* — was the holding up of five open fingers on either hand, preferably the right, and one upward thrust of the fist, preferably the left: "B" was six; "C" was five fingers and two thrusts, or seven; "D" was eight, "F" nine and "G" ten, or both hands held up with all fingers open — provided you had all ten (if someone had nine or eleven fingers, it still counted as ten, but all of us had ten). "H" was eleven — hands up once and one thrust; "J" was twelve and "K" thirteen. "V" was twenty-four and "W" for Wilberto, as Omar Cabezas would say, poking fun at my middle name, was twenty-five; twenty-six was "X" and "Z" was twenty-eight.

The complete primitive cipher, undecipherable — at least for the enemy — was:

A=1, E=2, I=3, O=4, U=5, B=6, C=7, D=8, F=9, G=10, H=11, J=12, K=13, L=14, Ll=15, M=16, N=17, Ñ=18, P=19, Q=20, R=21, S=22, T=23, V=24, W=25, X=26, Y=27, Z=28

They say the first code used by the Yankee police — based on numbers — was devised by the poet Edgar Allan Poe. His famous story, "The Gold Bug," is written this way.

Wherever possible, we transmitted written messages. Numbers were converted into letters to form words and slashes were used to separate the words. *Uno*, for example, was written 5 17 4. To see if you understand, translate:

22 3/ 2 17 23 2 17 8 3 4/ 2 22 7 21 3 6 1/ 1 14/ 1 19 1 21
23 1 8 4/ 5 17 4/ 17 5 2 24 2/ 8 4 22/ 17 5 2 24 2/ 16 1 17
1 10 5 1/ 17 3 7

[Translation of deciphered message: IF YOU UNDERSTOOD, WRITE TO BOX 1929, MANAGUA, NIC.]

We could speak as well as write it. Thus, when we wanted to communicate with each other at the at the Court Martial we would recite numbers, and to separate words we would say: *pared* ["slash"]. The only thing we couldn't do was sing in numbers. I don't know how we could have interpreted *Esa maldita pared*, our favorite off-key rendition after *Solamente una vez*, which was the one we sang most frequently.

The New International Information Order, founded in Algeria in 1973, had not yet appeared. We were pioneers in confronting the vertical, authoritarian practices of disinformation and isolation, and I believe we were a step ahead of satellite communications, telecommunications and memory banks. Precursors of independent radio for the deaf, transmitting messages in Arabic with our hands over long distances. Our mute transmitter was more powerful than the VOA. We were mute only in a certain sense: we were silent but not voiceless, so we were not mute.

We'd signal the location of message drops in the large patio where we sunned ourselves at different hours. There we'd leave lengthy messages that included poems, stories and news. This procedure reduced our physical exercise. The officials were astonished that I was so well-informed. That's to say nothing of Marcio who was born to be silent. He didn't talk to anyone but me.

René Núñez was chief of press and secret information. He patiently transmitted to me the latest news picked up on a clandestine radio receiver that had survived all searches, both routine and extraordinary. The latter were undertaken while the prisoners were sunning themselves. The transistor radios — there were several of them — were hidden by the most improbable means on the routine search days, when we left the cell blocks. They were wrapped in plastic and tossed into the bushes of the patio, and then were retrieved when wanted with fishhooks and line. Had anyone witnessed that scene, he would have shaken his head in amazement or smiled with pity at that surrealistic fishing expedition, like a scene from the days of silent films.

Another way of hiding forbidden objects, including the transistor radios, was to cover them with filthy rags that to all appearances had been carelessly tossed into a corner. If the rags happed to be covered with shit, so much the better. Infallible.

Not everyone was cognizant of our wireless telephone, of the precision that entertained Marcio and me but which for the participating Sandinistas in the other cell blocks was a boring exercise, since they had ready access to chess, conversation, horseplay and the latest jokes.

The leading protagonist, as I've said, was René Núñez. One quiet morning, a comrade who wasn't in on the secret saw René punching the air. When you'd make a mistake, you would wipe off an invisible blackboard on the walls with a towel, which meant, "start over." When I said something that made René laugh, his horrified cellmate went running off to communicate his sad discovery that René had gone mad to a group that was also laughing, having just heard the latest Pepito joke. The man — Alejandro López Guillén ("Catirrín") of Totogalpa, who had been arrested for collaborating with Omar Cabezas — was weeping and could not utter a word. René Núñez inspires — has always inspired — affection, respect and admiration for 258 different reasons, one of which is his honesty and another his modesty — which may be synonymous — and I won't refer to the remaining 256 reasons. Besides, René was justifiably famed for his common sense.

It is true, of course, that one has to be half mad to defy imperialism and the National Guard, but of all the crazies René was the sanest, notwithstanding the fact that he was penned up with the craziest.

"Brothers, René has gone mad. Incredible!" Comrade Catirrín told them. One of those present — Luis ("Chiri") Guzmán — who knew the details of the punches and erasures, couldn't say anything; he had to keep the secret and he tried to shrug the incident off. But Catirrín insisted, "I tell you he's freaked out and he's laughing like a lunatic. Give me a glass of water."

Those who weren't in on the secret also grew worried. There was no alternative but to explain the mysterious language. It became the joke of the week.

It wasn't until a week later that Juan José Ubeda was able to finish the Pepito joke, which also occasioned much laughter. When we were finally reunited — that's another chapter — Juan José told us the joke:

The schoolteacher, young, innocent, that is, with nice legs and a permanently surprised expression on her face asks: "Rodolfo, what do you want to be when you grow up?"

"An engineer, teacher."

"Very good; I congratulate you. It's a profession of immense skyscrapers, I mean great prospects. And you, Edgar?"

"A doctor, teacher."

"I knew it! You're a sensible boy. You'll operate on people, take out appendixes, cut off mangled legs. Do you want to be like Chiri Guzmán's wife?"

"No, that turns my stomach. I'm only going to prescribe antihistamines, broad spectrum antibiotics and antipyretics."

Edgar Lang asks Juan José what's so funny about that and how the hell is a small boy supposed to know what "broad spectrum" and "antipyretics" mean?

"Hang on, be patient," Juan José laughs, asking for a cup of coffee.

"And you, Pepito?" The teacher rests her elbows on the desk and gazes fondly at the incorrigible little rascal...

"Hurry up," says Rodolfo Amador. The teacher is impatient at the interruption, runs her fingers through her hair.

"Me, teacher?" Juan José drags the words out. "I want to be the afternoon."

We and the teacher gaze at Pepito in bewilderment.

408

"The afternoon? You mean you'd like to write poetry or paint rainbows?"

"Come on...cut the crap," Roberto ("Pirica") McEwan looks impatiently at the teacher and at Juan José.

"...or perhaps you'd like to paint a canvas of the sun setting in the west."

"No, teacher, I don't want to be a poet or a painter; I just want to be..."

"What is it you want to be, then?" the teacher explodes, as does Marcio, who never says a word.

"I already told you: I want to be the afternoon."

"Explain yourself." By now the teacher's on guard.

"Ah, it's because whenever you're late getting to class, you always say: 'Forgive me, children, but I was waylaid by the afternoon.'"

Chapter
Thirty-Six

1

My hunger strike culminated in the hospital. It was July, 1977.

One Tuesday afternoon they take me out of the cell. I stagger along, drunk with weakness. I see my arms: they look like dental floss. I can't avoid feelings of self-pity and vanity. I pass between two rows of armed men who look at me as if I were the protagonist of "Shane." Near the main entrance of the Tipitapa Prison, a police van awaits me. In a low voice someone carelessly mentions the Military Hospital. The duty officer gestures, gives an order. I climb in and before I can say a word the rear door slams with a dull thud. So begins another episode in the difficult trajectory of the hunger strike I had started fifty days earlier.

The van, escorted by several BECAT patrol vehicles, heads along the Northern Highway. Without the strength to crawl, I drag myself forward until I can peer out through the front windshield. It is nearly sunset. When we reach the Las Mercedes neighborhood on the outskirts of Managua, I can see people leaving work, waiting at bus stops or rapidly walking home. Pairs of young lovers hold hands, gaze into each others eyes, smile. At some point, a barefoot boy dashes across in front of us, instants before the slamming of brakes and the driver's curses. We stop for a red light, as an elderly, heavyset man waves at a girl vainly wearing too much makeup. To the left, at the corner of La Esperanza pharmacy, there's a minor ruckus: perhaps a fight, or an accident. We continue on. The traffic's heavy.

I devour each instant, each face, the street noises. More than anything, I want to hear voices, to hear a phrase — just one — that isn't tinged with hatred, but I see only the movement of lips. The van leaves behind the kindly eyes of an old lady. Beyond the railway station lie the open wounds of the city crucified by an earthquake. One by one, the ruins are gradually disappearing. There's the Bank of America, which remained intact. The van passes by the

Intercontinental Hotel whose lights have already been turned on and where Howard Hughes once found refuge. A living vampire, a sordid, recurrent type. I'm surprised and troubled by this out-of-context thought.

The director of the Military Hospital, Colonel Castellón, awaits me in the reception hall. I know him. I am hurried into a small, windowless room. The door at the end of the hall, with taciturn glass panes, is nailed shut with wooden planks. A man with his face hidden behind a cloth mask and a penetrating voice characteristic of people who hide behind cloth masks orders me to lie down on a thick-mattressed bed with the unmistakable cradle or coffin shape of all hospital beds. In brief seconds I am manacled to the headboard, naked. They dress me in white pajamas. A young man who looks like a recently married doctor approaches and says to me, blushing: "I have orders to give you an I.V. Please don't make this situation more difficult than it already is. If you resist, they're going to restrain you and put you to sleep."

A male nurse injects a white fluid into my hip and minutes later I drowsily feel the needle penetrating my median cubital vein, which, because I'm skinny, because I'm dying, resembles an insignificant, blue rivulet running down my forearm. Suddenly I become conscious of the intense light that pours down like fiery rain from the ceiling, illuminating the bare walls. I am restless and move my arm violently. A male nurse arrives a few minutes later. "The needle's pulled out," he says. "We're going to have to tie you down."

I lie still and they don't tie me. Hypnotized, I watch the drops of serum falling lethargically. I feel sleepy, but the spotlight, the heat, the discomfort won't let me sleep.

Hours later, around midnight, a man's authoritarian voice comes in through the doorway leading to the corridor. "Don't move!" he shouts. "Don't turn your head even for a second. Did ya hear me, scum bucket?"

"Yeah, I heard you," I reply without concealing my anger. "I'm not deaf and I haven't the slightest desire to see your face."

"Don't think I'm afraid of you, you prick," he says to me.

As he approaches I ask myself why he's telling me he's not afraid of me, and I hear the sound of the handcuffs as he closes them hastily. The steel sinks into my flesh but I don't complain; I'm used to it.

When the sunlight undresses itself behind the opaque panes of the barred door, I see the silhouette of a man with a submachine gun pacing back and forth. The I.V. bottle is nearly empty. The male nurse closes the valve and the drops stop falling. He doesn't remove the needle and I give him a questioning look. They turn off the light. It's daytime. A boy approaches carrying an appetizing breakfast tray. I refuse it. A little later, the doctor arrives. I recognize him. It's Dr. López, a forensic specialist. I complain of the discomfort, of the cruel combination of handcuffs, I.V., the spotlight, the heat, the hostility and the prohibition of looking behind me.

"Is it my relationship to Lot's family, Doctor?"

The forensic specialist says he understands, but that in order for him to be able to help me, I must eat. Suddenly, I shudder. Why a forensic doctor? Then I am dying, Mamma, and I didn't want that to happen. A forensic specialist comes to examine the dead, or to observe those who are on the verge of dying. Besides, Dr. López has the jaw of a gravedigger.

Late in the day they open the valve and just when I think I'm finally going to get some rest, they hang another bottle. How naive! I didn't know it at the time but we'd barely begun. The hostility grows more obvious on invisible faces.

"This man pisses too much. Tell him to stop being such a pain in the ass."

"It's the I.V.," the doctor explains. "It makes you want to urinate frequently."

"So? I give a shit. Tell him not to piss, that's all!"

Another bottle; this one's a yellowish color. Then a reddish one. The next one's white. An intramuscular injection, the I.V. valve closes and opens; the intravenous needle comes out and I rest for a moment. I sit up and manage to read the label on the bottle: "Patient: Special Room." (I have no reserves of humor left to laugh at this original pseudonym.) "Pathology: Dehydration. Treatment: Dextrose" (and other illegible words).

Farther down I seem to make out the word "Prednisone." I vaguely recall the name of a hormone to combat arthritis, to stimulate the appetite and... stimulate the appetite? I'm not sure, though, that that chemical product was actually written on the label. But the reddish liquid is undoubtedly Vitamin B complex. And then there are the appetizing dishes and the persistent: "Eat."

It's the sweet voice of a nurse with hair the color of old gold.

"Eat." The threatening voice of the invisible face.

"Eat." The neutral voice of the male nurse.

"Eat, eat, eat..."

"Ah! He doesn't want to eat," comes a voice from the hallway. "They ought to put a bullet through his heart... Pass this up through the window." (What can it be? Come on, don't panic now.) "You open her up all the way and when he crosses the street..." [Blackmail.] "...he dies like an animal." I hear hands clapping, think I might be delirious.

Words that light up, vials that turn off, cold sweat, hunger... I'm hungry! No, I will not eat. I won't eat that plate of chopped beef, the splendorous rice, the blushing slices of tomato. No, I will not.

Red, intramuscular liquid. My arms and buttocks are inflamed. Prednisone, the needle in my vein, the cold, humiliating manacle on my wrist, the hot air, my shoulders ache, the mattress is an oven, my relationship to Lot's family, please give me some air, the light that penetrates my closed eyes, pass me the water pitcher, you're a pain in the ass, the droplets fall silently like a cat's footsteps in the night, what unbearable suffering, I'm hungry; my God, I'm hungry!

Green serum, red serum, yellow serum, white, one day, two days, three days.

A man appears. He's dressed in civilian clothes but must be an officer: the guards call him "Sir."

"What is it you want, Tomás?" His voice is courteous, almost kindly. "We're interested in resolving your problem."

"I've been in solitary confinement for eighteen months," I reply, "locked up in a two-by-four cell and discriminated against. At times, sometimes, once in a long time — understand? — I have a one-hour visit. The rest of the time I'm not allowed to speak to anyone."

I do a quick summation: "Of the 168 hours in a week, I do not hear a human voice for 167 — if I hear one at all. I've asked myself many times what is the reason for this treatment, and the only answer

I come up with is that they want to drown me in a pit of hatred and rancor. They've traced a thorny path for Marcio Jaén and me that is unacceptable. We're isolated. Why? To murder us when circumstances permit. You must remember that so-called human rights, more than an issue of generosity or sadism, are a matter of common sense. You have Marcio in solitary confinement, despite the fact that he was only sentenced to five years and the only reason for that was not to draw public attention to my particular case. I've been sentenced to almost 200 years. Do you see the difference? You have sacrificed Marcio in order to vent your rage on me. I demand that this isolation cease and that you stop subjecting us to additional punishments that in any other country would be considered cruel and inhuman; punishments I might endure were I not condemned to death and unwilling to be an accomplice in my own liquidation. I've been in solitary confinement for more than 500 days, during which I was handcuffed for more than 5000 hours and hooded for 270 days."

The officer thought for a moment and then said: "It is not up to a person of my rank to resolve this problem. I assure you, however, that I don't find your demands exaggerated and there's almost a 100 percent probability that they will be met. Your statement that we are going to kill you is subjective. Nevertheless, the first step you must take, as a gesture of good faith and a sign that your hunger strike has no political purpose, is to accept food. I'm sure that once you have recovered and return to the Model Prison, you will receive a just and reasonable response to your demands."

Four days later, the application of serum, the heat, the handcuffs and the hostility all continue. My hunger has multiplied. Who says that during a hunger strike one stops feeling hunger? Five days, six days of accumulated suffering. My blood pressure drops to dangerous levels. A nurse tells me so in a whisper as she kisses me next to one of the ears God gave me and which, I think, must now look ridiculous. They take my blood pressure every two hours. On the sixth night I detect genuine preoccupation on the faces of the group of doctors who speak in low voices and eye me clinically, suspiciously. I have a stethoscope attached to me all the time, but now I'm no longer manacled. A group of officers arrives, led by a captain, all of them carrying submachine guns. They have a threatening air and say they wanted *to meet me*. The lieutenants say they were fellow cadets of the officer I killed in an armed encounter. They promise to return.

Day seven: "I'm not going to handcuff you so you can rest," says someone with a soft, persuasive voice. "They're going to bathe and shave you."

They bathe me and shave me. I'm very weak. The fellow with the soft, persuasive voice comes up behind me. "Here's some chicken," he passes the plate under my nose and I feel a tremor in my gut as I smell the delicious fragrance. "We prepared it especially for you."

I feel myself weakening. So many days without eating. Nobody can say you're a weakling, that you fail to keep your promises. Human resistance has its limits. The guy with the soft, persuasive voice says something I barely hear, that doesn't interrupt but reinforces my reflections: They've promised to resolve the prison problem, and the hunger strike is not an end in itself. What would you say, my love? You, who believe me to be strong... If I eat, they'll turn off the light, they'll let me urinate in peace — people have no idea how delicious it is to urinate in peace — they'll leave the handcuffs off, maybe they'll even permit family visits. Mamma, I need some rest. I could die and there'd still be a world to make out there in what remains a puddle of spit, a circle of fangs.

No, my brothers; no, my love; I will not eat. That isn't chicken meat; it's the flesh of an old alcoholic who died of syphilis. Look at it, it's the skin of his decaying arms; those are his mashed brains, because he was run over by a truck, and the meat, how revolting, how delicious! The plate still seemed a magical portion delivered by special messenger from paradise. The promises they are making you are false. To be sure, solidarity has increased both inside the country and abroad. Hunger is your sentry, but where is your strength? You could die, of course, but who has told you you're indispensable? But yet... perhaps everything has been resolved. They know that if they keep you in solitary, if they continue the discrimination, you're not going to resign yourself to it, nobody would. The demands will continue, the protests, the international condemnation. If they put you in with the others, nothing will happen. On the contrary, everything will be peaceful. To accede to such an elementary demand doesn't undermine the principle of authority. Maybe they've understood that. It doesn't make sense for them to overestimate the danger of your being with your comrades. But they also hate you, detest you. Haven't you understood that, you idiot?

Again the voice draws near. "You must eat. Do you want to die? There's a remedy for everything but death. Your comrades await you. It's your fault that your family is suffering. Basically, your attitude is pure vanity and egoism. You only think of yourself, not your loved ones. And why? So they'll think you're a hero? Let's be realistic. Your hunger strike is simply to improve your own situation. In principle, that's already been resolved, so why should you continue to suffer?"

The murmuring, persuasive voice filters through my gut. I feel like hitting him, shaking his hand, weeping.

"The sun shines for everyone and it will shine for you, I promise. Tonight they'll turn out the lights, you can forget the cuffs, but you will have to continue with the I.V. Of course, if you start eating, when the doctor decides, that won't be necessary either."

He sets the plate under my nose. Next to the meat is a luminous serving of rice, toast, butter, and what looks to be an apple tart. The fragrance reaches my nostrils, settles in my innards. From the corners of my mouth two tears of saliva dribble down towards the territory of surrender and delight.

"Are you sure," I ask, "that they are going to respond to my situation in the Tipitapa Prison?"

"I don't have the authority to answer that, but it's almost certain."

"Alright, leave the plate on the chair."

There's a great silence. The fellow with the soft, persuasive voice leaves. Behind me, I hear him speaking in a different tone of voice to another invisible face: "He's eating."

There's cruel, wounding laughter out in the hallway.

They gave me 32,000 ccs of serum — the young doctor told me so in a conspiratorial tone and that he was recently married and that his wife was expecting a baby — and dozens of intramuscular injections. They take me, manacled, back to the Tipitapa Prison.

418

Once again I see the street. I don't know why I now feel an infinite tenderness for the men, women and children who throng the sidewalks, wait for buses, love one another, laugh and suffer, unaware of my small tragedy. They, too, have their tragedies. How I love them!

Chapter
Thirty-Seven

1

To put an end to our isolation, we began a new hunger strike. It was May 1978 and for me it was the fourth.

A few weeks earlier, Marcio Jaén's mother went on a hunger strike at the Red Cross headquarters, and dozens of mothers, workers and students joined her. There was a flurry of activity by the prison warden and guards and National Guard patrols pursued students who roamed the streets and gathered in the plazas. The students called a general strike. I am moved whenever I recall the graffiti — still intact after the revolutionary victory — painted on the walls of every city: IF TOMAS DIES... Those dots and that phrase might have been an epitaph, and perhaps they are, because maybe we are dead, after all, surviving only in a dream where colors alternate with the desire to live.

One morning they take Marcio out to the patio and give him a soccer ball. It's an old trick. They signal him from the windows and Marcio understands that he's supposed to kick the ball and does so wearily, out of discipline. The following day, in *Novedades,* the famous prisoner appears transformed into a Pelé kicking the ball in a futile attempt to put an end to the protests.

An officer appears with a list of prisoners who will be transferred to our cell block. We reject the list and propose our own. We bargain, reach an agreement, and one day, smiling, understanding the risk and sacrifice they are making and for which they have volunteered, there appear Edgar Lang, Rodolfo Amador, Juan José Ubeda, Luis ("Chiri") Guzmán and Roberto McEwan, carrying their miserable belongings. We had won.

We organized ourselves to do physical exercises, to study history, English and urban guerrilla warfare. The program was so intense that after fifteen days they all asked for a break, and I, who had not, because I was the chief, was delighted to have more time to read Gorky, Agatha Christie, to reread *Hopscotch*, *A Thousand and One Nights*, the *Bible*, Jarchel Poncela, the dictionary, elements of philosophy, scraps of newspaper that had been used to wrap laundry soap, the chemical formulas of medical products, the Penal Code, and the future in the lines of my empty hands.

Bayardo writes to encourage me. He speaks of projects to free us. He makes no mention yet — as he will later — of the project to seize the National Palace while the deputies are in session. A secret I keep, despite the severe temptation to share it so as to raise the hopes of my comrades.

He gives me the good news that Camilo Ortega is showing a serious commitment to unity and that he has even sent some weapons to the GPP.*

I did pass this bit of news on to the others.

Camilo was very young. Because he disseminated affection, because he had no selfish appetites, because of these qualities I dubbed him the "Apostle of Unity."

On February 26, 1978, I've been in prison two years. Carlos Fonseca has been dead for fifteen months. The prison official, Munguía, brings me a television set so I can watch the news. I find this strange and his attitude puts me on guard. The news program announces the death of Camilo Ortega. I watch his mother, brokenhearted, sobbing, exclaim: "My God! It's true. It's Camilo." I walk to the cell door and catch Munguía slinking away, laughing.

2

Edgar made the discovery. Two kittens — the little boy kitten Meow and the little girl kitten Mew — insignificant creatures resembling two lumps of striped shit with a couple of spots of light. They were deposited in an empty, unlocked cell by a surly, dissolute female with the appearance of a vendor of love potions and magic spells.

* TRANSLATORS' NOTE: The Prolonged Popular War (GPP) tendency, led by Tomás Borge, was one of three factions into which the FSLN was split until a few months before the revolutionary triumph.

We put them in a cardboard box. Edgar tore up his new blue shirt for rags to keep Meow and Mew warm.

The mother cat reappeared with her accumulated load of sorcery on her paws and the flanks of her tail while we were locked in our cells. There was nothing we could do to prevent her from carrying off Meow between her impressive fangs. We tried to frighten her and she gave us a ferocious, contemptuous glare.

The following day, Robert McEwan took Mew to his cell. We immediately held a name contest and for some reason christened her Helen.

Helen was the new baby. We'd whistle at her, call "kitty, kitty," stroke her sparrow-sized head and give her milk diluted with water. Helen dominated each and every one of us with her amiable claws and innocent, perfidious fangs.

Helen had pointed ears; her steely pupils contracted in the vertical rays of light. The poor creature hadn't come from Angora, rather from an eastern neighborhood of Managua.

Helen grew lazy, gluttonous, presumptuous, a self-satisfied, voluntary prisoner. Like the ancient Egyptians, we deified Helen and, if one day we arrive at the temple of Bubastis or that of Beni Hassan, we will select her burial site after embalming her. She was little Helen, our own little goddess Pasht. We were not the first to love cats. Before us was little Ana Josefina, and long before her, among other paragons of strength with feline weaknesses were Richelieu, who kept a dozen black, white and gray cats, and Théophile Gautier, friend of Baudelaire and author of *Captain Failure*. Baudelaire himself was a cat lover, as was T.S. Eliot, with his treatise on cats, and Cortázar, with his philosopher cat named Teodoro W. Adorno. Hemingway, with his prolific cat refuge in Cuba, fifty in all, including Angoras and half-breeds — Boise, Missouri, Spendy — all named with sibilant esses. And the poet Carlos Martínez Rivas, who cannot live without caressing metaphors and two well-mannered, submissive little cats. I've already mentioned how I was with Ricardo Morales at the time of the earthquake when shortly after the initial shock a cat as black as a Peruvian witch scurried between the two of us and Ricardo assured me that there would soon be another...and before he could say "earthquake," the second shock hit us.

Helen was a cleanly cat. With her tongue she preened her fur, showered, put deodorant on her feet and her spotless little asshole. Later, she went into exile in Cuba, since, when we were liberated by the operation against the National Palace, we took her with us in defiance of feline immigration laws and the fact that she did not appear on the list of prisoners.

3

By that time, the Front was divided into factions; but sectarian passions were shattered against the walls of common sense.

One day, I don't know why, listening to the euphoria that takes possession of people who believe they own the truth, I expressed myself in harsh terms with regard to other comrades holed up in their respective ideological shelters. Juan José Ubeda asked me: "Is Pedro Antonio a counterrevolutionary?"

"No, of course not," I replied.

"In that case," he called me to order, "you have to treat him as a brother, even though he may be mistaken. And perhaps he's not. From here it's impossible to judge reality. The future will give us the answer."

I told him he was right, and I do not regret it.

Chapter
Thirty-Eight

1

In November 1975, Raquel Valladares, a guerrilla candidate, watched Agatón get out of the car and stride into the building where the school's instructors and students were gathered. Inside, new combatants of the Pablo Ubeda Brigade were being trained.

Raquel didn't know where the school was located, because she had arrived blindfolded and because she wasn't curious and because that's the way things were. It wasn't until recently that she learned the guerrilla school was close to Managua, not very far from the old highway to León.

Carlos Fonseca ("Agatón") was discovered by the young guerrilla apprentices in the same way one discovers a moonlit bay. We couldn't avoid it: his air of authority, the timber of his voice, the affection in his eyes, all denounced him.

We taught tactics with the self-importance of recent military graduates, the most insufferable individuals in military academies and ballrooms. We also gave weapons instruction. Carlos left his students — as he would have left anyone — with their mouths and eyes wide open and their minds ready for cultivation when he gave lessons on political strategy. For him, war — as Clausewitz had already stated — did not contradict politics, although in both practice and theory there is a tendency to forget this. War is the continuation of politics by other means, the German strategist said, and Lenin adorned that concept profusely with gems of his own. And sometimes politics is a continuation of war by other means, anyone fond of word games might add, or any explorer of ideas.

For us, it was impossible to confront the Somoza dictatorship by organizing ourselves as a political party. The circumstances did not permit it, nor would the neighboring governments or other parties, left or right. Besides that, we were crazy, sentimental adventurers, petty-bourgeois anarchists and senselessly messianic, according to the weekly and biweekly magazines, the daily press and the girl rolling her eyes on the television screen. There was no alternative but to continue politics by other means.

The contradiction was still premature when they wounded Carlos at El Chaparral. None of his later enemies understood that the bullet that pierced his lung had not felled Carlos, rather the existing conceptions about methods of struggle. His manner of understanding the revolution linked armed struggle to that of the workers who were half-shod, half-literate, half-naked, half-starved and half-enraged. Only the workers and the peasants will go the whole way, Sandino had said, and that phrase was taken up by Carlos Fonseca; only they could go from nothing to half and from half to total change.

From the moment the FSLN was founded — Carlos pointed this out — the law of confrontation was not to be decided by the dictatorship. It's absurd, he maintains, for the people to counter force with laws, bayonets with the Criminal Code. We would be idiots if we did not realize that the only defense against force is force, and that law books do not shield one from bayonets, either physically or morally.

The study of Sandinismo as thought and practice was either obsessive or worthless. A movement's roots cannot be explored haphazardly or without the guidance of someone experienced in measuring voltages and pratfalls. You could not understand the guerrilla war against the National Guard except as a continuation of the war sustained by the "Crazy Little Army" against Somoza's riffraff and the Yankee invaders.

By now, no one can doubt what the founder of the FSLN stubbornly maintained: that victory is impossible without a mass insurrection. Just as it is inadmissible to conceive of or understand the existence of the FSLN and the unique, riotous procession of July 19th without Carlos Fonseca.

"The armed, popular insurrection is the essence of the struggle against the dictatorship."[1]

[1] Carlos Fonseca, "Breve análisis de la lucha popular nicaragüense contra la dictadura de Somoza," *Obras*, I, p. 52.

"And within our strategy, the masses without rifles are defeated, as are rifles without masses."[1]

The struggle that Carlos Fonseca directed was flavored with salt and multitudes. What multitudes? Many, in terms of quality.

There exists but one solid basis for assuring that the determination of all sectors to struggle is not sidetracked toward new deceptions by the ambitious and unscrupulous. That basis is the open participation of the masses and their conscientious fighting bodies.[2]

All Nicaragua was a battlefield: factories, villages, schools, suburbs, ranches hidden among the trees, poverty. Countryside and city. The countryside for the rural guerrilla, the city for the urban guerrilla and for the rear guard of the armed groups that, in the mountains, laid minimal ambushes to harass, contain and annihilate the enemy. The guerrilla struggle is not enough — right, Carlos? — and one must confront the enemy in all places and in all tenses.

The guerrilla struggle is difficult, like the initiation of love; arduous, like the continuation of love; long, like the culmination of love; a struggle that includes — Carlos insists on it, as does a sense of reality, which closely resembles common sense — the organization of labor unions and musical groups. Groups, alliances, international solidarity committees, safehouses, lawful smiles, sunburnt skins, perfect masks that spin like tops around points of phosphorous and blood.

Carlos' thought flowed like an untamed river; he kept in mind the programmatic line as well as the necessary adjustments and trapeze acts; the cumulative character he conceived for the revolutionary forces.

[1] Fonseca, "Mensaje del FSLN a los estudiantes revolucionarios," *op. cit.*, p. 70.
[2] Fonseca, "!Sandino si, Somoza no; Revolucion si, farsa electoral no!," *op. cit.*, p. 245.

430

As early as 1960, Carlos Fonseca foresaw that, in order for the masses thirsting for milk and honey to conclude their long march, a general strike and an insurrection would be required.

With the founding of the FSLN, the following principles are extracted like molten gold: the preeminence of armed struggle; the magical bond between the guerrilla's rifle and our history; the value of moral authority; the study of the scientific theory of society and its creative application.

In the voluminous file that Somoza's Office of Security had on Carlos was found a document, written in 1960, in which guerrilla warfare was proposed as the principal method of struggle. Carlos maintained that: "Armed struggle without the support of other forms of struggle cannot lead us to victory."[1]

It was necessary to use all means, including the scanty legal opportunities permitted by the dictatorship, to bring together the different revolutionary classes and sectors.

The decision to opt for armed struggle in order to achieve a substantive social change is the fruit of analysis. Throughout our history violence was the primary form of political response, not only in the relations between the dominant and the dominated sectors of society, but between the different sectors of the dominant class as well. The rebellion of the people was spontaneous. Carlos and the FSLN added, as though it were a flame, what the "experts" define as consciousness.

Special attention was paid to the exploits of Sandino as the principal, fertile antecedent. In various analyses, Carlos seeks obstinately to compile and pass on our patriotic experience: battles, manifestos, ideology, political junctures and the international situation during Sandino's struggle are all dissected, and not by some erudite academician.

Carlos affirmed:

> Guerrilla warfare by the people against the National
> Guard is a continuation of the struggle against that same
> army and against the Yankee invaders fought by the great

[1] Fonseca, "La lucha por la transformación de Nicaragua," *op. cit.*, p. 29.

patriot Sandino and his Army for the Defense of National Sovereignty. [1]

Emphasis on building the guerrilla force and revolutionary army in the countryside did not negate the importance of organizing in the cities nor the role of workers in the revolutionary struggle:

> What we say must not at any time be interpreted as an aberration that seeks to deny the working class its proper role as conductor of the revolution. [2]

The general insurrection was, for Carlos, the culmination. He believed that the decisive battles of the masses would take place in the cities.

By the end of the 1960s, a program had become indispensable. It is drafted and disseminated during a period of sweeping social upheaval: strikes by construction workers, textile workers, longshoremen and freight haulers. In the countryside some lands are occupied, while the Revolutionary Student Front was a source of valiant young men and women, invulnerable to fear and vacillation, who also joined the struggle.

Referring to the fifteen points of the *Program*, Carlos insisted that they not only gave FSLN cadres greater political and ideological cohesion, but also gave the people a reason to live and to struggle. He said:

> We challenge any loudmouth to offer a program with better solutions to the Nicaraguan problem than those contained in the Program of the Sandinista National Liberation Front, FSLN, the program of the Sandinista Popular Revolution. [3]

No one took up the challenge.

---

[1] Ibid., p. 28.
[2] Fonseca, "Notas sobre la montaña y algunos otros temas," *op. cit.*, p. 137.
[3] Fonseca, "Proclama del FSLN," *op. cit.*, p. 268.

By the 1970s, and particularly after the successful action of 1974, Carlos perceived the development of pre-revolutionary conditions that could lead to a revolutionary crisis. The moral authority of the FSLN was recognized within the village and without. The dominated were no longer content in their prison.

Other sectors — merchants, industrialists, bankers — were no longer content with their profit margins. The FSLN had to be equal to the challenge of coming events:

> Having lived through the entire experience of building the Sandinista Front, Carlos had come to the conclusion that the struggle must now move toward the unleashing of a popular armed insurrection. And it was precisely the elements of that insurrection, its laws, its nature in the particular conditions of Nicaragua, its genesis in the heroic exploits of Sandino, that now occupied Carlos' attention. [1]

Carlos' perception of this qualitative change in the conditions of struggle move him to organize, among those comrades who were outside of the country, four working teams to investigate different aspects of a popular insurrection: the strategy employed in the struggle led by Gen. Sandino, a topic undertaken by Carlos himself together with Rufo Marín; the military strategy and tactics of the insurrection, coordinated by Humberto Ortega; the economic and social conditions of Nicaragua, directed by Camilo Ortega; and the organizational aspects of the FSLN, undertaken by Jaime Wheelock and Doris Tijerino. Angelita Morales Avilés was the group secretary.

For Carlos, victory was a dream that was possible if, and only if — as the mathematicians say — the principal enemy could be isolated, that is, Somoza and the pro-imperialist sector of the bourgeoisie; if other sectors could be neutralized and if all forces opposed to the dictatorship could be united. In order to accomplish this, a mass front had to be organized and political alliances established under the hegemony of the revolutionary forces. And this, my friend, was accomplished point by point.

[1] Jaime Wheelock, Prologue to Carlos Fonseca, "Viva Sandino," *op. cit.,* II, p. 16.

The unity of that broad opposition front had to be achieved on the basis of genuinely shared interests, not merely through formal agreements:

> Many points must be clarified with respect to unity in order to reach the conviction that this is not a formal, passive matter, rather a vital, essentially dynamic factor. We can go so far as to say that unity without action is not unity at all, but a grotesque caricature of unity. [1]

His conception of the political front derived from the existence of sectors and individuals opposed to the dictatorship. In this respect, one must not, "underestimate a certain progressive sector within the UDEL, or within sectors that have not yet separated completely from traditional political groups." [2]

It would be absurd to characterize Carlos Fonseca's political thought as a fish surviving in a dead, immutable sea after seeing the evidence of the 1960s and early '70s.

For Carlos, theory and practice go hand in hand. A revolution without theory is retarded and deformed, but revolutionary theory is insufficient if not accompanied by practice, which he demanded be concrete, combative and creative:

> The Sandinista knows that ideological correctness is worthless without consistent practical conduct, but positive practical conduct is also insufficient if unaccompanied by a revolutionary ideological definition. [3]

Carlos was a student of other revolutionary experience. His political formation was influenced by the North American intervention that overthrew the government of Jacobo Arbenz in Guatemala, in 1954, and his ideological formation by Che and his revolutionary experience. He had a profound knowledge of the

[1] Fonseca, "Breve analisis de la lucha popular," *op. cit.*, I, p. 53.
[2] Fonseca, "Síntesis de algunos problemas actuales," *op. cit.*, p. 117.
[3] Fonseca, *?Qué es un sandinista?* (Managua: National Secretariat of Propaganda and Political Education of the FSLN, 1980), p. 11.

Bolshevik Revolution and of the struggle of the Vietnamese people. He was an acute observer and prophet of the triumph and defeat of the Chilean people.

Immersed in the interplay of pawns and bishops, groping his way by the light of fireflies, Carlos achieves his full stature as a strategist and leader.

That was Carlos.

Chapter
Thirty-Nine

1

At the end of February 1976, Carlos ("Agatón") left Managua and headed north toward the mountains. He was accompanied by Inés Hernández ("Pedrito"), Juan de Dios Muñoz ("Juaquin"), Claudia Chamorro ("Luisa"), Facundo Picado ("Donaldo"), Marlon Urbina ("Vidal"), Rosa Argentina Ortiz ("Norma") and Celestina López ("Mayra"). There was also a handful of boys from León, workers from the San Felipe and Subtiava neighborhoods. I've only been able to recall the name of Benito Carvajal. Of the others, only the numbers remain that substituted for their pseudonyms: 111, 112, 113, 114, 115..., numbers I myself chose at random in the military school to disinform the enemy and which in the end disinformed ourselves, who wanted to connect the numbers to their pseudonyms and to their real names.

Agatón and his comrades entered the mountains, with the aid of peasant collaborator Juan López ("Ruperto"), in March 1976 at Bocaycito, in the department of Jinotega. From there, Carlos headed toward the Iyás river, where he planned to join Henry Ruiz ("Modesto"), chief of the Pablo Ubeda Brigade, who was awaiting him at the El Payú encampment, together with René Vivas ("José"), David Blanco ("Arcadia"), Carlos Agüero ("Rodrigo"), Nelson Suárez ("Anselmo"), William Ramírez, Hugo Torres, Edwin Cordero and other heroic, undernourished guerrillas.

Carlos planned to meet with Modesto and other leaders to look one another in the eye, erase misunderstandings and discuss different problems affecting the historic unity of the Sandinista movement. The meeting was scheduled for November 15th in Iyás and Carlos had proposed as well to take up two questions which, at that moment, were fundamental to the FSLN: the matter of internal organization and a reexamination of the political and military situations with a view to elaborating a new strategy.

Meanwhile, preparations were made to penetrate the southern boundary of the zone of operations. In a guerrilla struggle, nine months is a prudent time lapse, further dictated by the slowness of people on foot, for convening a meeting of leaders who are geographically dispersed. At that time, tactical concepts were also dispersed, which increased the distance to be covered. Months earlier the first steps of political stupidity had been taken, giving rise to divisions, to which I contributed my share of mistakes and intransigent attitudes. I wasn't the only one, of course. I remember clearly the firm and amiable manner in which Carlos, on his return to Nicaragua, pointed out the erroneous way in which we went about discussing things.

Ever cordial and incisive, he enumerated our streaks of arrogance, authoritarianism and deafness. In truth, we did not listen; we didn't understand. And it's time, now, to say so loudly and clearly, stressing each syllable. I say this here in my narrative, even though I'm aware that the problems which had already arisen had nothing to do with the drama of Carlos' death. Had they been germane, let there be no doubt that I would be obliged to say so.

The contributing factors were others: the fact that Inés Hernández — the best trail guide with the best nose for enemy ambushes — was carrying out another mission elsewhere; the betrayal by Tito Chamorro; the tactical ability of Capt. Enrique Munguía, chief of the National Guard patrol; and plain bad luck...

2

On April 30th, an FSLN squad operating in the area was attacked at Cerro Verde, Dipina, and Julián Roque Cuadra ("Pablo"), a veteran revolutionary militant, was killed, alerting the Guard to the guerrillas' presence.

In May, Tito Chamorro had left the mountains with real or feigned health problems and was captured in his own home in Granada. Chamorro provided the Guard with a detailed description of all the points transited by the guerrillas of Las Bayas. Chamorro's betrayal led to the death of Carlos Fonseca as well as to that of his own sister, Claudia.

Tito Chamorro revealed plans, routes, guerrilla methods of operation and survival — how they dressed, how they erased their trails, how they avoided the houses of local deputies — and he even betrayed his own wife, a loyal and lovely girl who served as a messenger for Carlos Agüero. He gave them true names, in countryside and city, everything he knew. This led to the death or imprisonment of hundreds of collaborators and militants. This Tito, this Chamorro, this Iscariot, had and still has blood so bad that not even the thirstiest of vampires would drink it.

3

In the first days of May, Agatón's guerrilla group had passed through La Lana, La Pioja and Yaosca and drew near La Posolera, close to Waslala. They headed for Los Chiles but were spotted and bombed by enemy planes. As a result, they had to detour toward the region of San José de las Bayas, where they established themselves early in June.

The encampment of Francisco Rivera ("Enrique") was located in Los Chiles, between Matagalpa and northern Zelaya. His squad's mission was to receive guerrilla fighters from the city and guide them on to Dipina, where Orlando Castellón ("Casimiro") incorporated them into the Pablo Ubeda Brigade.

The guerrilla group — three women and fourteen men — intensified their training. They remained in Las Bayas nearly two months — July through August. Two months is too long a time for a guerrilla group to remain in a populated zone.

Carlos guided his comrades' conduct, observed them, criticized them. "Things are never all right; there's always something." When he wasn't talking, he was listening to the news. He slept only the designated hours.

During those months of marching through the mountains, Carlos managed to accumulate an archive of documents and correspondence, which, wrapped in plastic, that living hero Francisco

Rivera carried on his back. It's assumed that these papers fell into the hands of the Guard, since the night before his death Carlos ordered them to be given to Crescencio Aguilar ("Danilo"), the peasant who died about twelve hours after Carlos. Some documents were recovered following the revolutionary victory.

Carlos organized the peasants who came to listen to him and, for lack of myrrh, to bring the group bananas, cooked beans and a local corn drink. And he assumed public administrative functions, marrying the guerrilla couple Francisco Rivera and Celestina López, who for some time had shared patrols, sentry duty and banana leaves beneath their hammock.

At the beginning of August, he ordered one group of guerrillas to move to the edge of the southern zone of operations so as to introduce new combatants and obtain supplies and ammunition. He was hoping that some members of the FSLN's National Directorate as well as senior cadres would make it to the Iyás meeting.

In El Pastal, the group that was marching south — comprising Juan de Dios Muñoz, Rosa Argentina Ortiz, Marlon Urbina and number 116 — was attacked and dispersed by a National Guard patrol. Juan de Dios was wounded — you have no idea what a saint he was — and lost an eye. A while later, he lost his life.

At the beginning of September, a second group, commanded by Carlos Agüero, also split off. Fonseca sent them to Iyás with the mission of locating Orlando Castellón's squad and making contact with Henry Ruiz. Carlos Agüero located Henry Ruiz and waited there for the arrival of the others. From that point on, Henry sent René Vivas every two weeks to a point nearby — a corpulent tree that also served as a drop — where Agatón was scheduled to come.

While Carlos Agüero's squad went to Iyás, local deputies discovered the Las Bayas encampment and attacked it. Marlon Urbina, Facundo Picado and Claudia Chamorro held them off, while Carlos and the rest of the group withdrew, fighting.

During the action, Carlos was wounded in the leg by a shotgun pellet. During the long nighttime withdrawal he concealed the fact. He didn't want to slow down the march. Only the following day, in a new encampment, did he reveal that he was wounded. Claudia

Chamorro extracted the pellet and bandaged him while she wept at the stoicism of the man they all loved.

News arrived that, on September 13th, Edgar Munguía Alvarez ("Lucky" or "Red Beard" as the peasants, especially the children, called him) had fallen in combat at El Ocote, near Los Chiles. This affected Agatón deeply. Months before, he had insisted on contacting Edgar because he was the one who maintained the link with Víctor Tirado López ("Rogelio" or "Gray Hair"), who was working in a region near Matagalpa. An exceptional revolutionary had been lost and Agatón knew it.

4

The group remained in Cola de Mico, near Waslala until the beginning of October, when they moved to Cusulí, where the Mendoza family gave them refuge. The head of the family was an old man who spoke of God as though he were the Pope, although he was only the pastor of the local church.

In Cusulí, Carlos preached and Francisco Rivera stored every word in his memory and in his conscience. In the background was the murmur of a brook, a short distance from the nightly bonfire that kept sadness and mosquitoes at bay. Carlos said:

> We are going to win in Nicaragua — as I have always said — when we manage to create boldness in the masses, and we will do that even at the cost of our own blood.
>
> Every militant Sandinista should relate to the people, win their friendship.
>
> You have to make comrades of your friends, convert your comrades into militants, militants into cadres, and cadres into our brothers.
>
> When you find yourself in difficult situations, when you feel disheartened, sad, ready to break down and weep, to desert, when you're feeling as low as you can, think of the FSLN, think of the thousands of children, women, men and elderly who are poverty-stricken, half-naked, barefoot, dressed in rags. We are their hope, their alternative. If you

remain conscious of all this, you'll find the strength to go on.

Seeing all of you, Juan de Dios, you, Francisco, and the other peasants, convinces me that there is no better school than the struggle itself. That success depends on the alliance of workers, peasants and students.

If they tell you everything's all right, that's a sign that something is wrong. If they tell you both the positive and the negative side, then things are going well.

You must note the good and the bad in us, the old cadres of the FSLN. What few good qualities we may have should only be taken as a reference point; you must be aware of our bad characteristics and not imitate them. Above all, you must not repeat mistakes we have made in the past or may make in the future.

We've had some internal problems that we haven't been able to resolve. We've failed, but we must rectify these errors and we are going to rectify them.

They are killing us off, one by one, and we haven't known how to make the proper responses; we're on the defensive. It's necessary to redouble our efforts and to wrest the initiative from the enemy. [1]

Carlos Fonseca analyzed events. He argued that it was necessary, with respect to contacts and supplies, that the guerrilla structure in the city accumulate strength, while the rural guerrilla forces diversified their sources of supply and tried, during 1977, to seize the initiative from the enemy. In a calm voice that softened the conspiracy, he outlined four operations to the assembled combatants:

First, to open a route along the Parpar river on the Honduran border and to turn it into a supply line replacing the one in the south. He appointed Inés Hernández and Víctor Manuel Urbina ("Juancito" or "The Humble Peasant") to carry out this mission.

Second, to make contact with what we called the southern periphery in order to bring in comrades from the National Directorate. Facundo Picado, Celestina López and number 116 would be responsible for this task.

[1] Testimony given the author by Francisco Rivera in 1989.

Third, Francisco Rivera, Claudia Chamorro, Leonel and number 113 would remain in the Las Bayas-Cusulí-Iyás area to insure continuity.

Fourth, Agatón, Crescencio Aguilar and Benito Carvajal would march along the Zinica-Sofana route to make contact with Casimiro's squad and join up with Modesto.

All of that movement is, more than a military project, a political one. Unity is more important than geography and sticks of dynamite; unity is more important than hierarchy and life itself.

Francisco Rivera, Inés Hernández and Facundo Picado thought that dispersal of the groups endangered the personal security of our founder because at that time the National Guard was moving through the area in small, heavily-armed units. Nevertheless, on November 5th the designated squads set out for their respective destinations. Carlos' and Francisco Rivera's groups remained in Cusulí until the night of November 7th. The founder of the FSLN issued orders for the different missions. That same night, Carlos and Francisco said good-bye to each other, and Carlos, beneath a driving rain, set off toward his death.

5

With Benito Carvajal and Crescencio Aguilar as guides, Carlos set off along the Las Bayas-Cusulí-Iyás route that Carlos Agüero and Francisco Rivera had discovered and explored. They had decided to limit the nighttime march to four hours, or the distance between the Mendoza ranch and the Cusulí river, taking into account the fact that Carlos' nearsightedness had reached such an extreme that it was very difficult for him to travel at night. The rest of the distance was to be covered by day, using secure trails.

Very little is known about what happened. What is certain is that on November 8, 1976, between 9 and 11 a.m.—and Francisco Rivera ("Rubén the Fox") hasn't the slightest doubt that this was the time of his sacrifice — Carlos Fonseca ("Agatón"), our chief, fell in combat with the National Guard. The worker, Benito Carvajal, died with him. Crescencio Aguilar managed to withdraw unwounded, but that same evening was ambushed and killed while attempting to return to their point of departure.

Until now, one of the few eye-witness accounts we have of the circumstances surrounding the death of the leader of the Sandinista Popular Revolution is that of the National Guards' guide, José Dolores Gómez Leytón, a member of the patrol that carried out the fatal ambush. His story is filled with reticence and ambiguities.

On November 8th, the Guard column commanded by Capt. Enrique Munguía ("Little Toad") and Lt. Francisco Cisneros ("The Rat") received information about guerrilla movements along the Zinica-Sofana route.

A pale, bearded man with yellow hair and the eyes of a recently hatched buzzard arrived at the encampment riding a mangy beast and conferred secretly with the officers. Munguía sent a patrol off to the northwest to investigate and ordered the rest of the contingent, under the command of Cisneros, to advance along the Boca de Piedra river to the house of Matías López, some 200 meters from the Cristo Rey chapel.

Matías' modest house is located at a crossroads. A traveler heading southeast comes from Zinica and goes toward Sofana. Whoever heads west goes toward El Garrobo peak. East of the crossroads is the river, on whose northeast bank, on elevated terrain about 80 meters from the house, lies the "opening," which is what they call the hellish paths leading to the purgatory of small mountain settlements. It was protected by a wire fence and met the river, almost perpendicular to it, passing almost immediately in front of the peasant's house.

The Guard laid their ambushes. An exchange of gunfire broke out at 9 a.m. and continued for nearly three hours.

The soldiers inspected the area. According to Capt. Enrique Munguía, Carlos' body was sprawled against the trunk of a tree with a grenade in one hand resting on its roots. When the Guards saw that man staring at them without blinking, they fired. One of the bullets hit the grenade, which fell harmlessly among the leaves. The man's eyes remained open, and always will, seeing beyond life and death.

The Guards returned to camp carrying the bloody cadaver of a man on a litter. They took him to the chapel, where the body was placed in a room.

At first, the patrol didn't know who he was, and they asked each other who the dead man might be. A few hours later, however, the news began to spread. Several helicopters agitated the leaves of the grieving trees. An enormous tear began to form.

6

René Vivas was passing through the area when a peasant informed him of Carlos' death. René rejected the possibility so strongly that he wasn't even concerned. When he reached the encampment, he was struck by the silence. Modesto greeted him with a gesture. Carlos Agüero was as distressed as if he had lost his mother, his father, his brothers and his own children. He chewed his calloused knuckles until nightfall darkened the scene. Hugo Torres wandered around with his eyes half shut.

Daniel Ortega was hiding in an eastern suburb of Managua. The details of the communique, reflecting the enemy's joy at what they thought to be the final defeat of the Sandinista movement, were sufficient to leave no doubts. Daniel stood up to bear the full force of the blow. The communique spoke of the deaths of both Carlos Fonseca and Eduardo Contreras.

As he listened to the radio, Omar Cabezas, who was in the mountains with two comrades, continued blowing on the coals of the fire over which he was attempting to roast a chicken, leaning closer and closer to the small fire until he singed his eyelashes in the flame of that truth.

Carlos Núñez reacted in the following manner to the news of Carlos' death:

> Christmas of 1975 has passed and we are waiting for a renewal of communications between the different commands of the Organization (as we called it). We're desperate; we can't stand so much uncertainty. Suddenly, Marco informs

me that he's been called to a meeting, in early January as I recall. He asks me if he should go, and I tell him he should. I don't remember the place; those were difficult days. Participants were picked up in an automobile and, for security reasons, ordered to close their eyes. They arrived at a house, got out, and there, standing with his back to them, was a tall, thin man. It was Carlos Fonseca.

Afterwards, Marco told me with his eyes shining: "Brother, our problems have ended; the Sandinista Front has been saved." Eleven months later came the bitter news. A day after the deaths of Eduardo Contreras, Carlos Roberto Huembes, Rogelio Picado and Silvio Reñazco, we would receive yet another hammer blow to the head: Carlos Fonseca had died. I remember passing through a safehouse in the San Judas neighborhood and a comrade, Doña Ada, said to me calmly when I told her the news was true: "No, it's just another lie of those sons-of-bitches. Carlos Fonseca cannot die." [1]

Francisco Rivera, who had heard the sounds of combat from where he was hiding, also came under attack on the morning of November 10th. He managed to escape the encirclement together with Claudia Chamorro. They wandered for days through the thickets of Cusulí until finally, on the 20th, they reached the Mendoza ranch. One of the daughters of the old pastor, who'd been arrested, told Francisco: "They killed Agatón and Benito Carvajal. Crescencio Aguilar was also killed. They buried them there," she said, pointing to Danilo's grave, a mound of moist earth darkened by the intensity of the interred remains. "Agatón went to heaven," she said, "but his body's there somewhere."

For almost three months Claudia and Francisco searched the vast territory of Cusulí for the Las Bayas guerrilla group.

On January 9, 1977, having taken cover in a cane field, they were resting while chewing on cane stalks, whose sugar soaked into their viscera like water into dry earth. The noise of gunshots surprised and scattered birds and deer. Claudia fired her carbine and asked

[1] Testimony of Carlos Nuñez.

Francisco to withdraw, because she was wounded. Francisco kept calling to her until the silence was once again interrupted by bursts from a Browning rifle.

We learned about it at our Court Martial. Silently, with burning eyes, we mourned Claudia's death. The traitor, Tito, received the news without changing his expression.

That night, in the solitude of my cell, I cradled her head on my lap. Let no one ask me about the intensity of my grief! Claudia was tall, svelte, with a slender waist, and eyes the size of discovery.

One day, under the roof of eternal confidence, she had told me about her love affair with Porritas. When Carlos Agüero showed up all her memories vanished and the two of them took possession of each other with all their egos, like a fountain gushing fruits and snails.

Carlos was dead. Claudia was dead. Eduardo Contreras was dead. The enemy said we were all dead and not a one of us was dead.

Chapter Forty

1

When I was notified in prison that Carlos Fonseca had died, I said to Col. Nicolás Valle Salinas: "Carlos is one of those dead who never die."

Lying on my back on the cot that was my home, I closed my eyes to see that crucified man navigating through a jungle of foam that engulfed nearly all of my stupor.

With my inner eye I contemplated his first communion, his contact lenses lost in a pile of manuscripts, the tractor starting up, the birth control pill he swallowed thinking it was an antipyretic, the way we jumped with joy upon seeing each other after so many years.

I saw his melancholy, the shotgun licking at his heels that were bruised and blistered from so much hiking, the sky closed in by rain, gunpowder penetrating gardens and projects. I also saw the pain, the attacks of conscience, his breast invaded by landscapes, the trickle of blood overflowing surprises, the panic of those who weren't sure about his death or our shared dreams.

Suddenly, I saw that you were a baby and that Doña Agustina was washing you and that your diapers smelled of soap; I saw your caramels offering themselves for the world to savor; I saw how you stole a lock to make a master key in your workshop of stone and wood; I saw your oaths, the outlines of life and death, the temple that you scoured clean of rubbish.

It was so clear that there were no hired mourners, no drawn curtains, no pontifical masses; it was obvious that the *cenzontles*[*] and the musicians wept, that the madrones and old people had dressed for mourning. The coffee trees ceased flowering and held their breath.

[*] Nicaragua's national bird.

Here in my cell I could indulge my grief without witnesses, drag the tiny statues through the gravel, consign your memory to Hell, my dear friend, so I could get some rest.

I could wait confidently for people to ask me one day who that man was who wept each February, who refused to attend weddings, who participated in the burials of the sacrificed, who was obsessed with babies and coffee plantations, with cotton and the buzzing of bees, who loved to read and share nougats and magnetized needles.

I learned about it this morning and I'm still a victim of anaesthesia; I touch my testicles, humiliated sparrows; I look at my heart, brother, and find it sad, as though it had turned to iodine; it's like a jungle under the rain at six in the afternoon; I'm stunned by foreboding; I feel remorse for my optimism.

I'm still confident about the avenues strung with banners, and it hurts so because you won't be there. Only your name, your specific weight, the silhouette of your glasses, your words, but you, what is called you — the scar on your chest, the ingrown toenail that Luz Danelia removed for you, those legs trained for interminable roads — you won't be there.

Your localisms won't be there, Matagalpa, wounded blood-red like nightmares and the juice of the *pitahaya* cactus. Where will your way of scratching your head be? And your drill trousers? Your hands tying the laces of your seven-league boots? Your fondness for coffee and *indioviejo* and the poetry of Pound?

The illustrious fertile races won't be there, nor the longed-for vanilla ice cream after yesterday's hard toil, the latest reflections on tomorrow's problems, the daily pause each evening to think about your mother, your children, and about the concreteness of the concrete laws of historical development in the here and now.

You're not going to be there when tolling bells announce the trumpet flourishes and the most beautiful of women smiles at the fiercest of the victors; when we lower you amidst hymns and salutes, dear chieftain, conqueror of death, and thousands of voices deposit caresses and kisses on your bones.

It's true. The dawn is no longer beyond our reach. Doña Agustina came to your funeral and in her eyes were volleys and tears. Carpenters came, and souvenir vendors and gymnasts, and grammar teachers and dreamers and tender children; they all came. The nine bore you on their shoulders. The entire people bore you toward the unfailing light.

Then hymns thundered and banners waved, repeating: Where are you, Carlos? Where are you, dearest brother? Because this world keeps on turning, brother, despite everything.